Catalan pocket dictionary

English-Catalan & Catalan-English

John Shapiro

Catalan pocket dictionary
by John Shapiro

First edition: March 2017

ENGLISH-CATALAN

A

a • *n* a *(f)*
aardvark • *n* porc formiguer *(m)*
abaca • *n* abacà *(m)*
abacus • *n* àbac *(m)*
abaft • *adv* a popa
abalone • *n* orella de mar *(f)*
abandon • *v* abandonar, deixar
abandoned • *adj* abandonat
abbacy • *n* abadia *(f)*
abbatial • *adj* abacial
abbess • *n* abadessa *(f)*
abbey • *n* abadia *(f)*
abbot • *n* abat
abbreviation • *n* abreviatura *(f)*
abdication • *n* abdicació *(f)*
abdomen • *n* abdomen *(m)*, buc *(m)*,
panxa *(f)*, ventre *(m)*
abdominal • *adj* abdominal
abecedary • *n* abecedari *(m)*, beceroles
aberrant • *adj* aberrant *(f)*
aberration • *n* aberració *(f)*
abhor • *v* avorrir
abiogenesis • *n* abiogènesi *(f)*, autogènesi
(f), generació espontània *(f)*
abjectly • *adv* abjectament
ablaze • *adj* rogent, cremant, ardent
abnormal • *adj* anormal
abnormality • *n* anormalitat *(f)*
abnormally • *adv* anormalment
abolish • *v* abolir, suprimir
abominable • *adj* abominable
abominate • *v* abominar
aboriginal • *adj* aborigen
abort • *n* avortament *(m)* • *v* avortar
abortion • *n* avort *(m)*, avortament *(m)*
abortive • *n* abortiu *(m)* • *adj* abortiu *(m)*,
abortiva *(f)*, avortiu *(m)*, avortiva *(f)*
about • *prep* sobre
above • *adv* dalt • *prep* damunt
abrasion • *n* abrasió *(m)*
abrasive • *adj* abrasiu
abridged • *adj* abreujat, resumit
abroad • *adv* a l'estranger
abrogate • *v* abrogar
abrupt • *adj* abrupte
abruptly • *adv* abruptament, precipitadament
abscissa • *n* abscissa *(f)*
abscond • *v* fugir, escapar-se, escapolir-
se, abscondir, amagar, ocultar, escondir
absence • *n* absència *(f)*
absent • *adj* absent • *v* absentar
absinthe • *n* absenta *(f)*, donzell *(m)*
absolute • *adj* absolut *(m)*

absolutely • *adv* absolutament
absolutist • *adj* absolutista *(f)*
absorb • *v* absorbir
absorbent • *n* absorbent *(m)* • *adj* absorbent
abstemious • *adj* abstemi
abstention • *n* abstenció *(f)*
abstersion • *n* abstersió *(f)*
abstersive • *adj* abstersiu
abstract • *n* resum, xifra, abstracció • *adj*
abstracte
abstraction • *n* abstracció *(f)*
abstractionism • *n* abstraccionisme *(m)*
abstractionist • *n* abstraccionista *(f)* • *adj*
abstraccionista *(f)*
absurd • *adj* absurd
absurdly • *adv* absurdament
abulia • *n* abúlia *(f)*
abulic • *adj* abúlic
abundant • *adj* abundant
abundantly • *adv* abundantment
abusive • *adj* abusiu
abusively • *adv* abusivament
abyss • *n* abisme *(m)*
acacia • *n* acàcia *(f)*
academic • *n* acadèmic *(m)* • *adj* acadèmic
academically • *adv* acadèmicament
academician • *n* acadèmic
acanthus • *n* acant *(m)*
accelerate • *v* accelerar
acceleration • *n* acceleració *(f)*
accelerometer • *n* acceleròmetre *(m)*
accent • *n* accent *(m)* • *v* accentuar
accentuate • *v* accentuar
accept • *v* acceptar
acceptability • *n* acceptabilitat *(f)*
acceptable • *adj* acceptable
acceptably • *adv* acceptablement
acceptor • *n* acceptant *(f)*
accessible • *adj* accessible
accident • *n* accident *(m)*
accidental • *n* accident *(m)* • *adj* accidental *(f)*
accidentally • *adv* accidentalment
accompaniment • *n* segona *(f)*, acompanyament *(m)*
accompany • *v* acompanyar
accomplice • *n* còmplice *(f)*
accordingly • *adv* apropiadament, tal
com correspon
accordion • *n* acordió *(m)*
accordionist • *n* acordionista *(f)*
accountability • *n* responsabilitat *(f)*
accountancy • *n* comptabilitat *(f)*

accretion • *n* acreció *(f)*
acculturation • *n* aculturació *(f)*
accurate • *adj* exacte, precís
accurately • *adv* exactament, precisament, acuradament
accusation • *n* acusació *(f)*
accusative • *n* acusatiu *(m)*, cas acusatiu *(m)* • *adj* acusatiu
accuse • *v* acusar
accustomed • *adj* acostumat
ace • *n* as *(m)*, punt directe *(m)*
acerola • *n* acerola *(f)*
acetabulum • *n* acetàbul *(m)*
acetamide • *n* acetamida *(f)*, etanamida
acetate • *n* acetat *(m)*
acetone • *n* acetona *(f)*
achene • *n* aqueni *(m)*
achievable • *adj* assolible
achieve • *v* acomplir, obtenir, aconseguir
achromatic • *adj* acromàtic *(m)*
acid • *n* àcid *(m)* • *adj* àcid
acidic • *adj* àcid
acidify • *v* acidificar
acidimetry • *n* acidimetria *(f)*
acknowledgement • *n* reconeixement *(m)*, agraïment *(m)*
acolyte • *n* acòlit *(m)*
aconite • *n* acònit *(m)*, tora *(f)*
acorn • *n* gla *(f)*
acoustic • *adj* acústic
acoustics • *n* acústica *(f)*
acquaintance • *n* conegut *(m)*
acquirable • *adj* adquirible
acquire • *v* adquirir
acquisition • *n* adquisició *(f)*
acrimonious • *adj* aspre *(m)*, aspra *(f)*, mordaç
acrobat • *n* acròbata *(f)*, equilibrista *(f)*
acromion • *n* acromi *(m)*
acronym • *n* acrònim *(m)*
acrophobia • *n* acrofòbia *(f)*
acropolis • *n* acròpolis *(f)*
acrostic • *n* acròstic *(m)*
acrylic • *adj* acrílic
act • *v* actuar, portar, comportar • *n* acte *(m)*
actinium • *n* actini *(m)*
actinometer • *n* actinòmetre *(m)*
action • *n* acció *(f)*
actively • *adv* activament
activism • *n* activisme *(m)*
activity • *n* activitat *(f)*
actor • *n* actor *(m)*, actriu *(f)*
actress • *n* actriu *(f)*
actual • *adj* real
actually • *adv* de fet, en realitat
actuary • *n* actuari *(m)*

acupuncture • *n* acupuntura *(f)*
acute • *adj* agut, tancat
acyclic • *adj* acíclic
adaptable • *adj* adaptable
adaptation • *n* adaptació *(f)*
adapter • *n* adaptador *(m)*
adaptive • *adj* adaptatiu *(m)*
add • *v* afegir, sumar
adder • *n* escurçó *(m)*
addict • *n* addicte *(m)*
addictive • *adj* addictiu
addition • *n* addició *(f)*
additional • *adj* addicional
additionally • *adv* addicionalment
additive • *n* additiu *(m)*
address • *v* adreçar • *n* adreça *(f)*
adenoid • *n* adenoide *(f)*
adequate • *adj* adequat
adequately • *adv* adequadament
adhere • *v* adherir
adherent • *adj* adherent *(f)*, adhesiu
adhesive • *n* adhesiu *(m)* • *adj* adhesiu
adiabatic • *adj* adiabàtic
adjacency • *n* adjacència *(f)*
adjacent • *adj* adjacent
adjectival • *adj* adjectiu
adjectivally • *adv* adjectivament
adjective • *n* adjectiu *(m)* • *adj* adjectiu
adjourn • *v* ajornar, posposar, suspendre
adjudicate • *v* adjudicar, jutjar
adjustable • *adj* ajustable
adjustment • *n* ajust *(m)*, ajustment *(m)*
administer • *v* administrar
administrative • *adj* administratiu
administratively • *adv* administrativament
administrator • *n* administrador *(m)*, administradora *(f)*
admirable • *adj* admirable
admirably • *adv* admirablement
admiral • *n* almirall
admire • *v* admirar
admissible • *adj* admissible
admission • *n* admissió
adobe • *n* tova *(f)*
adolescence • *n* adolescència *(f)*
adolescent • *n* adolescent *(f)* • *adj* adolescent
adoptive • *adj* adoptiu
adorable • *adj* adorable
adorably • *adv* adorablement
adrenaline • *n* adrenalina, epinefrina
adulation • *n* adulació *(f)*
adult • *n* adult
adulterer • *n* adúlter *(m)*
adultery • *n* adulteri *(m)*
advantage • *n* avantatge *(m)*, benefici *(m)*

advantageous • *adj* avantatjós
advection • *n* advecció *(f)*
adventitious • *adj* exogen, adventici, aquirit, ectòpic
adventure • *n* aventura, aventura *(f)*
adventurer • *n* aventurer *(m)*
adventurous • *adj* aventurer
adverb • *n* adverbi *(m)*
adverbial • *adj* adverbial
adverbially • *adv* adverbialment
adversity • *n* adversitat *(f)*
advertisement • *n* anunci *(m)*
advice • *n* consell *(m)*
advisable • *adj* aconsellable
adze • *n* aixa *(f)*
aeolian • *adj* eòlic
aerial • *n* antena *(f)* • *adj* aeri
aerobic • *adj* aeròbic
aerodrome • *n* aeròdrom *(m)*
aerodynamic • *adj* aerodinàmi
aerodynamics • *n* aerodinàmica *(f)*
aerometer • *n* aeròmetre *(m)*
aeronautics • *n* aeronàutica *(f)*
aerosol • *n* aerosol *(m)*
aesthetic • *adj* estètic
aesthetics • *n* estètica *(f)*
aetiology • *n* etiologia *(f)*
affect • *v* afectar • *n* afecte *(m)*
affection • *n* afecte *(m)*, afecció *(f)*
affectionate • *adj* afectuós
affirmation • *n* afirmació *(f)*, autosuggestió *(f)*
affirmatively • *adv* afirmativament
afraid • *adj* por
after • *adv* més tard, després, acabat, en acabat • *conj* després que, acabat que, en acabat que • *prep* després de, acabat de, en acabat de
afterlife • *n* més enllà *(m)*, inframón *(m)*, ultratomba *(f)*
afternoon • *n* tarda *(f)*
afterwards • *adv* després
again • *adv* una altra vegada, de nou
against • *prep* contra, davant, en contra
agate • *n* àgata *(f)*
age • *v* envellir • *n* edat *(f)*
agency • *n* agència *(f)*
agent • *n* agent *(m)*
aggressive • *adj* agressiu
aggressively • *adv* agressivament
aggressiveness • *n* agressivitat *(f)*
aghast • *adj* horroritzat
agile • *adj* àgil
agilely • *adv* àgilment
agility • *n* agulla *(f)*, agilitat *(f)*
agnosia • *n* agnòsia *(f)*
agnosticism • *n* agnosticisme *(m)*

agonize • *v* agonitzar
agora • *n* àgora *(f)*
agoraphobia • *n* agorafòbia *(f)*
agreeable • *adj* agradable, tractable
agreeably • *adv* agradablement
agreed • *interj* d'acord
agreement • *n* acord *(m)*, pacte *(m)*, contracte *(m)*, conveni *(m)*, concordança *(f)*
agricultural • *adj* agrícola *(f)*
agriculture • *n* agricultura *(f)*
agriculturist • *n* agricultor *(m)*, agricultora *(f)* • *adj* agrícola
aground • *adv* encallat
ahead • *adv* en front de, al davant de
aim • *v* apuntar
aioli • *n* allioli
air • *n* aire *(m)*
airborne • *adj* transportat per l'aire
aircraft • *n* aeronau *(f)*
airplane • *n* avió *(m)*
airport • *n* aeroport *(m)*
airtight • *adj* hermètic
aisle • *n* nau, passadís, corredor
akimbo • *adj* en gerres
akin • *adj* semblant *(f)*
alabaster • *n* alabastre *(m)* • *adj* alabastrí
alarm • *v* alarmar • *n* alarma *(f)*, despertador *(m)*
alarming • *adj* alarmant
alarmism • *n* alarmisme *(m)*
alas • *interj* ai las
albatross • *n* albatros *(m)*
albedo • *n* albedo *(m)*
albeit • *conj* encara que, tanmateix, però
albino • *n* albí *(m)* • *adj* albí *(m)*
albite • *n* albita *(f)*
albumen • *n* albumen *(m)*, clara *(f)*
alcazar • *n* alcàsser *(m)*
alchemist • *n* alquimista *(f)*
alchemy • *n* alquímia *(f)*
alcohol • *n* alcohol *(m)*
alcoholic • *n* alcohòlic *(m)* • *adj* alcohòlic
alcoholism • *n* alcoholisme *(m)*
alder • *n* vern *(m)*
alembic • *n* alambí
alert • *v* alertar • *n* alerta *(f)* • *adj* vigilant
algebra • *n* àlgebra *(f)*
algebraic • *adj* algebraic
algebraically • *adv* algèbricament, algebraicament
algorithm • *n* algorisme *(m)*
alibi • *n* coartada
alien • *n* estrany *(m)*, estranya *(f)*, foraster *(m)*, forastera *(f)*, extraterrestre *(f)* • *adj* aliè, alié, estrany *(m)*, estranya *(f)*
alienate • *v* alienar
alienation • *n* alienació *(f)*

aliphatic • *adj* alifàtic
alive • *adj* viu, vivent
alkalimetry • *n* alcalimetria *(f)*
alkaloid • *n* alcaloide *(m)*
all • *n* tot
allege • *v* al·legar
alleged • *adj* presumpte
allegedly • *adv* presumptament
allegorical • *adj* al·legòric
allegorically • *adv* al·legòricament
allegory • *n* al·legoria *(f)*
allele • *n* al·lel *(m)*
allemande • *n* alemanda, alemanya
allergic • *adj* al·lèrgic
allergy • *n* al·lèrgia *(f)*
alleviate • *v* mitigar, pal·liar
alley • *n* carreró *(m)*
alliance • *n* aliança *(f)*
alligator • *n* al·ligàtor *(m)*
alliteration • *n* al·literació *(f)*
allochthonous • *adj* al·lòcton *(m)*
allodium • *n* alou
allow • *v* deixar
alloy • *n* aliatge *(m)*, lliga *(f)*
allusion • *n* al·lusió *(f)*
allusive • *adj* al·lusiu
alluvial • *n* al·luvió *(m)* • *adj* al·luvial
alluvium • *n* al·luvió *(m)*
almanac • *n* almanac *(m)*
almighty • *adj* omnipotent
almond • *n* ametlla *(f)*, ametller *(m)*
almost • *adv* gairebé, quasi
alms • *n* almoina *(f)*
alone • *adj* sol, únic • *adv* sol, tot sol, només
alopecia • *n* alopècia *(f)*
alpaca • *n* alpaca *(m)*
alpha • *n* alfa *(f)*
alphabet • *n* alfabet *(m)*, abecedari *(m)*
alphabetical • *adj* alfabètic
alphabetically • *adv* alfabèticament
alphanumeric • *adj* alfanumèric
alpine • *adj* alpí *(m)*
already • *adv* ja
also • *adv* també
altar • *n* altar *(m)*
alter • *v* alterar
alteration • *n* alteració *(f)*
alternative • *adj* alternatiu
alternatively • *adv* alternativament
although • *conj* tot i que, malgrat que
altimeter • *n* altímetre *(m)*
altitude • *n* altitud *(f)*, alçada *(f)*
altogether • *adv* totalment, completament, en total
altruism • *n* altruisme *(m)*
altruist • *n* altruista *(f)*

altruistic • *adj* altruista
alveolus • *n* alvèol *(m)*
always • *adv* sempre
amaranth • *n* amarant *(m)*
amaryllis • *n* amaril·lis
amazon • *n* amazona *(f)*
ambassador • *n* ambaixador *(m)*
amber • *n* ambre *(m)*
ambergris • *n* ambre gris *(m)*
ambidextrous • *adj* ambidextre *(f)*
ambient • *n* ambient *(m)* • *adj* ambient
ambiguity • *n* ambigüitat *(f)*
ambiguous • *adj* ambigu
ambiguously • *adv* ambiguament
ambitious • *adj* ambiciós
ambitiously • *adv* ambiciosament
amblyopia • *n* ambliopia *(f)*
ambo • *n* ambó *(m)*
ambulance • *n* ambulància *(f)*
ambulatory • *n* deambulatori *(m)* • *adj* ambulatori
amen • *interj* amén
amendment • *n* esmena
amenity • *n* amenitat *(f)*, comoditat *(f)*
americium • *n* americi
amicable • *adj* amigable
amicably • *adv* amigablement
ammeter • *n* amperímetre *(m)*, amperòmetre *(m)*
ammonium • *n* amoni *(m)*
amnesia • *n* amnèsia *(f)*
amnion • *n* amni *(m)*
amniotic • *adj* àmnic, amniòtic
amorous • *adj* amorós
amorously • *adv* amorosament
amorphous • *adj* amorf
ampere • *n* ampere *(m)*
ampersand • *n* i comercial *(f)*, et *(m)*
amphibian • *n* amfibi
amphibious • *adj* amfibi
amphitheater • *n* amfiteatre *(m)*
amphora • *n* àmfora *(f)*
amplitude • *n* amplitud *(f)*
amputate • *v* amputar
amputation • *n* amputació *(f)*
amuse • *v* divertir, entretenir, distreure
amusing • *adj* divertit, entretingut
amygdala • *n* amígdala *(f)*
amylase • *n* amilasa *(f)*
an • *art* un *(m)*, una *(f)*
anachronism • *n* anacronisme *(m)*
anacrusis • *n* anacrusi *(f)*
anadromous • *adj* anàdrom
anagram • *n* anagrama *(m)*
anal • *adj* anal
analgesia • *n* analgèsia *(f)*, anàlgia *(f)*
analgesic • *n* analgèsic *(m)* • *adj* analgèsic

analogously • *adv* anàlogament
analogy • *n* analogia *(f)*
analysis • *n* anàlisi *(f)*
analytic • *adj* analític
analytically • *adv* analíticament
analyze • *v* analitzar
anamorphic • *adj* anamòrfic *(m)*, anamòr-fica *(f)*
anapest • *n* anapest *(m)*
anaphoric • *adj* anafòric
anarchic • *adj* anàrquic *(m)*
anarchically • *adv* anàrquicament
anarchism • *n* anarquisme *(m)*
anarchy • *n* anarquia *(f)*
anastomosis • *n* anastomosi *(f)*
anatomical • *adj* anatòmic
anatomically • *adv* anatòmicament
anatomy • *n* anatomia *(f)*
ancestor • *n* avantpassat *(m)*
ancestral • *adj* ancestral
ancestry • *n* llinatge *(m)*, ascendència *(f)*
anchor • *v* ancorar • *n* àncora *(f)*, enllaç *(m)*
ancient • *adj* antic, vetust
anciently • *adv* antigament
ancillary • *adj* auxiliar
and • *conj* i
andiron • *n* capfoguer *(m)*
androgynous • *adj* androgin
anecdotal • *adj* anecdòtic, anecdotari
anemia • *n* anèmia *(f)*
anemic • *adj* anèmic
anemometer • *n* anemòmetre *(m)*
aneurysm • *n* aneurisma
anew • *adv* de nou, novament
angel • *n* àngel *(m)*
angelic • *adj* angèlic, angelical
angelically • *adv* angèlicament
anger • *v* enfadar, enutjar, cabrejar • *n* ira *(f)*, còlera *(f)*, ràbia *(f)*, enfat *(m)*, enuig *(m)*
angiography • *n* angiografia *(f)*
angle • *n* angle *(m)*, racó *(m)*, cantonada *(f)*, punt de vista *(m)*
angler • *n* rap
angry • *adj* enfadat, enutjat
animadversion • *n* animadversió *(f)*
animal • *n* animal *(m)*, bèstia *(f)* • *adj* animal
animalcule • *n* animàlcul *(m)*
animate • *v* animar • *adj* animat *(m)*
animated • *adj* animat
animation • *n* animació *(f)*
anime • *n* anime
animism • *n* animisme *(m)*
anise • *n* anís *(m)*, matafaluga *(f)*
ankle • *n* turmell *(m)*
anklebone • *n* astràgal *(m)*

annatto • *n* annato *(m)*
annelid • *n* anèl·lid *(m)*
annex • *n* annex *(m)* • *v* annexar
announce • *v* anunciar
annoy • *v* molestar
annual • *n* anuari *(m)* • *adj* anual, anyal
annually • *adv* anualment
annular • *adj* anular
annulus • *n* anell *(m)*
anode • *n* ànode *(m)*
anodyne • *n* analgèsic, calmant • *adj* anodí
anomalous • *adj* anòmal
anonymous • *adj* anònim
anonymously • *adv* anònimament
anorexia • *n* anorèxia *(f)*
anorexic • *n* anorèxica *(f)*
anorthite • *n* anortita *(f)*
answer • *n* resposta *(f)* • *v* respondre
ant • *n* formiga *(f)*
antacid • *n* antiàcid *(m)* • *adj* antiàcid *(m)*, antiàcida *(f)*
antagonism • *n* antagonisme *(m)*
antagonist • *n* antagonista *(f)*, antagonista *(m)*
antagonistic • *adj* antagonista
antaphrodisiac • *n* anafrodisíac *(m)*, anafrodisíaca *(f)*, antiafrodisíac *(m)*, antiafrodisíaca *(f)* • *adj* anafrodisíac *(m)*
antebellum • *adj* d'avantguerra
antecedent • *n* antecedent *(m)*
antediluvian • *adj* antediluvià
antefix • *n* antefixa *(f)*
antelope • *n* antílop *(m)*
antenna • *n* antena *(f)*
antepenultimate • *adj* antepenúltim
anthem • *n* himne *(m)*
anthill • *n* formiguer *(m)*, termiter *(m)*
anthrax • *n* àntrax *(m)*
anthropocentric • *adj* antropocèntric
anthropocentrism • *n* antropocentrisme *(m)*
anthropoid • *n* antropoide • *adj* antropoide
anthropologist • *n* antropòleg *(m)*
anthropology • *n* antropologia *(f)*
anthropometry • *n* antropometria *(f)*
anthropomorphic • *adj* antropomorf, antropomòrfic
anthropomorphism • *n* antropomorfisme *(m)*
antibacterial • *n* antibacterià *(m)* • *adj* antibacterià
antibiotic • *n* antibiòtic *(m)* • *adj* antibiòtic
antibody • *n* anticòs *(m)*
antichrist • *n* anticrist *(m)*

anticyclone • *n* anticicló *(m)*
antidepressant • *n* antidepressiu *(m)* • *adj* antidepressiu
antidote • *n* antídot *(m)*
antihero • *n* antiheroi *(m)*
antihistamine • *n* antihistamínic *(m)*
antimony • *n* antimoni *(m)*
antineutron • *n* antineutró *(m)*
antioxidant • *n* antioxidant *(m)* • *adj* antioxidant
antiparallel • *adj* antiparal·lel
antiparticle • *n* antipartícula *(f)*
antiphlogistic • *n* antiinflamatori *(m)* • *adj* antiinflamatori
antiphony • *n* antífona *(f)*
antipodean • *n* antípoda *(f)* • *adj* antípoda
antiproton • *n* antiprotó *(m)*
antiquated • *adj* antiquat
antique • *n* antic • *adj* antic, antiquat
antiseptic • *n* antisèptic • *adj* antisèptic
antitank • *adj* antitanc *(f)*
antithetically • *adv* antitèticament
antiviral • *adj* antivíric, antivirus
antonomasia • *n* antonomàsia *(f)*
antonym • *n* antònim *(m)*
antonymous • *adj* antònim
antonymy • *n* antonímia *(f)*
antrum • *n* antre *(m)*
anus • *n* anus *(m)*
anvil • *n* enclusa *(f)*
anxiety • *n* ansietat *(f)*
anxious • *adj* ansiós
anxiously • *adv* ansiosament
any • *pron* algun, qualque
anyhow • *adv* en qualsevol cas, tot i així
anything • *pron* qualsevol cosa, alguna cosa, quelcom, tot, res
anywhere • *adv* onsevulga
aorta • *n* aorta *(f)*
apartheid • *n* apartheid *(m)*
apartment • *n* pis *(m)*
apathetic • *adj* apàtic
apathetically • *adv* apàticament
apathy • *n* apatia *(f)*
apatite • *n* apatita *(f)*
apex • *n* àpex *(m)*
aphasia • *n* afàsia *(f)*
aphorism • *n* aforisme *(m)*
apiary • *n* apiari *(m)*
apocalypse • *n* apocalipsi *(m)*
apocalyptic • *adj* apocalíptic
apocarpous • *adj* apocàrpic
apocryphal • *adj* apòcrif
apogee • *n* apogeu *(m)*
apograph • *n* apògraf *(m)*
apologetic • *adj* apologètic
apologetically • *adv* apologèticament

apologize • *v* apologitzar
apology • *n* disculpa *(f)*
aponeurosis • *n* aponeurosi
apophysis • *n* apòfisi *(f)*
apostatize • *v* apostatar
apostle • *n* apòstol *(m)*
apostrophe • *n* apòstrof *(m)*, apòstrofe *(m)*
apothegm • *n* apotegma *(m)*
apparent • *adj* aparent
apparently • *adv* aparentment
appeal • *v* abellir
appear • *v* aparèixer, sortir, semblar
appearance • *n* aparició, aparença
appendectomy • *n* apendicectomia *(f)*
appendix • *n* apèndix, apèndix *(m)*
appetite • *n* gana
appetizing • *adj* apetitós
applause • *n* aplaudiment *(m)*
apple • *n* poma *(f)*
applet • *n* miniaplicació *(f)*
applied • *adj* aplicat
appointment • *n* nomenament *(m)*, nomenament *(f)*, compromís *(m)*, cita *(f)*, consulta *(f)*
appraisal • *n* avaluació *(f)*, valoració *(f)*
appreciably • *adv* apreciablement
apprehend • *v* aprehendre
apprehensive • *adj* aprensiu
apprenticeship • *n* aprenentatge *(m)*
approach • *v* aproximar-se
appropriately • *adv* apropiadament
approve • *v* aprovar
approximate • *adj* aproximat
approximately • *adv* aproximadament
apricot • *n* albercoc *(m)*, albercoquer *(m)*
apron • *n* davantal *(m)*
apse • *n* absis *(m)*
aquatic • *adj* aquàtic
aquatint • *n* aiguatinta *(f)*
aqueduct • *n* aqüeducte *(m)*
aquifer • *n* aqüífer *(m)*
aquiline • *adj* aguilenc, aquilí
arabesque • *n* arabesc *(m)*
arable • *adj* cultivable
arachnid • *n* aràcnid *(m)*
arbitrary • *adj* arbitrari
arc • *n* arc *(m)*
arcade • *n* arcada *(f)*
arcane • *adj* arcà *(m)*, secret *(m)*
arch • *v* arquejar • *n* arc *(m)*
archaeological • *adj* arqueològic
archaeologist • *n* arqueòleg *(m)*
archaeology • *n* arqueologia *(f)*
archaic • *adj* arcaic
archangel • *n* arcàngel *(m)*
archbishop • *n* arquebisbe

archbishopric • *n* metròpolis *(f)*, metròpoli *(f)*
archdeacon • *n* ardiaca *(m)*, arxidiaca *(m)*
archduchess • *n* arxiduquessa *(f)*
archduke • *n* arxiduc *(m)*
archer • *n* arquer *(m)*
archetypal • *adj* arquetípic
archetype • *n* arquetip *(m)*
archipelago • *n* arxipèlag *(m)*
architect • *n* arquitecte *(f)*
architectural • *adj* arquitectònic
architecture • *n* arquitectura
architrave • *n* arquitrau *(m)*
archive • *n* arxiu *(m)*
archlute • *n* arxillaüt *(m)*
arduous • *adj* ardu
area • *n* àrea *(f)*
areola • *n* arèola *(f)*
argent • *n* plata *(f)*, argent *(m)*
argentite • *n* argentita *(f)*
arginine • *n* arginina
argon • *n* argó *(m)*
arguable • *adj* arguïble, discutible
argument • *n* argument *(m)*, disputa *(f)*, argumentació *(f)*
arid • *adj* àrid
aristocracy • *n* aristocràcia *(f)*
aristocrat • *n* aristòcrata *(f)*
aristocratic • *adj* aristocràtic
aristocratically • *adv* aristocràticament
arithmetic • *n* aritmètica
arithmetically • *adv* aritmèticament
arm • *n* braç *(m)*, arma *(f)* • *v* armar
armadillo • *n* armadillo *(m)*
armed • *adj* armat
armiger • *n* escuder *(m)*
armistice • *n* armistici *(m)*
armor • *n* arnès *(m)*, armadura *(f)*
armored • *adj* blindat
armpit • *n* aixella *(f)*, axilŭla *(f)*
army • *n* exèrcit *(m)*, host *(f)*
aromatic • *adj* aromàtic
around • *prep* al voltant de, passant
arrange • *v* organitzar, planificar, arreglar, arrenjar
arrangement • *n* arreglada, acord *(m)*, arrangement *(m)*
array • *v* arreglar
arrest • *n* arrest *(m)*
arrhythmia • *n* arítmia *(f)*
arrhythmic • *adj* arítmic
arrive • *v* arribar
arrogance • *n* arrogància *(f)*
arrogant • *adj* arrogant
arrogantly • *adv* arrogantment
arrow • *n* fletxa *(f)*, sageta *(f)*
arsenic • *n* arsènic

arterial • *adj* arterial
arteriole • *n* arteriola *(f)*
artery • *n* artèria *(f)*
arthritic • *adj* artrític
arthritis • *n* artritis *(f)*
arthropod • *n* artròpode *(m)*
artichoke • *n* carxofera *(f)*, carxofa
article • *n* article *(m)*
articulate • *adj* articulat *(m)*
articulately • *adv* articuladament
articulation • *n* articulació *(f)*
artifact • *n* artefacte *(m)*
artificial • *adj* artificial, fals
artificially • *adv* artificialment
artillery • *n* artilleria *(f)*
artilleryman • *n* artiller *(m)*
artisan • *n* artesà *(m)*
artist • *n* artista *(f)*
artistic • *adj* artístic
artistically • *adv* artísticament
as • *adv* tan • *conj* com, com que, ja que • *prep* com
asbestos • *n* asbest *(m)*, amiant *(m)*
ascend • *v* ascendir
ascension • *n* ascensió *(f)*
ascertain • *v* trobar, encertar
ascites • *n* ascites *(f)*
asexuality • *n* asexualitat
ash • *n* cendra *(f)*, cendre
ashamed • *adj* avergonyit
ashlar • *n* carreu *(m)*, carreuada *(f)*
ask • *v* preguntar, demanar
asleep • *adj* adormit
asparagus • *n* esparreguera *(f)*
aspen • *n* trèmol *(m)*
asphalt • *n* asfalt
aspirin • *n* aspirina *(f)*
ass • *n* cul *(m)*
assassin • *n* assassí *(m)*
assassinate • *v* assassinar
assassination • *n* assassinat *(m)*
assegai • *n* atzagaia *(f)*
assembly • *n* assemblea *(f)*
assertion • *n* asserció *(f)*, afirmació *(f)*
assertive • *adj* assertiu
assertiveness • *n* assertivitat *(f)*
assess • *v* avaluar
asseveration • *n* asseveració *(f)*
assiduously • *adv* assíduament
assimilate • *v* assimilar
assist • *n* assistència *(f)*
assistance • *n* assistència *(f)*
assistant • *n* assistente *(f)* • *adj* auxiliar
associate • *v* associar • *n* associat *(m)*
association • *n* associació *(f)*
associative • *adj* associatiu
astatine • *n* àstat

asterisk • *n* asterisc *(m)*
asteroid • *n* asteroide *(m)*, planetoide
asthenosphere • *n* astenosfera *(f)*
asthma • *n* asma *(f)*
asthmatic • *adj* asmàtic
astigmatism • *n* astigmatisme *(m)*
astonishing • *adj* sorprenent
astonishment • *n* estorament *(m)*, sorpresa *(f)*
astragalus • *n* astràgal *(m)*
astray • *adv* desencaminadament
astrological • *adj* astrològic
astrology • *n* astrologia *(f)*
astronaut • *n* astronauta *(f)*
astronomer • *n* astrònom *(m)*, astrònoma *(f)*
astronomically • *adv* astronòmicament
astronomy • *n* astronomia *(f)*
astrophysical • *adj* astrofísic
astrophysicist • *n* astrofísic *(m)*
astrophysics • *n* astrofísica *(f)*
astute • *adj* astut
astutely • *adv* astutament
asylum • *n* asil *(m)*
asymmetrical • *adj* asimètric
asymmetrically • *adv* asimètricament
asymptomatic • *adj* asimptomàtic
asymptote • *n* asímptota *(f)*
at • *prep* a
ataraxia • *n* ataràxia *(f)*
ataxia • *n* atàxia *(f)*
atheism • *n* ateisme *(m)*
atheist • *n* ateu *(m)*
atheistic • *adj* ateístic, ateu
athlete • *n* atleta *(f)*
atlas • *n* atles *(m)*
atmosphere • *n* atmosfera *(f)*, aerosfera *(f)*, ambient *(m)*
atmospheric • *adj* atmosfèric
atoll • *n* atol *(m)*
atom • *n* àtom *(m)*
atomic • *adj* atòmic
atonement • *n* redempció *(f)*
atrium • *n* atri *(m)*
atrocious • *adj* atroç
atrocity • *n* atrocitat *(f)*
atrophy • *v* atrofiar • *n* atròfia *(f)*
attack • *v* atacar • *n* atac *(m)*
attacker • *n* atacant *(m)*
attain • *v* aconseguir
attempt • *n* temptativa *(f)*
attend • *v* atendre, assistir
attention • *n* atenció *(f)*
attentive • *adj* atent
attentively • *adv* atentament
attenuate • *v* atenuar
attic • *n* golfes, àtic *(m)*

attitude • *n* positura *(f)*, actitud *(f)*
attorney • *n* advocat
attraction • *n* atracció *(f)*
attractive • *adj* atractiu
atypical • *adj* atípic
auction • *v* subhastar • *n* subhasta *(f)*
audacious • *adj* audaç
audible • *adj* oïble
audience • *n* públic *(m)*
audio • *adj* àudio
audiometer • *n* audiòmetre *(m)*, acúmetre *(m)*
audiometry • *n* audiometria *(f)*
audiovisual • *adj* audiovisual
audit • *n* auditoria *(f)*
auger • *n* barrina *(f)*
augite • *n* augita *(f)*
augment • *v* augmentar
aunt • *n* tia *(f)*
aura • *n* aura *(f)*
aureole • *n* aurèola *(f)*
auriferous • *adj* aurífer
aurochs • *n* ur *(m)*
aurora • *n* aurora *(f)*
auspicious • *adj* propici *(m)*, propícia *(f)*, favorable *(f)*
austerely • *adv* austerament
australopithecine • *adj* australopitecí *(m)*
authentic • *adj* autèntic
authentically • *adv* autènticament
authentication • *n* autenticació *(f)*
authenticity • *n* autenticitat *(f)*
author • *n* autor *(m)*, autora *(f)*
authoritarian • *adj* autoritari
authoritatively • *adv* autoritàriament
authorize • *v* autoritzar
autism • *n* autisme *(m)*
autistic • *n* autista *(f)* • *adj* autista
autobiographer • *n* autobiògraf *(m)*
autobiographical • *adj* autobiogràfic
autobiography • *n* autobiografia *(f)*
autocrat • *n* autòcrata *(f)*
autocratic • *adj* autocràtic
autocratically • *adv* autocràticament
autoeroticism • *n* autoerotisme *(m)*
autogamy • *n* autogàmia *(f)*
autograph • *v* autografiar • *n* autògraf *(m)*
autoimmune • *adj* autoimmune
autoimmunity • *n* autoimmunitat *(f)*
autolysis • *n* autòlisi *(f)*
automatic • *adj* automàtic
automatically • *adv* automàticament
automation • *n* automatització *(f)*
automatism • *n* automatisme *(m)*
automobile • *n* automòbil *(m)*
autonomous • *adj* autònom

autonomy • *n* autonomia *(f)*, autonomy *(f)*
autopsy • *n* autòpsia *(f)*
autumn • *n* tardor *(f)*
autumnal • *adj* autumnal
auxiliary • *adj* auxiliar
available • *adj* disponible
avalanche • *n* allau
avarice • *n* avarícia *(f)*, cobdícia *(f)*, avidesa *(f)*
avaricious • *adj* avariciós
avariciously • *adv* avariciosament
avenge • *v* venjar
avenue • *n* avinguda *(f)*
average • *n* mitjana *(f)*
aversion • *n* aversió *(f)*
avian • *adj* aviari
aviary • *n* aviari *(m)*
avidly • *adv* àvidament
avocado • *n* alvocat *(m)*, alvocater *(m)*
await • *v* esperar

awake • *v* llevar-se, despertar • *adj* despert, llevat
award • *v* fallar, decretar, sentenciar, premiar, guardonar • *n* veredicte *(m)*, premi *(m)*, trofeu *(m)*, medalla *(f)*, guardó *(m)*
aware • *adj* conscient
awareness • *n* consciència *(f)*
awful • *adj* horrorós
awkward • *adj* maldestre *(m)*
awl • *n* alena *(f)*
axillary • *adj* axil·lar
axiom • *n* axioma *(m)*
axiomatic • *adj* axiomàtic
axiomatically • *adv* axiomàticament
axis • *n* eix *(m)*, axis *(m)*
axle • *n* eix *(m)*
axon • *n* àxon *(m)*, axó *(m)*
azalea • *n* azalea *(f)*
azimuth • *n* azimut *(m)*
azure • *n* atzur *(m)* • *adj* atzur

B

baa • *v* belar • *n* bel *(m)*
baboon • *n* babuí *(m)*
baby • *n* nadó *(m)*, bebè *(m)*, benjamí *(m)*
babysitter • *n* cangur
baccarat • *n* bacarà
bacchanal • *n* bacanal *(f)* • *adj* bacanal
bachelor • *n* solter *(m)*
back • *n* esquena *(f)*
backboard • *n* tauler *(m)*
backbone • *n* columna vertebral *(f)*, espina dorsal *(f)*, espinada *(f)*
backdrop • *n* escenari *(m)*
backgammon • *n* backgammon *(m)*
background • *n* bagatge *(m)*, fons *(m)*, antecedents
backhand • *n* cop de revés *(m)* • *adj* de revés
backpack • *n* motxilla *(f)*
backspin • *n* efecte de retrocés *(m)*
backward • *adv* enrere
bacon • *n* cansalada *(f)*
bacterial • *adj* bacterià
bacteriological • *adj* bacteriològic
bacteriologist • *n* bacteriòleg *(m)*
bacteriology • *n* bacteriologia *(f)*
bad • *adj* mal, dolent
badge • *n* medalla *(f)*
badger • *n* teixó *(m)*
badly • *adv* malament, mal
badminton • *n* bàdminton *(m)*
badness • *n* bua *(f)*

bag • *n* bossa *(f)*, coixí *(m)*
bagatelle • *n* bagatel·la *(f)*
bagpipes • *n* cornamusa *(f)*, gaita *(f)*
bait • *n* esquer *(m)*
baize • *n* feltre *(m)*
bake • *v* fornejar
baker • *n* forner *(m)*
bakery • *n* fleca *(f)*, forn *(m)*
baklava • *n* baclaua
balalaika • *n* balalaica *(f)*
balance • *v* equilibrar, compensar • *n* equilibri *(m)*, balança *(f)*, balanç *(m)*
balcony • *n* balcó *(m)*
bald • *adj* calb
baldness • *n* calvície *(f)*, calbesa *(f)*
ball • *n* bola *(f)*, pilota *(f)*, pilotes *(f)*
ballerina • *n* ballarina *(f)*
ballistic • *adj* balístic
ballistics • *n* balística *(f)*
balloon • *n* globus *(m)*, baló *(m)*
ballot • *n* papereta de vot *(f)*
balls • *n* ous
bamboo • *n* bambú *(m)*
banal • *adj* banal
banana • *n* banana *(f)*, plàtan *(m)*
banderilla • *n* banderilla *(f)*
bandoleer • *n* canana *(f)*
banish • *v* bandejar
banjo • *n* banjo *(m)*
bank • *n* banc *(m)*
banker • *n* banquer *(m)*

banner • *n* bandera *(f)*, banderola *(f)*, estendard *(m)*, gomfaró *(m)*, pancarta *(f)*, banner *(m)*
baptism • *n* baptisme *(m)*
baptismal • *adj* baptismal
baptist • *n* baptista *(f)*
baptize • *v* batejar
barbarian • *n* bàrbar *(m)* • *adj* bàrbar
barbel • *n* barb *(m)*
barbican • *n* barbacana *(f)*
barefoot • *adv* descalç
barely • *adv* a penes
baritone • *n* baríton *(m)*, baríton
barium • *n* bari *(m)*
bark • *v* lladrar, bordar • *n* lladruc *(m)*, escorça *(f)*
barley • *n* ordi *(m)*
barnacle • *n* percebe *(m)*
barometer • *n* baròmetre *(m)*
barometric • *adj* baromètric
baron • *n* baró *(m)*
baroness • *n* baronessa *(f)*
baronial • *adj* baronial
barony • *n* baronia *(f)*
barque • *n* bricbarca *(m)*, veler *(m)*
barrack • *n* caserna *(f)*
barrel • *n* bóta *(f)*, canó *(m)*, quart *(m)*
barrow • *n* túmul *(m)*
bartender • *n* bàrman *(f)*
baryon • *n* barió *(m)*
basalt • *n* basalt *(m)*
base • *v* basar • *n* base *(f)*, fonament *(m)*, principi *(m)*, caserna *(f)*, seu *(f)*, basament *(m)* • *adj* baix, abjecte, vil, indigne, innoble, immoral, vulgar
baseball • *n* beisbol *(m)*
basement • *n* soterrani *(m)*
basic • *adj* bàsic
basically • *adv* bàsicament
basil • *n* alfàbrega *(f)*, alfàbega *(f)*
basilica • *n* basílica *(f)*
basilisk • *n* basilisc *(m)*
basin • *n* pica *(f)*, conca *(f)*
bask • *v* gaudir, disfrutar
basket • *n* cistell *(m)*, cistella *(f)*, cistella, bàsquet, encistellada, bàsquet *(m)*
basketball • *n* bàsquet *(m)*, basquetbol *(m)*
bassoon • *n* fagot *(m)*
bassoonist • *n* baixó
bastard • *n* bastard *(m)*, bord *(m)*, fill de puta *(m)* • *adj* bastard *(m)*, bord *(m)*, fill de puta *(m)*
bastion • *n* bastió *(m)*
bat • *n* ratpenat *(m)*, ratapinyada *(f)*, muricec *(m)*, bat *(m)*
bath • *n* bany

bathometer • *n* batímetre *(m)*, batòmetre *(m)*
bathrobe • *n* barnús *(m)*
bathroom • *n* bany *(m)*, servei *(m)*, vàter *(m)*, servici *(m)*
bathymetric • *adj* batimètric
bathymetry • *n* batimetria *(f)*
bathyscaphe • *n* batiscaf *(m)*
bathysphere • *n* batisfera *(f)*
batik • *n* bàtik
baton • *n* porra *(f)*, batuta *(f)*, testimoni *(m)*
batter • *n* batut *(m)*, batedor *(m)*
battery • *n* bateria *(f)*
battle • *v* batallar • *n* batalla *(f)*
battlefield • *n* camp de batalla *(m)*
battleship • *n* cuirassat *(m)*
bay • *n* badia *(f)*, bai
bayonet • *n* baioneta
bazaar • *n* basar
be • *v* estar, ser, ésser, fer
beach • *n* platja *(f)*
bead • *n* dena *(f)*
beak • *n* bec *(m)*
bean • *n* mongeta *(f)*, fesol *(m)*
bear • *n* ós *(m)*, bear • *v* portar, suportar
bearable • *adj* suportable
beard • *v* barbar • *n* barba *(f)*
beast • *n* bèstia *(f)*, fera *(f)*
beastly • *adj* bestial, animal
beautiful • *adj* bell *(m)*, bella *(f)*, formós *(m)*, formósa *(f)*, bonic *(m)*, bonica *(f)*
beautifully • *adv* bellament
beauty • *n* bellesa *(f)*
beaver • *n* castor, conillet *(m)*
because • *conj* perquè, ja que, car, puix, puix que
become • *v* esdevenir, escaure
bed • *v* allitar-se • *n* llit *(m)*, capa, buc *(m)*
bedbug • *n* xinxa *(f)*
bedouin • *n* beduí *(m)*
bedroom • *n* dormitori *(m)*, cambra *(f)*
bedspread • *n* colxa *(f)*, manta *(f)*, vànova *(f)*
bee • *n* abella *(f)*, be *(f)*
beech • *n* faig
beef • *n* vedella *(f)*
beehive • *n* arna *(f)*, buc *(m)*, casera *(f)*, rusc *(m)*
beekeeper • *n* apicultor *(m)*, abeller *(m)*
beer • *n* cervesa *(f)*, birra *(f)*
beeswax • *n* cera d'abelles *(f)*
beetle • *n* escarabat *(m)*
before • *adv* abans, davant • *prep* abans de, abans que, davant, abans
beg • *v* pidolar, mendicar, suplicar, pregar

beget • *v* engendrar, concebre
beggar • *n* mendicant (f), captaire (f)
begin • *v* començar, iniciar
beginner • *n* principiant
beginning • *n* començament (m), inici (m), principi (m)
begrime • *v* ensutzar
beguile • *v* embetumar
behavior • *n* conducta (f), comportament (m)
behead • *v* decapitar
behind • *adv* darrere • *prep* darrere
behold • *v* mirar, vigilar
being • *n* ésser (m)
belch • *v* rotar
belief • *n* creença (f)
believably • *adv* creïblement
believe • *v* creure
believer • *n* creient (f)
bell • *n* campana (f)
bellows • *n* manxa (f)
belly • *n* buc (m), abdomen (m), panxa (f), ventre
beloved • *adj* estimat (m), estimada (f)
below • *adv* sota, ensota • *prep* sota
belt • *n* cinturó (m), corretja (f), cop (f), regió (f)
bench • *n* banc (m), banqueta (f)
beneath • *adv* sota • *prep* sota
benefactor • *n* benfactor (m)
beneficial • *adj* beneficiós
benefit • *v* beneficiar • *n* benefici (m)
benevolence • *n* benevolència (f)
benevolent • *adj* benevolent (m), benèfic (f)
benevolently • *adv* benèvolament
bent • *adj* tort
benzene • *n* benzè (m)
bereavement • *n* dol (m)
berkelium • *n* berkeli (m)
berry • *n* baia (f)
berth • *n* camarot (m)
beryl • *n* beril (m)
beryllium • *n* beril·li (m)
besides • *adv* a més, a més a més, d'altra banda
besiege • *v* assetjar
best • *adj* millor
bestiality • *n* bestialitat (f)
bestiary • *n* bestiari (m)
bet • *v* apostar • *n* aposta (f)
beta • *n* beta (f)
betel • *n* bètel (m)
betray • *v* trair
better • *v* millorar • *adj* millor
between • *prep* entre
bewitch • *v* embruixar
bezant • *n* besant (m)

bias • *n* biaix (m)
biblical • *adj* bíblic
bibliographic • *adj* bibliogràfic
bibliography • *n* bibliografia (f)
bicameral • *adj* bicameral
bicycle • *n* bicicleta (f)
biface • *n* bifaç (m)
big • *adj* gran
bigamy • *n* bigàmia (f)
bike • *n* bici (f), moto (f)
bikini • *n* biquini (m)
bilabial • *adj* bilabial
bilateral • *adj* bilateral
bilberry • *n* nabiu (m), nabinera (f)
bile • *n* bilis (f), fel (f)
bilingual • *adj* bilingüe
bill • *n* bec (m), factura (f)
billiards • *n* billar (m)
bimolecular • *adj* bimolecular
bimonthly • *adv* bimestral
binary • *adj* binari
bingo • *n* bingo (m)
binoculars • *n* binocles (m)
binomial • *n* binomi (m)
biochemical • *adj* bioquímic
biochemistry • *n* bioquímica (f)
biodegradable • *adj* biodegradable
biogenesis • *n* biogènesi (f)
biographer • *n* biògraf (m)
biography • *n* biografia (f)
biological • *adj* biològic
biologist • *n* biòleg (m), biòloga (f)
biology • *n* biologia (f)
bioluminescence • *n* bioluminescència (f)
biomedicine • *n* biomedicina (f)
bioremediation • *n* bioremediació (f)
biotic • *adj* biòtic
biotite • *n* biotita (f)
bipolar • *adj* bipolar (f)
birch • *n* bedoll (m)
bird • *n* au (m), ocell (m), noia (f)
birth • *n* naixença (f), part (m)
birthday • *n* aniversari (m), natalici (m)
bisexual • *n* bisexual • *adj* bisexual
bishop • *n* bisbe (m), alfil (m)
bishopric • *n* bisbat (m)
bismuth • *n* bismut (m)
bistro • *n* bistrot
bit • *n* mos (m), mica (f), poquet (m)
bitch • *n* gossa (f)
bite • *v* mossegar • *n* mossegada (f)
bitter • *adj* amarg
bitterly • *adv* amargament
bittersweet • *n* dolçamara (f)
bizarre • *adj* estrany, estrafolari
blab • *v* xafardejar

blabber • *v* xafardejar • *n* xafarder
black • *n* negre *(m)*, negra *(f)* • *adj* negre, fosc
blackberry • *n* esbarzer *(m)*, móra *(f)*
blackbird • *n* merla *(f)*, tord negre *(m)*
blackboard • *n* pissarra *(f)*
blacken • *v* ennegrir
blackish • *adj* negrós, negrenc
blackmail • *n* xantatge *(m)*
blackmailer • *n* xantatgista *(f)*
blackness • *n* negror *(f)*
blacksmith • *n* ferrer *(m)*
bladder • *n* bufeta *(f)*
bladderpod • *n* tabac indi
blame • *n* culpa *(f)* • *v* culpar
blameworthy • *adj* culpable
blanket • *n* manta *(f)*
blasphemy • *n* blasfèmia *(f)*
bleed • *v* sagnar
blend • *n* mescla *(f)*
blender • *n* batidora *(f)*
blepharitis • *n* blefaritis *(f)*
bless • *v* beneir
blind • *v* cegar • *n* persiana *(f)* • *adj* cec, orb
blindly • *adv* cegament
blindness • *n* ceguesa *(f)*
blip • *n* parpelleig *(m)*
block • *v* bloquejar, blocar • *n* cub *(m)*, bloc *(m)*, illa *(f)*, bloqueig *(m)*
blockade • *v* bloquejar • *n* bloqueig *(m)*
blond • *n* ros *(m)*
blood • *n* sang *(f)*
bloodily • *adv* cruentament
bloody • *adj* sagnant
blossom • *v* florir • *n* flor *(f)*, floració *(f)*
blow • *v* bufar, llepar
blowgun • *n* sarbatana
blowtorch • *n* bufador *(m)*
blue • *n* blau *(m)* • *adj* blau, verd
blue-eyed • *adj* ullblau
blueberry • *n* nabiu *(m)*, mirtil *(m)*, nabinera *(f)*
blueness • *n* blavor *(f)*
bluish • *adj* blavós, blavenc, blavís
blunderbuss • *n* trabuc
blunt • *adj* rom
blurred • *adj* borrós
blush • *v* posar-se vermell, tornar-se vermell • *n* coloret *(m)*
boa • *n* boa *(f)*, boà *(m)*
boar • *n* verro *(m)*
board • *n* mesa *(f)*
boarder • *n* pensionista *(m)*, intern *(m)*
boarding • *n* càrrega contra la tanca *(f)*
boards • *n* tanca *(f)*
boastful • *adj* vanagloriós

boat • *n* vaixell *(m)*
bobcat • *n* linx roig *(m)*
bocce • *n* boccia *(f)*
body • *n* cos *(m)*, buc *(m)*
bodybuilder • *n* culturista *(f)*
bodybuilding • *n* culturisme *(m)*
bodyguard • *n* guardaespatlles *(f)*
bodywork • *n* buc *(m)*
bogeyman • *n* home del sac *(m)*
boggle • *v* confondre's, estar confós
boggy • *adj* pantanós
boil • *v* bullir
boiling • *adj* bullent
boisterous • *adj* sorollós *(m)*, escandalós *(m)*
bold • *adj* agosarat, negreta *(f)*
bolometer • *n* bolòmetre *(m)*
bolt • *n* llampec *(m)*
bomb • *v* bombardejar • *n* bomba *(f)*, tartana *(f)*, monument *(m)*
bombard • *n* bombarda *(f)* • *v* bombardejar
bond • *n* aparell *(m)*
bone • *v* desossar • *n* os *(m)*
bongo • *n* bongo *(m)*
bonk • *n* bony
bonnet • *n* capó
bony • *adj* ossi
boo • *v* esbroncar • *n* esbroncada *(f)* • *interj* bu, ua
boob • *n* pit *(m)*
book • *v* reservar, anotar • *n* llibre *(m)*, àlbum *(m)*, llibres
bookseller • *n* llibreter *(m)*, llibretera *(f)*, llibrer *(m)*
bookshop • *n* llibreria *(f)*
boom • *n* boom *(m)*
boomerang • *n* bumerang *(m)*
boot • *v* vomitar • *n* bota *(f)*
bootleg • *n* contraban
bootstrap • *n* llengüeta *(f)*, arrencada *(f)*
borage • *n* borratja *(f)*
borax • *n* bòrax *(m)*
border • *v* vorejar • *n* vora *(f)*, orla *(f)*, sanefa *(f)*, frontera *(f)*
bore • *v* barrinar, perforar, foradar, avorrir • *n* rissaga *(f)*
bored • *adj* avorrit
boric • *adj* bòric
boring • *adj* avorrit
born • *adj* nat
borne • *adj* cargar amb
bornite • *n* bornita *(f)*
boron • *n* bor *(m)*
borrow • *v* manllevar, amprar • *n* caiguda *(f)*
borrower • *n* manllevador *(m)*

boson • *n* bosó *(m)*
boss • *n* patró *(m)*
bossy • *adj* manaire
botanical • *adj* botànic
botanist • *n* botànic *(m)*
botany • *n* botànica *(f)*
bother • *v* molestar
bottle • *v* embotellar • *n* ampolla *(f)*, botella *(f)*, coratge *(m)*, audàcia *(m)*
bottom • *n* fons *(m)*, cul *(m)*
bouillon • *n* brou *(m)*
boulder • *n* bloc *(m)*
bounce • *v* botre
bound • *n* límit *(m)*
boundary • *n* frontera *(f)*
bourgeois • *adj* burgès
bourgeoisie • *n* burgesia *(f)*
boutique • *n* boutique *(f)*
bovine • *adj* boví
bow • *v* corbar, doblegar, vinclar • *n* arc *(m)*, corba, arc, reverència *(f)*, inclinació *(f)*, proa *(f)*
bowels • *n* intestins
bowl • *n* bol *(m)*
bowler • *n* jugador de bitlles *(m)*, bitllaire *(f)*
bowling • *n* bitlles *(m)*
bowsprit • *n* bauprès *(m)*
box • *v* empaquetar, encapsar, boxejar, boxar • *n* capsa *(f)*, caixa *(f)*, llotja *(f)*, garita *(f)*, boix *(m)*, cop de puny *(m)*
boxer • *n* boxador *(m)*, boxejador
boxing • *n* boxa
boxwood • *n* boix *(m)*
boy • *n* minyó *(m)*, noi *(m)*, alůlot *(m)*, xiquet *(m)*, xic *(m)*, xicot *(m)*, home *(m)*
boycott • *v* boicotejar • *n* boicot *(m)*
boyfriend • *n* xicot *(m)*, amic *(m)*
bra • *n* sostenidor *(m)*
bracelet • *n* braçalet *(m)*
bracken • *n* falguera aquilina *(f)*, falaguera aquilina *(f)*
bract • *n* bràctea *(f)*
bradycardia • *n* bradicàrdia *(f)*
braggart • *n* fanfarró *(m)*
braille • *n* braille *(m)*
brain • *n* cervell *(m)*
brake • *n* fre
bramble • *n* esbarzer
branch • *n* branca *(f)*
brandish • *v* brandar, brandejar
brandy • *n* brandi *(m)*, conyac *(m)*
brass • *n* llautó, metall *(m)*, pasta *(f)*
brave • *adj* valent, coratjós, audaç
bravely • *adv* valentament, coratjosament
bravery • *n* bravesa *(f)*, bravor *(f)*, bravura *(f)*

bray • *v* bramar • *n* bram *(m)*
bread • *n* pa *(m)*
breadfruit • *n* arbre del pa *(m)*
breakable • *adj* trencable
breakfast • *v* esmorzar • *n* esmorzar *(m)*
breakwater • *n* escullera *(f)*
bream • *n* brema *(f)*
breast • *n* pit *(m)*
breath • *n* respiració *(f)*, alè *(m)*
breathe • *v* respirar, alenar
breeches • *n* calçons
breed • *v* criar, engendrar • *n* raça *(f)*, varietat *(f)*
breeze • *n* brisa *(f)*
breezily • *adv* airosament
breezy • *adj* airejós, airós
brew • *v* destilar
brick • *n* maó *(m)*
bricklayer • *n* paleta *(f)*
bridal • *adj* nupcial
bride • *n* núvia *(f)*
bridegroom • *n* nuvi *(m)*
bridge • *n* pont *(m)*, bridge *(m)*
bridle • *n* brida *(f)*
brief • *adj* breu, concís
briefcase • *n* cartera *(f)*
briefly • *adv* breument
brig • *n* bergantí *(m)*, calabós *(m)*
bright • *adj* brillant, clar
brilliant • *adj* brillant, clar
brilliantly • *adv* brillantment
brim • *n* vora *(f)*
bring • *v* portar
brittle • *adj* fràgil, trencadís
broadcast • *v* emetre, transmetre • *n* emissió *(f)*
broadcasting • *n* radiodifusió *(f)*
broccoli • *n* bròquil *(m)*
brochure • *n* fullet *(m)*, opuscle *(m)*, prospecte *(m)*
broke • *adj* pelat
broken • *adj* trencat
bromine • *n* brom
bronchiole • *n* bronquíol *(m)*
bronchus • *n* bronqui *(m)*
bronze • *n* bronze *(m)* • *adj* bronze *(m)*
broom • *n* escombra *(f)*, ginesta
broth • *n* brou *(m)*
brother • *n* germà *(m)*
brother-in-law • *n* cunyat *(m)*
brotherhood • *n* fraternitat *(f)*
brouhaha • *n* gatzara *(f)*, aldarull *(m)*, cridòria *(f)*, rebombori *(m)*, brogit *(m)*, avalot *(m)*
browbeat • *v* intimidar
brown • *n* marró *(m)* • *adj* marró
bruise • *n* blau *(m)*

brush • *n* raspall *(m)*, raspallar
brutal • *adj* brutal
bubble • *n* bombolla *(f)*
bubo • *n* bubó *(m)*
bubonic • *adj* bubònic
buck • *n* cérvol *(m)*, boc *(m)*
bucket • *n* cubell *(m)*, galleda *(f)*, cubellada *(f)*, catúfol *(m)*
buckle • *n* sivella *(f)*
buckler • *n* escut *(m)*
bucolic • *adj* bucòlic
bud • *v* gemar • *n* brot *(m)*, gema *(f)*, borró *(m)*, colúlega *(f)*
budgerigar • *n* periquito *(m)*
budget • *n* pressupost *(m)*
buffalo • *n* búfal *(m)*, bisó *(m)*
bufflehead • *n* morell capblanc
bug • *n* xinxa *(f)*, cuca *(f)*, error *(m)*, defecte *(m)*, febre *(f)*, mania *(f)*
bugle • *n* clarí *(m)*
bugler • *n* corneta *(m)*
build • *v* construir, edificar
building • *n* construcció *(f)*, edifici *(m)*
built • *v* construït
bulb • *n* bulb *(m)*
bulk • *adj* massiu
bulky • *adj* voluminós
bull • *n* toro *(m)*, butlla *(f)*, segell *(m)*
bullet • *n* bala *(f)*
bulletproof • *adj* antibales, infalúlible *(f)*
bullring • *n* plaça de toros *(f)*, plaça de bous *(f)*
bullseye • *n* fitó *(m)*, ull de bou *(m)*
bullshit • *n* collonades
bumblebee • *n* borinot *(m)*
bumper • *n* para-xocs *(m)*
bun • *n* panellet *(m)*, pasta *(m)*, brioix *(m)*, llesca *(m)*, monya *(f)*, trossa *(f)*
bunch • *n* raïm *(m)*
bundle • *n* feix *(m)*, farcell *(m)*
bunion • *n* galindó *(m)*
bunker • *n* búnquer *(m)*, carbonera *(f)*
bunny • *n* catxap *(m)*, conillet *(m)*, conilleta *(f)*
bunt • *n* toc *(m)*
buoy • *n* boia *(f)*

burden • *n* càrrega *(f)*, carga
burdensome • *adj* gravós
bureaucracy • *n* burocràcia *(f)*
bureaucratic • *adj* burocràtic
burette • *n* bureta *(f)*
burglar • *n* lladre *(f)*
burial • *n* enterrament *(m)*
buried • *adj* enterrat *(m)*
burin • *n* burí *(m)*
burn • *v* cremar • *n* cremada *(f)*
burning • *adj* ardent
burnisher • *n* brunyidor *(m)*
burp • *n* rot *(m)*
burrow • *n* cau *(m)*
bury • *v* enterrar
bus • *n* autobús *(m)*, bus *(m)*
bush • *n* arbust *(m)*
business • *n* negoci *(m)*
bust • *n* bust *(m)*
bustard • *n* avitarda *(f)*
busy • *adj* ocupat
but • *conj* menys, excepte, però, encara que
butcher • *n* carnisser *(m)*, carnissera *(f)*
butler • *n* sommelier *(m)*, majordom *(m)*
butt • *n* natja *(f)*, punta *(f)*, burilla *(f)* • *v* tossar
butter • *n* mantega *(f)*
butterfly • *n* papallona *(f)*, papalló *(m)*, papaió *(m)*, babaiana *(f)*, paloma *(f)*, palometa *(f)*
buttermilk • *n* sèrum de mantega *(m)*
buttery • *adj* mantegós
buttock • *n* natja *(f)*
button • *v* botonar • *n* botó *(m)*, poncella *(f)*
buttress • *n* contrafort *(m)*
buy • *v* comprar
buzzard • *n* aligot *(m)*, zopilot *(m)*
bye • *interj* adéu
bypass • *n* apartador *(m)*, variant *(f)*, camí secundari *(m)*, ronda *(m)*, desviació *(f)*, derivació *(f)*, canal de derivació, canal d'alimentació, bypass *(m)*, anastomosi de derivació per a revascularització cardíaca

C

cabaret • *n* cabaret *(m)*
cabbage • *n* col *(f)*
cabinet • *n* armari *(m)*, gabinet *(m)*
cable • *v* cablejar, lligar • *n* cable *(m)*, cable
cacao • *n* cacau

cactus • *n* cactus *(m)*
cadastral • *adj* cadastral
cadaver • *n* cadàver *(m)*
cadaveric • *adj* cadavèric
cadaverous • *adj* cadavèric
caddie • *n* cadi *(f)*

caddy • *n* cadi *(f)*
cadence • *n* cadència *(f)*
cadmium • *n* cadmi *(m)*
caecum • *n* cec *(m)*
caesura • *n* cesura *(f)*
cafeteria • *n* cafeteria *(f)*
caffeine • *n* cafeïna *(f)*
cage • *v* engabiar • *n* gàbia *(f)*
cake • *n* pastís *(m)*
calcaneal • *adj* calcani
calcine • *v* calcinar *(m)*
calcite • *n* calcita *(f)*
calcium • *n* calci *(m)*
calculable • *adj* calculable
calculate • *v* calcular
calculation • *n* càlcul *(m)*
calculator • *n* calculadora *(f)*, calculadora
calculus • *n* càlcul *(m)*, càlcul
calendar • *n* calendari *(m)*, calendàriu, agenda *(f)*
calf • *n* vedell *(m)*, panxell *(m)*
calibration • *n* calibratge *(m)*
californium • *n* californi
calipers • *n* calibrador *(m)*
caliph • *n* califa *(m)*
call • *v* cridar, xisclar, xillar, telefonar, trucar, tocar, visitar, dir-se • *n* telefonada *(f)*, trucada *(f)*, visita *(f)*, crit *(m)*, crida *(f)*, xiscle *(m)*
calligrapher • *n* calŭlígraf *(m)*
calligraphic • *adj* calŭligràfic
calligraphy • *n* calŭligrafia *(f)*
calm • *v* calmar • *n* calma *(f)* • *adj* calm
calmly • *adv* calmosament
calorimeter • *n* calorímetre *(m)*
calorimetric • *adj* calorimètric
calorimetry • *n* calorimetria *(f)*
calque • *n* calc *(m)*
calyx • *n* calze *(m)*
camaraderie • *n* camaraderia *(f)*
camel • *n* camell *(m)*
camera • *n* càmera *(f)*
cameraman • *n* cameràman *(f)*
campaign • *n* campanya *(f)*
camphor • *n* càmfora *(f)*
campus • *n* campus *(m)*
can • *v* poder, enllaunar • *n* llauna *(f)*
canal • *n* canal *(m)*
canary • *n* canari *(m)*
cancellation • *n* cancelŭlació *(f)*
cancer • *n* càncer *(m)*
cancerous • *adj* cancerós
candelabrum • *n* canelobre *(m)*
candidate • *n* candidat *(m)*
candle • *n* espelma *(f)*, candela *(f)*
candlestick • *n* candeler *(m)*
candy • *n* caramel *(m)*, llaminadura *(f)*

cane • *n* canya *(f)*, canya
canine • *adj* caní
cannabis • *n* cànem *(m)*
cannibal • *n* caníbal *(f)*
cannibalism • *n* antropofàgia *(f)*, canibalisme *(m)*
cannon • *n* canó *(m)*
canoe • *n* canoa *(f)*
canonize • *v* canonitzar, santificar
cant • *n* argot *(m)*
cantaloupe • *n* meló cantalup *(m)*
canvas • *n* lona *(f)*, llenç *(m)*, tela *(f)*
canyon • *n* congost
cap • *n* gorra *(f)*
capable • *adj* capaç
capacitor • *n* condensador *(m)*
capacity • *n* capacitat *(f)*
cape • *n* cap *(m)*, capa *(f)*
capercaillie • *n* gall fer *(m)*, gall salvatge *(m)*, gall de bosc *(m)*
capillary • *n* capilŭlar *(m)*
capital • *n* capital *(m)*, capitell *(m)* • *adj* capital, excelŭlent, majúscula
capitalism • *n* capitalisme
capitalist • *adj* capitalista
caprice • *n* capritx *(m)*, caprici *(m)*
capsize • *v* sotsobrar
capsule • *n* càpsula *(f)*
captain • *n* capità *(m)*
capture • *v* capturar • *n* captura *(f)*
capybara • *n* capibara *(m)*
car • *n* cotxe *(m)*, automòbil *(m)*, vagó *(m)*, cabina *(f)*
caracal • *n* caracal *(m)*
carafe • *n* marraixa *(f)*, garrafa *(f)*
caramel • *n* caramel
carat • *n* quirat *(m)*
caravel • *n* caravelŭla *(f)*
carbide • *n* carbur *(m)*
carbohydrate • *n* carbohidrat *(m)*
carbon • *n* carboni *(m)*, carbó *(m)*
carburetor • *n* carburador *(m)*
card • *n* targeta *(f)*
cardia • *n* càrdies *(m)*
cardiac • *adj* cardíac
cardigan • *n* càrdigan *(m)*
cardinal • *adj* cardinal
cardiologist • *n* cardiòleg *(m)*
cardiology • *n* cardiologia *(f)*
cardiomyopathy • *n* miocardiopatia *(f)*, cardiomiopatia *(f)*
cardiovascular • *adj* cardiovascular
cardoon • *n* herbacol *(f)*
care • *n* cura *(f)*, compte *(m)*
career • *n* carrera *(f)*
carefree • *adj* despreocupat
careful • *adj* cautelós, curós

carefully • *adv* acuradament
careless • *adj* imprudent, negligent
caress • *v* carícia *(f)*
caretaker • *n* conserge *(m)*
cargo • *n* càrrega *(f)*
caricaturist • *n* caricaturista *(f)*
carillon • *n* carilló *(m)*
carmine • *n* carmí *(m)*, grana *(m)*, carmí
carnage • *n* carnatge *(m)*
carnal • *adj* carnal
carnival • *n* carnestoltes *(m)*, carnaval *(m)*
carnivore • *n* carnívor *(m)*
carnivorous • *adj* carnívor
carnotite • *n* carnotita *(f)*
carob • *n* garrover *(m)*, garrova *(f)*, garroví *(m)*, farina de garrova *(f)*
carotene • *n* carotè *(m)*
carotid • *n* caròtide *(f)*
carp • *n* carpa *(f)*
carpal • *adj* carpià
carpenter • *n* fuster *(m)*, fustera *(f)*
carpet • *n* moqueta *(f)*, catifa *(f)*
carriage • *n* carruatge *(m)*, cotxe *(m)*, vagó *(m)*
carrier • *n* portador *(m)*, portadora *(f)*
carrot • *n* pastanaga *(f)*
carry • *v* portar
cartilage • *n* cartílag *(m)*
cartographer • *n* cartògraf *(m)*
cartographic • *adj* cartogràfic
cartography • *n* cartografia *(f)*
carton • *n* bric *(m)*
cartoon • *n* tira còmica *(f)*, caricatura *(f)*, cartó *(m)*, dibuixos animats
cartridge • *n* cartutx *(f)*
carving • *n* entallament *(m)*
caryatid • *n* cariàtide *(f)*
case • *n* cas *(m)*, causa *(f)*, caixa *(f)*, capsa *(f)*, maleta *(f)*, vitrina *(f)* • *v* empaquetar
cash • *n* efectiu *(m)*
cashew • *n* anacard *(m)*
cashier • *v* destituir
cask • *n* bóta *(f)*, tina *(f)*
casket • *n* cofret *(m)*, escriny *(m)*, urna *(f)*
casserole • *n* casserola *(f)*, putxero *(m)*, olla *(f)*
cassette • *n* casset *(f)*
cast • *v* dirigir, llençar, fondre, votar • *n* llançament *(m)*, repartiment *(m)*, enguixat, motlle *(m)*
castanet • *n* castanyoles, castanyetes *(f)*, esclafidors
casting • *n* càsting *(m)*
castle • *n* castell *(m)*
castrate • *v* castrar
castration • *n* castració *(f)*
casual • *adj* casual, ocasional, informal

cat • *n* gat *(m)*, gata *(f)*, mix *(m)*, mixa *(f)*, moix *(m)*, moixa *(f)*, felí *(m)*, felina *(f)*
catacomb • *n* catacumba *(f)*
catalogue • *n* catàleg *(m)*
catalysis • *n* catàlisi *(f)*
catalytic • *adj* catalític
catapult • *v* catapultar • *n* catapulta *(f)*
catastrophe • *n* catàstrofe *(f)*
catastrophic • *adj* catastròfic
catcher • *n* receptor *(m)*
catechism • *n* catecisme *(m)*
catechumen • *n* catecumen
categorical • *adj* categòric
categorically • *adv* categòricament
category • *n* categoria *(f)*
caterpillar • *n* eruga *(f)*
catfish • *n* silur *(m)*
cathedral • *n* catedral *(f)*
cathode • *n* càtode *(m)*
cation • *n* catió *(m)*
catnip • *n* herba gatera
cattle • *n* bestiar *(m)*
cauliflower • *n* coliflor *(f)*
causal • *adj* causal
causality • *n* causalitat *(f)*
cause • *n* causa *(f)*
caustic • *adj* càustic
cauterization • *n* cauterització *(f)*
cauterize • *v* cauteritzar
cautious • *adj* cautelós
cautiously • *adv* cautelosament
cavalry • *n* cavalleria *(f)*
cave • *n* cova *(f)*
caveman • *n* cavernícola *(f)*
caviar • *n* caviar *(m)*
cavity • *n* cavitat *(f)*, càries *(f)*
cedar • *n* cedre
cedilla • *n* trencat *(m)*
ceiling • *n* sostre *(m)*
celebrate • *v* celebrar
celebration • *n* celebració *(f)*
celebrity • *n* celebritat *(f)*
celery • *n* api *(m)*
celesta • *n* celesta *(f)*
celibacy • *n* celibat *(m)*
cell • *n* pila *(f)*, calabós *(m)*, celůla *(f)*, celůla *(m)*, cèlůlula *(f)*
cello • *n* violoncel *(m)*
cellular • *adj* celůlular
cellulose • *n* celůlulosa *(f)*
cement • *n* ciment
cementum • *n* cement *(m)*
cenotaph • *n* cenotafi *(m)*
censer • *n* encenser *(m)*
census • *n* cens *(m)*
cent • *n* centau *(m)*, cèntim *(m)*
centaur • *n* centaure *(m)*

center • n pivot (f), central (m)
centipede • n centpeus
central • adj central
centralize • v centralitzar
centrally • adv centralment
centripetal • adj centrípet (m)
century • n segle (m), centúria (f)
ceramic • n ceràmica (f)
cerebellum • n cerebel (m)
cerebral • adj cerebral
ceremonial • adj cerimonial
ceremony • n cerimònia (f)
cerium • n ceri (m)
certain • adj cert
certainly • adv certament
certifiable • adj certificable, boig
certificate • n certificat (m)
certification • n certificació (f)
cerussite • n cerussita (f)
cervix • n cèrvix (f)
chafe • v desgastar, pelar, coure • n coïssor (f), ràbia (f)
chaff • n pallús (m)
chaffinch • n pinsà (m)
chain • n cadena (f)
chair • n cadira (f)
chalaza • n calaza (f)
chalcopyrite • n calcopirita (f)
chalice • n calze (m)
chalk • n creta (f), guix (m), magnèsia (f)
challenge • v desafiar • n desafiament (m), desafiu (m)
chamber • n cambra (f)
chameleon • n camaleó (m)
chamois • n isard
champagne • n xampany (m)
championship • n campionat (m)
chance • v arriscar-se • n oportunitat (f), atzar (m), probabilitat (f)
change • v canviar, modificar • n canvi (m)
chanterelle • n rossinyol (m)
chaos • n caos (m)
chaotic • adj caòtic
chaotically • adv caòticament
chapel • n capella (f)
chapter • n capítol (m), divisió (f)
character • n personatge (m), caràcter (m)
characteristic • n característica (f) • adj característic
characteristically • adv característicament
characterize • v caracteritzar
chard • n bleda (f)
charge • n càrrega (f), cost (m), preu (f), encàrrec (f)
chariot • n carro (m), carruatge (m), car-

rossa (f)
charismatic • adj carismàtic
charlatan • n xarlatà (m)
charm • n amulet (m), encant (m)
chase • n persecució (f)
chastely • adv castament
chastity • n castedat (f)
chat • v xerrar • n xat (m)
chauvinist • n xovinista • adj xovinista
chauvinistic • adj xovinista
cheat • v trampejar, mentir, enganyar • n trampós, truc
check • v comprovar, verificar, comparar • n inspecció (f)
checkered • adj escacat, endauat
checkmate • interj escac i mat
cheek • n galta (f)
cheekbone • n pòmul (m), zigoma (m)
cheers • interj salut
cheese • n formatge (m)
cheetah • n guepard
chef • n xef (m)
chelation • n quelació (f)
chemical • adj químic
chemically • adv químicament
chemist • n químic (m), química (f)
chemistry • n química (f)
cheque • n xec (m), taló (m)
cherry • n cirera (f), cirerer (m)
chert • n sílex
chervil • n cerfull (m)
chess • n escacs
chessboard • n àbac (m)
chest • n tòrax (m), pit (m)
chestnut • n castanya (f), castany (m), marró (m) • adj castany, marró
chew • v mastegar, masticar
chi • n khi (f)
chiasmus • n quiasme (m)
chicane • n xicana (f)
chick • n pollet (m), butza (f)
chicken • n pollastre (m), gallina (f), gall (m), butza (f)
chickpea • n cigronera (f), ciuró, cigró (m)
chief • n cap (m) • adj principal
chiefly • adv principalment
child • n nen
chilling • adj refrescant, esgarrifós, glaçador
chimera • n quimera (f)
chimney • n xemeneia (f)
chimpanzee • n ximpanzé (m)
chin • n mentó (m)
china • n porcellana (f)
chinchilla • n xinxilla (f)
chisel • n cisell
chitin • n quitina (f)

chiton • *n* quitó *(m)*
chlamys • *n* clàmide *(f)*
chlorate • *n* clorat *(m)*
chlorine • *n* clor
chlorophyll • *n* clorofilůla *(f)*
chocolate • *n* xocolata *(f)*, bombó *(m)*, xocolatina *(f)* • *adj* xocolata
choice • *n* tria *(f)*
cholera • *n* còlera *(f)*
choleric • *adj* colèric
choose • *v* triar, escollir, elegir
chopstick • *n* bastonet *(m)*
choral • *adj* coral
chordophone • *n* cordòfon *(m)*
chorea • *n* corea *(f)*
choreographer • *n* coreògraf *(m)*
choreographic • *adj* coreogràfic
choreography • *n* coreografia *(f)*
choroid • *n* coroide *(f)*
chromium • *n* crom
chromosomal • *adj* cromosòmic
chromosome • *n* cromosoma *(m)*
chromosphere • *n* cromosfera *(f)*
chronic • *adj* crònic
chronically • *adv* crònicament
chronogram • *n* cronograma *(m)*
chronological • *adj* cronològic
chronologically • *adv* cronològicament
chronologist • *n* cronologista *(f)*, cronòleg *(m)*
chronology • *n* cronologia *(f)*
chronometer • *n* cronòmetre *(m)*
chrysalis • *n* crisàlide *(f)*
chrysanthemum • *n* crisantem *(m)*, estrany *(m)*
chrysoberyl • *n* crisoberil *(m)*
chrysotile • *n* crisòtil *(m)*
chubby • *adj* grassonet, grosset
chufa • *n* xufa *(f)*, xufla *(f)*
church • *n* església *(f)*
churn • *n* manteguera *(f)*, lletera *(f)*
chyle • *n* quil *(m)*
chyme • *n* quim *(m)*
cicada • *n* cigala *(f)*
cigar • *n* cigar *(m)*
cigarette • *n* cigarret *(m)*
ciliate • *n* ciliat *(m)*
ciliated • *adj* ciliat
cinema • *n* cinema *(m)*
cinnabar • *n* cinabri *(m)*
cinnamon • *n* canyeller *(m)*, caneller *(m)*, canyella *(f)*, canella *(f)* • *adj* canyella *(f)*, canella *(f)*
cipher • *n* xifra *(f)*
circa • *prep* circa
circle • *n* cercle *(m)*, disc, òrbita *(f)*, ulleres
circular • *adj* circular

circularly • *adv* circularment
circulatory • *adj* circulatori
circumcise • *v* circumcidar
circumcision • *n* circumcisió *(f)*
circumference • *n* circumferència *(f)*
circumnavigate • *v* circumnavegar
circumnavigation • *n* circumnavegació *(f)*
circumspect • *adj* circumspecte
circumvent • *v* evitar, circumvalar, rodejar, bordejar, burlar, mofar
circumvention • *n* circumvalació *(f)*
circus • *n* circ *(m)*
cirrus • *n* cirrus *(m)*
cistern • *n* cisterna *(f)*
citadel • *n* ciutadella *(f)*
citizen • *n* ciutadà *(m)*
citizenship • *n* ciutadania *(f)*
citron • *n* poncem *(m)*
city • *n* ciutat *(f)*
civic • *adj* cívic
civil • *adj* civil
civility • *n* civilitat *(f)*
civilization • *n* civilització *(f)*
civilly • *adv* civilment
cladode • *n* cladodi *(m)*
claim • *n* pretensió
clairvoyance • *n* clarividència *(f)*
clam • *n* cloïssa *(f)*
clamor • *n* clamor *(m)*, clam *(m)*
clamp • *n* serjant *(m)*
clap • *v* fer mans balletes, aplaudir • *n* aplaudiment
clapper • *n* batall *(m)*
clapperboard • *n* claqueta
claptrap • *n* galimaties *(m)*, embull *(m)*, embrolla *(f)*, algaravia *(f)*
claque • *n* claca *(f)*
clarinet • *n* clarinet *(m)*
class • *n* classe *(f)*, promoció *(f)*, curs *(m)*
classicism • *n* classicisme *(m)*
classification • *n* classificació *(f)*
claustrophobia • *n* claustrofòbia *(f)*
claustrophobic • *adj* claustrofòbic
clavichord • *n* clavicordi *(m)*
clavicle • *n* clavícula *(f)*
claw • *n* urpa *(f)*, garra *(f)*
clay • *n* argila *(f)*, fang *(m)*
clean • *v* netejar, arreglar, ordenar • *adj* net, pur, sa
cleanliness • *n* netedat *(f)*
cleanly • *adv* netament
cleanup • *n* neteja *(f)*
clear • *v* aclarir-se, rebutjar • *adj* clar
clearance • *n* rebuig *(m)*
clearing • *n* clariana *(f)*, rebuig *(m)*
clearly • *adv* clarament

cleavage • *n* escot *(m)*
clef • *n* clau *(f)*
clergyman • *n* clergue
clever • *adj* llest
click • *v* clicar, fer clic • *n* clic *(m)*
client • *n* client *(f)*
cliff • *n* penya-segat *(m)*
climatic • *adj* climàtic
climatology • *n* climatologia *(f)*
climax • *n* clímax *(f)*, orgasme *(m)*
climb • *v* escalar
climber • *n* enfiladissa *(f)*
clink • *v* dringar • *n* dring *(m)*, trinc *(m)*
clinometer • *n* clinòmetre *(m)*
clitoris • *n* clítoris *(m)*
cloak • *n* capa *(f)*
clock • *v* cronometrar, mesurar • *n* rellotge *(m)*, comptaquilòmetres *(m)*
clog • *n* esclop *(m)*
cloister • *n* claustre *(m)*
clone • *v* clonar • *n* clon *(m)*
close • *v* cloure, tancar • *adj* pròxim
closed • *adj* tancat
closure • *n* clausura *(f)*
cloth • *n* drap *(m)*
clothes • *n* roba
clotheshorse • *n* estenedor *(m)*
clothesline • *n* estenedor *(m)*
clothing • *n* roba *(f)*
cloud • *n* núvol *(m)*
cloudberry • *n* romegueró de torbera *(m)*
cloudy • *adj* ennuvolat, nuvolós, nebulós
clove • *n* clau d'espècia *(f)*, clavell d'espècia *(m)*, all *(m)*
clover • *n* trèvol *(m)*
clown • *n* pallasso *(m)*
club • *v* bastonejar • *n* bastó *(m)*, club *(m)*, trèvol *(m)*
cluck • *v* cloquejar
clutch • *n* embragatge
coach • *n* entrenador *(m)*, autocar *(m)*
coachman • *n* cotxer *(m)*
coal • *n* carbó *(m)*
coalesce • *v* unir-se, ajuntar-se, incorporar-se
coarse • *adj* groller *(m)*, bast *(m)*, grollera *(f)*, basta *(f)*, brut *(m)*, bruta *(f)*
coast • *n* costa *(f)*
coastal • *adj* coster, costaner, costal
coat • *v* cobrir • *n* abric *(m)*, casaca *(f)*, cobertura *(f)*
cobalt • *n* cobalt *(m)*
cobblestone • *n* còdol, llamborda
coccyx • *n* còccix *(m)*
cochineal • *n* cotxinilla *(f)*
cochlea • *n* còclea *(f)*
cochlear • *adj* coclear *(f)*

cock-a-doodle-doo • *interj* quiquiriquic
cockade • *n* escarapelủla *(f)*
cockchafer • *n* escarabat de Sant Joan *(m)*
cockerel • *n* pollastre, pollet, butza
cockpit • *n* cabina *(f)*
cockroach • *n* escarabat *(m)*, panerola *(f)*
cocktail • *n* còctel *(m)*
coconut • *n* coco *(m)*
cocoon • *n* capoll *(m)*
cod • *n* bacallà *(m)*
code • *n* codi *(m)*, clau *(f)*
coercion • *n* coerció *(f)*, coerció
coexist • *v* coexistir
coexistence • *n* coexistència *(f)*
coffee • *n* cafè *(m)*, marró *(m)* • *adj* cafè, marró
coffer • *n* cofre *(m)*, cassetó *(m)*
coffin • *n* fèretre *(m)*, taüt *(m)*
cognac • *n* conyac *(m)*
coherent • *adj* coherent
coherently • *adv* coherentment
cohesive • *adj* cohesiu
cohort • *n* cohort
coin • *n* moneda *(f)*
cola • *n* cola *(f)*
cold • *n* fred *(m)*, constipat *(m)*, refredat *(m)* • *adj* fred
coldness • *n* fredor *(f)*
collaboration • *n* colủlaboració *(f)*
collage • *n* collage *(m)*
collar • *v* collar • *n* coll *(m)*, collar *(m)*, collera *(m)*, jou *(m)*
collate • *v* concedir un benefici eclesiàstic
colleague • *n* colủlega, company
collect • *v* reunir, ajuntar, recollir, agrupar, aplegar, arreplegar, replegar, colủleccionar
collection • *n* colủlecció *(f)*
collective • *adj* colủlectiu
collectively • *adv* colủlectivament
collector • *n* colủleccionador *(m)*, colủleccionista *(f)*
collegial • *adj* colủlegial
collegiate • *adj* colủlegiat
collider • *n* colủlisonador *(m)*
colloid • *n* colủloide *(m)*
colloquial • *adj* colủloquial
colloquy • *n* colloqui
cologne • *n* colònia
colon • *n* dos punts, còlon *(m)*
colonel • *n* coronel
colonial • *adj* colonial
colonialism • *n* colonialisme *(m)*
colonist • *n* colonitzador *(m)*, colon *(m)*
colonization • *n* colonització *(f)*
colonnade • *n* columnata *(f)*
colony • *n* colònia

color • *v* acolorir • *n* color *(f)*
colorimeter • *n* colorímetre *(m)*
colossus • *n* colós *(m)*
colt • *n* poltre *(m)*
columbine • *n* corniol *(m)*
column • *n* columna *(f)*
coma • *n* coma *(m)*
comb • *v* pentinar
combat • *v* combatre • *n* batalla *(f)*, combat *(m)*
combatant • *n* combatent *(f)*
combative • *adj* combatiu
combination • *n* combinació *(f)*
combustible • *n* combustible *(m)* • *adj* combustible
come • *v* venir, escórrer-se
comedy • *n* comèdia *(f)*
comet • *n* cometa *(m)*
comfortable • *adj* còmode
comfortably • *adv* còmodament
comitia • *n* comicis
comma • *n* coma *(f)*
command • *v* ordenar, manar • *n* ordre *(f)*, manat *(m)*
commandment • *n* manament *(m)*
commence • *v* començar
comment • *v* comentar • *n* comentari *(m)*
commentary • *n* comentari, comentari *(m)*
commerce • *n* comerç *(m)*
commercial • *n* anunci *(m)* • *adj* comercial
commercially • *adv* comercialment
common • *n* comuna *(f)* • *adj* comú *(m)*, comuna *(f)*, comú
commoner • *n* plebeu *(m)*, plebea *(f)*
commonly • *adv* comunament
commotion • *n* commoció *(f)*, avalot *(m)*, esvalot *(m)*, aldarull *(m)*
communism • *n* comunisme *(m)*
communist • *n* comunista *(f)*
community • *n* comunitat *(f)*
commute • *v* commutar
companion • *n* acompanyant *(m)*
company • *n* companyia *(f)*
comparable • *adj* comparable
comparative • *n* comparatiu *(m)* • *adj* comparatiu
comparatively • *adv* comparativament
comparison • *n* comparació *(f)*
compass • *n* brúixola *(f)*, àrea *(f)*, àmbit *(m)*
compassion • *n* compassió *(f)*
compassionate • *adj* compassiu
compatible • *adj* compatible
compelling • *adj* convincent
compendium • *n* compendi *(m)*

compensation • *n* compensació *(f)*
compete • *v* competir
competence • *n* competència *(f)*
competently • *adv* competentment
competition • *n* competència *(f)*, competició *(f)*
competitive • *adj* competitiu
complacent • *adj* complaent
complain • *v* queixar-se
complaint • *n* queixa *(f)*
complement • *v* complementar
complementary • *adj* complementari
complete • *v* complir • *adj* complet *(m)*, completa *(f)*, complet
completely • *adv* completament, totalment
complex • *n* complex *(m)* • *adj* complex
complexity • *n* complexitat *(f)*
complicated • *adj* complicat
composer • *n* compositor *(m)*, compositora *(f)*
composition • *n* redacció *(f)*
comprehensible • *adj* comprensible
comprehension • *n* comprensió *(f)*
comprehensively • *adv* comprensivament
compression • *n* compressió *(f)*
compromise • *n* compromís *(m)*
compulsory • *adj* obligatori
computational • *adj* computacional
compute • *v* computar
computer • *n* ordinador *(m)*, computador *(m)*, calculador *(m)*
comrade • *n* camarada *(f)*
con • *n* contra *(m)*
concave • *adj* còncau
concavity • *n* concavitat *(f)*
conceited • *adj* presumptuós
concentrate • *v* concentrar
concentration • *n* concentració *(f)*
concept • *n* concepte *(m)*
conception • *n* concepció *(f)*
conceptual • *adj* conceptual *(f)*
conceptually • *adv* conceptuosament
concern • *v* preocupar • *n* preocupació *(f)*, consternació *(f)*
concertina • *n* concertina *(f)*
concise • *adj* concís
concisely • *adv* concisament
conclave • *n* conclave *(m)*, conclau *(m)*
conclude • *v* concloure
conclusion • *n* conclusió *(f)*
conclusive • *adj* concloent
conclusively • *adv* conclusivament
concordance • *n* concordança, concordança *(f)*
concrete • *n* formigó • *adj* concret

concretion • *n* concreció *(f)*
concurrent • *adj* concurrent
concurrently • *adv* concurrentment
condemn • *v* condemnar
condescending • *adj* condescendent
condition • *v* condicionar • *n* condició *(f)*
conditional • *n* condicional *(m)* • *adj* condicional
conditionally • *adv* condicionalment
conditioning • *n* condicionament *(m)*
condom • *n* preservatiu *(m)*, condó *(m)*, condom *(m)*
condor • *n* còndor *(m)*
conduct • *n* conducta *(f)*
conductor • *n* director *(m)*
conduit • *n* conducte *(m)*
condyle • *n* còndil *(m)*
cone • *n* con *(m)*, pinya *(f)*
confederacy • *n* confederació
confidence • *n* confiança *(f)*
confident • *adj* confiat
confidentially • *adv* confidencialment
confidently • *adv* confidentment
configuration • *n* configuració *(f)*
confiscate • *v* confiscar
conflagration • *n* conflagració *(f)*
conflict • *n* conflicte
conformity • *n* conformitat *(f)*
confused • *adj* confús *(m)*, desconcertat, confús
confusing • *adj* confús
confusion • *n* confusió *(f)*
conga • *n* conga *(f)*
congenital • *adj* congènit
congratulations • *interj* felicitats
congregate • *v* congregar
congressman • *n* congressista *(f)*
conifer • *n* conífera *(f)*
coniform • *adj* coniforme
conjugally • *adv* conjugalment
conjugate • *v* conjugar
conjugation • *n* conjugació *(f)*
conjunction • *n* conjunció *(f)*
conjunctiva • *n* conjuntiva *(f)*
connotation • *n* connotació *(f)*
connotative • *adj* connotatiu
connote • *v* connotar
conquer • *v* conquistar
conscious • *adj* conscient
consciously • *adv* conscientment
consecutive • *adj* consecutiu
consecutively • *adv* consecutivament
consent • *n* consentiment *(m)*
consequence • *n* conseqüència *(f)*
consequently • *adv* conseqüentment
conservatism • *n* conservadorisme *(m)*
conservative • *adj* conservador, republicà

considerable • *adj* apreciable, considerable
considerate • *adj* considerat
considerately • *adv* consideradament
consistency • *n* consistència *(f)*
consistent • *adj* consistent
consistently • *adv* consistentment
consolidate • *v* consolidar
consonant • *n* consonant *(f)* • *adj* consonant
conspicuously • *adv* conspícuament
constant • *n* constant *(f)* • *adj* constant
constantly • *adv* constantment, constanment
constellation • *n* constel·lació *(f)*
constipation • *n* restrenyiment *(m)*
constituency • *n* circumscripció *(f)*
constituent • *adj* constituent
constitutional • *adj* constitucional
constitutionalism • *n* constitucionalisme *(m)*
constructive • *adj* constructiu
constructivism • *n* constructivisme *(m)*
consular • *adj* consular
consulate • *n* consolat *(m)*
consumer • *n* consumidor *(m)*
consumption • *n* consum *(m)*
contagious • *adj* contagiós, encomanadís
contain • *v* contenir
container • *n* contenidor *(m)*
contaminate • *v* contaminar
contamination • *n* contaminació *(f)*
contemn • *v* menyspreuar, desdenyar
contemporary • *n* contemporani • *adj* contemporani
content • *n* contingut *(m)* • *adj* content
contentious • *adj* controvertit, contenciós
contestant • *n* concursant *(f)*
contiguity • *n* contigüitat
contiguous • *adj* contigu
continent • *n* continent *(m)*
continually • *adv* continuadament
continue • *v* continuar
continuity • *n* continuïtat *(f)*
continuous • *adj* continu
continuously • *adv* contínuament
contortionist • *n* contorsionista *(f)*
contrabassoon • *n* contrafagot *(m)*
contraceptive • *n* anticonceptiu • *adj* anticonceptiu
contract • *n* contracte *(m)* • *v* contreure
contraction • *n* contracció *(f)*
contradict • *v* contradir
contradiction • *n* contradicció *(f)*
contradictorily • *adv* contradictòriament
contradictory • *adj* contradictori
contrarily • *adv* contràriament

contribution • *n* contribució *(f)*
contrite • *adj* contrit
contrived • *adj* artificial, forçat
control • *v* controlar • *n* control *(m)*
controllable • *adj* controlable
controversial • *adj* controvertit
contumelious • *adj* contumeliós
contusion • *n* contusió *(f)*
convection • *n* convecció *(f)*
convenience • *n* conveniència *(f)*
convenient • *adj* convenient
conveniently • *adv* convenientment
convention • *n* convenció
conventional • *adj* convencional
conventionalism • *n* convencionalisme *(m)*
convergence • *n* convergència *(f)*
convergent • *adj* convergent
conversation • *n* conversa *(f)*, conversació *(f)*
conversion • *n* transformació *(f)*
convert • *v* convertir
convertible • *n* descapotable • *adj* convertible
convex • *adj* convex
convexity • *n* convexitat *(f)*
convince • *v* convèncer
convinced • *adj* convençut
convincing • *adj* convincent
convoluted • *adj* complicat, enrevessat
convolution • *n* circumvolució *(f)*
convulsion • *n* convulsió *(f)*
cook • *v* cuinar, coure, coure's • *n* cuiner *(m)*, xef *(m)*
cookie • *n* coca *(f)*, galeta *(f)*
cool • *adj* fresc, fred *(m)*, freda *(f)*, guai, guai *(f)*, tranqui
cooper • *n* boter
cooperate • *v* cooperar
cooperative • *n* cooperativa *(f)* • *adj* cooperatiu
coot • *n* fotja *(f)*
copilot • *n* copilot *(f)*
copper • *n* coure *(m)*, aram *(m)* • *adj* courenc
copra • *n* copra *(f)*
coprolite • *n* copròlit *(m)*
copy • *v* copiar • *n* còpia *(f)*
coquettishly • *adv* coquetament
coral • *n* corall *(m)*, de, color *(m)*, corall, coralĺí • *adj* coralĺí
cord • *n* corda *(f)*, cordill *(m)*, cable *(m)*
corkscrew • *n* llevataps *(m)*
cormorant • *n* corb marí *(m)*
corncob • *n* panotxa
cornea • *n* còrnia *(f)*
corneal • *adj* corneal

corner • *v* arraconar
cornet • *n* corneta *(f)*
cornice • *n* cornisa *(f)*
coronation • *n* coronació *(f)*
corporal • *adj* corporal • *n* caporal *(f)*, corporal *(m)*
corporeal • *adj* corpori
corpse • *n* cadàver *(m)*
corpus • *n* corpus *(m)*
correct • *v* corregir • *adj* correcte
correctable • *adj* corregible
correction • *n* correcció *(f)*
correctly • *adv* correctament
correspondence • *n* correspondència *(f)*
corresponding • *adj* corresponent
corrode • *v* corroir
corrosion • *n* corrosió *(f)*
corrosive • *adj* corrosiu
corrugated • *adj* ondulat
corrupt • *v* corrompre • *adj* corrupte
corruptible • *adj* corruptible
corruption • *n* corrupció *(f)*
corruptly • *adv* corruptament
corsair • *n* corsari *(m)*, corsària *(f)*
cortex • *n* còrtex *(m)*
cortisone • *n* cortisona *(f)*
corvette • *n* corbeta *(f)*, bricbarca *(f)*
cosine • *n* cosinus *(m)*
cosmetic • *n* cosmètic *(m)*
cosmetics • *n* cosmètica *(f)*
cosmic • *adj* còsmic
cosmogony • *n* cosmogonia *(f)*
cosmologist • *n* cosmòleg *(m)*
cosmology • *n* cosmologia *(f)*
cosmopolitan • *n* cosmopolita • *adj* cosmopolita
cosmos • *n* cosmos *(m)*
cost • *n* preu *(m)*, cost *(m)* • *v* costar
costly • *adj* costós
cosy • *adj* acollidor
cotton • *n* cotó *(m)* • *adj* cotó *(m)*
cough • *v* tossir • *n* tos *(f)*
coulomb • *n* coulomb
council • *n* consell *(m)*
count • *v* comptar, valdre • *n* comptatge *(m)*, compte *(m)*, comte *(m)*
counter • *n* fitxa *(f)*, getó *(m)*, comptador *(m)*, comptavoltes *(m)*
counterespionage • *n* contraespionatge *(m)*
counteroffer • *n* contraoferta *(f)*
counterproductive • *adj* contraproduent
counterrevolution • *n* contrarevolució *(f)*
counterrevolutionary • *n* contrarevolucionari • *adj* contrarevolucionari
countertenor • *n* contratenor *(m)*
countess • *n* comtessa *(f)*

country • *n* país *(m)*, camp *(m)* • *adj* campestre
county • *n* comtat *(m)*, comarca *(f)*
couple • *n* parella
courage • *n* coratge *(m)*, valor *(m)*
courageous • *adj* coratjós, valent
course • *v* cursar, recórrer • *n* curs *(m)*, itinerari *(m)*, ruta *(f)*, recorregut *(m)*, plat *(m)*, trajectòria *(f)*, rumb *(m)*
court • *v* cortejar • *n* pati *(m)*, cort *(f)*, tribunal *(m)*, pista de joc *(f)*
courteous • *adj* cortès
courteously • *adv* cortesament
courtesy • *n* cortesia *(f)*
courthouse • *n* palau de justícia
cousin • *n* cosí *(m)*, cosina *(f)*
covariance • *n* covariància *(f)*
cove • *n* cala
cover • *n* tapa *(f)*
covered • *adj* cobert
cow • *n* vaca *(f)*, bruixa *(f)*, foca *(f)*, marró *(m)*, pedra *(f)*
coward • *n* covard
cowardice • *n* covardia *(f)*
cowardly • *adj* covard • *adv* covardament
cowherd • *n* vaquer *(m)*
coyote • *n* coiot *(m)*
crab • *n* cranc *(m)*, carranc *(m)*, cabra
crack • *n* esquerda *(f)*, badall *(m)*
cradle • *v* bressolar, bressar • *n* bressol *(m)*
craft • *v* fet a mà
craftsman • *n* artesà *(m)*
cranberry • *n* nabiu de grua *(m)*, nabiu
cranial • *adj* cranial
crank • *n* maneta *(f)*
crash • *n* xoc *(m)*, patacada *(f)*
crass • *adj* cras
crave • *v* ansiar
craving • *n* ànsia
crawl • *v* arrossegar-se, gatejar
crayfish • *n* cranc del riu *(m)*
crayon • *n* llapis de color *(m)*
craziness • *n* bogeria *(f)*, insanitat *(f)*
crazy • *adj* boig
cream • *n* nata *(f)*
creamy • *adj* cremós
create • *v* crear
creation • *n* creació *(f)*
creationism • *n* creacionisme *(m)*
creative • *n* creatiu • *adj* creatiu
creativity • *n* creativitat *(f)*
creator • *n* creador *(m)*
credible • *adj* creïble
creditor • *n* creditor *(m)*, anglès *(m)*
credulous • *adj* crèdul
creek • *n* cala *(f)*, rierol *(m)*, riera *(f)*

creepy • *adj* esborronador
creole • *n* crioll *(m)*
crepuscular • *adj* crepuscular
crepuscule • *n* crepuscle
cretinous • *adj* cretí
crew • *n* tripulació *(f)*, marineria *(f)*, equip *(m)*, tripulant *(m)*, banda *(f)*, colla *(f)*
cricket • *n* grill *(m)*, criquet *(m)*
crime • *n* crim *(m)*, delicte *(m)*
criminal • *n* criminal *(f)* • *adj* criminal
criminally • *adv* criminalment
criminologist • *n* criminòleg *(m)*
criminology • *n* criminologia *(f)*
crimson • *n* carmesí
crippled • *adj* esguerrat
crisis • *n* crisi *(f)*
criterion • *n* criteri *(n)*
critic • *n* crític *(m)*
critical • *adj* crític
critically • *adv* críticament
croak • *v* raucar • *n* rauc *(m)*
crockery • *n* vaixella *(f)*
crocodile • *n* cocodril *(m)*
cromlech • *n* cromlec *(m)*
crone • *n* vella *(f)*, àvia *(f)*, iaia *(f)*
crooked • *adj* tort, tortuós
croquette • *n* croqueta *(f)*
cross • *n* creu *(f)*
cross-eyed • *adj* guerxo
cross-stitch • *n* punt de creu *(m)*
crossbar • *n* travesser *(m)*
crossbow • *n* ballesta *(f)*
crossroads • *n* encreuament *(m)*, cruïlla *(f)*
crow • *n* còrvid *(m)*, corb *(m)*
crowd • *n* multitud *(f)*
crown • *n* corona *(f)*, capçada *(f)*
crucial • *adj* crucial
crucifix • *n* crucifix *(m)*
cruciform • *adj* cruciforme
crucify • *v* crucificar
crude • *adj* cru, groller
cruel • *adj* cruel
cruelly • *adv* cruelment
cruelty • *n* crueltat *(f)*
cruet • *n* setrill *(m)*, setrilleres, vinagrera *(f)*, canadella *(f)*
cruise • *n* creuer *(m)*
cruiser • *n* creuer *(m)*
crumb • *n* engruna *(f)*, mica *(f)*, molla *(f)*
crumble • *v* esmicolar-se, fer-se miques, desmoronar-se, derrumbar-se
crusade • *n* croada *(f)*
crust • *n* crosta *(f)*, massa *(f)*, escorça *(f)*
crustacean • *n* crustaci *(m)*
crutch • *n* crossa *(f)*
cry • *v* plorar

cryogenic • *adj* criogènic
crystal • *n* cristall *(m)*
crystalline • *adj* cristalŭlí
crystallize • *v* cristalŭlitzar
cube • *n* cub *(m)*
cubic • *adj* cúbic
cubism • *n* cubisme
cuboid • *adj* cuboide
cuckold • *n* cornut *(m)*
cuckoo • *n* cucut *(m)*
cucumber • *n* cogombre *(m)*, cogombrera *(f)*
cue • *n* tac *(m)*
cuff • *n* puny *(m)*
cuirass • *n* cuirassa *(f)*, buc *(m)*
cuisine • *n* cuina *(f)*
culinary • *adj* culinari
culpable • *adj* culpable
cultivate • *v* conrear, cultivar
cultural • *adj* cultural
culture • *n* cultura *(f)*
cum • *v* escórrer-se, ejacular • *n* llet *(f)*, escorreguda *(f)*, semen *(m)*, sement *(f)*
cumin • *n* comí *(m)*
cuneiform • *n* cuneïforme *(m)*
cunning • *adj* astut, murri
cunt • *n* cony *(m)*
cup • *n* tassa *(f)*, copa *(f)*
cupboard • *n* canterano *(m)*, calaixera *(f)*, armari *(m)*
cupola • *n* cúpula *(f)*
curfew • *n* toc de queda *(m)*
curious • *adj* curiós *(m)*, curiosa
curiously • *adv* curiosament
curium • *n* curi *(m)*
curlew • *n* becut *(m)*, polit *(m)*
curly • *adj* arrissat
currant • *n* grosella *(f)*
currency • *n* moneda *(f)*

current • *n* riu *(m)*, corrent *(m)* • *adj* actual
currently • *adv* actualment
curry • *n* curri *(m)*
curse • *n* maledicció
cursive • *n* cursiva *(f)* • *adj* cursiu
curtain • *n* cortina *(f)*, teló *(m)*
curve • *n* revolt *(m)*, corba *(f)*, corbes
cushion • *n* coixí *(m)*
custard • *n* crema *(f)*
custom • *n* costum *(m)*
custom-built • *adj* personalitzat
custom-made • *adj* personalitzat
customarily • *adv* consuetudinàriament
customer • *n* client *(f)*
cut • *v* tallar, retallar
cutaneous • *adj* cutani, epidèrmic, dermatològic
cute • *adj* bufó, maco
cutter • *n* cúter *(m)*
cutting • *adj* mordaç
cuttlefish • *n* sípia *(f)*, sépia *(f)*, sèpia *(f)*
cyborg • *n* ciborg
cycle • *n* cicle *(m)*
cyclic • *adj* cíclic
cycling • *n* ciclisme *(m)*
cyclist • *n* ciclista *(f)*
cyclone • *n* cicló *(m)*
cyclonic • *adj* ciclònic
cyclops • *n* ciclop
cylinder • *n* cilindre *(m)*
cylindrical • *adj* cilíndric
cymbal • *n* platerets
cynically • *adv* cínicament
cynicism • *n* cinisme *(m)*
cypress • *n* xiprer *(m)*
cysteine • *n* cisteïna *(f)*
cytology • *n* citologia *(f)*
cytoplasm • *n* citoplasma *(m)*

D

dacha • *n* datxa *(f)*
dactylology • *n* dactilologia *(f)*
dagger • *n* daga *(f)*, punyal *(m)*
dahlia • *n* dàlia *(f)*
daikon • *n* daikon, rave blanc, rave japonès, rave xinès, lo bok, mooli
daily • *n* diari *(m)* • *adj* diari • *adv* diàriament
dalmatic • *n* dalmàtica *(f)*
damage • *v* danyar • *n* dany *(m)*
damaging • *adj* perjudicial
damask • *n* domàs *(m)*
damn • *v* maleir • *adj* maleït • *adv* malaï-

dament • *interj* cagondena
damp • *n* humitat *(f)* • *adj* humit
dance • *v* ballar, dansar • *n* ball *(m)*, dansa *(f)*
dancer • *n* ballador *(m)*, ballarí *(m)*
dandelion • *n* dent de lleó *(f)*
dandruff • *n* caspa *(f)*, arna *(f)*
danger • *n* perill *(m)*
dangerous • *adj* perillós
dangerousness • *n* perillositat
daredevil • *adj* temerari
daring • *adj* agosarat
dark • *n* foscor *(f)*, obscuritat *(f)* • *adj* fosc,

obscur
dark-skinned • *adj* bru
darkness • *n* foscor *(f)*, tenebres, negror *(f)*
darling • *n* estimat *(m)*, estimada *(f)*
darnel • *n* jull *(m)*, zitzània *(f)*
dash • *v* esprintar • *n* guió, ratlla *(f)*
data • *n* informació *(f)*, dades
database • *n* base de dades *(f)*
date • *n* dàtil *(m)*, data *(f)*, cita *(f)* • *v* sortir, quedar
datum • *n* dada *(f)*
daughter • *n* filla *(f)*
daughter-in-law • *n* nora *(f)*
dawn • *v* clarejar, néixer • *n* aurora *(f)*, alba *(m)*, albada *(f)*, albors
day • *n* dia *(m)*, jorn *(m)*, jornada *(f)*
daybreak • *n* alba *(f)*
daylight • *n* llum del dia *(f)*, dia *(m)*
daytime • *n* dia *(m)*
dazed • *adj* estabornit, atordit
deacon • *n* diaca *(m)*
dead • *adj* mort, mort *(m)*
deadly • *adj* mortal, letal, mortífer
deaf • *adj* sord
deafen • *v* ensordir
deafening • *adj* ensordidor
deafness • *n* sordesa *(f)*
deal • *v* repartir, comerciar, vendre, comprar, tractar • *n* tracte *(m)*
dean • *n* degà *(m)*
dear • *adj* estimat, benvolgut, car
death • *n* mort *(f)*, la mort
debt • *n* deute *(m)*
debtor • *n* deutor *(m)*, deutora *(f)*
debut • *v* debutar • *n* debut *(m)*
decade • *n* dècada *(f)*, decenni *(m)*
decadent • *adj* decadent
decagon • *n* decàgon *(m)*
decahedron • *n* decaedre *(m)*, decàedre *(m)*
decapitate • *v* decapitar
decapitation • *n* decapitació *(f)*
decathlon • *n* decatló *(m)*
decease • *n* defunció *(f)*
deceased • *n* difunt, mort • *adj* difunt, mort
deceive • *v* decebre
decently • *adv* decentment
decentralize • *v* descentralitzar
deceptive • *adj* enganyós, decebedor, deceptiu
decibel • *n* decibel *(m)*
decide • *v* decidir
decidedly • *adv* decididament
deciduous • *adj* caduc, decidu
decision • *n* decisió *(f)*

decisive • *adj* decisiu
decisively • *adv* decisivament
deck • *n* terra *(m)*, baralla *(f)*, coberta *(f)*
declaration • *n* declaració *(f)*
declension • *n* declinació *(f)*
decline • *v* declinar-se, debilitar-se, declinar, refusar • *n* declivi *(m)*, caiguda *(f)*
decolonization • *n* descolonització *(f)*
decompose • *v* descompondre
decomposition • *n* descomposició *(f)*
decontamination • *n* descontaminació *(f)*
decorative • *adj* decoratiu
decrease • *v* decréixer, disminuir • *n* disminució *(f)*, decreixença *(f)*
deed • *n* fet *(m)*, acte *(m)*, escriptura *(f)*, acta *(f)*
deep • *adj* profund, pregon, greu, intens, fondo
deepen • *v* profunditzar, profunditzar-se
deeply • *adv* profundament
deer • *n* cérvol *(m)*
defamation • *n* difamació *(f)*
defamatory • *adj* difamador, difamant, difamatori
defeat • *v* vèncer • *n* venciment *(m)*, derrota *(f)*
defect • *n* defecte *(m)*
defective • *adj* defectiu, defectuós
defender • *n* defensor *(m)*
defense • *n* defensa *(f)*
defenseless • *adj* indefens
deficiency • *n* deficiència *(f)*
deficient • *adj* deficient
deficit • *n* dèficit *(m)*
defile • *v* embrutar, contaminar, polůluir
definite • *adj* definit *(m)*
definition • *n* definició *(f)*
definitive • *adj* definitiu
deflation • *n* deflació *(f)*
deflect • *v* desviar, desviar-se
deforestation • *n* desforestació *(f)*
deformation • *n* deformació *(f)*
defraud • *v* estafar, defraudar
degree • *n* grau *(m)*, títol *(m)*, diploma *(m)*
dehiscence • *n* dehiscència *(f)*
dehydration • *n* deshidratació *(f)*
deification • *n* deïficació *(f)*
deify • *v* deïficar
deity • *n* deïtat *(f)*, divinitat *(f)*
delegate • *n* delegat *(m)*, delegada *(f)*
deleterious • *adj* deleteri
deliberate • *adj* deliberat
deliberately • *adv* deliberadament, prudentment
delicate • *adj* delicat
delicious • *adj* deliciós, gustós, saborós
deliciously • *adv* deliciosament

delight • *n* delit *(m)*, plaer *(m)*
delighted • *adj* encantat *(m)*
delightful • *adj* encantador
deliquescent • *adj* deliqüescent
delirium • *n* deliri *(m)*
delta • *n* delta *(f)*
delude • *v* enganyar
deluge • *n* diluvi *(m)*
demand • *v* exigir
demeanor • *n* comportament *(m)*, conducta *(f)*
demigod • *n* semidéu *(m)*, semideessa *(f)*
demijohn • *n* damajoana *(f)*
democracy • *n* democràcia *(f)*
democrat • *n* demòcrata *(f)*
democratic • *adj* democràtic
democratically • *adv* democràticament
democratization • *n* democratització *(f)*
demographer • *n* demògraf *(m)*
demographic • *adj* demogràfic
demography • *n* demografia *(f)*
demon • *n* dimoni, diable
demonstrate • *v* demostrar
demoralize • *v* desmoralitzar
den • *n* cau *(m)*
dendrite • *n* dendrita *(f)*
denial • *n* desmentiment *(m)*
denier • *n* diner *(m)*
denominator • *n* denominador
denounce • *v* denunciar
dense • *adj* dens
densely • *adv* densament
dental • *adj* dental
denticulate • *adj* denticulat
dentist • *n* dentista
deny • *v* denegar, negar
deodorant • *n* desodorant *(m)*
deodorize • *v* desodorar, desodoritzar
deoxyribose • *n* desoxiribosa
depart • *v* departir, deixar
dependable • *adj* fiable
depiction • *n* representació *(f)*
depletion • *n* exhauriment *(m)*
deplorably • *adv* deplorablement
deposit • *v* dipositar • *n* jaciment *(m)*, dipòsit *(m)*
depot • *n* dipòsit *(m)*
deprecated • *adj* desaprovat, rebaixat
depress • *v* deprimir
depressed • *adj* deprimit
depressing • *adj* depriment
depression • *n* depressió *(f)*
depressive • *adj* depressiu *(m)*
depth • *n* profunditat
derange • *v* pertorbar
derive • *v* derivar
dermatologist • *n* dermatòleg *(f)*

dermatology • *n* dermatologia *(f)*
dermis • *n* derma *(m)*, dermis *(f)*
derogate • *v* derogar
derogatory • *adj* pejoratiu, despectiu, derogatori
descend • *v* descendir
descendant • *n* descendent *(m)*
descent • *n* baixada *(f)*
describe • *v* descriure
description • *n* descripció *(f)*
descriptively • *adv* descriptivament
desert • *n* desert *(m)* • *v* desertar
deserter • *n* desertor *(m)*
deserve • *v* merèixer, meritar
deserving • *adj* mereixedor
design • *v* dissenyar • *n* disseny *(m)*
designer • *n* dissenyador *(m)*
desirable • *adj* desitjable
desire • *v* desitjar • *n* desig *(m)*
desktop • *n* escriptori *(m)*, sobretaula *(m)*
despair • *n* desesperació
desperate • *adj* desesperat
desperately • *adv* desesperadament
despicable • *adj* menyspreable
despise • *v* menysprear
despite • *prep* malgrat, tot i que, encara que, tot i
despotism • *n* despotisme *(m)*
dessert • *n* postres, darreries
destiny • *n* destí *(m)*, planeta *(f)*
destitution • *n* indigència *(f)*
destroyer • *n* destructor *(m)*
destructible • *adj* destructible
destructive • *adj* destructiu
destructively • *adv* destructivament
detail • *n* detall *(m)*
detain • *v* detenir, detindre
detect • *v* detectar
detection • *n* detecció *(f)*
detective • *n* detectiu *(m)*
deterioration • *n* deterioració *(f)*
determine • *v* determinar
determined • *adj* determinat
determinedly • *adv* determinadament
detour • *n* marrada *(f)*
deuce • *n* iguals
devastate • *v* devastar
develop • *v* desenvolupar
development • *n* desenvolupament *(m)*
device • *n* dispositiu *(m)*, mecanisme *(m)*
devil • *n* dimoni *(m)*, diable *(m)*
devise • *v* divisar, copçar, preveure
devote • *v* consagrar
devour • *v* devorar
dew • *n* rosada *(f)*
dexterity • *n* destresa *(f)*
dexterous • *adj* destre

diabetes • *n* diabetis *(f)*
diabetic • *n* diabètic *(m)* • *adj* diabètic
diabolical • *adj* diabòlic
diabolically • *adv* diabòlicament
diachronic • *adj* diacrònic
diacritical • *adj* diacrític *(m)*
diagnostic • *adj* diagnòstic
diagonal • *n* diagonal *(f)* • *adj* diagonal
diagonally • *adv* diagonalment
dialect • *n* dialecte *(m)*
dialectically • *adv* dialècticament
dialogue • *v* dialogar
diameter • *n* diàmetre *(m)*
diametrically • *adv* diametralment
diamond • *n* diamant *(m)*, camp interior *(m)*
diaper • *n* bolquer, bolquers, bolcall *(m)*, bolcalls *(m)*, llençolet *(m)*
diary • *n* diari *(m)*
diatom • *n* diatomea
diatomic • *adj* diatòmic
dichotomy • *n* dicotomia *(f)*
dichroic • *adj* dicroic *(m)*
dichroism • *n* dicroisme *(m)*
dick • *n* carall *(m)*, polla *(f)*, titola *(f)*
dictatorship • *n* dictadura *(f)*
diction • *n* dicció *(f)*
dictionary • *n* diccionari *(m)*
didactic • *adj* didàctic
didactically • *adv* didàcticament
die • *v* morir • *n* dau *(m)*, encuny *(m)*
diencephalon • *n* diencèfal *(m)*
diet • *n* dieta *(f)*
dietary • *adj* dietètic
difference • *n* diferència *(f)*
different • *adj* diferent
differently • *adv* diferentment
difficult • *adj* difícil
difficulty • *n* dificultat *(f)*
dig • *v* cavar, excavar • *n* excavació *(f)*
digestible • *adj* digerible
digestive • *n* digestiu *(m)* • *adj* digestiu
digger • *n* excavadora *(f)*, excavador *(m)*
digit • *n* dit *(m)*, xifra *(f)*
digital • *adj* digital
digitally • *adv* digitalment
digitization • *n* digitalització *(f)*
dignified • *adj* digne
dignity • *n* dignitat *(f)*
digress • *v* desviar-se
digression • *n* digressió *(f)*
dildo • *n* consolador *(m)*, olisbe *(m)*
dilettantism • *n* diletantisme *(m)*
diligently • *adv* diligentment
dill • *n* anet *(m)*
dimension • *n* dimensió *(f)*
dimer • *n* dímer *(m)*

dinghy • *n* bot *(m)*, bot pneumàtic *(m)*
dinner • *n* sopar *(m)*, dinar *(m)*
dinosaur • *n* dinosaure *(m)*
diode • *n* díode *(m)*
diorite • *n* diorita *(f)*
dioxide • *n* diòxid *(m)*
diphtheria • *n* diftèria *(f)*
diphthong • *n* diftong *(m)*
diplodocus • *n* diplodoc *(m)*
diplomacy • *n* diplomàcia *(f)*
diplomat • *n* diplomàtic *(m)*, diplomàtica *(f)*
diplomatic • *adj* diplomàtic
diplomatically • *adv* diplomàticament
diptych • *n* díptic *(m)*
direct • *v* dirigir, adreçar • *adj* directe
direction • *n* direcció *(f)*
directly • *adv* directament
director • *n* director *(m)*, directora *(f)*
dirge • *n* complanta *(f)*, plany *(m)*, cant fúnebre *(m)*
dirt • *n* terra *(f)*
dirtiness • *n* brutícia *(f)*
dirty • *v* embrutar • *adj* brut
disabled • *adj* invàlid, minusvàlid
disappearance • *n* desaparició
disappointed • *adj* decebut
disaster • *n* desastre *(m)*
disastrous • *adj* desastrós
disastrously • *adv* desastrosament
disbelieve • *v* descreure
disclose • *v* divulgar
disconcerting • *adj* desconcertant
disconcertingly • *adv* desconcertantment
discontinuity • *n* discontinuïtat *(f)*
discover • *v* descobrir
discovery • *n* descobriment *(m)*
discreetly • *adv* discretament
discriminatory • *adj* discriminatori
discursion • *n* digressió *(f)*
discuss • *v* discutir, debatre
discussion • *n* discussió *(f)*
disdainfully • *adv* desdenyosament
disease • *n* malaltia *(f)*
disgust • *v* fer fàstic • *n* fàstic
disgusting • *adj* fastigós, repugnant, menyspreable
dish • *n* vaixella *(f)*, plat *(m)*, antena parabòlica *(f)*
dishonest • *adj* deshonest
dishonestly • *adv* deshonestament
dishwasher • *n* rentaplats *(m)*
disinfection • *n* desinfecció *(f)*
disinter • *v* desenterrar
disinterested • *adj* desinteressat
disinterestedly • *adv* desinteressadament
disinterment • *n* desenterrament *(m)*

disk • *n* disc *(m)*, disc dur *(m)*
disloyal • *adj* deslleial
disloyally • *adv* deslleialment
disloyalty • *n* deslleialtat *(f)*
dismiss • *v* destituir, acomiadar, despedir, rebutjar
disobedient • *adj* desobedient
disobey • *v* desobeir
disorder • *n* desordre *(m)*, trastorn *(m)*
disorderly • *adj* desordenat
disorganization • *n* desorganització *(f)*
disorganized • *adj* desorganitzat
dispel • *v* dissipar
disperse • *v* dispersar
displace • *v* desnonar, suplantar, desplaçar, desallotjar
displacement • *n* desplaçament *(m)*
display • *v* exhibir • *n* espectacle *(m)*, monitor *(m)*
disproportionate • *adj* desproporcionat
disproportionately • *adv* desproporcionadament
disruption • *n* interrupció *(f)*, desordre *(m)*
dissatisfied • *adj* insatisfet
dissect • *v* dissecar
dissection • *n* dissecció *(f)*
dissident • *n* dissident *(f)*, dissident
dissociate • *v* dissociar
dissuasive • *adj* dissuasiu
distance • *v* allunyar • *n* distància
distant • *adj* distant
distillery • *n* destilleria
distinct • *adj* distint
distinction • *n* distinció *(f)*
distinctive • *adj* distintiu
distinctly • *adv* distintament
distinguish • *v* distingir
distinguishable • *adj* distingible
distinguished • *adj* distingit
distract • *v* distreure
distraction • *n* distracció *(f)*
district • *n* comarca *(f)*, districte
disturb • *v* molestar
diurnal • *adj* diürn
dive • *n* estirada *(f)*
diver • *n* bus *(f)*
divergence • *n* divergència *(f)*
diverse • *adj* divers
diversification • *n* diversificació *(f)*
diversify • *v* diversificar
divert • *v* desviar
diverticulum • *n* diverticle *(m)*
divine • *adj* diví
diving • *n* salts
divinity • *n* deïtat *(f)*, divinitat *(f)*
divorce • *v* divorciar • *n* divorci *(m)*

divorced • *adj* separat, divorciat
divot • *n* gleva *(f)*
divulge • *v* divulgar
dizzy • *adj* marejat, vertiginós
do • *v* fer, fotre-li, fer-ho • *n* do *(m)*
dobra • *n* dobra
docility • *n* docilitat *(f)*
doctor • *n* metge *(m)*, metgessa *(f)*
doctrinal • *adj* doctrinal
doctrinally • *adv* doctrinalment
doctrine • *n* doctrina *(f)*
document • *v* documentar • *n* document *(m)*
documentary • *n* documental *(m)* • *adj* documental
documentation • *n* documentació *(f)*
dodecagon • *n* dodecàgon *(m)*
dodecahedron • *n* dodecàedre, dodecaedre *(m)*
dog • *n* gos, ca *(m)*, gossa *(f)*, cutxu
dogma • *n* dogma *(m)*
dogmatic • *adj* dogmàtic
dogmatism • *n* dogmatisme *(m)*
dogwood • *n* sanguinyol *(m)*
doll • *n* nina *(f)*
dollar • *n* dòlar *(m)*
dolor • *n* dolor
dolphin • *n* dofí *(m)*
dome • *n* cúpula
domestic • *adj* domèstic, interior
domesticated • *adj* domesticat *(m)*
domesticity • *n* domesticitat *(f)*
domicile • *n* domicili *(m)*
dominate • *v* dominar
dominical • *adj* dominical
donation • *n* donació *(f)*, donatiu *(m)*
donkey • *n* ase *(m)*, somera *(f)*, burro *(m)*, burra *(f)*, ruc *(m)*, ruca *(f)*
doom • *v* damnar
door • *n* porta *(f)*
doorbell • *n* timbre
dormant • *adj* latent
dormouse • *n* liró
dose • *n* dosi *(f)*
dot • *n* punt *(m)*
double • *v* doblar • *adj* doble
doubles • *n* dobles
doublet • *n* gipó
doubly • *adv* doblement
doubt • *v* dubtar • *n* dubte *(m)*
doubtful • *adj* dubtós
doubtfully • *adv* dubtosament
dough • *n* pasta *(f)*, massa *(f)*
doughnut • *n* dònat *(m)*
dove • *n* colom *(m)*
down • *n* intent *(m)* • *adj* deprimit, moix, baix • *adv* avall

downturn • *n* daltabaix *(m)*
dowry • *n* dot *(f)*
drachma • *n* dracma *(f)*
draconian • *adj* draconià
draft • *n* esborrany *(m)*, esbós *(m)*
drag • *v* arrossegar
dragon • *n* drac *(m)*, víbria *(f)*
dragonfly • *n* libèlůlula *(f)*, cavall de serp *(m)*, espiadimonis *(m)*, tallanassos *(m)*, teixidor *(m)*, barratgina *(f)*
dragoon • *n* dragó *(m)*
dramatically • *adv* dramàticament
drastic • *adj* dràstic
draught • *n* tiro *(m)*, corrent *(f)*, correntia *(f)*, calat *(m)*, dama *(f)*
draughts • *n* dames
draw • *v* dibuixar, empatar
drawer • *n* calaix *(m)*
drawing • *n* dibuix *(m)*
dread • *v* témer
dream • *v* somiar • *n* somni *(m)*
dredge • *v* dragar • *n* draga *(f)*
dregs • *n* pòsit *(m)*, solatge *(m)*
drenched • *adj* xop
dress • *v* vestir, vestir-se • *n* vestit *(m)*
dribble • *v* conduir, driblar • *n* driblatge *(m)*, conducció *(f)*
drift • *n* vagar, vagarejar
drill • *v* perforar, foradar
drink • *v* beure • *n* beguda *(f)*, glop *(m)*
drinkable • *adj* potable
drinker • *n* bevedor *(m)*, bevedora *(f)*, abeurador *(m)*
drive • *v* conduir
drivel • *v* bavejar • *n* ximpleries
driver • *n* conductor *(m)*, controlador de dispositiu *(m)*
droll • *adj* divertit *(m)*
dromedary • *n* dromedari *(m)*
drop • *n* gota *(f)*
droplet • *n* goteta *(f)*
drought • *n* sequera *(f)*, secada *(f)*, seca *(f)*
drown • *v* ofegar, submergir
drug • *n* droga *(f)*
druid • *n* druida *(m)*
drum • *v* tamborinejar • *n* tambor *(m)*, barril *(m)*
drunk • *n* borratxo *(m)*, embriac *(m)* • *adj* borratxo, embriac
drunkard • *n* borratxo *(m)*
drunkenness • *n* embriaguesa *(f)*, turca *(f)*, borratxera *(f)*

dry • *adj* eixut, sec
dryer • *n* assecadora *(f)*
dryness • *n* sequedat *(f)*, eixutesa *(f)*, secor *(f)*, eixutor *(f)*
dubitation • *n* dubte *(m)*
ducat • *n* ducat *(m)*
duchess • *n* duquessa *(f)*
duchy • *n* ducado, ducat *(m)*
duck • *n* ànec *(m)*
duckling • *n* aneguet *(m)*
dud • *n* fracàs *(m)*, pífia *(f)*
dude • *n* paio *(m)*, tio *(m)*
duel • *v* batre, duel • *n* duel *(m)*
duet • *n* duo *(m)*, duet *(m)*
duke • *n* duc *(m)*, duc
dulcimer • *n* dulcimer *(m)*
dull • *adj* insuls *(m)*, fat
duly • *adv* degudament
dumpling • *n* mandonguilla *(f)*, nyoqui *(m)*
dung • *n* adob *(m)*, fem *(m)*
dungeon • *n* calabós *(m)*, masmorra *(f)*
dunk • *v* esmaixar • *n* esmaixada *(f)*
duodecimo • *n* dotzè *(m)*
duodenum • *n* duodè *(m)*
duplicate • *v* duplicar • *n* duplicat *(m)*
duplication • *n* duplicació *(f)*
durability • *n* durabilitat *(f)*
durable • *adj* durable, durador
duration • *n* durada *(f)*, duració *(f)*
durian • *n* durian *(m)*
during • *prep* durant
dusk • *n* crepuscle *(m)*, capvespre *(m)*
dust • *n* pols *(f)*
dustpan • *n* recollidor *(m)*
duty • *n* obligació, deure *(m)*, servei, taxa
dwarf • *n* nan *(m)*, nano *(m)*, nana *(f)*
dwarfism • *n* nanisme *(m)*
dwelling • *n* habitatge, vivenda
dye • *v* tenyir • *n* tint *(m)*
dynamic • *n* dinàmica *(f)* • *adj* dinàmic *(m)*
dynamically • *adv* dinàmicament
dynamite • *v* dinamitar • *n* dinamita *(f)*
dynastic • *adj* dinàstic *(m)*
dynasty • *n* dinastia *(f)*
dyne • *n* dina *(f)*
dysentery • *n* disenteria *(f)*
dyslexia • *n* dislèxia *(f)*
dysphoria • *n* disfòria *(f)*
dysprosium • *n* disprosi

E

e • *n* e *(f)*
eagle • *n* àliga *(f)*, àguila *(f)*
ear • *n* orella *(f)*, espiga *(f)*
eardrum • *n* timpà *(m)*
early • *adj* d'hora • *adv* aviat
earn • *v* guanyar, cobrar
earnest • *adj* seriós
earring • *n* arracada *(f)*
earth • *n* terra *(f)*
earthenware • *n* pisa *(f)*
earthquake • *n* terratrèmol *(m)*
earthworm • *n* cuc de terra *(m)*, llambric *(m)*
earwig • *n* tisoreta, papaorelles
easel • *n* cavallet *(m)*
easement • *n* servitud
easily • *adv* fàcilment
east • *n* est
eastern • *adj* oriental, llevant
easy • *adj* fàcil
easygoing • *adj* calmat, tranquil, relaxat
eat • *v* menjar
eater • *n* menjador
eaves • *n* ràfec *(m)*
ebony • *n* eben *(m)*, banús *(m)*
eccentric • *adj* excèntric
ecclesiastical • *adj* eclesiàstic
echidna • *n* equidna *(m)*
echinoderm • *n* equinoderm *(m)*
echo • *n* eco *(m)*
eclectic • *adj* eclèctic
eclipse • *v* eclipsar • *n* eclipsi *(m)*
ecliptic • *n* eclíptica *(f)*
ecological • *adj* ecològic
ecologically • *adv* ecològicament
ecologist • *n* ecòleg *(m)*
ecology • *n* ecologia *(f)*
economic • *adj* econòmic
economically • *adv* econòmicament
economics • *n* economia *(f)*
economist • *n* economista *(f)*
ecosystem • *n* ecosistema *(m)*
ecumenical • *adj* ecumènic
edge • *n* vora *(f)*
edible • *adj* comestible
edit • *v* editar • *n* edició *(f)*, modificació *(f)*
editing • *n* edició *(f)*
edition • *n* edició *(f)*
editorial • *adj* editorial
educated • *adj* educat
education • *n* educació *(f)*
educational • *adj* educatiu, didàctic
eel • *n* anguila *(f)*
eerie • *adj* misteriós, espantós
effect • *n* efecte *(m)*
effective • *adj* eficaç, efectiu

effectiveness • *n* eficàcia *(f)*
effervescent • *adj* efervescent
efficacy • *n* eficàcia *(f)*
efficiency • *n* eficiència *(f)*, rendiment *(m)*
efficient • *adj* eficient
efficiently • *adv* eficientment
effort • *n* esforç *(m)*
effortless • *adj* fàcil
egalitarianism • *n* igualitarisme *(m)*
egg • *n* ou
egg-shaped • *adj* ovoide
eggplant • *n* albergínia *(f)*, alberginiera *(f)*
eggshell • *n* closca *(f)*, ou *(m)*
ego • *n* jo *(m)*
egocentric • *adj* egocèntric
egret • *n* agró *(m)*, martinet *(m)*
eight • *n* vuit *(m)*, huit *(m)*
eighteenth • *n* divuitè *(m)*, dihuitè *(m)* • *adj* divuitè *(m)*, dihuitè *(m)*
eighth • *adj* vuitè
einsteinium • *n* einsteini *(m)*
either • *adv* tampoc
ejaculate • *v* ejacular, escórrer-se
ejaculation • *n* ejaculació *(f)*
ejection • *n* ejecció *(f)*
el • *n* ela *(f)*
elastic • *adj* elàstic
elasticity • *n* elasticitat *(f)*
elbow • *n* colze *(m)*
elder • *n* grans *(m)*, ancian *(m)*, saüc *(m)*
elderly • *adj* ancià *(m)*
election • *n* elecció *(f)*
elector • *n* elector *(m)*
electoral • *adj* electoral
electric • *adj* elèctric
electrical • *adj* elèctric
electrically • *adv* elèctricament
electricity • *n* electricitat *(f)*
electrode • *n* elèctrode *(m)*
electrodynamometer • *n* electrodinamòmetre *(m)*
electrolyte • *n* electròlit *(m)*
electromagnetic • *adj* electromagnètic
electromagnetism • *n* electromagnetisme *(m)*
electron • *n* electró *(m)*
electronic • *adj* electrònic
electronically • *adv* electrònicament
electronics • *n* electrònica, electrònica *(f)*
electroscope • *n* electroscopi *(m)*
electrum • *n* electre *(m)*
elegant • *adj* elegant
elegantly • *adv* elegantment
elemental • *adj* elemental
elephant • *n* elefant *(m)*
elevation • *n* elevació *(f)*, alçat *(m)*

eleventh • *n* onzè *(m)*, onzena *(f)* • *adj* onzè *(m)*
eligible • *adj* elegible
eliminate • *v* eliminar
elite • *n* elit *(f)*
elitist • *n* elitista *(f)* • *adj* elitista
elixir • *n* elixir *(m)*
elm • *n* om *(m)*, olm *(m)*
eloquence • *n* eloqüència *(f)*
eloquent • *adj* eloqüent
else • *adj* més, altre
elsewhere • *adv* en un altre lloc
emancipate • *v* emancipar
emancipation • *n* emancipació *(f)*
emasculate • *v* emascular
embarrassed • *adj* avergonyit *(m)*, avergonyida *(f)*
embarrassment • *n* avergonyiment *(m)*
embassy • *n* ambaixada *(f)*
embed • *v* encastar
ember • *n* brasa *(f)*
embezzle • *v* malversar
emblematic • *adj* emblemàtic
embrace • *v* abraçar • *n* abraçada *(f)*
embrasure • *n* tronera *(f)*
embroider • *v* brodar
embroidery • *n* brodat
embryo • *n* embrió *(m)*
embryonic • *adj* embrionari
emerald • *n* maragda *(f)*, esmaragda *(f)*
emerge • *v* emergir, sorgir
emergence • *n* emergència *(f)*, propietats emergents *(f)*
emergency • *n* emergència *(f)*, urgència *(f)*
emeritus • *adj* emèrit *(m)*
emigrate • *v* emigrar
eminence • *n* eminència *(f)*
emirate • *n* emirat *(m)*
emission • *n* emissió
emit • *v* emetre
emotion • *n* emoció *(f)*
emotional • *adj* emocional
emotionally • *adv* emocionalment
empathy • *n* empatia *(f)*
emperor • *n* emperador *(m)*
emphasis • *n* èmfasi *(f)*
emphasize • *v* emfatitzar
emphatic • *adj* emfàtic
emphatically • *adv* emfàticament
empire • *n* imperi *(m)*
employee • *n* empleat *(m)*
empress • *n* emperadriu *(f)*
emptiness • *n* buidor *(f)*, buidesa *(f)*
empty • *v* buidar • *adj* buit
emu • *n* emú
en • *n* ena *(f)*

enable • *v* habilitar
enamel • *v* esmaltar • *n* esmalt *(m)*
enamor • *v* enamorar
enchantment • *n* encanteri
encouraging • *adj* encoratjador
encroach • *v* usurpar, ocupar, envair
encyclopedia • *n* enciclopèdia
encyclopedic • *adj* enciclopèdic
end • *v* acabar • *n* final *(m)*, fi *(f)*
endearment • *n* tendresa, afecte
endeavor • *n* esforç *(m)*
endemic • *adj* endèmic
endless • *adj* interminable, inacabable
endocardium • *n* endocardi *(m)*
endocrine • *adj* endocrí
endocrinology • *n* endocrinologia *(f)*
endometrium • *n* endometri *(m)*
endorphin • *n* endorfina *(f)*
endothelium • *n* endoteli *(m)*
enema • *n* ènema *(m)*
enemy • *n* enemic *(m)* • *adj* enemic
energetic • *adj* enèrgic, ple d'energia, energètic
energetically • *adv* enèrgicament
energy • *n* energia *(f)*
engine • *n* motor *(m)*
engineer • *n* enginyer *(m)*
engineering • *n* enginyeria
engrave • *v* gravar
engraving • *n* gravat
engrossed • *adj* absort
enigma • *n* enigma *(m)*
enigmatic • *adj* enigmàtic
enjoy • *v* gaudir
enormous • *adj* enorme
enormously • *adv* enormement
enough • *adv* suficientment, prou • *interj* prou! • *pron* prou
entangle • *v* enredar
enter • *v* entrar
enterprise • *n* empresa *(f)*
entertain • *v* entretenir, divertir, distreure
entertaining • *adj* divertit
enthusiastic • *adj* entusiàstic
enthusiastically • *adv* entusiàsticament
entire • *adj* enter
entirely • *adv* totalment, enterament
entomological • *adj* entomològic
entomologist • *n* entomòleg *(m)*
entomology • *n* entomologia *(f)*
entrance • *n* entrada *(f)*
entresol • *n* entresòl *(m)*
envelope • *n* sobre *(m)*, sobre de carta *(m)*
environment • *n* medi *(m)*, ambient *(m)*, entorn *(m)*, medi ambient *(m)*
environmental • *adj* ambiental, mediambiental

environmentalist • n ecologista
environmentally • adv ambientalment
envy • v envejar • n enveja (f)
enzyme • n enzim (m)
epee • n espasa (f)
ephemeral • adj efímer
epicycle • n epicicle
epidemiologic • adj epidemiològic
epidemiologist • n epidemiòleg (m)
epidemiology • n epidemiologia (f)
epidermis • n epidermis (f)
epididymis • n epidídim (m)
epiglottis • n epiglotis (f)
epigraph • n epígraf (m)
epigraphy • n epigrafia (f)
epilepsy • n epilèpsia (f)
epilogue • n epíleg (m)
epiphysis • n epífisi (f)
episode • n episodi (m)
epistle • n epístola (f), Epístola (f)
epitaph • n epitafi (m)
epithelial • adj epitèlic, epitelial
epithelium • n epiteli (m)
epoch • n època (f)
eponymous • adj epònim (m)
epsilon • n èpsilon (f)
equal • adj igual
equality • n igualtat (f)
equally • adv igualment
equation • n equació (f)
equator • n equador (m)
equestrian • adj eqüestre
equilibrium • n equilibri (m)
equinox • n equinocci (m)
equipment • n equipament (m), equipatge (m), equip (m)
equipollence • n equipolůlència (f), equivalència (f)
equity • n patrimoni net (m)
era • n era (f), època (f), període (m)
eraser • n goma (f), goma d'esborrar (f)
erbium • n erbi (m)
erect • adj erecte
erectile • adj erèctil
erection • n erecció (f)
erg • n erg (m)
ergonomic • adj ergonòmic
ermine • n ermini
erosion • n erosió (f)
erotic • adj eròtic
erotically • adv eròticament
errand • n encàrrec (m)
erroneous • adj erroni
eruption • n erupció (f)
escape • v escapar, eludir • n fuita (f)
eschatology • n escatologia (f)
escort • n escorta (f)

esoteric • adj esotèric
especially • adv sobretot, especialment
espionage • n espionatge (m)
essence • n bessó (m)
essential • adj essencial
essentiality • n essencialitat (f)
essentially • adv en essència
establish • v establir
establishment • n establiment (m)
estate • n propietat (f), béns
ester • n èster (m)
estival • adj estival
eta • n eta (f)
etch • v gravar
etching • n aiguafort (m)
eternal • adj etern, eternal
eternity • n eternitat (f)
ethane • n età (m)
ethical • adj ètic
ethics • n ètica (f)
ethnic • adj ètnic, pagà
ethnicity • n ètnia (f)
ethnocentric • adj etnocèntric
ethnocentrism • n etnocentrisme (m)
ethnography • n etnografia (f)
ethyl • n etil (m)
etymological • adj etimològic
etymologist • n etimòleg (m), etimòloga (f), etimologista (f)
etymology • n etimologia (f)
eucalyptus • n eucaliptus (m)
eugenics • n eugènsia (f)
eukaryote • n eucariota (m)
euphemism • n eufemisme (m)
euphonium • n eufoni (m)
euphoria • n eufòria (f)
euphoric • adj eufòric
eureka • interj eureka
europium • n europi
euthanasia • n eutanàsia (f)
even • adj pla, igual, parell • adv fins i tot, encara
evening • n tarda (f), vespre (m)
eventually • adv finalment
everybody • pron tothom
everyone • pron tothom, cada u, cadascú
everything • pron tot
everywhere • adv tot arreu
evict • v desdonar
eviction • n desallotjament, desnonament (m)
evidence • n prova (f)
evident • adj evident
evil • n mal (m) • adj malvat, dolent, maliciós, malèfic, roí
evolution • n evolució (f)
evolve • v progressar, desenvolupar

ewe • *n* ovella *(f)*
ewer • *n* pitxer *(m)*
ex • *n* ics *(f)*
exact • *adj* exacte, precís
exactly • *adv* exactament
exaggerate • *v* exagerar
examination • *n* examen *(m)*
example • *n* exemple *(m)*
exasperate • *v* exasperar
excavation • *n* excavació *(f)*
excavator • *n* excavador *(m)*
exceed • *v* excedir
excel • *v* excelŀlir
excellence • *n* excelŀlència *(f)*
excellent • *adj* excelŀlent
excellently • *adv* excelŀlentment
exception • *n* excepció *(f)*
exceptional • *adj* excepcional
exceptionally • *adv* excepcionalment
excess • *n* excés *(m)*
excessive • *adj* excessiu
exchange • *n* intercanvi *(m)* • *v* intercanviar
excitable • *adj* excitable, entusiasmadís
excited • *adj* emocionat, excitat
exciting • *adj* excitant
exclaim • *v* exclamar
exclude • *v* excloure
exclusive • *adj* exclusiu
excommunicate • *v* excomunicar
excrement • *n* femta *(f)*
excrete • *v* excretar
excretory • *adj* excretori
execute • *v* executar
executioner • *n* botxí *(m)*, botxina *(f)*
exegesis • *n* exegesi *(f)*
exempt • *adj* exempt
exercise • *v* exercitar, exercir • *n* exercici *(m)*
exhalation • *n* exhalació *(f)*
exhausted • *adj* exhaust
exhaustive • *adj* exhaustiu
exhibit • *v* exhibir, exposar
exhibitionism • *n* exhibicionisme *(m)*
exhibitionist • *n* exhibicionista *(f)* • *adj* exhibicionista
exhumation • *n* exhumació *(f)*
exhume • *v* exhumar
exigent • *adj* exigent *(f)*
exile • *v* exiliar, bandejar, desterrar • *n* exili *(m)*, bandejament *(m)*, desterrament *(m)*, exiliat *(m)*, bandejat *(m)*
exist • *v* existir
existence • *n* existència *(f)*
existent • *adj* existent
existing • *adj* existent
exit • *v* sortir • *n* sortida *(f)*

exorcise • *v* exorcitzar
exorcism • *n* exorcisme
exorcist • *n* exorcista *(f)*
exoskeleton • *n* exosquelet *(m)*
exosphere • *n* exosfera *(f)*
exotic • *adj* exòtic
expel • *v* expelŀlir
expenditure • *n* despesa *(f)*
expensive • *adj* car
expensively • *adv* carament, costosament
experimental • *adj* experimental
explain • *v* explicar
explanation • *n* explicació *(f)*
explicit • *adj* explícit
explicitly • *adv* explícitament
explode • *v* esclatar, explotar
exploit • *v* explotar • *n* fita *(f)*, proesa *(f)*, gesta *(f)*
exploration • *n* exploració *(f)*
explore • *v* explorar
explorer • *n* explorador *(m)*
explosion • *n* explosió *(f)*
explosive • *n* explosiu *(m)* • *adj* explosiu
express • *v* expressar
expression • *n* expressió *(f)*
expressionist • *n* expressionista *(f)* • *adj* expressionista
expressive • *adj* expressiu *(m)*
expressively • *adv* expressivament
exquisite • *adj* exquisit
extant • *adj* existent *(f)*
extend • *v* extendre
extension • *n* extensió *(f)*
extensive • *adj* extens
extensively • *adv* extensament
external • *adj* extern *(m)*, externa *(f)*
extinct • *adj* extint
extinction • *n* extinció
extinguish • *v* extingir, apagar
extracellular • *adj* extracelŀlular
extract • *v* extreure
extraordinary • *adj* extraordinari
extraterrestrial • *adj* extraterrestre
extravagant • *adj* extravagant
extreme • *n* extrem *(m)* • *adj* extrem
extremism • *n* extremisme *(m)*
extremist • *n* extremista • *adj* extremista
extremity • *n* extremitat *(f)*
exult • *v* exultar
exultant • *adj* exultant
eye • *n* ull *(m)*
eyebrow • *n* cella *(f)*
eyelash • *n* pestanya *(f)*
eyelid • *n* parpella *(f)*
eyesight • *n* vista *(f)*

F

fabulously • *adv* fabulosament
face • *n* cara *(f)*, faç *(f)*, rictus *(m)*, gest *(m)*, cara, faceta *(f)*
fact • *n* fet
factitious • *adj* factici
fag • *n* marieta *(m)*, marica *(m)*, maricó *(m)*
fail • *v* fracassar
failure • *n* fracàs *(m)*
faint • *v* acubar-se • *n* desmai • *adj* feble *(f)*, dèbil *(f)*, tènue *(f)*
fainting • *n* desmai
fair • *adj* bell, just, equitatiu
fairly • *adv* francament, verdaderament, justament, força
fairway • *n* carrer *(m)*
fairy • *n* fada *(f)*
faith • *n* fe *(f)*
faithful • *adj* fidel, lleial
faithfully • *adv* fidelment
fake • *v* falsejar
falcon • *n* falcó *(m)*
fall • *v* caure • *n* caiguda *(f)*
fallacy • *n* falŀlàcia *(f)*
fallibility • *n* falŀlibilitat *(f)*
fallible • *adj* falŀlible
false • *adj* fals, incorrecte, postís, artificial
falsely • *adv* falsament
falsify • *v* falsificar, falsejar
fame • *n* fama *(f)*
familiar • *adj* familiar
familiarize • *v* familiaritzar
familiarly • *adv* familiarment
family • *n* família *(f)*, familiar • *adj* marieta *(m)*
famous • *adj* famós, cèlebre
fan • *v* ventar • *n* ventall *(m)*, vano *(m)*, palmito *(m)*, ventilador *(m)*
fanatical • *adj* fanàtic
fanatically • *adv* fanàticament
fancy • *n* fantasia *(f)*
fanfare • *n* fanfara *(f)*
fang • *n* ullal *(m)*
fantastic • *adj* fantàstic
fantasy • *n* fantasia *(f)*
far • *adj* llunyà, extrem • *adv* lluny, enllà, ença
far-flung • *adj* remot, estès
farewell • *n* adéu • *interj* adéu
farm • *n* granja *(f)*
farmer • *n* granger *(m)*
faro • *n* faraó *(m)*
fart • *v* petar • *n* pet *(m)*
fascinating • *adj* fascinador, fascinant

fascism • *n* feixisme *(m)*
fascist • *n* feixista
fast • *adj* ferm, ràpid, veloç • *adv* fermament, ràpid, ràpidament, veloçment • *v* dejunar
fat • *adj* gras
fatal • *adj* fatal
fatalism • *n* fatalisme *(m)*
fate • *n* destí *(m)*, planeta *(f)*
father • *n* pare *(m)*
father-in-law • *n* sogre *(m)*
fatherland • *n* pàtria *(f)*
fathom • *v* abraçar, sondejar, comprendre • *n* braça *(f)*
fatigues • *n* roba militar *(f)*
fattening • *adj* engreixador
fault • *n* errada *(f)*, culpa *(f)*, defecte *(m)*, error *(m)*, falta, falla *(f)*, falta *(f)*
faun • *n* faune *(m)*
fauna • *n* fauna *(f)*
favorite • *adj* favorit, preferit
fawn • *n* cervatell *(m)*
fax • *n* fax
fear • *n* por *(f)*, paüra *(f)*, basarda *(f)*, temor *(f)*, temor *(m)*, respecte *(m)*
feasible • *adj* factible
feast • *n* festa *(f)*
feather • *n* ploma *(f)*
feature • *n* tret *(m)*
federal • *adj* federal
feeble • *adj* feble *(f)*, dèbil *(f)*
feed • *v* alimentar • *n* pinso
feedback • *n* resposta *(f)*
feign • *v* fingir
feijoa • *n* feijoa *(f)*
feldspar • *n* feldspat *(m)*
feline • *adj* felí
fellatio • *n* felŀlació *(f)*
felon • *n* delinqüent
felt • *n* feltre *(m)*
female • *n* femella *(f)* • *adj* femení *(m)*, femenina *(f)*, femella
feminine • *n* femení *(m)*
femininity • *n* feminitat *(f)*
feminism • *n* feminisme *(m)*
femoral • *adj* femoral
femur • *n* fèmur *(m)*
fence • *n* tanca *(f)*
fencing • *n* esgrima
fennel • *n* fonoll *(m)*
ferment • *n* ferment *(m)*
fermentation • *n* fermentació *(f)*
fermion • *n* fermió *(m)*
fermium • *n* fermi *(m)*

fern • *n* falguera *(f)*, falaguera *(f)*
ferocious • *adj* ferotge
ferret • *n* furó, fura
ferric • *adj* fèrric
ferromagnetic • *adj* ferromagnètic
ferromagnetism • *n* ferromagnetisme
ferry • *n* bac *(m)*, rai *(m)*
fertile • *adj* fèrtil
fertilization • *n* fertilització *(f)*, fecundació *(f)*
fertilize • *v* fertilitzar
fertilizer • *n* adob *(m)*
fetal • *adj* fetal
fetid • *adj* fètid
fetter • *v* engrillonar, impedir • *n* grilló *(m)*, obstacle *(m)*
feud • *n* feu
fever • *n* febre *(f)*
feverish • *adj* febril
feverishly • *adv* febrilment
fiasco • *n* fiasco *(m)*
fibrous • *adj* fibrós
fibula • *n* fíbula *(f)*
fickle • *adj* inconstant
fiction • *n* ficció *(f)*
fictional • *adj* ficcional *(f)*
fictitious • *adj* fictici
fidget • *n* belluguet *(m)*, ballaruga *(f)*
fiduciary • *n* fiduciari
fief • *n* feu *(m)*
field • *n* camp *(m)*, terreny *(m)*, cos *(m)*
fiend • *n* dimoni, diable
fierce • *adj* ferotge, feroç
fiercely • *adv* feroçment
fife • *n* pifre
fifteenth • *adj* quinzè *(m)*
fifth • *n* cinquè *(m)*, quint *(m)*, quinta *(f)* • *adj* cinquè *(m)*, quint *(m)*
fiftieth • *n* cinquantè • *adj* cinquantè
fig • *n* figuera *(f)*, figa *(f)*
fight • *v* lluitar, barallar-se, combatre • *n* lluita *(f)*, combat *(m)*
figuratively • *adv* figurativament
figure • *v* figurar-se • *n* figura *(f)*, xifra *(f)*
figurehead • *n* mascaró de proa *(m)*
file • *n* arxiu *(m)*, fitxer *(m)*, llima *(f)*
filigree • *v* filigranar • *n* filigrana *(f)*
filly • *n* poltra *(f)*
film • *n* pel·lícula *(f)*
filter • *v* filtrar • *n* filtre *(m)*
filth • *n* immundícia, porqueria *(f)*
filthy • *adj* impur, obscè, groller
fin • *n* aleta *(f)*
final • *n* final *(m)*, final *(f)* • *adj* final *(f)*
finalist • *n* finalista *(f)*
finally • *adv* finalment
finance • *n* finances

financial • *adj* financer
financially • *adv* financerament
finch • *n* pinsà *(m)*
find • *v* trobar
fineness • *n* llei *(m)*
finger • *n* dit *(m)*
fingering • *n* digitació *(f)*, inserció del dit *(f)*
fingernail • *n* ungla *(f)*
fingertip • *n* punta dels dits
finish • *v* acabar, finir, terminar, finalitzar • *n* meta *(f)*, fita *(f)*, fi *(f)*
finite • *adj* finit
fir • *n* avet
fire • *v* coure, acomiadar, disparar • *n* foc *(m)*, incendi *(m)*
firearm • *n* arma de foc *(f)*
fireplace • *n* xemeneia *(f)*, foganya *(f)*
firewood • *n* llenya *(f)*
firework • *n* for d'artifici *(m)*, foc d'artifici *(m)*
fireworks • *n* focs artificials
firm • *n* firma *(f)* • *adj* ferm
firmness • *n* fermesa *(f)*
first • *n* primer *(m)* • *adj* primer *(m)* • *adv* primer *(m)*
firstborn • *n* primogènit *(m)*, primogènita *(f)* • *adj* primogènit *(m)*
fiscal • *adj* fiscal
fish • *n* peix *(m)* • *v* pescar
fishbone • *n* espina *(f)*
fisher • *n* pescador *(m)*
fisherman • *n* pescador *(m)*
fishhook • *n* ham *(m)*
fishing • *n* pesca *(f)*
fishmonger • *n* peixater
fissure • *n* fissura *(f)*
fist • *v* apunyalar • *n* puny *(m)*
fit • *adj* adequat, apte
five • *n* cinc *(m)*, cinc *(f)*
fix • *v* arreglar
fixed • *adj* fix
fjord • *n* fiord *(m)*
flag • *n* bandera *(f)*
flageolet • *n* flageolet
flagstone • *n* llosa *(f)*
flail • *n* flagell *(m)*
flake • *n* ascla *(f)*
flamboyant • *adj* flamant
flame • *n* flama *(f)*
flamenco • *n* flamenc *(m)*
flamethrower • *n* llançaflames *(m)*
flamingo • *n* flamenc *(m)*
flannel • *n* franel·la *(f)*
flashlight • *n* llanterna *(f)*
flask • *n* matràs *(m)*
flat • *n* bemoll, punxada, avaria • *adj* pla,

xato (m)
flatten • v planejar
flattering • adj afalagador
flatulent • adj flatulent
flawless • adj perfecte
flawlessly • adv perfectament
flax • n lli (m)
flea • n puça (f)
flee • v fugir
fleece • n velló (m), vell (m), pelfa (f)
flesh • n carn (f)
fleshy • adj carnós, polpós
flexibility • n flexibilitat (f)
flexible • adj flexible
flight • n vol (m)
flint • n sílex, pedrenyal (m), pedrenyera (f), pedra foguera (f)
float • v flotar
flock • n bandada (f), ramat (m), floc (m)
floe • n banquisa (f)
flood • n inundació (f)
floor • n sòl (m), terra (m)
floral • adj floral
florist • n florista (f)
flotation • n flotació (f)
flour • v enfarinar • n farina (f)
flow • v fluir • n flux (m), cabal (m)
flower • v florir • n flor (f)
fluctuate • v fluctuar
fluently • adv fluidament
flugelhorn • n fiscorn (m)
fluid • n fluid (m)
fluke • n xamba (f)
fluorine • n fluor
flute • n flauta (f)
flutter • v onejar
fly • n mosca (f)
flying • v volador (m), voladora (f)
foal • n pollí, poltre (m)
foam • n escuma (f)
focal • adj focal
focus • v enfocar • n focus (m)
fodder • n farratge (f), pinso (m)
fog • n boira (f)
foggy • adj enboirat (m)
foil • n full (m), paper d'alumini (m), floret (m)
fold • v doblegar, plegar • n plegament (m), plec (m), séc (m)
folklore • n folklore (m)
follicle • n folŭlicle (m)
follow • v seguir
following • adj següent
fondle • v acaronar, acariciar
font • n fosa (f)
fontanelle • n fontanelŭla (f)
food • n menjar (m), aliment (m)

foodstuff • n aliment (m)
fool • v enganar • n beneit (m), idiota, el boig
foolish • adj ximple
foot • n pota (m), peu (m)
football • n futbol (m), pilota de futbol (m), pilota (m)
footpath • n senda (f), sendera (f), sender (m), viarany (m)
footprint • n petjada (f)
for • conj per • prep per, per a
forbidden • adj prohibit (m)
force • n força (f)
forced • adj forçat
forcibly • adv forçadament
forearm • n avantbraç (m)
forecast • n calendari (m)
forecastle • n castell
forefinger • n índex (m)
forefront • n avantguarda (f)
forehand • n cop de dreta (m)
forehead • n front (m)
foreign • adj estrany (m), estranya (f), foraster (m), forastera (f), estranger (m), estrangera (f)
foreigner • n foraster (m), forastera (f), estranger (m), estrangera (f)
foreland • n avantpaís
foremast • n trinquet (m)
forensic • adj forense
foresee • v pronosticar
foreseeable • adj previsible
forest • n bosc (m), forest (f), selva
forested • adj boscós
forge • n farga (f), forja (f) • v forjar
forget • v oblidar, descuidar-se, oblidar-se
forgetful • adj oblidadís, oblidós
forgettable • adj oblidable
forgive • v perdonar
fork • n forca (f), forquilla (f), bifurcació (f)
form • v formar • n forma (f), formulari (m)
formal • adj formal, solemne, convencional
formally • adv formalment
former • adj previ
formula • n fórmula (f)
fort • n fort (m)
forth • adv envant
fortieth • n quaranté (m) • adj quaranté, quadragèsim
fortnightly • adj quinzenal • adv quinzenalment
fortress • n fortalesa (f)
fortunately • adv afortunadament, feliç-

ment
fortune • *n* fortuna *(f)*, destí *(m)*
forum • *n* fòrum *(m)*, fòrum
forward • *n* atacant *(m)*, davanter *(m)*, ala *(f)*, aler *(m)*
fossil • *n* fòssil *(m)*
fossilization • *n* fossilització *(f)*
foster • *v* criar, cultivar
foul • *n* falta
foundation • *n* fundació *(f)*, fonaments
founder • *n* fonedor *(m)*
fountain • *n* font
four • *n* quatre *(m)*
fourfold • *v* quadruplicar
fourteenth • *adj* catorzè
fourth • *adj* quart
fox • *n* guineu *(f)*, guilla *(f)*, rabosa *(f)*
foxglove • *n* didalera *(f)*
fractal • *n* fractal *(m)* • *adj* fractal
fraction • *n* fracció
fragile • *adj* fràgil
fragility • *n* fragilitat *(f)*
fragment • *v* fragmentar • *n* fragment *(m)*
fragmentary • *adj* fragmentari
fragrance • *n* perfum *(m)*
fragrant • *adj* fragant
frame • *v* emmarcar • *n* estructura *(f)*, constitució, marc
framework • *n* infraestructura *(f)*
franc • *n* franc *(m)*, franc
francium • *n* franci *(m)*
frank • *adj* franc
frantically • *adv* frenèticament
fraternal • *adj* fratern
fraternization • *n* confraternització *(f)*
fraternize • *v* fraternitzar
fraud • *n* frau *(m)*
fraudulence • *n* fraudulència *(f)*
fraudulent • *adj* fraudulent
fraudulently • *adv* fraudulentament
fray • *v* desfilar-se
freckle • *n* piga *(f)*
free • *v* alliberar • *adj* lliure, desocupat
freedom • *n* llibertat *(f)*
freely • *adv* lliurement
freeze • *v* gelar, glaçar, congelar • *n* glaçada *(f)*, gelada *(f)*
frenetic • *adj* frenètic
frenzy • *n* frenesí
frequency • *n* freqüència *(f)*
frequent • *v* freqüentar
frequently • *adv* freqüentment
fresco • *n* fresc *(m)*
fresh • *adj* fresc, fresc *(m)*, fresca *(f)*
freshness • *n* frescor *(f)*
friar • *n* frare *(m)*
friction • *n* fricció *(f)*

friend • *n* amic *(m)*, amiga *(f)*, conegut *(m)*, coneguda *(f)*
friendly • *adj* amistós
friendship • *n* amistat *(f)*
frieze • *n* fris *(m)*
frigate • *n* fragata *(f)*
frighten • *v* espantar, espaventar
frightened • *adj* atemorit
fringe • *n* orla *(f)*, perifèria *(f)*, radical, serrell, pelussa • *adj* marginal
frivolity • *n* frivolitat *(f)*
frivolous • *adj* frívol, tonto, trivial
frivolously • *adv* frívolament
frog • *n* granota *(f)*
from • *prep* de, des de
front • *n* front *(m)*, cara *(f)*, façana principal *(f)*
frontal • *adj* frontal
frontier • *n* frontera *(f)* • *adj* fronterer
frontispiece • *n* frontispici *(m)*
frost • *n* gelada *(f)*, glaçada *(f)*, gebre *(m)*
frowsy • *adj* desendreçat
frozen • *adj* gelat
fructose • *n* fructosa *(f)*
frugal • *adj* frugal
fruit • *n* fruit *(m)*, fruita *(f)*, marieta, maricó
fruitless • *adj* infructuós
frustrated • *adj* frustrat
frustum • *n* tronc *(m)*
fry • *v* fregir • *n* aleví *(m)*
fuchsia • *n* fúcsia
fuck • *v* follar, cardar, fotre, fer un clau, fotre un clau, tirar-se, cagar-la • *n* clau *(m)* • *interj* merda!
fucker • *n* follador *(m)*
fudge • *n* caramel
fuel • *n* carburant *(m)*, combustible *(m)*
fulfill • *v* complir
full • *adj* ple, complet, total, sencer, tip
fully • *adv* plenament, completament
fun • *adj* divertit
function • *v* funcionar • *n* funció *(f)*
fundamental • *n* fonamental *(f)* • *adj* fonamental
fundamentalism • *n* fonamentalisme *(m)*
funeral • *n* enterrament *(m)*, funeral *(m)*, funerals
funerary • *adj* funerari
fungible • *adj* fungible
fungus • *n* fong
funnel • *n* embut *(m)*
funny • *adj* divertit
furious • *adj* furiós
furnish • *v* fornir
furnished • *adj* equipat, moblat
furrow • *n* solc *(m)*

furthermore • *adv* a més, a més a més, endemés

fuselage • *n* buc *(m)*

fuss • *n* rebombori *(m)*, gatzara *(f)*, brogit *(m)*, cridòria *(f)*, aldarull *(m)*

fussy • *adj* perepunyetes

futile • *adj* fútil

futility • *n* futilitat *(f)*, futilesa *(f)*

future • *n* futur *(m)* • *adj* futur

futurism • *n* futurisme *(m)*

futuristic • *adj* futurista

fuzzy • *adj* arrissat, borrós

G

gable • *n* gablet *(m)*

gadolinium • *n* gadolini *(m)*

gaga • *adj* boig *(m)*

galactic • *adj* galàctic *(m)*, galàctica *(f)*

galactose • *n* galactosa *(m)*

galaxy • *n* galàxia *(f)*

galena • *n* galena *(f)*

galleon • *n* galió *(m)*

galley • *n* galera *(f)*

gallium • *n* gal·li *(m)*

galvanize • *v* galvanitzar

galvanometer • *n* galvanòmetre *(m)*

gambler • *n* jugador *(m)*

game • *n* joc *(m)*, partida *(f)*

gamete • *n* gàmeta *(m)*

gamma • *n* gamma *(f)*

gamut • *n* gamma *(f)*

ganglion • *n* gangli *(m)*

gannet • *n* mascarell *(m)*

garage • *n* garatge *(m)*

garden • *n* jardí *(m)*, parc *(m)*, jardí públic

gardener • *n* jardiner *(m)*, jardinera *(f)*

garganey • *n* xarrasclet *(m)*

gargoyle • *n* gàrgola

garlic • *n* all *(m)*

garnet • *n* granat *(m)*

garnish • *v* guarnir • *n* guarnició *(f)*, guarniment *(m)*

garrison • *n* guarnició

garter • *n* lligacama *(m)*

gaseous • *adj* gasós

gasoline • *n* gasolina *(f)*, benzina *(f)*

gastric • *adj* gàstric

gastritis • *n* gastritis *(f)*

gastrointestinal • *adj* gastrointestinal

gastronomic • *adj* gastronòmic

gastronomy • *n* gastronomia *(f)*

gate • *n* taquilla *(f)*, porta *(f)*, reixat *(m)*

gateway • *n* passarel·la *(f)*

gather • *v* recollir

gaucho • *n* gautxo *(m)*

gay • *n* gai *(m)* • *adj* gai, gaia

gazette • *n* gaseta *(f)*

gecko • *n* dragó *(m)*

gee • *n* ge *(f)*

gelatinous • *adj* gelatinós

gem • *n* gemma *(f)*

gender • *n* gènere *(m)*, sexe *(m)*

genealogically • *adv* genealògicament

genealogist • *n* genealogista *(f)*

genealogy • *n* genealogia *(f)*

general • *n* general *(m)* • *adj* general

generally • *adv* generalment

generic • *adj* genèric

generous • *adj* generós

genet • *n* geneta *(f)*

genetic • *adj* genètic

genetically • *adv* genèticament

geneticist • *n* genetista *(f)*

genetics • *n* genètica *(f)*

genitive • *n* genitiu *(m)* • *adj* genitiu

genius • *n* geni *(m)*

genocide • *n* genocidi *(m)*

genome • *n* genoma *(m)*

genre • *n* gènere *(m)*

gently • *adv* suaument

genuine • *adj* genuí

genus • *n* gènere *(m)*

geographer • *n* geògraf *(m)*

geographically • *adv* geogràficament

geography • *n* geografia *(f)*

geologically • *adv* geològicament

geologist • *n* geòleg *(m)*

geology • *n* geologia *(f)*

geometer • *n* geòmetra *(f)*

geometric • *adj* geomètric

geometry • *n* geometria *(f)*

geriatrics • *n* geriatria *(f)*

germ • *n* germen *(m)*

germane • *n* germà *(m)*

germanium • *n* germani *(m)*

germinal • *adj* germinal

germinate • *v* germinar

gerund • *n* gerundi *(m)*

gesticulate • *v* gesticular

get • *v* aconseguir, obtindre, rebre, convertir-se en, esdevenir, arribar, entendre, comprendre, ser

geyser • *n* guèiser *(m)*

gherkin • *n* cogombret *(m)*

giant • *n* gegant *(m)*, gegant • *adj* gegant
gibbet • *n* forca *(f)*
giddy • *adj* marejat, marejador
gift • *n* regal
gig • *n* carrossí
gigantic • *adj* gegantí, gegantesc
gigantism • *n* gigantisme *(m)*, gegantisme *(m)*
gild • *v* daurar
gill • *n* brànquia *(f)*
gimel • *n* guímel *(f)*
gin • *n* ginebra *(f)*, gin *(m)*
ginger • *n* gingebre *(m)* • *adj* pèl-roig
gingivitis • *n* gingivitis *(f)*
giraffe • *n* girafa *(f)*
girl • *n* noia *(f)*, nena *(f)*, xiqueta, alůlota *(f)*
girlfriend • *n* nòvia *(f)*, xicota *(f)*, amiga *(f)*
give • *v* donar
gizzard • *n* pedrer
glacial • *adj* glacial
glacier • *n* glacera
glad • *adj* alegre
glade • *n* clar *(m)*
gladiator • *n* gladiador *(m)*
gladiolus • *n* gladiol *(m)*
gladly • *adv* gustosament
glance • *n* cop d'ull *(m)*
gland • *n* glàndula *(f)*
glandular • *adj* glandular
glans • *n* gland *(m)*
glass • *n* vidre *(m)*, got, vas *(m)*
glassworks • *n* cristalleria
glee • *n* alegria *(f)*, joia *(f)*
glider • *n* planador *(m)*
global • *adj* globular, mundial, global
globally • *adv* globalment
globetrotter • *n* rodamón *(f)*
glockenspiel • *n* carilló
glorious • *adj* gloriós
glottis • *n* glotis *(f)*
glove • *n* guant *(m)*
glowworm • *n* lluerna *(f)*
glucose • *n* glucosa *(f)*
gluon • *n* gluó *(m)*
glutamine • *n* glutamina *(f)*
gluttony • *n* gola *(f)*
glycine • *n* glicina *(f)*
glycolysis • *n* glicòlisi *(f)*
glycoprotein • *n* glicoproteïna
gnat • *n* mosquit *(m)*
gnaw • *v* rosegar
gnome • *n* gnom *(m)*, follet *(m)*, nan *(m)*
gnu • *n* nyu *(m)*
go • *v* anar, funcionar, desaparèixer, anar-se, destruir, dir, fer, sortir amb • *n* volta

(f), torn *(m)*, temptativa *(f)*, intent *(m)*, aprovació *(f)*, go *(m)*
goal • *n* objectiu *(m)*, meta *(f)*, porteria *(f)*, gol *(m)*
goalkeeper • *n* porter *(m)*
goat • *n* cabra *(f)*
goblet • *n* calze
goblin • *n* follet *(m)*
god • *n* déu *(m)*
goddaughter • *n* fillola *(f)*
goddess • *n* deessa *(f)*
godfather • *n* padrí *(m)*
godson • *n* fillol *(m)*
gold • *n* or *(m)*, moneda d'or *(f)*, daurat, medalla dor *(f)* • *adj* daurat
goldcrest • *n* reietó *(m)*
golden • *adj* d'or *(m)*, daurat, daurada *(f)*, daurat *(m)*
goldfinch • *n* cadernera *(f)*
golf • *n* golf *(m)*
golfer • *n* golfista *(f)*
gondola • *n* góndola *(f)*
gong • *n* gong *(m)*
goniometer • *n* goniòmetre
gonorrhea • *n* gonocòccia *(f)*
good • *adj* bo, bon • *n* bo *(m)*, bona *(f)*, bo
goodbye • *interj* adéu, adéu-siau
goodness • *n* bondat *(f)*, bonesa *(f)*
goods • *n* béns
goose • *n* oca *(f)*
gooseberry • *n* agrassó *(m)*
gorge • *v* devorar • *n* gola *(f)*, gargamella
gorgeous • *adj* esplèndit, magnífic, maquíssim
gorget • *n* gola *(f)*
gorilla • *n* gorilůla *(m)*
gorse • *n* gatosa *(f)*
gosh • *interj* ostres *(f)*
goshawk • *n* astor *(m)*
gospel • *n* evangeli *(m)*
gossip • *v* xafardejar • *n* xafarder, xafarderia *(f)*
goth • *n* gòtic *(m)*
goutte • *n* gota *(f)*
govern • *v* governar
government • *n* govern *(m)*
governmental • *adj* governamental
governor • *n* governador *(m)*
goy • *n* Goy
gracefully • *adv* graciosament
gradual • *adj* gradual
gradually • *adv* gradualment
gram • *n* gram *(m)*
grammar • *n* gramàtica *(f)*, gramàtica
grammatical • *adj* gramatical
granary • *n* graner
granddaughter • *n* néta *(f)*

grandeur • *n* grandesa *(f)*
grandfather • *n* avi *(m)*
grandiloquent • *adj* grandiloqüent *(n)*
grandiose • *adj* grandiós
grandmother • *n* àvia *(f)*, iaia *(f)*
grandson • *n* nét *(m)*
granitic • *adj* granític
grape • *n* raïm *(m)*
grapefruit • *n* aranger *(m)*, aranja *(f)*
graph • *n* gràfic *(m)*
graphic • *n* gràfic *(m)*, gràfics • *adj* gràfic
grappa • *n* grappa
grasp • *v* comprendre
grass • *n* herba *(f)*
grasshopper • *n* llagosta *(f)*, saltamartí *(m)*
grassy • *adj* herbaci
grateful • *adj* agraït
gratefulness • *n* agraïment
grater • *n* ratllador
gratitude • *n* gratitud *(f)*
grave • *n* sepulcre *(m)* • *adj* seriós, greu
gravedigger • *n* enterramorts
gravel • *n* grava *(f)*
gravely • *adv* greument
gravestone • *n* làpida *(f)*
gravitation • *n* gravitació *(f)*
gravitational • *adj* gravitacional, gravitatori
gravity • *n* gravetat *(f)*
gravure • *n* gravat *(m)*
gray • *n* gris *(m)* • *adj* gris
greasy • *adj* greixós
great • *adj* gran, enorme, genial, fabulós
great-uncle • *n* besoncle *(m)*
greed • *n* avarícia *(f)*, cobdícia *(f)*
greedy • *adj* avariciós, cobdiciós, cobejós, avar, àvid
green • *n* verd *(m)* • *adj* verd
greenish • *adj* verdós
greet • *v* saludar
gregarious • *adj* gregari
grenade • *n* granada *(f)*
greyhound • *n* llebrer *(m)*
grid • *n* quadrícula *(f)*
griffin • *n* griu *(m)*, grif *(m)*
grime • *n* brutícia *(f)*, sutge *(m)*, sutja *(f)*
grind • *v* moldre, triturar
grip • *v* agafar, empunyar
groan • *v* gemegar
grog • *n* grog *(m)*
groin • *n* engonal *(m)*

groovy • *adj* genial
gross • *n* grossa
grotto • *n* gruta *(f)*
ground • *n* terra *(m)*, sòl *(m)*, fons *(m)*, camp *(m)*, punt de terra *(m)*, terra *(f)*
group • *n* grup *(m)*
grovel • *v* arrossegar
grow • *v* créixer, cultivar
growing • *adj* creixent
grudge • *v* recar
grumpy • *adj* rondinaire
guarantee • *v* garantir • *n* garantia
guard • *n* escorta *(f)*, guarda
guerrilla • *n* guerrilla *(f)*
guess • *v* endevinar, obtenir, suposar • *n* conjetura *(f)*
guest • *n* convidat *(m)*, hoste *(m)*, invitat *(m)*
guillotine • *v* guillotinar • *n* guillotina *(f)*, guillotina
guilt • *n* culpabilitat, culpa *(f)*
guilty • *adj* culpable, reprovable
guitar • *n* guitarra *(f)*
guitarist • *n* guitarrista *(f)*
gulag • *n* gulag *(m)*
gulf • *n* golf *(m)*
gull • *n* gavina, gavià
gullet • *n* esòfag *(m)*
gum • *n* geniva *(f)*
gun • *v* disparar • *n* pistola *(m)*, escopeta *(f)*, canó *(m)*, obús *(m)*
gunboat • *n* canonera *(f)*
gunner • *n* artiller *(m)*
gunpowder • *n* pólvora
guru • *n* guru *(m)*
gust • *n* ratxe
gustatory • *adj* gustatiu, gustatori
guts • *n* pebrots
gutter • *n* canal, canal *(m)*
guy • *n* paio *(m)*
gymnasium • *n* gimnàs *(m)*
gymnast • *n* gimnasta *(f)*
gymnastic • *adj* gimnàstic
gymnastics • *n* gimnàstica *(f)*
gynecological • *adj* ginecològic
gynecology • *n* ginecologia *(f)*
gypsum • *n* guix *(m)*, parrell *(m)*
gypsy • *n* gitano *(m)*
gyre • *n* gir *(m)*, gir oceànic *(m)*
gyrus • *n* circumvolució *(f)*

H

habit • *n* costum, hàbit *(m)*
habitable • *adj* habitable
habitat • *n* hàbitat *(m)*
habitually • *adv* habitualment
hackamore • *n* xàquima *(f)*
hackberry • *n* lledoner
hadal • *adj* hadal
hadron • *n* hadró *(m)*
haemophilic • *adj* hemofílic
hafnium • *n* hafni *(m)*
hail • *n* calamarsa
hair • *n* cabell *(m)*, pèl *(m)*
hairnet • *n* ret *(m)*
hake • *n* lluç *(m)*
halberd • *n* alabarda *(f)*
halberdier • *n* alabarder *(m)*
halcyon • *n* blauet *(m)*, alció *(m)*
half • *n* meitat *(f)* • *adj* mig
half-mast • *n* mig pal
hallelujah • *interj* alŭleluia
hallowed • *adj* sagrat
hallucination • *n* alŭlucinació *(f)*
hallucinogen • *n* alŭlucinogen *(m)*
hallucinogenic • *n* alŭlucinogen *(m)* • *adj* alŭlucinogen
halogen • *n* halogen *(m)*
halyard • *n* drissa *(f)*
ham • *n* pernil *(m)*
hamburger • *n* hamburguesa *(f)*
hamlet • *n* poblet *(m)*
hammer • *v* martellejar, clavar • *n* martell *(m)*
hammock • *n* hamaca *(f)*
hamster • *n* hàmster *(m)*
hand • *n* mà *(f)*, busca *(f)*, maneta *(f)*, agulla *(f)*
hand-held • *adj* mac
handball • *n* handbol *(m)*
handcuffs • *n* manilles
handful • *n* grapat *(m)*
handicap • *v* handicapar
handkerchief • *n* mocador *(m)*
handle • *n* nansa *(f)*, mànec *(m)*, maneta *(m)*, maneta *(f)*, tirador *(f)*
handling • *n* manipulació
handsaw • *n* xerrac *(m)*
handy • *adj* pràctic, a mà
hang • *v* penjar, encallar-se, bloquejar-se, penjar-se, encallar, bloquejar
hanger • *n* perxa *(f)*
hangman • *n* penjat *(m)*
hangnail • *n* repeló
hangover • *n* ressaca *(f)*
haploid • *adj* haploide
happen • *v* passar, ocórrer, succeir
happily • *adv* feliçment, alegrement, afortunadament

happiness • *n* felicitat *(f)*
happy • *adj* feliç, content, alegre, afortunat, satisfet
harass • *v* molestar, fastiguejar, vexar
harbinger • *v* anunciar • *n* anunciador *(m)*, herald *(m)*
hard • *adj* dur, complicat, difícil, dur *(m)*, dura
harden • *v* endurir-se, endurir
hardly • *adv* a penes
hardship • *n* dificultats
hardware • *n* maquinari *(m)*
hardworking • *adj* treballador
hare • *n* llebre *(f)*
harem • *n* harem *(m)*
harlequin • *n* arlequí *(m)*
harm • *n* dany *(m)*
harmful • *adj* nociu
harmless • *adj* inofensiu
harmonica • *n* harmònica *(f)*
harmoniously • *adv* harmoniosament
harmonium • *n* harmònium *(m)*
harmonize • *v* harmonitzar
harness • *n* arnès *(m)*
harp • *n* arpa *(f)*
harpoon • *v* arponar • *n* arpó *(m)*
harpooner • *n* arponer *(m)*
harpsichord • *n* clavicèmbal *(m)*, clavecí *(m)*
harpsichordist • *n* clavecinista *(f)*
harpy • *n* harpia *(f)*
harrier • *n* arpella *(f)*
harsh • *v* criticar • *adj* aspre *(f)*, sever *(m)*, severa *(f)*
harvestman • *n* frare
hashish • *n* haixix *(m)*
haste • *n* pressa *(f)*
hasty • *adj* precipitat
hat • *n* barret *(m)*, capell *(m)*
hate • *v* odiar
hateful • *adj* odiós
hatred • *n* odi *(m)*
haughty • *adj* superb, orgullós, arrogant
have • *v* tenir
hawk • *n* falcó *(m)*, aligot *(m)*
hawthorn • *n* arç blanc *(m)*
hay • *n* fenc *(m)*
haystack • *n* paller *(m)*
hazardous • *adj* atzarós
hazel • *n* avellaner
hazelnut • *n* avellana *(f)*
he • *pron* ell
head • *v* comandar, dirigir, encapçalar, liderar, cabotejar • *n* cap *(m)*, seny *(m)*, ment *(f)*, punta *(f)*, líder *(f)*, director *(m)*, directora *(f)* • *adj* cap
header • *n* cop de cap

headlight • *n* far *(m)*
headquarters • *n* quarter general *(m)*, central *(m)*, seu *(f)*
headscarf • *n* mocador de cap
headwind • *n* vent de proa *(m)*
health • *n* salut, sanitat *(f)*
healthily • *adv* saludablement
healthy • *adj* salubre
hear • *v* sentir, oir
hearing • *n* oïda *(f)*
heart • *n* cor, cor *(m)*, si *(m)*
hearth • *n* llar, llar *(f)*
heat • *n* calor
heating • *n* calefacció *(f)*
heaven • *n* cel
heavy • *adj* pesat, greu
hebdomadary • *n* hebdomadari *(m)*
hectare • *n* hectàrea *(f)*
hectic • *adj* frenètic, febril
heddle • *n* collador *(m)*
hedge • *n* tanca viva *(f)*
hedgehog • *n* eriçó *(m)*
hedonism • *n* hedonisme *(m)*
hedonist • *n* hedonista *(f)*
heel • *v* estalonar • *n* taló *(m)*, crostó *(m)*
hegemonic • *adj* hegemònic
heighten • *v* aixecar
heir • *n* hereu *(m)*
helicon • *n* helicó *(m)*
helicopter • *n* helicòpter *(m)*
heliometer • *n* heliòmetre *(m)*
heliosphere • *n* heliosfera *(f)*
helium • *n* heli *(m)*
helix • *n* hèlix *(f)*
hello • *interj* hola, digui, si, mani'm, na maria?, conill!
helm • *n* timó *(m)*
helmet • *n* casc *(m)*, elm *(m)*
help • *n* ajuda *(f)* • *v* ajudar, aidar
helper • *n* ajudant *(m)*, ajudador *(m)*
helpful • *adj* útil
helpless • *adj* indefens
hem • *n* vora *(f)*
hematologic • *adj* hematològic
hemiplegia • *n* hemiplegia *(f)*
hemisphere • *n* hemisferi *(m)*
hemlock • *n* tsuga *(f)*, cicuta *(f)*
hemorrhoid • *n* hemorroide *(f)*
hemp • *n* cànem
hen • *n* gallina *(f)*, au
hendiadys • *n* hendíadis
hepatic • *adj* hepàtic
hepatitis • *n* hepatitis *(f)*
heptagon • *n* heptàgon *(m)*
heraldry • *n* heràldica *(f)*
herb • *n* herba *(f)*
herbaceous • *adj* herbaci

herbarium • *n* herbari
herbivore • *n* herbívor *(m)*
herbivorous • *adj* herbívor
herborize • *v* herboritzar
herd • *n* ramat *(m)*
here • *adv* aquí, ací
hereditary • *adj* hereditari
heresy • *n* heretgia *(f)*
heretic • *n* heretge *(f)*
heretical • *adj* herètic
heretofore • *adv* fins ara
hermaphrodite • *n* hermafrodita
hermit • *n* ermità *(m)*
hero • *n* heroi *(m)*, heroïna *(f)*
heroic • *adj* heroic
heroin • *n* heroïna *(f)*
heroine • *n* heroïna *(f)*
heroism • *n* heroisme *(m)*
heron • *n* agró
herpes • *n* herpes *(m)*
herpetology • *n* herpetologia *(f)*
herring • *n* areng *(m)*
herself • *pron* es, mateix
hesitate • *v* hesitar, dubtar, titubejar
hesitation • *n* hesitació *(f)*, vacil·lació *(f)*
heterogeneous • *adj* heterogeni
heterosexism • *n* heterosexisme
heterosexual • *adj* heterosexual
heterosexuality • *n* heterosexualitat *(f)*
heuristic • *n* heurística *(f)* • *adj* heurístic
hexagon • *n* hexàgon *(m)*
hexahedron • *n* hexaedre *(m)*, hexàedre *(m)*
hey • *interj* ep, ei, eh
hi • *interj* hola
hiatus • *n* hiat *(m)*
hibernate • *v* hibernar
hibernation • *n* hibernació *(f)*
hiccup • *n* singlot *(m)*
hidden • *adj* amagat
hide • *v* amagar
hieroglyph • *n* jeroglífic *(m)*
hieroglyphic • *adj* jeroglífic
high • *adj* alt, elevat, drogat
highbrow • *adj* intel·lectual
highlight • *v* emfasitzar, remarcar, ressaltar, marcar, subratllar • *n* llum *(f)*
highly • *adv* altament
hight • *v* dir-se
hike • *n* caminada *(f)*
hilarious • *adj* hilarant
hilarity • *n* hilaritat *(f)*
hill • *n* puig *(m)*, turó *(m)*
hilly • *adj* muntanyós
hilt • *n* empunyadura *(f)*
hilum • *n* hil *(m)*
himself • *pron* es, mateix

hind • *adj* posterior
hinder • *v* destorbar, dificultar
hinge • *n* polleguera *(f)*
hip • *n* maluc *(m)*
hippocampus • *n* hipocamp *(m)*
hippodrome • *n* hipòdrom *(m)*
hippopotamus • *n* hipopòtam *(m)*
hire • *v* llogar, contractar
his • *pron* el seu *(m)*, la seva *(f)*, els seus, les seves
historian • *n* historiador *(m)*
historic • *adj* històric
historical • *adj* històric
historically • *adv* històricament
history • *n* història *(f)*, historial *(m)*
histrionic • *adj* histriònic
hit • *v* colpejar, batre, pegar, xocar, encertar • *n* cop *(m)*, èxit *(m)*
hoard • *v* acaparar, abassegar
hobo • *n* rodamón *(f)*
hockey • *n* hoquei *(m)*
hoe • *n* aixada
hog • *n* suid *(m)*, marrà *(m)*, tacany *(m)*
hoist • *v* hissar
hold • *v* aguantar, sostenir
hole • *v* foradar • *n* forat *(m)*
holiday • *n* festa *(f)*, dia de festa, dia feriat, vacances
holistic • *adj* holístic
holly • *n* grèvol *(m)*
holmium • *n* holmi *(m)*
holy • *adj* sagrat, sagrada *(f)*, sant *(m)*, santa *(f)*
homage • *n* homenatge
home • *n* llar *(m)*, casa *(f)*
homeless • *adj* sense llar
homeopath • *n* homeòpata *(f)*
homeopathy • *n* homeopatia *(f)*
homesick • *adj* enyorat
homework • *n* deures
homicide • *n* homicidi *(m)*
homogeneous • *adj* homogeni
homograph • *n* homògraf *(m)*
homologate • *v* homologar
homonym • *n* homònim *(n)*
homonymous • *adj* homònim
homonymy • *n* homonímia *(f)*
homophobia • *n* homofòbia *(f)*, antropofòbia *(f)*
homophone • *n* homòfon
homophony • *n* homofonia *(f)*
homosexual • *n* homosexual *(f)* • *adj* homosexual
homosexuality • *n* homosexualitat *(f)*
hone • *n* esmoladora *(f)*
honestly • *adv* honestament
honesty • *n* honradesa *(f)*, honestedat *(f)*

honey • *n* mel *(f)*
honeycomb • *n* bresca *(f)*
honeymoon • *n* lluna de mel *(f)*
honeysuckle • *n* lligabosc *(m)*
honor • *n* honor *(m)*
honorable • *adj* honorable
honorary • *adj* honorari
hood • *n* caputxa *(f)*
hoof • *n* peülla *(f)*
hook • *v* enganxar • *n* garfi *(m)*, ganxo *(m)*
hooked • *adj* ganxut
hooker • *n* prostituta, talonador *(m)*
hoop • *n* cèrcol *(m)*
hoopoe • *n* puput *(f)*, palput
hop • *n* llúpol *(m)*
hope • *n* esperança *(f)* • *v* esperar
hopeless • *adj* desesperat
horizon • *n* horitzó *(m)*
horizontal • *adj* horitzontal
horizontally • *adv* horitzontalment
hormonal • *adj* hormonal
hormone • *n* hormona *(f)*
horn • *n* banya *(f)*, corn *(m)*, clàxon *(m)*
hornbeam • *n* carpí *(m)*
horny • *adj* corni, calent
horology • *n* orologia
horoscope • *n* horòscop *(m)*
horrible • *adj* horrible, hòrrid, esgarrifós
horribly • *adv* horriblement
horse • *n* cavall *(m)*, euga *(f)*
horseradish • *n* rave picant
horseshoe • *n* ferradura *(f)*
horticulture • *n* horticultura *(f)*
hosanna • *interj* ossanna, hosanna
hose • *n* mànega *(f)*
hospital • *n* hospital *(m)*
hospitalization • *n* hospitalització *(f)*
host • *v* allotjar • *n* amfitrió *(m)*, amfitriona *(f)*
hostage • *n* ostatge *(f)*
hostel • *n* alberg *(m)*
hostile • *adj* hostil
hot • *adj* calent
hotel • *n* hotel *(m)*
hour • *n* hora *(f)*
house • *v* allotjar • *n* casa *(f)*
housefly • *n* mosca comuna *(f)*
household • *n* seguici *(m)*, familiars
housekeeper • *n* casera
hovel • *n* enfony *(m)*
hovercraft • *n* aerolliscador *(m)*
how • *adv* com, que
however • *adv* tanmateix, nogensmenys
howitzer • *n* obús *(m)*
howl • *v* udolar • *n* udol *(m)*
hubbub • *n* gatzara *(f)*, aldarull *(m)*,

cridòria (f), rebombori (m), brogit (m), avalot (m)
hug • v abraçar • n abraçada (f)
huge • adj enorme
hull • n buc (m)
human • n humà (m), ésser humà (m) • adj humà
humane • adj humà
humanism • n humanisme (m)
humanistic • adj humanístic
humanitarian • adj humanitari (m), humanitària (f)
humanity • n humanitat (f)
humble • v humiliar • adj humil (f), humil
humbly • adv humilment
humdrum • adj avorrit, tediós
humerus • n húmer (m)
humid • adj humit
hummingbird • n colibrí (m)
hump • n gep (m)
humpback • n geperut (m), geperuda (f)
hunch • n pressentiment (m)
hundreds • n cents (m)
hundredth • n centèsim (m) • adj centèsim
hunger • n gana (f), fam (m)
hungry • adj afamat
hunt • v caçar • n caça (f), cacera (f)
hunter • n caçador (m)
hurdle • n obstacle
hurricane • n huracà (m)
hurry • v fer via, accelerar, apressar • n presa (f)
hurt • v doldre, doler, ferir
husband • n marit (m)
husk • n clofolla (f), closca (f), clovella (f)
husky • adj ronc (m)
hussar • n hússar (m)
hybrid • n híbrid (m) • adj híbrid
hydraulic • adj hidràulic
hydraulics • n hidràulica (f)
hydride • n hidrur (m)
hydrocarbon • n hidrocarbur (m)
hydrodynamic • adj hidrodinàmic
hydrodynamics • n hidrodinàmica (f)

hydrogen • n hidrogen (m)
hydrosphere • n hidrosfera (f)
hydrostatic • adj hidrostàtic
hyena • n hiena (f)
hygiene • n higiene (f)
hygienic • adj higiènic
hygrometer • n higròmetre (m)
hymen • n himen (m)
hymn • n himne (m)
hymnal • n himnari (m)
hypallage • n hipàlůlage (f)
hyperactive • adj hiperactiu
hyperbaton • n hipèrbaton
hyperbola • n hipèrbola (f), hipèrbole (f)
hyperbole • n hipèrbole (f)
hyperbolic • adj hiperbòlic
hyperglycemia • n hiperglucèmia, hiperglicèmia
hypernym • n hiperònim (m)
hypersensitivity • n hipersensibilitat (f)
hypertext • n hipertext (m)
hypertrophy • n hipertròfia (f)
hyphen • n guionet (m)
hypnosis • n hipnosi (f)
hypnotic • n hipnòtic (m) • adj hipnòtic
hypnotism • n hipnotisme (m)
hypnotist • n hipnotitzador (m)
hypocaust • n hipocaust (m)
hypochondria • n hipocondria (f)
hypocrisy • n hipocresia (f)
hypocrite • n hipòcrita
hypocritical • adj hipòcrita (f)
hypodermic • adj hipodèrmic
hyponym • n hipònim (m)
hypotenuse • n hipotenusa (f)
hypothalamic • adj hipotalàmic
hypothalamus • n hipotàlem (m)
hypothesis • n hipòtesi (f)
hypothetical • adj hipotètic
hypothetically • adv hipotèticament
hypoxia • n hipòxia (f)
hysterectomy • n histerectomia (f)
hysteria • n histèria (f)
hysterical • adj histèric
hysterically • adv histèricament

I

i • n i (f)
iamb • n iambe (m)
iambic • adj iàmbic
ibex • n cabra alpina (f)
ibis • n ibis (m)
ibuprofen • n ibuprofèn (m)

ice • n gel (m)
iceberg • n iceberg (m)
icebreaker • n trencaglaç (m)
ichthyologist • n ictiòleg (m)
ichthyology • n ictiologia (f)
icicle • n caramell (f)

icing • *n* refús prohibit *(m)*
icon • *n* icona *(f)*
icosahedron • *n* icosaedre *(m)*, icosàedre *(m)*
idea • *n* idea *(f)*
ideal • *n* ideal *(m)* • *adj* ideal
idealization • *n* idealització *(f)*
ideally • *adv* idealment
identical • *adj* idèntic
identically • *adv* idènticament
identifiable • *adj* identificable
identification • *n* identificació *(f)*
identify • *v* identificar, identificar-se
identity • *n* identitat *(f)*
ideogram • *n* ideograma *(m)*
ideograph • *n* ideograma *(m)*
ideology • *n* ideologia
idiocy • *n* idiòcia
idiolect • *n* idiolecte *(m)*
idiom • *n* idiotisme *(m)*
idiosyncratic • *adj* idiosincràtic
idiot • *n* idiota *(f)*
idle • *adj* inactiu, desocupat, aturat
idol • *n* ídol *(m)*
idolater • *n* idòlatra *(f)*
idolatrous • *adj* idòlatra
idolatry • *n* idolatria *(f)*
idyll • *n* idili *(m)*
idyllic • *adj* idíl·lic
if • *conj* si
igloo • *n* iglú *(m)*
ignorance • *n* ignorància *(f)*
ignorant • *adj* ignorant
ileum • *n* ili *(m)*
iliac • *adj* ilíac
ilium • *n* ili *(m)*, os ilíac *(m)*
ill • *adj* malalt
illegal • *adj* il·legal
illegally • *adv* il·legalment
illegible • *adj* illegible, il·legible
illegitimate • *adj* il·legítim
illicit • *adj* il·lícit
illiteracy • *n* analfabetisme *(m)*
illiterate • *n* analfabet *(m)* • *adj* illetrat, analfabet
illness • *n* malaltia *(f)*
illogical • *adj* il·lògic
illogically • *adv* il·lògicament
illusion • *n* il·lusió *(f)*, illusió
illustrious • *adj* il·lustre
image • *n* imatge *(f)*
imagery • *n* imatgeria *(f)*
imaginary • *adj* imaginari
imagination • *n* imaginació *(f)*
imaginative • *adj* imaginatiu
imagine • *v* imaginar
imam • *n* imam *(m)*

imbecile • *n* imbècil *(f)*
imbecility • *n* imbecil·litat *(f)*
imbricate • *v* imbricar
imbue • *v* imbuir, impregnar
imitate • *v* imitar
imitation • *n* imitació *(f)*
immaterial • *adj* immaterial
immateriality • *n* immaterialitat *(f)*
immature • *adj* immadur
immaturity • *n* immaduresa *(f)*
immediacy • *n* immediatesa *(f)*
immediate • *adj* immediat, pròxim
immediately • *adv* immediatament
immense • *adj* immens
immensity • *n* immensitat *(f)*
immigrant • *n* immigrant *(f)*
imminence • *n* imminència *(f)*
imminent • *adj* imminent
immobile • *adj* immoble, immòbil
immolate • *v* immolar, sacrificar
immoral • *adj* immoral
immorally • *adv* immoralment
immortal • *adj* immortal
immortality • *n* immortalitat *(f)*
immune • *adj* immune
immunity • *n* immunitat *(f)*
immunological • *adj* immunològic
immunologist • *n* immunòleg *(m)*
immunology • *n* immunologia *(f)*
impact • *v* impactar
impala • *n* impala *(m)*
impartial • *adj* imparcial
impartially • *adv* imparcialment
impassable • *adj* infranquejable
impatient • *adj* impacient
impatiently • *adv* impacientment
impeccable • *adj* impecable *(f)*
impeccably • *adv* impecablement
impenetrability • *n* impenetrabilitat *(f)*
imperceptible • *adj* imperceptible
imperceptibly • *adv* imperceptiblement
imperfect • *n* imperfet *(m)* • *adj* imperfecte
imperfection • *n* imperfecció *(f)*
imperfectly • *adv* imperfectament
imperial • *adj* imperial, majestuós
imperialist • *n* imperialista • *adj* imperialista
imperialistic • *adj* imperialista
imperil • *v* arriscar
imperious • *adj* imperiós
impermeable • *adj* impermeable
impersonally • *adv* impersonalment
impertinent • *adj* impertinent
impetuous • *adj* impetuós
implausible • *adj* inversemblant
implicit • *adj* implícit, absolut

implicitly • *adv* implícitament
implosion • *n* implosió *(f)*
imply • *v* implicar, insinuar
important • *adj* important
importantly • *adv* notablement, importantment
importunate • *adj* importú
impossible • *n* impossible • *adj* impossible, insuportable
impossibly • *adv* impossiblement
impotent • *adj* impotent
impracticability • *n* impracticabilitat *(f)*
impracticable • *adj* impracticable
impressed • *adj* impressionat, imprès, requisat
impression • *n* impressió *(f)*
impressionable • *adj* impressionable
impressionism • *n* impressionisme *(m)*
impressionist • *n* impressionista *(f)*
impressive • *adj* impressionant
impressively • *adv* impressionantment
imprison • *v* empresonar
imprisonment • *n* empresonament *(m)*
improbability • *n* improbabilitat *(f)*
improbable • *adj* improbable
improper • *adj* impropi
improve • *v* millorar
improvement • *n* millora *(f)*
improvisation • *n* improvisació
improvise • *v* improvisar
imprudence • *n* imprudència *(f)*
imprudent • *adj* imprudent
imprudently • *adv* imprudentment
impudence • *n* impudència *(f)*
impudent • *adj* impudent
impulse • *n* impuls *(m)*, antull *(m)*, capritx *(m)*, caprici *(m)*, impulsió *(f)*
impulsive • *adj* impulsiu
impure • *adj* impur
impurity • *n* impuresa *(f)*
in • *prep* en, dins, d'aquí a • *adv* dins, cap endintre
inaccessibility • *n* inaccessibilitat *(f)*
inaccessible • *adj* inaccessible
inaccurate • *adj* imprecís
inaccurately • *adv* desacuradament
inaction • *n* inacció *(f)*
inactive • *adj* inactiu
inactivity • *n* inactivitat *(f)*
inadequate • *adj* inadequat
inadequately • *adv* inadequadament
inadmissible • *adj* inadmissible
inalienable • *adj* inalienable
inanimate • *adj* inanimat
inapplicable • *adj* inaplicable
inappropriate • *adj* inapropiat
inaugural • *adj* inaugural

inauguration • *n* inauguració *(f)*
inborn • *adj* innat
incandescent • *adj* incandescent
incapable • *adj* incapaç
incarceration • *n* encarcerament
incarnation • *n* encarnació *(f)*
incautiously • *adv* incautament
incendiary • *adj* incendiari
incense • *n* encens *(m)*
incentive • *n* incentiu *(m)*
inception • *n* inici *(m)*
incessant • *adj* incessant
incestuous • *adj* incestuós
inch • *n* polzada *(f)*, centímetre *(m)*
incinerate • *v* incinerar
incision • *n* incisió *(f)*
incisive • *adj* incisiu
incisor • *n* incisiu *(m)*, dent incisia *(f)*
inclination • *n* inclinació *(f)*, desnivell *(m)*
incline • *v* inclinar
inclusion • *n* inclusió *(f)*
inclusive • *adj* inclusiu
incoherent • *adj* incoherent
incoherently • *adv* incoherentment
incombustible • *adj* incombustible
incomparable • *adj* incomparable
incompatible • *adj* incompatible
incompetent • *adj* incompetent
incomplete • *adj* incomplet
incompletely • *adv* incompletament
incomprehensible • *adj* incomprensible
inconceivable • *adj* inconcebible
incongruous • *adj* incongruent
inconsiderate • *adj* inconsiderat
inconsiderately • *adv* inconsideradament
inconspicuously • *adv* desapercebudament
inconstancy • *n* inconstància *(f)*
inconstant • *adj* inconstant
inconvenience • *n* inconveniència *(f)*
inconvenient • *adj* inconvenient
inconveniently • *adv* inconvenientment
incorporate • *v* incorporar
incorrect • *adj* incorrecte
incorrectly • *adv* incorrectament
increase • *v* augmentar • *n* augment *(m)*
incredible • *adj* increïble
incredibly • *adv* increïblement
incredulous • *adj* incrèdul
incremental • *adj* incremental
incubation • *n* incubació *(f)*, covament *(m)*
incubator • *n* incubadora *(f)*
incubus • *n* íncub *(m)*, íncube *(m)*
incumbent • *n* titular *(f)* • *adj* titular
incurable • *adj* incurable
incus • *n* enclusa *(f)*

indebted • *adj* endeutat
indebtedness • *n* endeutament *(m)*
indecent • *adj* indecent
indecisive • *adj* indecís
indefensible • *adj* indefensable
indefinite • *adj* indefinit
indefinitely • *adv* indefinidament
indelible • *adj* indeleble
independence • *n* independència *(f)*
independent • *adj* independent
independently • *adv* independentment
indescribable • *adj* indescriptible
indestructible • *adj* indestructible
index • *n* índex *(m)*
indicative • *adj* indicatiu
indifferent • *adj* indiferent, mediocre
indigenous • *adj* indígena
indigent • *n* indigent • *adj* indigent
indignant • *adj* indignat
indignation • *n* indignació *(f)*
indignity • *n* indignitat *(f)*
indirect • *adj* indirecte
indirectly • *adv* indirectament
indiscreet • *adj* indiscret
indiscriminate • *adj* indiscriminat
indispensable • *adj* indispensable
indisputable • *adj* indiscutible
indistinct • *adj* indistint
indistinguishable • *adj* indistingible
indium • *n* indi *(m)*
individual • *n* individu *(m)* • *adj* individual
individually • *adv* individualment
indivisible • *adj* indivisible
indoctrination • *n* adoctrinament
indolent • *adj* indolent
indomitable • *adj* indomable
indubitable • *adj* indubtable
induce • *v* induir
indulgent • *adj* indulgent
industrial • *adj* industrial
industrialism • *n* industrialisme *(m)*
industrialized • *adj* industrialitzat
inedible • *adj* immenjable, incomestible
ineffective • *adj* ineficaç
inelastic • *adj* inelàstic
inept • *adj* inepte
ineptitude • *n* ineptitud *(f)*
inequality • *n* desigualtat *(f)*
inert • *adj* inert
inertia • *n* inèrcia *(f)*
inessential • *adj* inessencial *(f)*, extern *(m)*, extern *(f)*
inevitable • *adj* inevitable
inevitably • *adv* inevitablement
inexact • *adj* inexacte
inexcusably • *adv* inexcusablement

inexorable • *adj* inexorable
inexpensive • *adj* barat
inexperienced • *adj* inexpert
inexplicable • *adj* inexplicable
infallibility • *n* infalůlibilitat *(f)*
infallible • *adj* infalůlible
infamous • *adj* infame
infamy • *n* infàmia *(f)*
infantile • *adj* infantil
infatuation • *n* infatuació *(f)*
infection • *n* infecció *(f)*
infectious • *adj* infecciós
infelicitous • *adj* infeliç *(f)*, desgraciat, maldestre, inadequat, impropi
inferiority • *n* inferioritat *(f)*
infidel • *n* infidel *(f)*
infidelity • *n* infidelitat *(f)*
infielder • *n* interior *(f)*
infiltrate • *v* infiltrar
infinite • *adj* infinit
infinitive • *n* infinitiu *(m)*
infinity • *n* infinitat *(f)*
inflammable • *adj* inflamable, combustible
inflammation • *n* inflamació *(f)*
inflate • *v* inflar, unflar
inflection • *n* flexió *(f)*, inflexió *(f)*
inflexibility • *n* inflexibilitat *(f)*
inflexible • *adj* inflexible
inflexibly • *adv* inflexiblement
inflorescence • *n* inflorescència *(f)*
influence • *n* influència *(f)*
influenza • *n* grip *(f)*
informal • *adj* informal
informality • *n* informalitat *(f)*
informally • *adv* informalment
information • *n* informació *(f)*
informative • *adj* informatiu
infrared • *n* infraroig *(m)* • *adj* infraroig
infrastructure • *n* infraestructura *(f)*
infrequent • *adj* infreqüent
infusion • *n* infusió *(f)*
ingenious • *adj* enginyós
ingenuity • *n* enginy *(m)*
ingot • *n* lingot *(m)*
ingredient • *n* ingredient *(m)*
inhabit • *v* habitar
inhabitant • *n* habitant *(m)*
inhalation • *n* inhalació *(f)*
inhale • *v* inhalar, aspirar, inspirar
inherent • *adj* inherent
inherit • *v* heretar
inhibit • *v* inhibir
inhibition • *n* inhibició *(f)*
inhuman • *adj* inhumà
inhumation • *n* inhumació *(f)*
initial • *n* inicial, inicials, caplletra, ober-

tura • *adj* inicial
initiative • *n* iniciativa *(f)*
inject • *v* injectar
injection • *n* injecció *(f)*
injure • *v* ferir
injury • *n* ferida *(f)*
ink • *v* tintar, signar, tatuar • *n* tinta *(f)*, tinta *(m)*
inkwell • *n* tinter *(m)*
inmate • *n* internat *(m)*, intern *(m)*, resident *(f)*
innate • *adj* innat
inner • *adj* interior
inning • *n* entrada *(f)*
innocence • *n* innocència *(f)*
innocent • *adj* innocent
innocently • *adv* innocentment
innocuous • *adj* innocu
innovative • *adj* innovador
inoffensive • *adj* inofensiu
inorganic • *adj* inorgànic
inquiry • *n* indagació *(f)*, perquisició *(f)*
insanity • *n* insanitat *(f)*, bogeria *(f)*
insatiable • *adj* insaciable
inscribe • *v* inscriure
inscription • *n* inscripció *(f)*
inscrutable • *adj* inescrutable, insondable
insect • *n* insecte
insecure • *adj* insegur
insemination • *n* inseminació *(f)*
insensible • *adj* insensible
insensitive • *adj* insensible
inseparable • *adj* inseparable
inseparably • *adv* inseparablement
insertion • *n* inserció *(f)*
inside • *n* interior *(m)* • *adj* dins • *adv* dins • *prep* dins
insignificant • *adj* insignificant
insipid • *adj* insípid
insipidly • *adv* insípidament
insistence • *n* insistència *(f)*
insolent • *adj* insolent
insoluble • *adj* insoluble
insolvent • *adj* insolvent
insomnia • *n* insomni *(m)*
insomniac • *adj* insomne
inspect • *v* inspeccionar
inspection • *n* inspecció *(f)*
inspiring • *adj* inspirador
instability • *n* inestabilitat *(f)*
install • *v* instal·lar
installation • *n* instal·lació *(f)*
instantaneous • *adj* instantani
instigation • *n* instigació *(f)*
instinctive • *adj* instintiu
instruction • *n* instrucció *(f)*
instructive • *adj* instructiu

instrumentalist • *n* instrumentista *(f)*
insufficient • *adj* insuficient
insufficiently • *adv* insuficientment
insular • *adj* insular, aïllat, isolat
insulate • *v* aïllar, isolar
insulin • *n* insulina
insult • *v* insultar • *n* insult *(m)*
insulting • *adj* insultant
insurance • *n* assegurança *(f)*
insurgent • *n* insurgent *(f)* • *adj* insurgent
intact • *adj* intacte
intangible • *adj* intangible
integer • *n* enter
integrate • *v* integrar
integrity • *n* integritat *(f)*, enteresa *(f)*
intellectual • *n* intel·lectual *(f)* • *adj* intel·lectual
intelligence • *n* intel·ligència *(f)*, seny *(m)*, llestesa *(f)*
intelligent • *adj* intel·ligent
intelligently • *adv* intel·ligentment
intelligibility • *n* intel·ligibilitat *(f)*
intelligible • *adj* intel·ligible
intelligibly • *adv* intel·ligiblement
intempestivity • *n* intempestivitat
intense • *adj* intens
intensely • *adv* intensament
intensify • *v* intensificar
intensity • *n* intensitat *(f)*
intensive • *adj* intensiu
intensively • *adv* intensivament
intention • *n* intenció *(f)*
intentional • *adj* intencionat
intentionally • *adv* intencionadament
inter • *v* enterrar
interaction • *n* interacció *(f)*
intercalary • *adj* intercalar
interception • *n* intercepció *(f)*
interchangeable • *adj* intercanviable
intercontinental • *adj* intercontinental
interdisciplinary • *adj* interdisciplinari
interest • *n* interès *(m)*
interested • *adj* interessat
interesting • *adj* interessant
interfere • *v* interferir
interference • *n* interferència *(f)*
intergalactic • *adj* intergalàctic
interim • *adj* interí
interior • *n* interior *(m)* • *adj* interior
interjection • *n* interjecció *(f)*
interlude • *n* interludi *(m)*
intermediate • *adj* intermedi
interment • *n* enterrament *(m)*
interminable • *adj* interminable
intermittent • *adj* intermitent
intermittently • *adv* intermitentment
internal • *adj* intern

internally • *adv* internament, interiorment

international • *adj* internacional

internationally • *adv* internacionalment

interpersonal • *adj* interpersonal

interplanetary • *adj* interplanetari

interpolate • *v* interpolar

interpret • *v* interpretar

interpreter • *n* intèrpret *(f)*, intèrpret *(m)*

interrogatively • *adv* interrogativament

interrupt • *v* interrompre

intersexual • *n* intersexual • *adj* intersexual

intervene • *v* intervenir

intervention • *n* intervenció *(f)*

interview • *v* entrevistar • *n* entrevista *(f)*, interviu *(m)*

interviewer • *n* entrevistador *(m)*

intestinal • *adj* intestinal

intestine • *n* intestí *(m)*, budell *(m)*

intimacy • *n* intimitat *(f)*

intimate • *adj* íntim

intimidate • *v* intimidar

intolerable • *adj* intolerable

intolerant • *adj* intolerant

intonation • *n* entonació *(f)*

intracellular • *adj* intracel·lular

intransitive • *adj* intransitiu

intransitively • *adv* intransitivament

intravenous • *adj* intravenós

intrepid • *adj* intrèpid

intricate • *adj* intricat

intrigue • *v* intrigar • *n* intriga

intriguing • *adj* intrigant

intrinsic • *adj* intrínsec

introduction • *n* introducció *(f)*, presentació *(f)*

introductory • *adj* introductori

introspective • *adj* introspectiu

intuition • *n* intuïció *(f)*

intuitive • *adj* intuïtiu

inundate • *v* inundar

invade • *v* envair

invader • *n* invasor

invalid • *adj* invàlid

invalidate • *v* invalidar

invariable • *adj* invariable

invasion • *n* invasió *(f)*

invasive • *adj* invasiu

invent • *v* inventar

invention • *n* invenció *(f)*

inventive • *adj* inventiu, enginyós

inventory • *v* inventariar • *n* inventari *(m)*

inverse • *adj* invers

invert • *v* invertir

invertebrate • *n* invertebrat *(m)* • *adj* invertebrat

invest • *v* invertir, investir

investigate • *v* investigar

investigation • *n* investigació *(f)*

inveterate • *adj* inveterat

invincible • *n* invencible • *adj* invencible

invisibility • *n* invisibilitat *(f)*

invisible • *adj* invisible

invisibly • *adv* invisiblement

invite • *v* invitar, convidar • *n* invitació

invoke • *v* invocar

involuntarily • *adv* involuntàriament

involuntary • *adj* involuntari

invulnerable • *adj* invulnerable

iodine • *n* iode

ion • *n* ió *(m)*

ionic • *adj* iònic

ionosphere • *n* ionosfera *(f)*

iota • *n* iota *(f)*

irate • *adj* irat

ire • *n* ira *(f)*

iridescence • *n* iridescència *(f)*

iridium • *n* iridi *(m)*

iris • *n* iris *(m)*

iron • *v* planxar • *n* ferro *(m)*, planxa *(f)* • *adj* ferro

ironclad • *n* cuirassat

ironic • *adj* irònic

ironically • *adv* irònicament

irony • *n* ironia *(f)*

irrational • *adj* bèstia, irracional

irrationally • *adv* irracionalment

irrefutable • *adj* irrefutable

irregular • *adj* irregular

irregularity • *n* irregularitat *(f)*

irregularly • *adv* irregularment

irremediable • *adj* irremeiable

irreparable • *adj* irreparable

irreparably • *adv* irreparablement

irreplaceable • *adj* irreemplaçable, insubstituïble

irrepressible • *adj* irreprimible

irresistible • *adj* irresistible

irresponsible • *adj* irresponsable

irreverent • *adj* irreverent

irrigate • *v* irrigar

irritability • *n* irritabilitat *(f)*

irritable • *adj* irritable

irritating • *adj* irritant

irritation • *n* irritació *(f)*

irruption • *n* irrupció *(f)*

is • *v* és, està

ischium • *n* isqui *(m)*, ísquium *(m)*

island • *n* illa *(f)*

islander • *n* illenc *(m)*, illenca *(f)*

isolate • *v* aïllar, isolar

isolated • *adj* aïllat

isolation • *n* aïllament *(m)*, isolament *(m)*, isolació *(f)*
isolationism • *n* aïllacionisme *(m)*
isometric • *adj* isomètric
isotonic • *adj* isotònic
isotope • *n* isòtop *(m)*
issue • *v* lliurar
isthmus • *n* istme *(m)*

italic • *n* cursiva *(f)*
iterative • *adj* iteratiu
itinerant • *adj* itinerant
itself • *pron* es, mateix
ivory • *n* ivori *(m)*, vori *(m)*, marfil *(m)*, ivori, vori
ivy • *n* heura *(f)*, hedra *(f)*

J

jack • *n* gat *(m)*, bolig *(m)*
jackal • *n* xacal *(m)*
jackdaw • *n* gralla
jacket • *n* jaqueta *(f)*
jackrabbit • *n* llebre *(f)*
jacquerie • *n* germania *(f)*
jade • *n* jade *(m)*
jam • *n* esmaixada *(f)*
jargon • *n* argot *(m)*
jasper • *n* jaspi *(m)*
javelin • *n* javelina *(f)*
jaw • *n* mandíbula *(f)*, maixella *(f)*
jay • *n* gaig
jazz • *n* jazz *(m)*
jealous • *adj* gelós
jealously • *adv* gelosament
jeer • *n* burleria *(f)*
jejunum • *n* jejú *(m)*
jelly • *n* gelatina *(f)*, melmelada *(f)*
jellyfish • *n* medusa *(f)*
jeopardize • *v* posar en perill, amenaçar
jeopardy • *n* perill *(m)*, risc *(m)*
jerboa • *n* jerbu *(m)*
jerk • *n* sobreacceleració *(f)*
jet • *n* atzabeja *(f)*, gaieta *(f)*
jeweler • *n* joier *(m)*
jib • *n* floc *(m)*
jihad • *n* jihad *(m)*
job • *n* treball *(m)*, feina *(f)*
jockey • *n* joquei *(m)*, genet *(m)*
join • *v* unir-se, afegir-se • *n* unió
joiner • *n* fuster *(m)*
joint • *n* juntura *(f)*, articulació *(f)*, cau *(m)*, porret *(m)* • *adj* conjunt
jointly • *adv* conjuntament
joke • *n* acudit *(m)*, broma *(f)*
joker • *n* comodí, jòquer *(m)*

joule • *n* joule *(m)*
journal • *n* diari *(m)*, gaseta *(f)*
journalism • *n* periodisme *(m)*
journalist • *n* periodista *(f)*
journalistic • *adj* periodístic
joust • *v* justar
jovial • *adj* jovial
joy • *n* alegria *(f)*, joia *(f)*
joyful • *adj* joiós
judge • *v* jutjar • *n* jutge *(m)*, àrbitre *(m)*
judgment • *n* judici, seny *(m)*, esma *(f)*, coneixement *(m)*, judici *(m)*, veredicte *(m)*
judicial • *adj* judicial, judiciari
judo • *n* judo *(m)*
jug • *n* gerra *(f)*, popa *(f)*, pitrera *(f)*
juggler • *n* malabarista *(f)*
juggling • *n* malabarisme *(m)*
juice • *n* suc *(m)*
juicy • *adj* sucós
jujube • *n* gínjol *(m)*, ginjoler *(m)*
jump • *v* saltar, sobresaltar • *n* salt *(m)*, sobresalt *(m)*
jungle • *n* jungla *(f)*
juniper • *n* ginebre
juror • *n* jurat *(m)*
jury • *n* jurat *(m)*
just • *adj* just • *adv* simplement, només, sols, acabar de, just
justice • *n* justesa *(f)*, justícia *(f)*, justícia *(m)*
justifiable • *adj* justificable
justification • *n* justificació *(f)*
justified • *adj* justificat *(m)*
justify • *v* justificar
justly • *adv* justament
jute • *n* jute *(m)*

K

kaki • *n* caqui *(m)*
kale • *n* col arrissada
kaleidoscope • *n* calidoscopi
kamikaze • *n* kamikaze
kangaroo • *n* cangur *(m)*
kaon • *n* kaó *(m)*
kappa • *n* kappa *(f)*
kaput • *adj* caput
karat • *n* quirat *(m)*
kayak • *n* caiac *(m)*
kazoo • *n* mirlitó *(m)*
keel • *n* quilla *(f)*
keen • *adj* entusiasta
keep • *v* desar, guardar, seguir, continuar • *n* torre mestra *(f)*, torre de l'homenatge *(f)*, homenatge *(m)*
keg • *n* barril *(m)*, bóta *(f)*
kelp • *n* varec *(m)*
kestrel • *n* falcó *(m)*, xoriguer *(m)*, xoriguer gros *(m)*, xoriguer comú *(m)*
ketose • *n* cetosa *(f)*
kettle • *n* caldera *(f)*
key • *n* clau *(f)*, tecla *(f)* • *adj* clau
keyboard • *v* teclejar • *n* teclat *(m)*
keystone • *n* clau de volta *(f)*
khaki • *n* caqui *(m)*
kibbutz • *n* quibuts *(m)*
kick • *n* cop de peu *(m)*, puntada de peu *(f)*
kicker • *n* xutador *(m)*
kid • *n* cabrit *(m)*
kidnap • *v* segrestar, raptar • *n* segrest, rapte
kidnapping • *n* segrest *(m)*
kidney • *n* ronyó *(m)*
kill • *n* assassinat *(m)*, assassinat, mort
kilobyte • *n* quilooctet *(m)*
kilogram • *n* quilogram *(m)*
kiloton • *n* quilotona *(f)*
kilovolt • *n* quilovolt *(m)*
kilowatt • *n* quilowatt *(m)*

kimono • *n* quimono *(m)*
kind • *n* tipus *(m)*, gènere *(m)*, classe *(f)*, tipus • *adj* maco, amable
kindly • *adv* amablement
kindness • *n* bondat *(f)*, cortesia *(f)*, gentilesa *(f)*
kinetic • *adj* cinètic
king • *v* coronar • *n* rei *(m)*
kingdom • *n* regne *(m)*
kingfisher • *n* blauet *(m)*, arner *(m)*, alció *(m)*, botiguer *(m)*
kiss • *v* besar, petonejar • *n* petó *(m)*, bes *(m)*, besada *(f)*
kitchen • *n* cuina *(f)*
kite • *n* milà, estel
kith • *n* conegut, amistat, parentela *(f)*
kitten • *n* moixet *(m)*, moixeta *(f)*, gatet *(m)*, gateta *(f)*
kiwi • *n* kiwi *(m)*
klaxon • *n* claxon *(m)*, botzina *(f)*
kleptomania • *n* cleptomania *(f)*
knead • *v* amassar
knee • *n* genoll *(m)*
knife • *v* acoltellar, apunyalar • *n* ganivet *(m)*, coltell *(m)*, daga *(f)*, punyal *(m)*
knight • *n* cavaller *(m)*, cavall *(m)*
knock • *v* colpejar, batre • *n* cop *(m)*
knot • *n* nus *(m)*, grop *(m)*, territ gros *(m)*
knotty • *adj* nuós
know • *v* saber
know-it-all • *n* setciències
knowledge • *n* coneixement *(m)*, coneixements
known • *adj* conegut
knuckle • *n* artell *(m)*
koala • *n* coala *(m)*
koine • *n* koiné *(f)*
kolkhoz • *n* kolkhoz *(m)*
koumiss • *n* kumis *(m)*
krypton • *n* criptó

L

la • *n* la *(m)*
label • *v* etiquetar • *n* etiqueta *(f)*
labial • *adj* labial *(f)*
laboratory • *n* laboratori
laborious • *adj* laboriós
laboriously • *adv* laboriosament
labyrinth • *n* laberint *(m)*, dèdal *(m)*
labyrinthine • *adj* laberíntic
labyrinthitis • *n* labirintitis *(f)*
lace • *n* cordó *(m)*
laceration • *n* laceració *(f)*

lack • *v* faltar, mancar • *n* falta *(f)*, manca *(f)*
lackluster • *adj* deslluït
lacquer • *n* laca *(f)*
lacrimal • *adj* lacrimal
lacrosse • *n* lacrosse *(m)*
lactose • *n* lactosa *(f)*
ladder • *n* escala *(f)*, carrera *(f)*
ladle • *n* cullerot *(m)*
lady • *n* senyora
lake • *n* llac *(m)*, laca *(f)*

lama • *n* lama *(m)*
lamb • *n* xai *(m)*, anyell, corder *(m)*
lambda • *n* lambda *(f)*
lame • *adj* coix
lament • *v* lamentar • *n* lament *(m)*
lamia • *n* làmia
lamp • *n* làmpada *(f)*
lamppost • *n* farola *(f)*
lamprey • *n* llampresa *(f)*
lance • *n* llança *(f)*
lancer • *n* llancer *(m)*
lancet • *n* llanceta
land • *v* aterrar, atracar • *n* terra *(f)*, terra, terreny
landfill • *n* abocador
landlocked • *adj* sense litoral
landowner • *n* terratinent *(f)*
landscape • *n* paisatge *(m)*, apaïsat *(m)*
landslide • *n* ensulsiada
language • *n* idioma *(m)*, llengua *(f)*, llenguatge *(m)*
languid • *adj* lànguid
languish • *v* llanguir
lanthanum • *n* lantani *(m)*
lap • *n* doblec *(m)*
lapse • *n* lapsus *(m)*
laptop • *n* ordinador portàtil *(m)*, portàtil *(m)*
lapwing • *n* fredeluga *(f)*
larboard • *n* babor
larch • *n* làrix
lard • *n* llard
larder • *n* rebost *(m)*
large • *adj* llarg
large-scale • *adj* a gran escala
lark • *n* alosa *(f)*
laryngopharynx • *n* laringofaringe *(f)*
larynx • *n* laringe *(f)*
lasagna • *n* lasanya *(f)*
laser • *n* làser *(m)*
late • *adj* tard • *adv* tard
later • *adv* posteriorment • *interj* fins aviat
latex • *n* làtex *(m)*
lather • *n* sabonera *(f)* • *v* ensabonar
latitude • *n* latitud *(f)*
latrine • *n* latrina *(f)*, comuna *(f)*
latter • *adj* segon
laugh • *v* riure, riure's de • *n* riure *(m)*
laughter • *n* riure, rialla, rialla *(f)*, riure *(m)*
launch • *v* llançar • *n* llançament, llanxa *(f)*
laurel • *n* llorer *(m)*, llorer
lava • *n* lava *(f)*
lavender • *n* espígol *(m)*
law • *n* llei *(f)*, llei, dret
lawrencium • *n* laurenci *(m)*

lawsuit • *n* plet *(m)*, litigi *(m)*
lawyer • *n* advocat *(m)*, advocada *(f)*
lay • *adj* profà, laic
layer • *n* capa *(f)*
lazily • *adv* mandrosament, peresosament
lazy • *adj* mandrós, peresós
lead • *n* plom *(m)* • *v* dirigir, conduir, portar, encapçalar, anar al capdavant
leader • *n* líder *(f)*, dirigent *(m)*
leaf • *n* fulla *(f)*, full *(m)*
league • *n* lliga *(f)*
lean • *v* inclinar, abocar, repenjar-se, recolsar-se, arrambar-se • *adj* magre
leap • *v* saltar • *n* salt
leapfrog • *n* viola *(f)*
learn • *v* aprendre, estudiar
learner • *n* aprenent
learning • *n* aprenentatge
leash • *n* corretja
leather • *n* cuir *(m)*
leave • *n* permís *(m)*, comiat *(m)*
leaven • *n* llevat *(m)*
lechery • *n* lubricitat *(f)*
lecithin • *n* lecitina *(f)*
ledge • *n* imposta *(f)*
ledger • *n* llibre de comptabilitat *(m)*
leech • *n* sangonera *(f)*
leek • *n* porro *(m)*
lees • *n* pòsit *(m)*
left • *n* esquerra *(f)* • *adj* esquerre, esquerrà
left-handed • *n* esquerrà
leg • *n* cama *(f)*, petge *(m)*
legal • *adj* legal
legality • *n* legalitat *(f)*
legalization • *n* legalització *(f)*
legally • *adv* legalment
legend • *n* llegenda *(f)*
legendary • *adj* llegendari
legible • *adj* llegible
legion • *n* legió *(f)*
legislate • *v* legislar
legislation • *n* legislació *(f)*
legislative • *adj* legislatiu
legislator • *n* legislador
legitimate • *adj* legítim
legitimately • *adv* legítimament
legume • *n* llegum *(m)*
leisure • *n* lleure *(m)*, oci *(m)*
lemming • *n* lèmming *(m)*
lemon • *n* llimona *(f)*, llimoner *(m)*, llimonera *(f)*, llimona
lemonade • *n* llimonada *(f)*, gasosa *(f)*
lemur • *n* lèmur *(m)*
lender • *n* prestador *(m)*
length • *n* longitud *(f)*

lens • *n* lent *(f)*
lentil • *n* llentilla *(f)*, llentilla
leprosy • *n* lepra *(f)*
lepton • *n* leptó *(m)*
lesbian • *n* lesbiana *(f)* • *adj* lesbiana *(f)*, lesbià *(m)*
lesion • *v* lesionar • *n* lesió *(f)*
less • *adj* menys • *adv* menys • *prep* menys
let • *v* permetre, deixar
lethargic • *adj* letàrgic
lethargy • *n* letargia *(f)*
letter • *n* lletra *(f)*, caràcter *(m)*, carta *(f)*
lettuce • *n* enciam *(m)*, lletuga *(f)*
level • *adj* anivellat, uniforme
levitation • *n* levitació *(f)*
levy • *n* lleva *(f)*
lewd • *adj* lasciu
lexeme • *n* lexema *(m)*
lexical • *adj* lèxic
lexicographer • *n* lexicògraf *(m)*, lexicògrafa *(f)*
lexicographic • *adj* lexicogràfic
lexicography • *n* lexicografia *(f)*
lexicology • *n* lexicologia *(f)*
liabilities • *n* passius
liability • *n* responsabilitat *(f)*
liable • *adj* responsable, subjecte
libation • *n* libació *(f)*, libació
liberate • *v* alliberar
liberation • *n* alliberament *(m)*, alliberació *(f)*
liberty • *n* llibertat *(f)*
libidinal • *adj* libidinal
libidinous • *adj* libidinoso
librarian • *n* bibliotecari *(m)*
library • *n* biblioteca *(f)*
libretto • *n* llibret *(m)*
lichen • *n* liquen *(m)*
lick • *v* llepar • *n* llepada *(f)*
licorice • *n* regalèssia *(f)*
lid • *n* tapa *(f)*
lie • *v* jeure, trobar-se, mentir • *n* situació *(f)*, mentida *(f)*
liege • *n* senyor *(m)*, vassall *(m)*
lieutenant • *adj* tinent *(m)*
life • *n* vida *(f)*
lifeboat • *n* bot salvavides *(m)*
lifeguard • *n* socorrista *(f)*
lifetime • *n* eternitat *(f)*
lift • *v* alçar • *n* ascensor *(m)*
ligament • *n* lligament *(m)*
light • *n* llum *(f)*, llum *(m)*, flama *(f)*, metxa *(f)* • *v* encendre, il·luminar • *adj* clar, tallat, lleuger
lighten • *v* alleujar, alleugerir
lighter • *n* encenedor *(m)*
lighthouse • *n* far *(m)*

lightly • *adv* lleugerament
lightning • *n* llampec *(m)*, rellamp *(m)*, llamp *(m)*
lignite • *n* lignit *(m)*
like • *v* agradar • *n* preferències • *adj* semblant *(f)* • *adv* com • *prep* com
likelihood • *n* versemblança *(f)*
lilac • *n* lila • *adj* lila
lily • *n* lliri *(m)*
limb • *n* membre
limestone • *n* pedra calcària
limit • *n* límit *(m)* • *v* limitar
limitless • *adj* il·limitat
limousine • *n* limusina *(f)*
limp • *adj* flàccid *(m)*, flàccida *(f)* • *v* coixejar • *n* coixesa *(f)*
linden • *n* tell
line • *n* recta
lineage • *n* llinatge *(m)*
linebacker • *n* rerelínia *(f)*
linen • *n* lli *(m)*
ling • *n* bruguerola *(f)*
linger • *v* romandre, perviure, rumiar
linguist • *n* lingüista *(f)*
linguistic • *adj* lingüístic
linguistics • *n* lingüística *(f)*
lining • *n* folre *(m)*
link • *v* lligar, enllaçar, vinclar • *n* enllaç *(m)*, vincle *(m)*, baula *(f)*, link *(m)*, torxa *(f)*
lintel • *n* llinda *(f)*
lion • *n* lleó *(m)*
lioness • *n* lleona *(f)*
lip • *n* llavi *(m)*
lipid • *n* lípid *(m)*
lipstick • *n* pintallavis *(m)*
liquid • *n* líquid *(m)* • *adj* líquid
liquidate • *v* liquidar
list • *v* llistar, allistar • *n* llista *(f)*
listen • *v* escoltar
listless • *adj* apàtic
literally • *adv* literalment
literary • *adj* literari
literate • *adj* alfabet, lletrat
literature • *n* literatura *(f)*
lithic • *adj* lític
lithium • *n* liti *(m)*
lithosphere • *n* litosfera *(f)*
litigate • *v* litigar
litotes • *n* lítote *(f)*
little • *adj* petit • *adv* poc
liturgical • *adj* litúrgic
liturgy • *n* litúrgia *(f)*
live • *v* viure • *adj* viu, en viu • *adv* en viu
lively • *adj* vivaç *(f)*
liver • *n* fetge *(m)*, fetge
liverwort • *n* fetgera *(f)*
livestock • *n* bestiar *(m)*

living • *adj* viu
lizard • *n* llangardaix *(m)*, sargantana *(f)*
llama • *n* llama *(f)*
load • *v* carregar
loam • *n* marga *(f)*
loan • *v* prestar • *n* préstec *(m)*
loathe • *v* detestar
loathing • *n* aversió *(f)*
lob • *v* bombar, fer un globus • *n* globus *(m)*
lobe • *n* lòbul *(m)*
lobster • *n* llagosta *(f)*, llamàntol *(m)*, escamarlà *(m)*
local • *adj* local
localize • *v* localitzar
locally • *adv* localment
location • *n* ubicació
lock • *n* cadenat *(m)*, resclosa *(f)*, floc *(m)*, ble *(m)*
locker • *n* armari
locket • *n* medalló *(m)*
locksmith • *n* manyà *(m)*
locomotive • *n* locomotora *(f)*
locust • *n* llagosta *(f)*
logarithm • *n* logaritme *(m)*
logical • *adj* lògic
logically • *adv* lògicament
logistic • *adj* logístic
logorrhea • *n* logorrea *(f)*
lonely • *adj* solitari *(m)*
long • *adj* llunyà, llong • *v* enyorar
longbow • *n* arc llarg *(m)*
longitude • *n* longitud *(f)*
loo • *n* vàter *(m)*
look • *v* mirar, semblar, cercar, buscar, encarar • *n* ullada *(f)*, cop d'ull *(m)*, mirada *(f)*
loop • *n* bucle *(m)*, cicle *(m)*
loophole • *n* espitllera *(f)*
loose • *v* deslligar, descordar, afluixar, alliberar, tirar
loosely • *adv* en termes generals, sense ésser estrictes
lord • *v* senyorejar • *n* castellà, senyor, senyor *(m)*
lore • *n* saviesa *(f)*
lose • *v* perdre
loss • *n* pèrdua *(f)*
lost • *adj* perdut
loud • *adj* fort, alt, estrident, cridaner
loudly • *adv* sorollosament
loudspeaker • *n* altaveu *(m)*

louse • *n* poll *(m)*
lousy • *adj* pèssim, horrible, pollós
louvar • *n* luvar *(m)*
louver • *n* persiana *(f)*
lovable • *adj* amable
love • *n* amor *(f)*, res, zero *(m)*
love-in-a-mist • *n* niella o aranya
lovely • *adj* encantador, preciós
lover • *n* amant *(f)*, amistançat *(m)*
loving • *adj* amorós
low • *adj* baix • *adv* baix
lower • *v* baixar, abaixar, disminuir, reduir
lowering • *n* abaixament *(m)*
loyal • *adj* lleial
loyally • *adv* lleialment
loyalty • *n* lleialtat *(f)*
lozenge • *n* losange *(m)*, rombe *(m)*, pastilla *(f)*
lubricate • *v* lubricar
lubrication • *n* lubrificació *(f)*, lubricació *(f)*
lucid • *adj* lúcid
lucidity • *n* lucidesa *(f)*
luck • *n* sort *(f)*
lucky • *adj* afortunat
ludicrous • *adj* ridícul
luff • *n* orsa *(f)*
luggage • *n* equipatge *(m)*, bagatge *(m)*
lukewarm • *adj* tebi *(m)*, tèbia *(f)*
lullaby • *n* cançó de bressol *(f)*, vouverivou *(m)*
lumbago • *n* lumbago
lunatic • *adj* llunàtic
lunch • *v* dinar • *n* dinar *(m)*
lung • *n* pulmó *(m)*
lunula • *n* lúnula *(f)*
lurk • *v* aguaitar
lust • *n* luxúria *(f)*
lute • *n* llaüt *(m)*
lutetium • *n* luteci *(m)*
luxurious • *adj* luxuriós, luxós
lycanthropy • *n* licantropia *(f)*
lye • *n* lleixiu *(m)*
lymph • *n* limfa *(f)*
lymphatic • *adj* limfàtic
lynx • *n* linx *(m)*
lyophilize • *v* liofilitzar
lyre • *n* lira *(f)*
lysine • *n* lisina

M

macadamia • *n* macadàmia *(f)*
mace • *n* maça *(m)*, maça *(f)*
machicolation • *n* matacà *(m)*
machine • *n* màquina *(f)*, auto *(m)*, automòbil *(m)*
machismo • *n* masclisme
mackerel • *n* verat *(m)*, cavalla *(f)*
macula • *n* màcula
mad • *adj* boig *(m)*, boja *(f)*
madly • *adv* bojament
maelstrom • *n* voràgine *(f)*
magazine • *n* revista, arsenal, carregador
mage • *n* mag *(m)*, màgic *(m)*, fetiller *(m)*
maggot • *n* asticot *(m)*
magic • *n* màgia *(f)* • *adj* màgic *(m)*
magical • *adj* màgic
magically • *adv* màgicament
magician • *n* mag *(m)*, màgic *(m)*, fetiller *(m)*
magnanimous • *adj* magnànim
magnanimously • *adv* magnànimament
magnesium • *n* magnesi
magnet • *n* imant *(m)*
magnetic • *adj* magnètic
magnetism • *n* magnetisme *(m)*
magnetize • *v* magnetitzar
magnetometer • *n* magnetòmetre *(m)*
magnetosphere • *n* magnetosfera *(f)*
magnificent • *adj* magnífic *(m)*
magnificently • *adv* magníficament
magnolia • *n* magnòlia *(f)*
magpie • *n* garsa *(f)*
magus • *n* mag *(m)*
mahogany • *n* caoba *(f)*
maid • *n* criada *(f)*
mailman • *n* carter *(m)*
main • *adj* principal *(f)*
mainland • *n* continent *(m)*, terra ferma *(f)*
mainly • *adv* principalment
mainmast • *n* pal major *(m)*
maintain • *v* mantenir
maintenance • *n* manteniment *(m)*
majestic • *adj* majestuós
majestically • *adv* majestuosament
majesty • *n* majestat
major • *n* major *(m)* • *adj* major
majority • *n* majoria *(f)*, majoria d'edat *(f)*
make • *v* fer
maker • *n* fabricant *(m)*
makeshift • *adj* provisional
makeup • *n* maquillatge *(m)*
malacology • *n* malacologia *(f)*
maladroit • *adj* maldestre
male • *n* mascle *(m)* • *adj* masculí *(m)*, masculina *(f)*, mascle *(m)*, mascla *(f)*
malevolent • *adj* malèvol

malice • *n* malícia *(f)*
malicious • *adj* maliciós
maliciously • *adv* maliciosament
malignant • *adj* maligne
malleus • *n* martell *(m)*
mallow • *n* malva *(f)*
malt • *n* malt *(m)*
mamma • *n* mama *(f)*, mamella *(f)*
mammal • *n* mamífer *(m)*
mammography • *n* mamografia *(f)*, mastografia *(f)*
mammoth • *n* mamut *(m)* • *adj* mastodòntic
man • *n* home *(m)*
manage • *v* sortir-se'n
management • *n* administració *(f)*, gestió *(f)*, direcció *(f)*, gerència *(f)*, maneig *(m)*
managerial • *adj* directiu
manatee • *n* manatí
mandate • *n* mandat *(m)*
mandible • *n* mandíbula *(f)*
mandolin • *n* mandolina *(f)*
mandrake • *n* mandràgora
manganese • *n* manganès *(m)*
manger • *n* pessebre *(m)*
mango • *n* mango *(m)*
mangrove • *n* mangle *(m)*
mania • *n* mania *(f)*
maniacal • *adj* maníac
manifest • *v* manifestar • *n* manifest • *adj* manifest
manifesto • *n* manifest *(m)*
manipulate • *v* manipular
manipulative • *adj* manipulador
manly • *adj* viril
mannitol • *n* mannitol *(m)*
manometer • *n* manòmetre *(m)*
manslaughter • *n* homicidi involuntari *(m)*
mansuetude • *n* mansuetud *(f)*
mantissa • *n* mantissa *(f)*
manul • *n* gat de Pallas
manumit • *v* manumetre
manuscript • *n* manuscrit *(m)*, original *(m)* • *adj* manuscrit *(m)*
marathon • *n* marató *(f)*
marble • *n* marbre *(m)*, bala *(f)*
march • *v* marxar • *n* marxa *(f)*, manifestació *(f)*, pas *(m)*, marca *(f)*
marchioness • *n* marquesa *(f)*
mare • *n* euga *(f)*, egua *(f)*
margin • *n* marge *(m)*
margrave • *n* marcgravi *(m)*, marquès *(m)*
marijuana • *n* marihuana *(f)*
marine • *adj* marí
marital • *adj* marital
marjoram • *n* marduix *(m)*

mark • *n* marca *(f)*, marc *(m)*
markedly • *adv* marcadament
market • *n* mercat *(m)*
marmalade • *n* melmelada *(f)*
marmot • *n* marmota *(f)*
marquess • *n* marquès *(m)*
marquetry • *n* marqueteria *(f)*
marriage • *n* matrimoni *(m)*, casament *(m)*, boda *(f)*
married • *adj* casat
marrow • *n* medulŭla *(f)*, moll *(m)*
marry • *v* casar-se, casar, pegar
marsh • *n* aiguamoll *(m)*
marsupial • *n* marsupial *(m)* • *adj* marsupial
marten • *n* marta *(f)*
martyr • *n* màrtir *(f)*
marvelous • *adj* meravellós
marzipan • *n* massapà *(m)*
masculine • *adj* masculí, viril
mask • *v* emmascarar • *n* màscara *(f)*, careta *(f)*, mascarada *(f)*
masochism • *n* masoquisme *(m)*
masochist • *n* masoquista *(f)*
masochistic • *adj* masoquista
masonry • *n* maçoneria *(f)*
masquerade • *n* mascarada *(f)*
mass • *n* massa *(f)*, missa *(f)*
massacre • *v* massacrar • *n* massacre *(m)*
massage • *n* massatge *(m)*
masseur • *n* massatgista *(f)*
massive • *adj* massiu
mast • *n* pal *(m)*
mastectomy • *n* mastectomia *(f)*
master • *n* mestre *(m)*
masterpiece • *n* obra mestra
masturbation • *n* masturbació *(f)*, palla *(f)*
mat • *n* estora *(f)*
match • *v* coincidir, concordar, correspondre • *n* partit *(m)*, matx *(m)*, misto *(m)*
material • *adj* material
materialism • *n* materialisme *(m)*
materialist • *n* materialista
materialistic • *adj* materialista
materialization • *n* materialització *(f)*
mathematical • *adj* matemàtic *(m)*
mathematics • *n* matemàtiques, matemàtica
matriarchal • *adj* matriarcal
matrix • *n* matriu *(f)*
mattock • *n* aixada *(f)*
mattress • *n* matalàs *(m)*
mature • *v* madurar, vencer *(m)* • *adj* madur *(m)*, madura *(f)*, madura *(m)*, raonat *(m)*, raonada *(m)*
maturity • *n* maduresa *(f)*

maul • *n* mol *(m)*
mausoleum • *n* mausoleu *(m)*
maverick • *adj* individualista *(f)*
maw • *n* estómac *(m)*
maximum • *adj* màxim
maybe • *adv* potser
mayhem • *n* tumult *(m)*, avalot *(m)*, aldarull *(m)*, mutilació *(f)*
mayonnaise • *n* maionesa *(f)*
mayor • *n* alcalde *(f)*
maze • *v* desconcertar • *n* laberint *(m)*, dèdal *(m)*
me • *pron* em, me, mi
meadow • *n* prat *(m)*
meal • *n* àpat *(m)*
mean • *v* pretendre, significar, voler dir • *n* mitjana • *adj* mig *(m)*
meanwhile • *adv* mentrestant
measles • *n* xarampió *(m)*
measure • *v* mesurar, amidar • *n* mesura *(f)*
meat • *n* carn *(f)*, bessó *(m)*
meatball • *n* mandonguilla *(f)*
mechanical • *adj* mecànic
mechanics • *n* mecànica *(f)*
mechanism • *n* mecanisme *(m)*
medallion • *n* medalló *(m)*
median • *n* mitjana *(f)*
mediastinum • *n* mediastí *(m)*
mediator • *n* tercer
medical • *adj* mèdic
medicinal • *adj* medicinal
medieval • *adj* medieval
mediocre • *adj* mediocre
mediocrity • *n* mediocritat *(f)*
meditation • *n* meditació *(f)*
medium • *n* medi *(m)*, mitjà *(m)*, mèdium • *adj* mitjà
meet • *v* conèixer
meeting • *n* reunió *(f)*, trobada *(f)*
megalith • *n* megàlit *(m)*
megalomaniacal • *adj* megalòman
megalopolis • *n* megalòpolis *(f)*, megalòpoli *(f)*
meiosis • *n* meiosi *(f)*, miosi *(f)*
meiotic • *adj* meiòtic
melancholic • *adj* melancòlic
melissa • *n* melisse *(f)*
mellow • *adj* melós
melodic • *adj* melòdic
melodious • *adj* melodiós
melodramatic • *adj* melodramàtic
melon • *n* meló *(m)*
melt • *v* fondre
member • *n* membre *(m)*, membre viril *(m)*
membrane • *n* membrana *(f)*

membranous • *adj* membranós
meme • *n* mem *(m)*
memorable • *adj* memorable
memorably • *adv* memorablement
memorization • *n* memorització *(f)*
memorize • *v* memoritzar
memory • *n* memòria *(f)*, record *(m)*
mendelevium • *n* mendelevi
menhir • *n* menhir *(m)*
menial • *n* criat *(m)*, minyona *(f)* • *adj* labor *(f)*
meninx • *n* meninge *(f)*
meniscus • *n* menisc *(m)*
mental • *adj* mental
mentally • *adv* mentalment
menu • *n* menú *(m)*
meow • *v* miolar • *interj* mèu *(m)*
mercantile • *adj* mercantil
mercenary • *n* mercenari *(m)*
merchant • *n* mercader *(m)*
merciless • *adj* despietat
mercilessly • *adv* despietadament
mercury • *n* mercuri
mercy • *n* misericòrdia
mere • *adj* mer
merely • *adv* merament, simplement
mermaid • *n* sirena *(f)*
merman • *n* tritó *(m)*
merrymaking • *n* revetlla *(f)*
mesentery • *n* mesenteri *(m)*
mesh • *n* malla *(f)*
meson • *n* mesó *(m)*
mesosphere • *n* mesosfera *(f)*
mess • *n* garbuix *(m)*
message • *n* missatge *(m)*, notícia *(f)*
messenger • *n* missatger *(m)*, missatgera *(f)*
messiah • *n* messies *(m)*
metabolic • *adj* metabòlic
metabolism • *n* metabolisme *(m)*
metacarpal • *n* metacarpià *(m)* • *adj* metacarpià
metacarpus • *n* metacarp *(m)*
metal • *n* metall
metallic • *adj* metàl·lic
metallography • *n* metal·lografia *(f)*
metalloid • *n* metal·loide *(m)*
metallurgical • *adj* metal·lúrgic
metallurgy • *n* metal·lúrgia *(f)*
metaphor • *n* metàfora *(f)*
metaphorical • *adj* metafòric
metaphorically • *adv* metafòricament
metaphysics • *n* metafísica *(f)*
metatarsal • *n* metatarsià *(m)* • *adj* metatarsià
metatarsus • *n* metatars *(m)*
meteor • *n* meteor *(m)*

meteoric • *adj* meteòric
meteorite • *n* meteorit *(m)*
meteorology • *n* meteorologia *(f)*
methane • *n* metà *(m)*
methionine • *n* metionina *(f)*
method • *n* mètode *(m)*
methyl • *n* metil *(m)*
meticulous • *adj* meticulós, minuciós
meticulously • *adv* meticulosament
metro • *n* metro *(m)*
metrology • *n* metrologia *(f)*
metropolis • *n* metròpolis *(f)*, metròpoli *(f)*
metropolitan • *adj* metropolità
mi • *n* mi *(m)*
microbe • *n* microbi *(m)*
microbiology • *n* microbiologia *(f)*
microcosm • *n* microcosmos *(m)*
microcyte • *n* micròcit *(m)*
microfilm • *v* microfilmar • *n* microfilm *(m)*
microgram • *n* microgram *(m)*
micrometer • *n* micròmetre *(m)*
microorganism • *n* microorganisme *(m)*
microphone • *n* micròfon *(m)*
microprocessor • *n* microprocessador *(m)*
microscope • *n* microscopi *(m)*
microscopic • *adj* microscòpic
microscopy • *n* microscòpia *(f)*
microwave • *n* microona *(f)*
mid • *adj* mitjan
middle • *adj* mitjà
midfield • *n* centre del camp *(m)*
midnight • *n* mitjanit *(f)*
midwife • *n* llevadora *(f)*
mighty • *adj* poderós
migratory • *adj* migratori
mild • *adj* suau
milestone • *n* fita
militarily • *adv* militarment
military • *n* exèrcit *(m)* • *adj* militar
milkman • *n* lleter *(m)*
milkshake • *n* batut de llet *(m)*
milky • *adj* lletós
mill • *n* molí *(m)* • *v* moldre
millennium • *n* mil·lenni *(m)*
miller • *n* moliner
millet • *n* mill *(m)*
milligram • *n* mil·ligram *(m)*
millipede • *n* milpeu
millstone • *n* mola *(f)*
mind • *n* ment *(f)*
mine • *pron* el meu *(m)*, la meva *(f)* • *v* minar • *n* mina *(f)*
mineral • *n* mineral *(m)*, aigua mineral *(f)* • *adj* mineral *(f)*
mineralogist • *n* mineralogista *(f)*

mineralogy • *n* mineralogia *(f)*
minesweeper • *n* caçamines *(m)*, dragamines *(m)*
minimal • *adj* mínim, minimalista
minion • *n* adlàter
minister • *n* ministre de l'església *(m)*, ministre *(m)*
ministry • *n* ministeri *(m)*
minium • *n* mini
mink • *n* visó *(m)*
minority • *n* minoria, minoritat
minotaur • *n* minotaure *(m)*
mint • *v* encunyar • *n* seca *(f)*, menta *(f)*, menta • *adj* menta
minus • *conj* menys
minuscule • *adj* minúscul
minute • *n* minut *(m)* • *adj* menut, diminut, minúscul
miracle • *n* miracle *(m)*
miraculous • *adj* miraculós
miraculously • *adv* miraculosament
mirage • *n* miratge *(m)*
mirror • *v* duplicar, copiar • *n* mirall *(m)*, espill *(m)*, còpia *(f)*
misanthrope • *n* misantrop
misanthropic • *adj* misantròpic
misanthropy • *n* misantropia *(f)*
miscarriage • *n* avortament espontani
miscellaneous • *adj* miscel·lani
mischievous • *adj* entremaliat
misdeed • *n* pecat *(m)*
miserable • *adj* trist *(m)*, desgraciat *(m)*, miserable *(f)*
misery • *n* misèria *(f)*
misogamy • *n* misogàmia *(f)*
misogynist • *n* misogin *(m)*
misogyny • *n* misogínia *(f)*
misology • *n* misologia *(f)*
misopedia • *n* misopèdia *(f)*
miss • *v* trobar a faltar, enyorar
missile • *n* projectil *(m)*, míssil
mission • *n* missió *(f)*, missió
missionary • *n* missioner *(m)*
missive • *n* missiva *(f)*
mist • *n* boira *(f)*
mister • *n* senyor
mistletoe • *n* vesc *(m)*
mistress • *n* mestressa *(f)*, amistançada *(f)*
misunderstand • *v* malentendre
mite • *n* àcar *(m)*
mitigate • *v* mitigar
mitochondrion • *n* mitocondri *(m)*
mitosis • *n* mitosi *(f)*
mix • *v* barrejar, mesclar
mixer • *n* batedora *(f)*
mnemonic • *adj* mnemònic
moan • *v* gemegar, llamentar-se, plànyer-

se • *n* gemec *(m)*
moat • *n* fossat *(m)*
mob • *n* xusma *(f)*, xurma *(f)*
mobile • *adj* mòbil
mobility • *n* mobilitat *(f)*
mobilization • *n* mobilització
mode • *n* moda
model • *n* model *(f)*, maqueta *(f)*, model *(m)*
modem • *n* mòdem *(m)*
moderate • *v* moderar • *adj* moderat
moderately • *adv* moderadament
modern • *adj* modern *(m)*
modernization • *n* modernització *(f)*
modernize • *v* modernitzar
modest • *adj* modest
modestly • *adv* modestament
modify • *v* modificar
modulate • *v* modular
mogul • *n* magnat *(m)*
moist • *adj* humit *(m)*, humida *(f)*
moisture • *n* humitat *(f)*
molar • *adj* molar *(f)*
mold • *n* motlle *(m)*, motle *(m)*, floridura *(f)*
mole • *n* piga *(f)*, talp *(m)*, mol *(m)*
molecular • *adj* molecular
molecule • *n* molècula *(f)*
molest • *v* assetjar
molybdenum • *n* molibdèn
moment • *n* moment *(m)*, instant *(m)*, moment de força *(m)*
momentum • *n* impuls *(m)*, impuls
monarch • *n* monarca *(f)*
monarchist • *n* monàrquic *(m)*
monarchy • *n* monarquia *(f)*
monastery • *n* monestir *(m)*
monastic • *adj* monàstic, monacal
monasticism • *n* monaquisme *(m)*
monetary • *adj* monetari
money • *n* diner *(m)*
monitor • *n* monitor *(m)*
monk • *n* monjo *(m)*
monkey • *n* mico *(m)*
monkfish • *n* rap *(m)*
monochromatic • *adj* monocromàtic
monochrome • *adj* monocrom
monoecious • *adj* monoeci
monogamous • *adj* monògam
monogamy • *n* monogàmia *(f)*
monolingual • *adj* monolingüe, unilingüe
monolith • *n* monòlit *(m)*
monologue • *n* monòleg *(m)*
monomer • *n* monòmer *(m)*
monopolize • *v* monopolitzar
monopoly • *n* monopoli *(m)*

monosaccharide • *n* monosacàrid *(m)*
monosyllabic • *n* monosílůlab *(m)* • *adj* monosílůlab *(m)*, monosilůlàbic *(m)*
monotheism • *n* monoteisme *(m)*
monotheist • *n* monoteista *(f)*
monotheistic • *adj* monoteista
monotone • *adj* monòton
monotonous • *adj* monòton
monotony • *n* monotonia *(f)*
monotreme • *n* monotrema *(m)*
monoxide • *n* monòxid *(m)*
monster • *n* monstre *(m)*, dimoni *(m)* • *adj* monstruós
monstrous • *adj* monstruós
monstrously • *adv* monstruosament
month • *n* mes *(m)*
monthly • *adv* mensualment
monument • *n* monument *(m)*
monumental • *adj* monumental
moo • *v* mugir • *n* mugit *(m)*
mood • *n* humor *(f)*, ànim *(m)*
moon • *n* lluna *(f)*
moonlight • *n* llum de lluna *(f)*
moor • *n* erm *(m)*
moose • *n* ant *(m)*
moot • *v* plantejar • *adj* discutible, irrellevant
mop • *n* pal de fregar *(m)*, ganyota *(f)*
moped • *n* ciclomotor
morally • *adv* moralment
morbid • *adj* mòrbid *(m)*, mòrbida *(f)*
mordant • *v* mordentar • *n* mordent *(m)*
more • *adv* més
morgue • *n* dipòsit de cadàvers *(m)*
morion • *n* morrió
morning • *n* matí *(m)*, matinada *(f)*
morpheme • *n* morfema *(m)*
morphine • *n* morfina *(f)*
morphologically • *adv* morfològicament
morphology • *n* morfologia *(f)*
morrow • *n* l'endemà
mortal • *n* mortal *(f)* • *adj* mortal
mortality • *n* mortalitat *(f)*
mortar • *n* morter *(m)*
mortgage • *v* hipotecar • *n* hipoteca *(f)*
mosaic • *n* mosaic *(m)*
mosque • *n* mesquita *(f)*
mosquito • *n* mosquit *(m)*
moss • *n* molsa *(f)*
motel • *n* motel *(m)*
moth • *n* arna *(f)*
mother • *n* mare *(f)*
mother-in-law • *n* sogra *(f)*
motif • *n* motiu *(m)*
motivation • *n* motivació *(f)*
motive • *n* motiu *(m)*
motmot • *n* motmot *(m)*

motor • *n* motor *(m)* • *adj* motor
motorcycle • *n* motocicleta *(f)*, moto *(f)*
motorist • *n* motorista *(f)*
motto • *n* divisa *(f)*, lema *(m)*
mouflon • *n* mufló
mound • *n* mota *(f)*, túmul *(m)*
mountain • *n* muntanya *(f)*
mountaineer • *n* alpinista *(f)*
mountainous • *adj* muntanyós
mournful • *adj* planyívol *(m)*
mouse • *n* ratolí *(m)*
mousetrap • *n* ratera
moustache • *n* bigoti, mostatxo *(m)*
mouth • *n* boca *(f)*, embocadura *(f)*, desembocadura *(f)*
mouthful • *n* mossegada *(f)*, bocí *(m)*, mos *(m)*
movable • *adj* mobiliari *(m)*
move • *v* moure, mudar, traslladar, emocionar • *n* mudament *(m)*, mudança *(f)*
movement • *n* moviment *(m)*
movie • *n* pelůlícula *(f)*, film *(m)*
mow • *v* segar
mu • *n* mi *(f)*
much • *adv* molt
mucus • *n* moc *(m)*
mud • *n* fang *(m)*, llot *(m)*
muddy • *adj* fangós
mudguard • *n* parafang *(m)*
muffler • *n* silenciador *(m)*
mug • *n* tassa *(f)*
mugger • *n* cocodril persa *(m)*
mulberry • *n* morera *(f)*, móra *(f)*
mule • *n* mul
mull • *v* rumiar, sopesar, picar, encalentir, espiciar
mullet • *n* llíssera *(f)*, mújol *(m)*
multilingual • *adj* multilingüe, plurilingüe
multimedia • *n* multimèdia *(f)* • *adj* multimèdia, multimèdia *(f)*
multinational • *n* multinacional • *adj* multinacional
multiple • *n* múltiple • *adj* múltiple
multitude • *n* ramat *(m)*
mum • *n* mama
mummery • *n* momeria *(f)*
mummy • *n* mòmia *(f)*
municipal • *adj* municipal
municipality • *n* municipi
muon • *n* muó *(m)*
murder • *v* assassinar • *n* assassinat *(m)*, assassinat
murderer • *n* assassí *(m)*
murderous • *adj* assassí
murrey • *n* morat
muscle • *n* múscul *(m)*

muscovite • *n* moscovita *(f)*
muscular • *adj* muscular, musculós
museum • *n* museu *(m)*
mushroom • *n* bolet *(m)*, fong *(m)*
music • *n* música *(f)*
musical • *adj* musical *(f)*
musicality • *n* musicalitat *(f)*
musician • *n* músic *(m)*
musket • *n* mosquet *(m)*
musketeer • *n* mosqueter *(m)*
must • *v* deure
mustard • *n* mostassa *(f)*
mutant • *n* mutant *(m)* • *adj* mutant
mutation • *n* mutació *(f)*
mute • *n* mut *(m)*, muda *(f)* • *adj* mut
mutilation • *n* mutilació *(f)*
mutual • *adj* mutu
muzzle • *n* morrió *(m)*
mycologist • *n* micòleg *(m)*

mycology • *n* micologia *(f)*
myocardium • *n* miocardi *(m)*
myope • *n* miop
myopia • *n* miopia *(f)*
myopic • *adj* miop *(m)*
myriad • *n* miríada *(f)*
myrrh • *n* mirra *(f)*
myrtle • *n* murta *(f)*
myself • *pron* em, mateix
mysterious • *adj* misteriós
mysteriously • *adv* misteriosament
mystery • *n* misteri *(m)*
mystic • *adj* místic
mystical • *adj* místic
myth • *n* mite *(m)*, mites
mythical • *adj* mític
mythology • *n* mitologia *(f)*

N

nag • *n* haca *(f)*, rossí *(m)*
naiad • *n* nàiada *(f)*
nail • *n* ungla *(f)*, clau *(m)* • *v* clavar
naive • *adj* naïf
naked • *adj* despullat, nu
name • *v* anomenar, escollir, especificar, precisar, denominar • *n* nom *(m)*, reputació *(f)*
nanosecond • *n* nanosegon *(m)*
nap • *n* becaina *(f)*
nape • *n* bescoll *(m)*, nuca *(f)*, clatell *(m)*
naphthalene • *n* naftalina *(f)*
napkin • *n* tovalló *(m)*, torcaboques *(m)*
narcissist • *n* narcís *(m)*, narcisista *(f)*
narcissus • *n* narcís *(m)*
narcolepsy • *n* narcolèpsia *(f)*
narrate • *v* narrar, explicar
narrative • *n* narració *(f)*, narrativa *(f)* • *adj* narratiu
narrow • *adj* estret *(m)*, estreta *(f)*, angost
narthex • *n* nàrtex *(m)*
narwhal • *n* narval *(m)*
nasal • *adj* nasal
nasalization • *n* nasalització
nasturtium • *n* caputxina *(f)*
nasty • *adj* brut, menyspreable
nation • *n* nació *(f)*
national • *adj* nacional
nationalism • *n* nacionalisme *(m)*
nationalist • *adj* nacionalista
nationally • *adv* nacionalment
naturally • *adv* naturalment
nature • *n* natura *(f)*

naughty • *adj* trapella
nausea • *n* nàusea *(f)*
nauseating • *adj* nauseabund
nautical • *adj* nàutic
naval • *adj* naval
nave • *n* nau *(f)*
navel • *n* melic *(m)*, llombrígol *(m)*
navy • *n* marina *(f)*
neanderthal • *n* neandertal *(m)*
near • *v* apropar, aproximar
nearly • *adv* gairebé
neat • *adj* pulcre, sol, pur, net, enginyós
nebula • *n* nebulosa *(f)*
nebulous • *adj* nebulós
necessarily • *adv* necessàriament
necessary • *adj* necessari
necessity • *n* necessitat *(f)*
neck • *n* coll *(m)*, broc *(m)*
necklace • *n* collar *(m)*, collaret *(m)*
necktie • *n* corbata *(f)*
necromancy • *n* nigromància *(f)*
necropolis • *n* necròpolis *(f)*
necrosis • *n* necrosi *(f)*
nectar • *n* nèctar *(m)*
nectarine • *n* nectarina *(f)*
need • *n* necessitat *(f)* • *v* necessitar, requerir, haver de, caldre
needle • *n* agulla *(f)*
needless • *adj* innecessari
negative • *adj* negatiu *(m)*, estrictament negatiu *(m)*
neglect • *v* negligir • *n* negligència *(f)*
neglectful • *adj* negligent

negligence • *n* negligència *(f)*
negligent • *adj* negligent
negligently • *adv* negligentment
negligible • *adj* negligible
negotiable • *adj* practicable, negociable
negotiate • *v* negociar
negotiation • *n* negociació *(f)*
neigh • *v* renillar, eguinar, aïnar • *n* renill *(m)*, eguí *(m)*, aïnada *(f)*
neighborhood • *n* barri *(m)*
neoclassicism • *n* neoclassicisme *(m)*
neodymium • *n* neodimi
neologism • *n* neologisme *(m)*
neon • *n* neó
nephew • *n* nebot *(m)*
nepotism • *n* nepotisme *(m)*
neptunium • *n* neptuni
nereid • *n* nereida *(f)*
nerve • *n* nervi *(m)*
nervous • *adj* nerviós
nervously • *adv* nerviosament
nest • *n* niu *(m)*, niu
net • *n* xarxa *(f)*, malla *(f)* • *adj* net
netball • *n* netbol *(m)*
nettle • *n* ortiga *(f)*
network • *n* xarxa *(f)*
neural • *adj* neural
neuralgic • *adj* neuràlgic
neurasthenia • *n* neurastènia *(f)*
neurobiology • *n* neurobiologia *(f)*
neuroblast • *n* neuroblast *(m)*
neurological • *adj* neurològic
neurologist • *n* neuròleg *(m)*
neurology • *n* neurologia *(f)*
neuromotor • *adj* neuromotor
neuromuscular • *adj* neuromuscular
neurophysiology • *n* neurofisiologia *(f)*
neuropsychiatry • *n* neuropsiquiatria *(f)*
neurosis • *n* neurosi *(f)*
neurosurgeon • *n* neurocirurgià *(m)*
neurosurgery • *n* neurocirurgia *(f)*
neurotic • *n* neuròtic *(m)* • *adj* neuròtic
neurotransmitter • *n* neurotransmissor *(m)*
neurotropism • *n* neurotropisme *(m)*
neutral • *adj* neutral, neutre
neutrality • *n* neutralitat *(f)*
neutrino • *n* neutrí *(m)*
neutron • *n* neutró
never • *adv* mai
neverending • *adj* interminable
nevertheless • *adv* nogensmenys, no obstant, tanmateix
new • *adj* nou
newcomer • *n* nouvingut *(m)*, nouvinguda *(f)*, novell
newly • *adv* novament

news • *n* notícies, telenotícies *(m)*, informatiu *(m)*, diari *(m)*
newsagent • *n* estanc *(m)*, estanquer *(m)*
newspaper • *n* diari *(m)*, periòdic *(m)*
newt • *n* tritó *(m)*
next • *adj* proper, següent, que ve • *prep* al costat
nexus • *n* nexe *(m)*, centre *(m)*
nib • *n* plumí *(m)*, bec *(m)*
niche • *n* nínxol *(m)*
nickel • *n* níquel *(m)*
nickname • *n* sobrenom *(m)*
niece • *n* neboda *(f)*
night • *n* nit *(f)*, vetllada *(f)*, vespre *(m)*, fosca *(f)*, obscuritat *(f)*
nightfall • *n* capvespre *(m)*
nightgown • *n* camisa de dormir *(f)*
nightingale • *n* rossinyol *(m)*
nightmare • *n* malson *(m)*
nightshade • *n* morella *(f)*
nihilism • *n* nihilisme
nimble • *adj* àgil
nimbus • *n* nimbe *(m)*
nincompoop • *n* ximple, bovo, babau, tonto, fava, panoli, beneit, imbècil, idiota, estúpid
nine • *n* nou *(m)*
nineteenth • *adj* dinovè *(m)*
ninth • *n* novè *(m)*, novena *(f)* • *adj* novè, 9è
niobium • *n* niobi
nipple • *n* mugró *(m)*
nit • *n* llémena *(f)*
nitrogen • *n* nitrogen *(m)*
no • *n* negativa *(f)*, no *(m)*, no
nobelium • *n* nobeli
nobility • *n* noblesa *(f)*
noble • *adj* noble
nobody • *n* ningú *(f)*
nocturnal • *adj* nocturn
nod • *v* fer que sí amb el cap, assentir amb el cap, capejar • *n* capejada *(f)*
nodule • *n* nòdul *(m)*
noise • *n* soroll *(m)*
noisily • *adv* sorollosament
noisy • *adj* sorollós
nomad • *n* nòmada *(f)*
nomadic • *adj* nòmada
nomadism • *n* nomadisme *(m)*
nominate • *v* nominar
nominative • *adj* nominatiu *(m)*
nonagon • *n* enneàgon *(m)*
none • *pron* cap
nonexistence • *n* inexistència *(f)*
nonexistent • *adj* inexistent
nonius • *n* nònius *(m)*
nonsense • *n* bajanada *(f)*, bestiesa *(f)*, es-

tirabot *(m)*
nonstick • *adj* antiadherent *(f)*
noodle • *n* fideu *(m)*, cervell *(m)*
noon • *n* migdia *(m)*
noose • *n* llaç
noradrenaline • *n* noradrenalina *(f)*
noria • *n* sínia *(f)*
normal • *n* normal • *adj* normal
normally • *adv* normalment
normative • *adj* normatiu
north • *n* nord *(m)*, septentrió *(m)*
northeast • *n* nord-est
northern • *adj* septentrional
northwest • *n* nord-oest
nose • *n* nas *(m)*
nostalgia • *n* nostàlgia *(f)*
nostril • *n* nariu *(m)*
nosy • *adj* dotor
not • *adv* no
notable • *adj* notable
notably • *adv* notablement
notch • *v* oscar • *n* osca *(f)*
nothing • *pron* res
notice • *v* fixar-se en, notar, adonar-se
notification • *n* notificació *(f)*
notion • *n* noció *(f)*
notoriety • *n* notorietat *(f)*
notorious • *adj* notori
notoriously • *adv* notòriament
notwithstanding • *prep* no obstant
nought • *n* zero *(m)*
noun • *n* substantiu *(m)*
novel • *n* novel·la *(f)*

novelist • *n* novel·lista *(f)*
now • *n* ara *(m)* • *adv* ara • *interj* ara, ja • *conj* ara
nowadays • *adv* actualment, avui dia, avui en dia
nowhere • *adv* enlloc
nth • *adj* enèsim *(m)*
nu • *n* ni *(f)*
nuance • *n* matís *(m)*
nubile • *adj* núbil
nuclear • *adj* nuclear
nucleon • *n* nucleó *(m)*
nucleus • *n* nucli *(m)*
nude • *adj* nu
nudity • *n* nuesa *(f)*
number • *v* numerar, comptar, sumar • *n* nombre, xifra *(f)*, nombre *(m)*, número *(m)*
numeral • *n* número *(m)*, xifra
numerator • *n* numerador *(m)*
numerical • *adj* numèric
numerous • *adj* nombrós
numismatics • *n* numismàtica *(f)*
nun • *n* monja *(f)*
nurse • *v* alletar • *n* infermer *(m)*
nut • *n* nou *(f)*, ou
nuthatch • *n* pica-soques *(m)*
nutmeg • *n* túnel *(m)*
nutritional • *adj* nutritiu, nutricional
nutritious • *adj* nutritiu, nutrient, nutrici, alimentós, alimentador

O

o • *n* o *(f)*
o'clock • *adv* una *(f)*
oak • *n* roure *(m)*, roure
oar • *n* rem *(m)*
oasis • *n* oasi *(m)*
oat • *n* civada *(f)*
oath • *n* jurament *(m)*
obedience • *n* obediència
obedient • *adj* obedient
obelisk • *n* obelisc *(m)*
obese • *adj* obès
obesity • *n* obesitat
object • *n* objecte *(m)*
objective • *adj* objectiu *(m)*
obligatory • *adj* obligatori
oblige • *v* obligar
oblique • *adj* oblic
obliquity • *n* obliqüitat *(f)*
obliteration • *n* obliteració *(f)*

oblivious • *adj* inconscient, ignorant, oblidós, oblidadís
oblong • *adj* oblong
oboe • *n* oboè *(m)*
oboist • *n* oboista *(f)*
obscene • *adj* obscè
obscenely • *adv* obscenament
obscenity • *n* obscenitat *(f)*
obscurantism • *n* obscurantisme *(m)*
obsequious • *adj* obsequiós
observation • *n* observació *(f)*, registre *(m)*, anotació *(f)*, comentari *(m)*
observatory • *n* observatori *(m)*
observe • *v* observar, seguir
obsession • *n* obsessió *(f)*
obsidian • *n* obsidiana *(f)*
obsolescence • *n* obsolescència *(f)*
obsolete • *adj* obsolet, rudimentari
obstacle • *n* obstacle *(m)*

obstetric • *adj* obstètric
obstinate • *adj* obstinat
obstinately • *adv* obstinadament
obstructive • *adj* obstructiu
obtuse • *adj* obtús
obverse • *n* anvers *(m)* • *adj* anvers *(m)*
obvious • *adj* obvi
obviously • *adv* òbviament
obviousness • *n* obvietat *(f)*
ocarina • *n* ocarina *(f)*
occasional • *adj* ocasional
occasionally • *adv* ocasionalment
occipital • *n* occipital *(m)* • *adj* occipital
occiput • *n* occípit *(m)*
occult • *v* ocultar, amagar • *n* ocultisme, ocult • *adj* ocult, amagat
occupation • *n* ocupació *(f)*
ocean • *n* oceà *(m)*
oceanic • *adj* oceànic
oceanographer • *n* oceanògraf *(m)*
oceanography • *n* oceanografia *(f)*, oceanologia *(f)*
ocelot • *n* ocelot *(m)*
octagon • *n* octàgon *(m)*
octahedron • *n* octaedre *(m)*, octàedre *(m)*
octave • *n* octava *(f)*, vuitada *(f)*
octavo • *n* octau *(m)*
octet • *n* octet *(m)*
octogenarian • *n* octogenari • *adj* octogenari
octopus • *n* pop *(m)*
ocular • *adj* ocular
odalisque • *n* odalisca *(f)*
odd • *adj* estrany *(m)*, imparell, senar, escaig
odious • *adj* odiós
odometer • *n* comptaquilòmetres *(m)*
of • *prep* de
offal • *n* víscera *(f)*
offensive • *adj* ofensiu *(m)*, ofensiva *(f)*
offer • *n* oferta *(f)* • *v* oferir
offering • *n* oferiment *(m)*
office • *n* oficina *(f)*
official • *n* funcionari *(m)* • *adj* oficial
officially • *adv* oficialment
offset • *n* decalatge *(m)*, decalatges
offside • *n* fora de joc *(f)*
often • *adv* sovint
ogre • *n* ogre *(m)*
oil • *v* greixar • *n* oli *(m)*, benzina *(f)*, petroli *(m)*
ointment • *n* pomada *(f)*
okapi • *n* ocapi *(m)*, okapi *(m)*
old • *adj* vell, antic, gran, tenir
oleander • *n* baladre *(m)*
olfaction • *n* olfacte *(m)*
olfactory • *adj* olfactiu, olfactori

oligarch • *n* oligarca *(f)*
oligarchic • *adj* oligàrquic
oligarchy • *n* oligarquia *(f)*
olive • *n* oliva *(f)*
omega • *n* omega *(f)*
omicron • *n* òmicron *(f)*
ominous • *adj* ominós
omission • *n* omissió *(f)*
omit • *v* ometre
omnidirectional • *adj* omnidireccional
omnipotence • *n* omnipotència *(f)*
omnipotent • *adj* omnipotent
omnipresence • *n* omnipresència *(f)*
omnipresent • *adj* omnipresent
omniscience • *n* omnisciència *(f)*
omniscient • *adj* omniscient
omnivore • *n* omnívor *(m)*
omnivorous • *adj* omnívor
on • *prep* sobre
onager • *n* onagre *(m)*
oncologist • *n* oncòleg *(m)*
oncology • *n* oncologia *(f)*
one • *n* u *(m)* • *adj* un, únic, u, mateix
one-armed • *adj* manc
one-eyed • *adj* borni, tort
oneirology • *n* oneirologia *(f)*
onerous • *adj* onerós
oneself • *pron* es
onion • *n* ceba *(f)*
onionskin • *n* paper ceba *(m)*
only • *adj* únic • *adv* només, sols, solament, únicament
onomatopoeia • *n* onomatopeia *(f)*
onomatopoeic • *adj* onomatopeic
ontological • *adj* ontològic
ontology • *n* ontologia *(f)*
onyx • *n* ònix *(m)*
oocyte • *n* oòcit *(m)*
oosphere • *n* oosfera *(f)*
opal • *n* òpal *(m)*
opaque • *adj* opac
opening • *n* obertura *(f)*
openly • *adv* obertament
operation • *n* operació *(f)*
operational • *adj* operatiu
operculum • *n* opercle *(m)*
ophicleide • *n* figle *(m)*
ophthalmic • *adj* oftàlmic
ophthalmologist • *n* oftalmòleg *(m)*, oftalmòloga *(f)*
ophthalmology • *n* oftalmologia *(f)*
opinion • *n* opinió *(f)*
opium • *n* opi
opponent • *n* oponent
opportune • *adj* oportú
opportunity • *n* oportunitat *(f)*
oppose • *v* oposar

opposite • *n* contrari *(m)* • *adj* oposat • *prep* davant de
opposition • *n* oposició *(f)*
oppression • *n* opressió
optic • *adj* òptic
optimism • *n* optimisme *(m)*
optimist • *n* optimista *(f)*
optimistic • *adj* optimista
option • *n* opció *(f)*
optional • *adj* opcional
opulence • *n* opulència *(f)*
opulent • *adj* opulent
or • *conj* o, o bé
oral • *adj* oral, bucal, verbal
orally • *adv* oralment
orange • *n* taronger *(m)*, taronja *(f)*, taronja *(m)* • *adj* ataronjat, carabassa
orangutan • *n* orangutan *(m)*
oratory • *n* oratòria *(f)*, oratori *(m)*
orbit • *v* orbitar • *n* òrbita *(f)*
orbital • *adj* orbital
orc • *n* orc
orchestra • *n* orquestra *(f)*
orchestral • *adj* orquestral
order • *v* ordenar, demanar • *n* ordre *(m)*, ordre *(f)*, comanda *(f)*, orde *(m)*
ordinary • *adj* ordinari
ordinate • *n* ordenada
ordnance • *n* artilleria *(f)*
ore • *n* mena *(f)*
oregano • *n* orenga *(f)*
organ • *n* òrgan *(m)*, orgue *(m)*
organelle • *n* orgànul *(m)*
organic • *adj* orgànic
organism • *n* organisme *(m)*
organization • *n* organització *(f)*
organize • *v* organitzar
organized • *adj* organitzat
orgasm • *n* orgasme *(m)*
orientalist • *n* orientalista
originality • *n* originalitat *(f)*
originally • *adv* originàriament
ornamental • *n* ornamental • *adj* ornamental
ornithological • *adj* ornitològic
ornithologist • *n* ornitòleg *(m)*
ornithology • *n* ornitologia *(f)*
orphan • *n* orfe *(m)*, òrfena *(f)*
orthodontics • *n* ortodòncia *(f)*, ortodontologia *(f)*
orthodox • *adj* ortodox
orthodoxy • *n* ortodòxia
orthogonal • *adj* ortogonal
orthographic • *adj* ortogràfic
orthopedic • *adj* ortopèdic
orthopedist • *n* ortopedista *(f)*, ortopèdic *(m)*

oryx • *n* òrix *(m)*
oscillate • *v* oscil·lar
oscillation • *n* oscil·lació *(f)*
oscilloscope • *n* oscil·loscopi *(m)*
osmium • *n* osmi
osmosis • *n* osmosi *(f)*
osmotic • *adj* osmòtic
osprey • *n* àguila pescadora *(f)*
osseous • *adj* ossi
ossicle • *n* ossicle *(m)*
ossify • *v* ossificar
ostentatious • *adj* ostentós
ostracism • *n* ostracisme *(m)*
ostrich • *n* estruç *(m)*
otalgia • *n* otàlgia *(f)*
others • *n* altres
otherwise • *adv* altrament
otic • *adj* òtic
otitis • *n* otitis *(f)*
otter • *n* llúdria *(f)*, llúdriga *(f)*
ouch • *interj* au
ounce • *n* unça *(f)*
ourselves • *pron* ens, mateix
out • *n* eliminació *(f)* • *adj* disponible
outcrop • *n* aflorament *(m)*
outfield • *n* camp exterior *(m)*
outfielder • *n* exterior *(f)*
outgoing • *adj* extrovertit, sortint
outlet • *n* sortida *(f)*, desguàs *(m)*, punt de venda *(m)*, endoll *(m)*
outrage • *v* indignar • *n* atrocitat *(f)*, ultratge *(m)*, ràbia *(f)*, indignació *(f)*
outrageous • *adj* xocant, cruel, immoral, escandalós
outright • *adv* completament, francament, immediatament, directament
outset • *n* inici *(m)*, començament *(m)*
outside • *adv* fora
outskirt • *n* afores
outstanding • *adj* destacat, excepcional, sobresortint, pendent
oval • *n* oval *(m)* • *adj* oval, ovular
ovary • *n* ovari *(m)*
oven • *n* forn *(m)*
overcoat • *n* abric
overeat • *v* sobremenjar
overestimate • *v* sobreestimar
oversight • *n* oblit *(m)*, supervisió *(f)*
overwhelm • *v* superar, agobiar
ovoid • *adj* ovoide
ovum • *n* òvul
owl • *n* òliba *(f)*, mussol *(m)*, gamarús *(m)*, gran duc *(m)*
own • *adj* mateix, propi
owner • *n* propietari *(m)*
ownership • *n* propietat *(f)*, possessió *(f)*
ox • *n* bou *(m)*

oxide • *n* òxid *(m)*

oxygen • *n* oxigen *(m)*

oxymoron • *n* oxímoron *(m)*

P

pace • *prep* amb tot el respecte per

pack • *v* fer (la maleta)

package • *v* empaquetar • *n* paquet *(m)*, empaquetatge *(m)*

packed • *adj* empaquetat, replet

pact • *n* pacte *(m)*

paddle • *n* pala *(f)*

padlock • *n* cadenat *(m)*

paella • *n* paella *(f)*

pagan • *n* pagà *(m)* • *adj* pagà

paganism • *n* paganisme *(m)*

page • *n* pàgina *(f)*, patge *(m)*

pagoda • *n* pagoda *(f)*

pain • *n* dolor *(m)*, pena *(f)*

painful • *adj* dolorós

painfully • *adv* dolorosament

painless • *adj* indolor

painstaking • *adj* acurat

paint • *v* pintar • *n* pintura *(f)*

painter • *n* pintor *(m)*

painting • *n* quadre *(m)*, pintura *(f)*

pair • *n* parella *(f)*

pajamas • *n* pijama *(m)*

palace • *n* palau *(m)*

paladin • *n* paladí *(m)*

palaestra • *n* palestra *(f)*

pale • *adj* pàlŭlid • *n* pal

paleoanthropology • *n* paleoantropologia *(f)*

paleobotany • *n* paleobotànica *(f)*

paleontological • *adj* paleontològic

paleontologist • *n* paleontòleg *(m)*

paleontology • *n* paleontologia *(f)*

paleozoology • *n* paleozoologia *(f)*

paletot • *n* abric *(m)*, gavany *(m)*, paltó *(m)*, sobretot *(m)*

palindrome • *n* palíndrom *(m)*

palisade • *n* palissada *(f)*

palladium • *n* palŭladi *(m)*

pallet • *n* palet *(m)*

palliate • *v* palŭliar, mitigar, atenuar, remeiar, encobrir, dissimular

palliative • *adj* palŭliatiu

pallid • *adj* pàlŭlid

palm • *n* palmell *(m)*

palpable • *adj* palpable

panacea • *n* panacea *(f)*

panache • *n* plomall *(m)*

pancake • *n* tortita *(f)*

pancreas • *n* pàncrees *(m)*

pancreatic • *adj* pancreàtic

pandora • *n* pagell *(m)*

panic • *n* pànic

panoramic • *adj* panoràmic

pantaloons • *n* calces, pantaló

pantheon • *n* panteó *(m)*

pantry • *n* rebost *(m)*

pants • *n* pantaló *(m)*, pantalons, calçons, bragues, calçotets, calçons blancs

papacy • *n* papat *(m)*, pontificat *(m)*

papal • *adj* papal

paper • *v* empaperar • *n* paper *(m)*, article *(m)*

paperboard • *n* cartonet *(m)*

papers • *n* papers

paperweight • *n* petjapapers *(m)*

paperwork • *n* paperassa *(f)*, paperada *(f)*

parable • *n* paràbola *(f)*

parabola • *n* paràbola *(f)*

parabolic • *adj* parabòlic

parachute • *n* paracaigudes *(m)*

parachutist • *n* paracaigudista *(f)*

paradigm • *n* paradigma *(m)*

paradise • *n* paradís *(m)*

paradox • *n* paradoxa *(f)*

paradoxical • *adj* paradoxal

paradoxically • *adv* paradoxalment

parakeet • *n* periquito *(m)*

parallel • *adj* paralŭlel

parallelepiped • *n* paralelepípede

parallelogram • *n* paralŭlelogram *(m)*

paralysis • *n* paràlisi *(f)*

paralytic • *n* paralític *(m)* • *adj* paralític

paralyze • *v* paralitzar

paramecium • *n* parameci *(m)*

paramilitary • *n* paramilitar • *adj* paramilitar

paranoid • *n* paranoic • *adj* paranoic

paranormal • *adj* paranormal

parapet • *n* ampit *(m)*

paraphrastic • *adj* parafràstic *(m)*, parafràstica *(f)*

paraplegia • *n* paraplegia *(f)*

paraplegic • *n* paraplègic *(m)* • *adj* paraplègic

parasite • *n* paràsit *(m)*

parasol • *n* para-sol *(m)*, ombrelŭla *(f)*

paratrooper • *n* paracaigudista *(f)*

parched • *adj* ressec, assedegat

pardon • *v* perdonar, indultar • *n* perdó

(m), indult *(m)* • *interj* perdó *(m)*
parenthesis • *n* parèntesi *(m)*
pariah • *n* pària *(f)*, intocable *(f)*
parish • *n* parròquia
park • *n* parc *(m)*, parc natural *(m)*, vedat *(m)*
parliament • *n* parlament *(m)*
parliamentary • *adj* parlamentari
parody • *v* parodiar • *n* paròdia *(f)*
parrot • *n* lloro *(m)*
parse • *v* analitzar
parsley • *n* julivert *(m)*
part • *n* part *(f)*
partial • *adj* parcial
partially • *adv* parcialment
participle • *n* participi *(m)*
particle • *n* partícula *(f)*
partridge • *n* perdiu *(f)*
party • *n* part *(f)*, festa *(f)*, sarau *(m)*
pass • *v* passar, aprovar
passable • *adj* transitable, passable
passage • *n* passatge *(m)*
passenger • *n* passatger *(m)*
passing • *adj* passatger
passionate • *adj* apassionat
passionately • *adv* apassionadament
passive • *adj* passiu *(m)*
passively • *adv* passivament
passivity • *n* passivitat *(f)*
passport • *n* passaport *(m)*
password • *n* contrasenya *(f)*
pasta • *n* pasta *(f)*
paste • *v* enganxar
pasteurize • *v* pasteuritzar
pastiche • *n* pastitx
pastille • *n* pastilla *(f)*
pastime • *n* passatemps *(m)*
pastry • *n* pastissos
pasture • *v* pasturar • *n* prat *(m)*
patent • *v* patentar • *n* patent • *adj* patent
paternal • *adj* patern *(m)*
path • *n* sender *(m)*, camí *(m)*
pathetic • *adj* commovedor, patètic
pathogen • *n* patogen *(m)*
pathological • *adj* patològic
pathology • *n* patologia *(f)*
patience • *n* paciència *(f)*, solitari *(m)*
patient • *n* pacient • *adj* pacient
patiently • *adv* pacientment
patina • *n* pàtina *(f)*
patriarch • *n* patriarca *(m)*
patriarchal • *adj* patriarcal
patriarchy • *n* patriarcat *(m)*, patriarquia *(f)*
patrician • *n* patrici *(m)*
patrimony • *n* patrimoni *(m)*
patriot • *n* patriota *(f)*

patriotic • *adj* patriòtic
patriotically • *adv* patriòticament
patriotism • *n* patriotisme *(m)*
patrol • *n* patrulla
patronymic • *n* patronímic
pattern • *n* mostra *(f)*, model *(m)*, patró
paunch • *n* panxa *(f)*, butza *(f)*
pave • *v* pavimentar, empedrar
pavement • *n* vorera
paw • *n* pota *(f)*
pawn • *n* peó *(m)* • *v* empenyorar
pawnshop • *n* casa de penyores *(f)*
pay • *v* pagar
payment • *n* pagament *(m)*
pea • *n* pesolera *(f)*, pèsol *(m)*
peace • *n* pau *(f)*
peaceable • *adj* pacifista
peaceful • *adj* pacífic, assossegat
peacefully • *adv* pacíficament
peach • *n* presseguer *(m)*, préssec *(m)*
peacock • *n* paó
peak • *n* pic *(m)*, cim *(m)*
peanut • *n* cacauet *(m)*
pear • *n* pera *(f)*, perera *(f)*
pearl • *n* perla *(f)*
peasant • *n* camperol
peat • *n* torba *(f)*
pebble • *n* còdol *(m)*
pectin • *n* pectina *(f)*
peculiar • *adj* peculiar
pecuniary • *adj* monetari
pedagogical • *adj* pedagògic
pedagogue • *n* pedagog *(m)*
pedal • *v* pedalejar • *n* pedal *(m)*
pedantic • *adj* pedant
pederast • *n* pederasta *(f)*
pederasty • *n* pederàstia *(f)*
pedestal • *n* pedestal *(m)*, peana *(f)*
pedestrian • *n* vianant *(m)*
pediment • *n* frontó *(m)*
pedometer • *n* podòmetre *(m)*, pedòmetre *(m)*
peduncle • *n* peduncle *(m)*
pee • *v* orinar
peephole • *n* espiera *(f)*
pegasus • *n* pegàs *(m)*
pejoratively • *adv* despectivament, pejorativament
pelican • *n* pelicà *(m)*
pellet • *n* pèl·let *(m)*, perdigó *(m)*
pelvic • *adj* pelvià
pelvis • *n* pelvis *(f)*
pen • *n* bolígraf *(m)*
penalty • *n* càstig *(m)*
penance • *n* penitència
pencil • *n* llapis *(m)*
pendant • *n* penjoll *(m)*

pending • *adj* pendent
penguin • *n* pingüí *(m)*
penicillin • *n* penicilůlina *(f)*
peninsula • *n* península *(f)*
penis • *n* penis *(m)*
penitent • *n* penitent • *adj* penedit, penitent
pensive • *adj* pensatiu
pentagon • *n* pentàgon *(m)*
pentahedron • *n* pentaedre *(m)*, pentàedre *(m)*
pentathlete • *n* pentatleta *(f)*
pentathlon • *n* pentatló *(m)*
pentatonic • *adj* pentatònic
penthouse • *n* àtic *(m)*
penultimate • *adj* penúltim
people • *v* poblar, poblar-se • *n* gent *(f)*, poble *(m)*, família *(f)*, els meus
pepper • *n* pebrotera *(f)*, pebre *(m)*, pebrot *(m)*
peptide • *n* pèptid *(m)*
per • *prep* per, via, segons
perceive • *v* percebre
percentage • *n* percentatge *(m)*
perception • *n* percepció *(f)*
percussion • *n* percussió *(f)*
perennial • *n* perennifoli • *adj* perenne
perfect • *v* perfeccionar
perfection • *n* perfecció *(f)*
perfectionism • *n* perfeccionisme *(m)*
perfectionist • *n* perfeccionista *(f)*
perfectly • *adv* perfectament
perfidy • *n* perfídia *(f)*
performance • *n* actuació *(f)*, execució *(f)*, representació *(f)*
perfume • *n* perfum *(m)*
perhaps • *adv* potser
peril • *n* perill *(m)*
perilous • *adj* perillós
perineum • *n* perineu *(m)*
period • *n* període *(m)* • *interj* i punt
periodically • *adv* periòdicament
periphery • *n* perifèria *(f)*
periphrasis • *n* perífrasi *(f)*
perish • *v* perir
peristyle • *n* peristil *(m)*
peritoneum • *n* peritoneu *(m)*
permafrost • *n* pergelisòl *(m)*
permanence • *n* permanència *(f)*
permanent • *adj* permanent
permanently • *adv* permanentment
permeable • *adj* permeable
permeate • *v* impregnar
permission • *n* permís *(m)*, autorització *(f)*
perpendicular • *adj* perpendicular
perpendicularly • *adv* perpendicularment

perpetrate • *v* perpetrar
perpetual • *adj* perpetu, perpetual
perpetually • *adv* perpètuament, perpetualment
perpetuate • *v* perpetuar
perseverance • *n* perseverança *(f)*
persevere • *v* perseverar
persimmon • *n* caquier, persimó, banús
person • *n* persona *(f)*
personal • *adj* personal, corporal
personally • *adv* personalment
personify • *v* personificar
perspicacious • *adj* perspicaç
perspicacity • *n* perspicàcia *(f)*
persuade • *v* persuadir
persuasive • *adj* persuasiu
persuasively • *adv* persuasivament
pertain • *v* pertànyer
peseta • *n* pesseta *(f)*
pessimism • *n* pessimisme *(m)*
pessimist • *n* pessimista *(f)*
pessimistic • *adj* pessimista
pest • *n* pesta *(f)*, plaga *(f)*
pesticide • *n* plaguicida *(m)*, pesticida *(m)*
pestle • *n* mà de morter *(f)*, maça *(f)*
pet • *n* mascota *(f)*
petal • *n* pètal *(m)*
petrify • *v* petrificar
petrochemical • *adj* petroquímic
phalanx • *n* falange *(f)*
phallic • *adj* fàlůlic
phallus • *n* falůlus *(m)*
phantom • *n* fantasma *(m)*
pharaoh • *n* faraó *(m)*
pharaonic • *adj* faraònic
pharmacist • *n* farmacèutic *(m)*
pharmacological • *adj* farmacològic
pharmacology • *n* farmacologia *(f)*
pharmacy • *n* farmàcia *(f)*
pheasant • *n* faisà *(m)*
phenomenal • *adj* fenomenal, fenomènic
phenomenon • *n* fenomen *(m)*
phi • *n* fi *(f)*
philanthropic • *adj* filantròpic
philanthropist • *n* filantrop *(m)*
philanthropy • *n* filantropia *(f)*
philatelic • *adj* filatèlic
philharmonic • *n* filharmònic
philistine • *adj* filisteu
philological • *adj* filològic
philologist • *n* filòleg *(m)*
philology • *n* filologia *(f)*
philosopher • *n* filòsof *(m)*, filòsofa *(f)*
philosophical • *adj* filosòfic
philosophically • *adv* filosòficament
philosophy • *n* filosofia

phlegm • *n* flegma *(f)*
phlegmatic • *adj* flegmàtic
phloem • *n* floema *(m)*
phoenix • *n* fènix *(m)*
phone • *n* telèfon *(m)*
phoneme • *n* fonema *(m)*
phonetic • *adj* fonètic
phonetically • *adv* fonèticament
phonetics • *n* fonètica *(f)*
phonic • *adj* fònic
phonological • *adj* fonològic
phonologist • *n* fonòleg *(m)*
phonology • *n* fonologia *(f)*
phosphate • *n* fosfat *(m)*
phosphorous • *adj* fosforós *(m)*
phosphorus • *n* fòsfor *(m)*
photo • *n* foto *(f)*
photochemical • *adj* fotoquímic
photocopier • *n* fotocopiadora *(f)*
photocopy • *v* fotocopiar • *n* fotocòpia *(f)*
photograph • *v* fotografiar • *n* fotografia *(f)*, foto *(f)*
photographer • *n* fotògraf *(m)*
photographic • *adj* fotogràfic
photographically • *adv* fotogràficament
photography • *n* fotografia *(f)*
photometer • *n* fotòmetre *(m)*
photon • *n* fotó *(m)*
photosphere • *n* fotosfera *(f)*
photosynthesis • *n* fotosíntesi *(f)*
photosynthetic • *adj* fotosintètic
photovoltaic • *adj* fotovoltaic *(m)*
phrase • *n* sintagma *(m)*, frase *(f)*
phraseology • *n* fraseologia *(f)*
phrenology • *n* frenologia *(f)*
phthisic • *adj* tísic *(m)*
phthisis • *n* tisi *(f)*
phylactery • *n* filacteri *(m)*, talismà *(m)*
phylogeny • *n* filogènia *(f)*
phylum • *n* fílum *(m)*
physical • *adj* físic
physically • *adv* físicament
physician • *n* metge *(m)*, metgessa *(f)*
physiological • *adj* fisiològic
physiologically • *adv* fisiològicament
physiologist • *n* fisiòleg *(m)*
physiology • *n* fisiologia *(f)*
phytophagous • *adj* fitòfag
pianist • *n* pianista *(f)*
piano • *n* piano *(m)*
picador • *n* picador *(m)*
pick • *n* pic *(m)*
pickle • *n* conserva *(f)*, envinagrat *(m)*
pickpocket • *n* carterista
picture • *n* foto *(f)*, fotografia *(f)*, cinema *(m)*
pie • *n* pastís *(m)*

piece • *n* peça *(f)*
pierce • *v* foradar
piercing • *n* pírcing
piety • *n* pietat *(f)*
piezometer • *n* piezòmetre *(m)*
pig • *n* porc *(m)*, golafre *(m)*
pigeon • *n* colom *(m)*
piglet • *n* garrí *(m)*, porcell *(m)*, porquet *(m)*
pigment • *v* pigmentar • *n* pigment *(m)*
pigsty • *n* cort de porcs *(f)*, porcatera *(f)*, porcellera *(f)*, soll *(f)*
pike • *n* pica *(f)*, lluç *(m)*
pilaster • *n* pilastra *(f)*
pile • *n* pila *(f)*
pilgrim • *n* pelegrí *(m)*, pelegrina *(f)*
pilgrimage • *n* pelegrinatge *(m)*
pill • *n* píndola *(f)*
pillar • *n* pilar *(m)*
pillory • *n* picota *(f)*
pillow • *n* coixí *(m)*
pilot • *v* pilotar, provar • *n* pilot *(f)* • *adj* pilot *(f)*
pimple • *n* bua *(f)*, buba *(f)*
pinch • *v* pessigar • *n* pessic
pincushion • *n* buirac *(m)*
pine • *n* pi *(m)*
pineapple • *n* ananàs *(m)*, pinya *(f)*
ping • *v* pinguejar
pink • *n* rosa *(m)* • *adj* rosa
pinna • *n* aurícula *(f)*, pavelló auricular *(m)*
pion • *n* pió *(m)*
pipa • *n* pipa *(m)*
pipette • *n* pipeta
pirate • *v* piratejar • *n* pirata *(m)*
piss • *v* pixar • *n* pixo *(m)*, pipí *(m)*, pixat *(m)*, pixada *(f)*
pistachio • *n* festuc *(m)*, pistatxer *(m)*, pistatxo *(m)*
pistol • *n* pistola *(f)*
pit • *n* pinyol *(m)*
pitch • *v* llançar • *n* llançament *(m)*
pitcher • *n* llançador *(m)*, gerra *(f)*
pitiful • *adj* lamentable, miserable
pituitary • *adj* pituïtari
pity • *n* llàstima *(f)*
pivot • *v* pivotar
pizza • *n* pizza *(f)*
pizzeria • *n* pizzeria *(f)*
place • *v* colůlocar • *n* lloc *(m)*, indret *(m)*
placebo • *n* placebo *(m)*
placenta • *n* placenta *(f)*
plagiarism • *n* plagi *(m)*
plain • *adj* senzill, natural, simple, net • *n* pla *(m)*
plait • *n* dobleg *(m)*, trena *(f)*

plan • *v* planejar
plane • *n* ribot *(m)*
planet • *n* planeta *(m)*
planetarium • *n* planetari *(m)*
planetary • *adj* planetari
plankton • *n* plàncton *(m)*
planner • *n* agenda *(f)*
planning • *n* planificació *(f)*
plant • *v* plantar • *n* planta *(f)*
plastic • *n* plàstic • *adj* plàstic
plasticity • *n* plasticitat *(f)*
plate • *n* plat *(m)*, matrícula *(f)*
platelet • *n* plaqueta *(f)*
platform • *n* tarima *(f)*, plataforma *(f)*, programa *(m)*, andana *(f)*
platinum • *n* platí *(m)*
platonic • *adj* platònic
platypus • *n* ornitorinc *(m)*
platyrrhine • *adj* camerí *(m)*, platirí *(m)*
plausible • *adj* plausible
play • *v* jugar, tocar, actuar, participar • *n* joc *(m)*, obra *(f)*
player • *n* jugador *(m)*
playwright • *n* dramaturg *(m)*, dramaturga *(f)*
plaza • *n* plaça
pleasant • *adj* agradable, plaent
pleasantly • *adv* agradablement
please • *v* plaure, complaure, agradar • *adv* si us plau, per favor
pleased • *adj* content
pledge • *v* prometre, penyorar, empenyorar • *n* promesa *(f)*, jurament *(m)*, penyora *(f)*, garantia *(f)*
plenary • *adj* plenari
plethora • *n* plètora *(f)*
plethoric • *adj* pletòric
plinth • *n* sòcol *(m)*
plosive • *n* oclusiva *(f)*
plot • *v* planejar, traçar, marcar, conspirar • *n* argument *(m)*, trama *(f)*, solar *(m)*, marjal *(m)*, terreny *(m)*, gràfica *(f)*, traçada *(f)*, complot *(m)*, conspiració *(f)*
plough • *v* llaurar • *n* arada *(f)*
plover • *n* corriol *(m)*
pluck • *n* perseverància *(f)*
plug • *n* clavilla *(f)*, endoll *(m)*
plum • *n* pruna *(f)*, pruner *(m)*, prunera *(f)*, color pruna, pilotes, ous
plumbic • *adj* saturní *(m)*
plunge • *n* immersió *(f)*
plunger • *n* desembossador
plural • *n* plural *(m)* • *adj* plural
plurality • *n* pluralitat *(f)*
plus • *adj* més, positiu • *conj* més
plutonium • *n* plutoni
pluviometer • *n* pluviòmetre *(m)*, udòme-

tre *(m)*
pneumatometer • *n* pneumatòmetre *(m)*
pneumonia • *n* pneumònia *(f)*, pulmonia *(f)*
pocket • *n* butxaca *(f)*, tronera *(f)*
pocketful • *n* butxacada *(f)*
pod • *v* pelar • *n* vaina *(f)*
poem • *n* poema *(m)*, poesia *(f)*, oda *(f)*
poet • *n* poeta *(f)*
poetaster • *n* poetastre *(m)*
poetess • *n* poetessa *(f)*
poetic • *adj* poètic *(m)*, poètica *(f)*
poetically • *adv* poèticament
poetry • *n* poesia *(f)*, poeticitat *(f)*
pogrom • *n* pogrom *(m)*
point • *n* punt *(m)*, endoll *(m)*
pointed • *adj* punxegut
pointer • *n* apuntador *(m)*
poison • *v* emmetzinar, enverinar • *n* verí *(m)*, metzina *(f)*
poisoning • *n* enverinament *(m)*
poisonous • *adj* verinós, tòxic
poker • *n* pòquer *(m)*
pokey • *n* garjola *(f)*
polecat • *n* turó
polemic • *adj* polèmic
polemical • *adj* polèmic
police • *n* policia *(f)*
policy • *n* política *(f)*
polite • *adj* cortès
politely • *adv* cortesament
politeness • *n* educació cortesia *(f)*
political • *adj* polític
politically • *adv* políticament
politician • *n* polític *(m)*, política *(f)*
politics • *n* política *(f)*
polka • *n* polca *(f)*
pollen • *n* polŭlen *(m)*
pollination • *n* polŭlinització *(f)*
pollutant • *n* contaminant *(m)*
pollution • *n* contaminació *(f)*, polŭlució *(f)*, polŭluent *(m)*
polo • *n* polo *(m)*
polonaise • *n* polonesa *(f)*
polonium • *n* poloni *(m)*
polychromatic • *adj* policrom, policromàtic
polyethylene • *n* polietilè *(m)*
polygamist • *n* polígam *(m)*
polygamy • *n* poligàmia *(f)*
polygon • *n* polígon *(m)*
polyhedron • *n* poliedre *(m)*, políedre *(m)*
polymer • *n* polímer *(m)*
polynomial • *n* polinomi *(m)* • *adj* polinomial
polyphosphate • *n* polifosfat *(m)*
polytheism • *n* politeisme *(m)*

polytheist • *n* politeista *(f)*
polytheistic • *adj* politeista
polyunsaturated • *adj* poliinsaturat
pomegranate • *n* magraner *(m)*, magrana *(f)*
pompous • *adj* pompós
pompously • *adv* pomposament
poncho • *n* ponxo *(m)*
pond • *n* bassa *(f)*
pontiff • *n* pontífex *(m)*
pony • *n* poni *(m)*
poodle • *n* canitx *(m)*
poop • *v* cagar
poor • *n* pobres • *adj* pobre
pop • *n* papi, papa *(m)*
popcorn • *n* crispeta *(f)*, rosa *(f)*, roseta *(f)*, gallet *(m)*
pope • *n* Papa *(m)*
poplar • *n* pollancre *(m)*, àlber *(m)*
poppy • *n* rosella *(f)*
popular • *adj* popular
population • *n* població *(f)*
porbeagle • *n* marraix *(m)*
porcelain • *n* porcellana *(f)*
porcine • *adj* porquí, porcí
porcupine • *n* porc espí *(m)*
pornographer • *n* pornògraf *(m)*, pornista *(f)*
pornographic • *adj* pornogràfic
pornography • *n* pornografia *(f)*
porosity • *n* porositat *(f)*
porous • *adj* porós
porpoise • *n* marsopa *(f)*
porridge • *n* farinetes
port • *n* port *(m)*
portability • *n* portabilitat *(f)*
portable • *adj* portàtil, portable
portion • *n* porció *(f)*
portrait • *n* retrat *(m)*
position • *n* posició *(f)*
positive • *n* positiu *(m)* • *adj* positiu
positively • *adv* positivament
positron • *n* positró *(m)*
possess • *v* posseïr
possession • *n* possessió *(f)*, propietat *(f)*
possessive • *adj* possessiu
possibility • *n* possibilitat *(f)*
possible • *adj* possible
possibly • *adv* possiblement
post • *n* pivot *(f)*
postcard • *n* targeta postal *(f)*, postal *(f)*
poster • *n* cartell *(m)*, pòster *(m)*
postern • *n* poterna *(f)*
posthumous • *adj* pòstum
postilion • *n* postilló *(m)*
postmodernism • *n* postmodernitat *(f)*
postnatal • *adj* postpart

postpone • *v* posposar, ajornar
postscript • *n* Postdata
pot • *n* olla *(f)*
potable • *adj* potable
potassium • *n* potassi *(m)*
potato • *n* patata *(f)*, creïlla *(f)*
potential • *n* potencial • *adj* potencial
potsherd • *n* padellàs *(m)*
potter • *n* terrissaire
pottery • *n* terrissa *(f)*
poultry • *n* aviram, volateria
pound • *n* lliura *(f)*
poverty • *n* pobresa *(f)*
power • *n* poder *(m)*, potència *(f)*
powerful • *adj* potent, poderós
powerfully • *adv* poderosament, potentment
pox • *n* buba *(f)*
practical • *adj* pràctic
practically • *adv* pràcticament
practice • *v* practicar • *n* pràctica *(f)*
pragmatic • *adj* pragmàtic *(m)*, pragmàtica *(f)*
praise • *v* lloar
praiseworthy • *adj* lloable, encomiable
praseodymium • *n* praseodimi *(m)*
pray • *v* resar, pregar
prayer • *n* oració, pregària, rés *(m)*
precarious • *adj* precari
precariously • *adv* precàriament
precariousness • *n* precarietat *(f)*
precedent • *n* precedent *(m)*
precious • *adj* preciós
precipice • *n* precipici *(m)*
precise • *adj* precís
precisely • *adv* precisament
precocious • *adj* precoç
preconceived • *adj* preconcebut
predecessor • *n* antecessor *(m)*
predestination • *n* predestinació *(f)*
predilection • *n* predilecció *(f)*
predominant • *adj* predominant
predominantly • *adv* predominantment
preface • *n* prefaci *(m)*
preferable • *adj* preferible
preferably • *adv* preferiblement
pregnancy • *n* embaràs *(m)*, prenyat *(m)*
pregnant • *adj* embarassada *(f)*, encinta *(f)*, prenyada *(f)*, prenyat
prehensile • *adj* prènsil
prehistoric • *adj* prehistòric
prehistory • *n* prehistòria *(f)*
preliminary • *adj* preliminar
prelude • *n* preludi *(m)*
prenatal • *adj* prenatal
prenuptial • *adj* antenupcial
prepared • *adj* preparat, disposat

preposition • *n* preposició *(f)*
prepuce • *n* prepuci *(m)*
presbyopia • *n* presbícia *(f)*, vista cansada *(f)*
present • *n* present *(m)* • *adj* actual, present • *v* presentar
presentable • *adj* presentable
presentiment • *n* pressentiment *(m)*
preserve • *v* preservar • *n* reserva natural *(f)*
presidency • *n* presidència *(f)*
president • *n* president *(m)*, presidenta *(f)*
presidential • *adj* presidencial
press • *n* premsa *(f)*, impressora *(f)* • *v* prémer
presumably • *adv* presumiblement
pretend • *v* fingir, fer veure
pretentious • *adj* pretenciós, ostentós
pretty • *adj* bonic • *adv* força
preventive • *adj* preventiu, profilàctic
previous • *adj* previ, anterior, prematur
previously • *adv* anteriorment, prèviament
prey • *n* presa
price • *n* preu *(m)*
priceless • *adj* no tenir preu
prickly • *adj* espinós, malhumorós
pride • *n* orgull, orgull *(m)*
priest • *n* sacerdot *(m)*
priestess • *n* sacerdotessa
prim • *adj* posturer *(m)*
primarily • *adv* primàriament
primary • *n* primària *(f)*, primari *(m)*, bàsic *(m)*, fonamental *(m)* • *adj* primari *(m)*, primària *(f)*
primate • *n* primat *(m)*
prime • *adj* primer
primeval • *adj* primigeni *(m)*
primitive • *adj* primitiu
primitively • *adv* primitivament
primrose • *n* prímula *(f)*, primavera *(f)*
prince • *n* príncep *(m)*
princess • *n* princesa *(f)*
printable • *adj* imprimible *(f)*
prison • *n* presó *(f)*
prisoner • *n* pres *(m)*, presoner *(m)*
pristine • *adj* primitiu, primer, pristí
privacy • *n* privacitat *(f)*, privadesa *(f)*
private • *adj* privat, personal
privately • *adv* privadament
privet • *n* troana *(f)*
privilege • *n* privilegi *(m)*
privileged • *adj* privilegiat
prize • *n* botí *(m)*, premi *(m)*
pro • *n* pro *(m)* • *prep* pro
probability • *n* probabilitat *(f)*
probable • *adj* probable

probably • *adv* probablement
problem • *n* problema *(m)*
proboscis • *n* probòscide *(f)*
procedure • *n* procediment *(m)*
process • *v* processar • *n* procés *(m)*
procession • *n* processió *(f)*
proclamation • *n* proclamació *(f)*
prodigious • *adj* prodigiós
prodigy • *n* prodigi *(m)*
produce • *v* produir
producer • *n* productor *(m)*, productora *(f)*
product • *n* producte *(m)*
productive • *adj* productiu
profane • *v* profanar • *adj* profà
profession • *n* professió *(f)*, ofici *(m)*
professional • *n* professional, professional *(f)* • *adj* professional, perit
professionally • *adv* professionalment
professor • *n* professor *(m)*, professora *(f)*
proficiency • *n* habilitat, competència *(f)*
proficient • *adj* perit, capaç, versat
profitable • *adj* profitós, rendible
progeny • *n* progènie *(f)*
prognathous • *adj* pRògnat *(m)*
program • *n* programa *(m)*
programmer • *n* programador *(m)*
progress • *n* progrés
progression • *n* progressió *(f)*
progressive • *adj* progressista, progressiu
progressivism • *n* progressisme *(m)*
prohibit • *v* prohibir
project • *n* projecte *(m)*
projectile • *n* projectil *(m)*
prolific • *adj* prolífic
prolix • *adj* prolix
prologue • *n* pròleg *(m)*
promethium • *n* prometi *(m)*
prominent • *adj* prominent
promiscuity • *n* promiscuïtat *(f)*
promiscuous • *adj* promiscu
promiscuously • *adv* promíscuament
promise • *v* prometre • *n* promesa *(f)*
promising • *adj* prometedor
prompt • *v* incitar • *adj* ràpid
prone • *adj* predisposat, propens, procliu
pronoun • *n* pronom *(m)*
pronounce • *v* pronunciar
pronunciation • *n* pronunciació *(f)*, pronúncia *(f)*
proof • *n* prova *(f)*
prop • *n* pilar *(f)*
propane • *n* propà *(m)*
propeller • *n* hèlice *(f)*
proper • *adj* adequat
property • *n* propietat *(f)*, possessió *(f)*, pertinença *(f)*

prophecy • *n* profecia *(f)*
prophesy • *v* profetitzar
prophet • *n* profeta *(f)*
prophetic • *adj* profètic
prophylactic • *adj* profilàctic
proportion • *n* proporció *(f)*
proportional • *adj* proporcional
proportionate • *adj* proporcional
proposal • *n* proposta
propose • *v* proposar
propriety • *n* propietat *(f)*
proscenium • *n* prosceni *(m)*
prose • *n* prosa *(f)*
prosecute • *v* perseguir
prosecutor • *n* fiscal *(m)*
prosimian • *n* prosimi *(m)*
prosody • *n* prosòdia *(f)*
prospect • *n* prospeccions
prosper • *v* prosperar
prosperous • *adj* pròsper
prostate • *n* pròstata *(f)*
prostatectomy • *n* prostatectomia *(f)*
prostatitis • *n* prostatitis *(f)*
prostitute • *n* prostituta *(f)*
prostitution • *n* prostitució *(f)*
prostyle • *n* pròstil *(m)*
protactinium • *n* protactini *(m)*
protagonist • *n* protagonista *(f)*
protect • *v* protegir
protection • *n* protecció *(f)*
protectorate • *n* protectorat *(m)*
protein • *n* proteïna *(f)*
protest • *v* protestar • *n* protesta *(f)*
prothrombin • *n* protrombina *(f)*
proton • *n* protó
protozoan • *n* protozou *(m)*
proturan • *n* protur *(m)*
proud • *adj* orgullós, arrogant
proudly • *adv* orgullosament
proverb • *n* proverbi *(m)*, dita *(f)*, refrany *(m)*, parèmia *(f)*
province • *n* província *(f)*
provisional • *adj* provisional
provisionally • *adv* provisionalment
provocative • *adj* provocador, provocatiu
prow • *n* proa *(f)*
prowl • *v* aguaitar
prudently • *adv* prudentment
prune • *n* pruna seca *(f)* • *v* podar
pry • *v* dotorejar
psalm • *v* salmejar, psalmejar • *n* salm *(m)*, psalm *(m)*
psalter • *n* saltiri *(m)*
psaltery • *n* saltiri *(m)*
pseudopod • *n* pseudòpode *(m)*
pseudoscience • *n* pseudociència *(f)*
psi • *n* psi *(f)*

psoriasis • *n* psoriasi *(f)*
psychedelic • *adj* psicodèlic
psychiatric • *adj* psiquiàtric
psychiatrist • *n* psiquiatre *(m)*
psychiatry • *n* psiquiatria *(f)*
psychoanalysis • *n* psicoanàlisi *(f)*
psychological • *adj* psicològic
psychologically • *adv* psicològicament
psychologist • *n* psicòleg *(m)*
psychology • *n* psicologia *(f)*
psychotherapy • *n* psicoteràpia *(f)*
psychrometer • *n* psicròmetre *(m)*
pterodactyl • *n* pterodàctil *(m)*
pterosaur • *n* pterosaure *(m)*
pub • *n* bar *(m)*, taverna *(f)*
puberty • *n* pubertat *(f)*
pubescent • *n* púber, pubescent
pubis • *n* pubis *(m)*
public • *adj* públic
publication • *n* publicació *(f)*
publicity • *n* publicitat *(f)*
publicly • *adv* públicament
publish • *v* publicar
puck • *n* disc *(m)*
puddle • *v* entollar • *n* bassiot *(m)*, toll *(m)*
pudor • *n* pudor *(m)*
pug-nosed • *adj* xato *(m)*
pugilist • *n* pugilista *(f)*
pugnacious • *adj* pugnaç
pull • *v* tirar
pulmonary • *adj* pulmonar
pulpit • *n* púlpit *(m)*
pulsar • *n* púlsar *(m)*
pumice • *n* pumicita *(f)*
pumpkin • *n* carbassera *(f)*, carabassera *(f)*, carbassa *(f)*, carabassa *(f)*
pun • *n* joc de paraules *(m)*
punch • *n* cop de puny *(m)*
punctual • *adj* puntual
punctuality • *n* puntualitat *(f)*
punctuation • *n* puntuació *(f)*
punish • *v* punir, castigar
punishment • *n* punició *(f)*, puniment *(m)*, càstig *(m)*
punitive • *adj* punitiu
punt • *n* xut al vol *(m)*
puny • *adj* feble, escarransit, desnerit
pupil • *n* pupil *(m)*, pupilůla *(f)*
pure • *adj* pur
purgative • *adj* purgatiu
purgatory • *n* purgatori *(m)*
purify • *v* purificar
purity • *n* puresa *(f)*
purple • *adj* porpra, purpuri
purr • *v* roncar, ronronejar
purse • *n* moneder *(m)*

pursuit • *n* perseguiment *(m)*
pus • *n* pus *(m)*
push • *v* empènyer
pussy • *n* cony *(m)*
put • *v* posar, ficar, metre
putative • *adj* putatiu
putrid • *adj* pútrid
putt • *v* fer un putt
puzzled • *adj* perplex

pyramid • *n* piràmide *(f)*
pyramidal • *adj* piramidal
pyromania • *n* piromania *(f)*
pyromaniac • *n* piròman
pyrometer • *n* piròmetre *(m)*
pyrotechnic • *adj* pirotècnic
pyrotechnics • *n* pirotècnia *(f)*

Q

quacksalver • *n* curandero *(m)*
quadrant • *n* quadrant *(m)*
quadrilateral • *n* quadrilàter *(m)* • *adj* quadrilàter
quadriplegia • *n* tetraplegia *(f)*
quadriplegic • *n* quadriplègic, tetraplègic
quadruple • *adj* quàdruple
quail • *n* guatlla *(f)*
quake • *v* tremolor *(f)*
qualification • *n* qualificació *(f)*
qualified • *adj* qualificat
qualitative • *adj* qualitatiu
quality • *n* qualitat *(f)*, quality *(f)*
quantity • *n* quantitat *(f)*
quantum • *n* quantitat *(f)*, quàntum *(m)*
quarantine • *n* quarantena *(f)*
quark • *n* quark *(m)*
quarrel • *v* barallar-se, discutir • *n* baralla *(f)*
quarry • *n* cantera *(f)*, presa *(f)*
quart • *n* quart *(m)*
quarter • *n* quart *(m)*, quarter *(m)*
quarterback • *n* rerequart *(m)*
quarterly • *adj* trimestral • *adv* trimestralment
quarto • *n* quart *(m)*
quartz • *n* quars *(m)*
quaternary • *adj* quaternari *(m)*, quaternària *(f)*

quaver • *n* corxera *(f)*
queen • *n* reina *(f)*, marieta *(f)*, gata *(f)*
queer • *adj* estrany, marieta *(m)*, marica *(m)*
quench • *v* sadollar
question • *n* pregunta *(f)*, qüestió *(f)*
questionnaire • *n* qüestionari *(m)*
quetzal • *n* quetzal *(m)*
quick • *n* carn viva *(f)* • *adv* corrents
quickly • *adv* ràpidament
quiet • *v* calmar • *adj* silenciós, tranquil, quiet, poc, mica
quietly • *adv* silenciosament
quill • *n* pua *(m)*
quinary • *adj* quinari *(m)*, quinària *(f)*
quince • *n* codony *(m)*, codonyer *(m)*
quinine • *n* quinina *(f)*
quintal • *n* quintar *(m)*
quintet • *n* quintet *(m)*
quire • *n* mà *(f)*
quit • *v* sortir, eixir, deixar, aturar
quite • *adv* completament, totalment, exactament, verdaderament, bastant
quiver • *n* buirac *(m)*, carcaix *(m)* • *v* tremolar
quixotic • *adj* quixotesc
quote • *n* citació
quotidian • *adj* quotidià

R

rabbi • *n* rabí *(m)*
rabbinical • *adj* rabínic
rabbit • *n* conill *(m)*
rabid • *adj* rabiós
rabies • *n* ràbia *(f)*
raccoon • *n* ós rentador *(m)*
race • *n* cursa *(f)*, raça *(f)*, arrel *(f)*
raceme • *n* raïm *(m)*
rachitic • *adj* raquític

racial • *adj* racial
racism • *n* racisme *(m)*
racist • *n* racista *(f)* • *adj* racista
rack • *n* poltre *(m)*, pitrera
racket • *n* raqueta *(f)*
radar • *n* radar *(m)*
radiant • *n* radiant *(m)* • *adj* radiant
radiation • *n* radiació *(f)*
radical • *n* radical *(f)*, radical *(m)* • *adj*

radical
radically • *adv* radicalment
radio • *n* ràdio *(f)*
radio-controlled • *adj* radiodirigit
radioactive • *adj* radioactiu
radioactivity • *n* radioactivitat *(f)*
radiocarbon • *n* radiocarboni *(m)*
radiolarian • *n* radiolari *(m)*
radiologist • *n* radiòleg *(m)*
radiometer • *n* radiòmetre *(m)*
radish • *n* ravenera *(f)*, rave *(m)*
radium • *n* radi *(m)*
radius • *n* radi *(m)*
radon • *n* radó *(m)*
raft • *n* rai *(m)*
rage • *n* ràbia *(f)*
rail • *n* carril *(m)*
rain • *v* ploure • *n* pluja *(f)*
rainbow • *n* arc de Sant Martí *(m)*, arc iris *(m)*
raindrop • *n* gota d'aigua
rainstorm • *n* tempesta
rainy • *adj* plujós
raisin • *n* pansa *(f)*
rake • *n* rampí *(m)*, rasclet *(m)*
rally • *n* intercanvi de cops *(m)*, piloteig *(m)*
ram • *n* marrà *(m)*
ramification • *n* ramificació *(f)*
rancid • *adj* ranci
random • *n* fulano *(m)* • *adj* aleatori
randomly • *adv* aleatòriament
ranger • *n* guardabosc *(m)*
rank • *adj* ranci
ranking • *n* rànquing *(m)*
ransom • *n* rescat *(m)*
rape • *n* violació *(f)*
rapier • *n* estoc *(m)*
rapt • *adj* embadalit, extasiat
rapture • *n* rapte, arravatament
rare • *adj* cru, rar
rarely • *adv* rarament
rash • *adj* arrauxat
raspberry • *n* gerdera *(f)*, gerd *(m)*
rather • *adv* preferiblement, força, bastant
ratiocination • *n* raciocinació *(f)*
rational • *adj* racional
rationally • *adv* racionalment
rattle • *n* sacsejador *(m)*
raven • *n* corb *(m)*
raw • *adj* cru
ray • *n* raig *(m)*, raig, rajada
razor • *n* navalla *(f)*
reaction • *n* reacció *(f)*
reactionary • *n* reaccionari • *adj* reaccionari
read • *v* llegir, llegir-se, sentir, estudiar

reader • *n* lector *(m)*
ready • *adj* llest, disposat
reagent • *n* reactiu
realism • *n* realisme
realistic • *adj* realista
reality • *n* realitat *(f)*
realize • *v* adonar-se
really • *adv* realment
realm • *n* domini *(m)*
ream • *v* barrinar
reap • *v* segar
rearguard • *n* rereguarda *(f)*
reason • *v* raonar • *n* raó *(f)*
reasonable • *adj* raonable
reasonably • *adv* raonablement
reasoning • *n* raonament *(m)*
reassure • *v* tranquilůlitzar
rebel • *n* rebel *(f)*
rebellion • *n* rebelůlió *(f)*
rebellious • *adj* rebel
rebound • *v* rebotre • *n* rebot *(m)*
rebuild • *v* reconstruir
rebuke • *v* esbroncar, reprendre, reganyar • *n* reprensió *(f)*, esbroncada *(f)*, esbronc *(m)*
recall • *v* recordar
recapitulation • *n* recapitulació *(f)*
receipt • *n* rebut *(m)*, rebuda *(f)*
receive • *v* rebre
recent • *adj* fresc, recent
recently • *adv* recentment
receptive • *adj* receptiu
recessive • *adj* recessiu
recidivate • *v* reincidir
recipe • *n* recepta *(f)*
reciprocal • *adj* recíproc, mutu, al revés, a l'inrevés
recklessly • *adv* temeràriament
recollect • *v* recordar, rememorar
recollection • *n* record *(m)*
recommend • *v* recomanar
reconstruct • *v* reconstruir
reconstructed • *adj* reconstruit
recorder • *n* flauta dolça *(f)*
recovery • *n* recuperació *(f)*
recruitment • *n* reclutament
rectangle • *n* rectangle *(m)*
rectangular • *adj* rectangular
rectory • *n* rectoria *(f)*, abadia *(f)*
red • *n* vermell *(m)*, roig *(m)*, roja *(f)*, vi negre *(m)* • *adj* roig, vermell, pèl-roig
reddish • *adj* rogenc, vermellós
redheaded • *adj* pèl-roig
redness • *n* rojor *(f)*, vermellor *(f)*
redoubt • *n* reducte *(m)*
reduce • *v* reduir
redundancy • *n* redundància *(f)*

redundant • *adj* redundant
redwood • *n* sequoia *(f)*
reed • *n* canya *(f)*
reef • *n* escull *(m)*
refectory • *n* refectori *(m)*
referendum • *n* referèndum *(m)*
refill • *v* reomplir
refine • *v* refinar
refined • *adj* refinat
reflection • *n* reflexió *(f)*
refraction • *n* refracció *(f)*
refractometer • *n* refractòmetre *(m)*
refrigerate • *v* refrigerar
refrigerator • *n* frigorífic *(m)*
refuge • *v* refugiar-se • *n* refugi *(m)*
refugee • *n* refugiat *(m)*
refuse • *n* rebuig *(m)* • *v* refusar, rebutjar
refute • *v* refutar
regain • *v* reconquerir
regal • *adj* reial
regardless • *adv* malgrat tot
regime • *n* règim *(m)*
regiment • *n* regiment *(m)*
region • *n* regió *(f)*
regional • *adj* regional
regrettable • *adj* lamentable
regularity • *n* regularitat *(f)*
regularly • *adv* regularment
rehearsal • *n* assaig *(m)*
rehearse • *v* reproduir, assajar
reign • *v* regnar • *n* regnat *(m)*
reimburse • *v* reemborsar
reimbursement • *n* reemborsament
rein • *n* regna *(f)*
reindeer • *n* ren *(m)*
reinforcement • *n* reforç
reinstall • *v* reinstalŀlar
reiterate • *v* reiterar
reject • *v* rebutjar, refusar
rejection • *n* rebuig *(m)*, refús *(m)*
rejuvenation • *n* rejoveniment *(m)*
relationship • *n* relació *(f)*
relative • *n* parent • *adj* relatiu
relatively • *adv* relativament
relax • *v* relaxar, afluixar
relaxation • *n* relaxació
relaxed • *adj* relaxat
relay • *v* rellevar • *n* relé *(m)*, relleus
release • *v* alliberar, estrenar, publicar, llançar, amollar • *n* alliberament *(m)*, versió *(f)*, estrena *(f)*, alliberat *(m)*
relentless • *adj* implacable
relevance • *n* rellevància *(f)*
relevant • *adj* rellevant, pertinent *(f)*
reliability • *n* fiabilitat *(f)*
relief • *n* consol *(m)*, alleujament *(m)*, relleu *(m)*

relieved • *adj* alleujat
religion • *n* religió *(f)*
religious • *adj* religiós
religiously • *adv* religiosament
reliquary • *n* reliquiari *(m)*
reluctance • *n* reluctància
remain • *v* quedar-se, restar
remaining • *adj* romanent, restant, sobrer
remarkable • *adj* remarcable
remedy • *v* remeiar • *n* remei *(m)*, correcció *(f)*, correctiu *(m)*
remember • *v* recordar, rememorar
remembrance • *n* recordatori *(m)*, memòria *(f)*
remind • *v* recordar
remorse • *n* remordiment *(m)*
remote • *adj* remot
removable • *adj* desmuntable, extraïble
remove • *v* treure
remuneration • *n* remuneració *(f)*, compensació *(f)*
renewable • *adj* renovable
rent • *v* llogar • *n* lloguer *(m)*
reorganize • *v* reorganitzar
reparation • *n* reparació *(f)*
repeat • *v* repetir
repeatable • *adj* repetible
repeatedly • *adv* repetidament
repeater • *n* repetidor *(m)*
repel • *v* rebutjar, refusar, repelŀlir
repellent • *adj* repelŀlent
repent • *v* penedir-se
repetition • *n* repetició *(f)*
replace • *v* reemplaçar
replaceable • *adj* reemplaçable
replete • *adj* replet *(m)*, repleta *(f)*
report • *v* informar, notificar, fer saber, ser responsable, presentar-se • *n* informe *(m)*
represent • *v* representar
representation • *n* representació *(f)*
reproductive • *adj* reproductiu *(m)*, reproductor
reptile • *n* rèptil *(m)*
republic • *n* república *(f)*
republican • *adj* republicà
reputation • *n* reputació *(f)*
request • *v* demanar • *n* petició *(f)*, solŀlicitud *(f)*
requirement • *n* requisit *(m)*, menester *(m)*, exigència *(f)*
rescue • *v* rescatar • *n* rescat *(m)*
research • *n* recerca *(m)*, investigació *(m)*
resemblance • *n* semblança *(f)*
resemble • *v* semblar
reserved • *adj* reservat *(m)*
reside • *v* residir

residence • *n* residència *(f)*, seu social *(f)*

residential • *adj* residencial

resilient • *adj* elàstic, resistent

resin • *n* resina *(f)*, reïna *(f)*

resinous • *adj* resinós

resistance • *n* resistència *(f)*

resistant • *n* resistent *(m)* • *adj* resistent

resistible • *adj* resistible

resistor • *n* resistent *(m)*, resistència *(f)*

resolute • *adj* resolut

resolve • *v* resoldre, solucionar • *n* resolució *(f)*

resounding • *adj* ressonant

respectable • *adj* respectable

respectful • *adj* respectuós

respective • *adj* respectiu

respectively • *adv* respectivament

respiratory • *adj* respiratori

respite • *n* respir *(m)*

respond • *v* respondre

responsibility • *n* responsabilitat *(f)*

responsible • *adj* responsable

responsibly • *adv* responsablement

rest • *n* descans *(m)*, repòs *(m)*, resta *(f)* • *v* descansar, reposar

restaurant • *n* restaurant *(m)*

restless • *adj* intranquil, inquiet, desvetllat

restrict • *v* restringir

restrictive • *adj* restrictiu

result • *n* resultat *(m)*

resume • *v* reprendre

resurrection • *n* resurrecció *(f)*

reticent • *adj* reticent

retinue • *n* seguici *(m)*

retire • *v* jubilar

retort • *n* retorta *(f)*

retouch • *n* retoc *(m)*

retractable • *adj* retractable

retrieve • *v* recuperar

retrovirus • *n* retrovirus *(m)*

return • *v* tornar, restar

reveal • *v* revelar

reveille • *n* diana *(f)*

revel • *n* revetlla *(f)*

revelry • *n* xerinola *(f)*

revenge • *v* revenjar-se • *n* revenja *(m)*

revenue • *n* rèdit

reverberate • *v* reverberar

revere • *v* reverir, reverenciar

reverence • *n* reverència *(f)*

reverent • *adj* reverent

revocation • *n* revocació *(f)*

revolt • *v* revoltar • *n* revolta *(f)*

revolting • *adj* repugnant

revolution • *n* revolució *(f)*

revolutionary • *n* revolucionari • *adj* revolucionari

revolver • *n* revòlver *(m)*

reward • *v* recompensar

rewarding • *adj* gratificant

rhenium • *n* reni *(m)*

rhetorical • *adj* retòric

rheumatic • *n* reumàtic *(m)* • *adj* reumàtic

rhinoceros • *n* rinoceront *(m)*

rhizome • *n* rizoma *(m)*

rho • *n* ro *(f)*

rhodium • *n* rodi *(m)*

rhombohedral • *adj* romboèdric

rhombohedron • *n* romboedre *(m)*, rombòedre *(m)*

rhombus • *n* rombe *(m)*

rhyme • *v* rimar • *n* rima *(f)*

rhythm • *n* ritme *(m)*

rhythmically • *adv* rítmicament

rib • *n* costella *(f)*, quaderna *(f)*

ribbon • *n* cinta *(f)*

ribose • *n* ribosa *(f)*

rice • *n* arròs *(m)*

rich • *adj* ric

richness • *n* ricor *(f)*, riquesa *(f)*

rickets • *n* raquitisme *(m)*

ricochet • *v* retopar

ride • *v* muntar, cavalcar, colcar

ridiculous • *adj* ridícul

riff • *n* riff, melodia *(f)*

rifle • *n* fusell *(m)*, rifle *(m)*

rig • *n* aparell *(m)*

rigging • *n* eixàrcia *(f)*, cordam *(m)*

right • *n* dret *(m)* • *adj* dret

right-handed • *n* dretà

rigid • *adj* rígid

rigidity • *n* rigidesa *(f)*, rigiditat *(f)*

rigidly • *adv* rígidament

rigorously • *adv* rigorosament

rind • *n* crosta *(f)*, escorça *(f)*, closca *(f)*

ring • *n* cèrcol *(m)*, anell *(m)*, anella, rodanxa, ring, pista, cercle, corona, anell • *v* dringar, trucar, fer sonar

ringworm • *n* tinya *(f)*

rinse • *v* esbandir

ripe • *adj* madur

ripple • *v* onejar • *n* ona *(f)*

rise • *v* pujar

rising • *n* rebel·lular-se • *adj* creixent, ixent, naixent

risk • *v* arriscar • *n* risc *(m)*

rite • *n* ritus *(m)*

ritual • *adj* ritual *(f)*

rival • *n* rival

rivalry • *n* rivalitat *(f)*

river • *n* riu *(m)*

riverbed • *n* buc *(m)*

road • *n* carretera *(f)*, camí

roar • *v* rugir
roast • *adj* rostit
robber • *n* lladre *(f)*
robe • *n* hàbit *(m)*, toga *(f)*
robin • *n* pit-roig *(m)*
robotics • *n* robòtica *(f)*
rock • *n* quer *(m)*, roc *(m)*, roca *(f)*, pedra *(f)*, pedra preciosa *(f)*, rock
rocket • *n* coet *(m)*, ruca *(f)*
rococo • *n* rococó *(m)*
rod • *n* verga *(f)*
rodent • *n* rosegador
romantic • *adj* romàntic
romantically • *adv* romànticament
roof • *n* teulada *(f)*, sostre *(m)*
rook • *n* graula *(f)*, torre *(f)*
room • *n* espai *(m)*, lloc *(m)*, cambra *(f)*, sala *(f)*, habitació *(f)*, peça *(f)*, aposento
roommate • *n* company d'habitació *(m)*
roomy • *adj* espaiós
rooster • *n* gall *(m)*
root • *n* arrel *(f)*
rope • *n* corda *(f)*
rosary • *n* rosari
rose • *n* roser *(m)*, rosa *(f)* • *adj* rosat
rosemary • *n* romaní *(m)*, romer *(m)*
rot • *v* podrir
rotten • *adj* podrit *(m)*
rough • *adj* aspre, aproximat, quasi, difícil, rude *(f)*, tosc *(m)*
roulette • *n* ruleta *(f)*
round • *n* volta *(f)* • *adj* rodó
roundabout • *n* rotonda *(f)*, carrussel *(m)*, cavallets
rounded • *adj* arrodonit
route • *n* ruta *(f)*
routine • *adj* rutinari
row • *v* remar
rowan • *n* moixera de guilla *(f)*

rowing • *n* remant, rem *(m)*
royal • *adj* reial
rub • *v* fregar
rubber • *n* cautxú *(m)*, goma *(f)*, condó *(m)*, placa del llançador *(f)*
rubidium • *n* rubidi
ruby • *n* robí *(m)*
ruckus • *n* commoció *(f)*, aldarull *(m)*
rudder • *n* timó *(m)*
ruddy • *adj* rubicund *(m)*, rubicunda *(f)*
rude • *adj* rude *(m)*, bast *(m)*, obscè *(m)*, robust
rue • *n* ruda *(f)*
ruin • *n* ruïna
ruinous • *adj* ruïnós
rule • *v* manar, governar, regnar • *n* regla *(f)*, norma *(f)*
ruler • *n* regla *(f)*, líder, governant
rum • *n* rom *(m)*
ruminant • *n* remugant *(m)* • *adj* remugant
rumor • *n* rumor *(m)*
run • *v* córrer, fer córrer, fluir, escolar-se, fer fluir, funcionar, fer funcionar • *n* córrer, recorregut *(m)*, ruta *(f)*, galopar, carrera *(f)*
runner • *n* corredor *(m)*
runway • *n* pista *(f)*
rupture • *n* ruptura
rural • *adj* rural
rust • *v* rovellar, oxidar • *n* rovell *(m)*, òxid *(m)*
rustic • *adj* rústic
rusty • *adj* rovellat
ruthenium • *n* ruteni *(m)*
rutherfordium • *n* rutherfordi *(m)*
ruthlessly • *adv* sense pietat
rye • *n* sègoll *(m)*

S

sabotage • *v* sabotejar • *n* sabotatge *(m)*
saccharin • *n* sacarina *(f)*
sack • *v* acomiadar, destituir, despedir
sackbut • *n* sacabutx *(m)*
sacral • *adj* sacre
sacred • *adj* sagrat *(m)*
sacrifice • *v* sacrificar, oferir, sacrificar-se • *n* sacrifici *(m)*
sacrificial • *adj* sacrificial
sacrilege • *n* sacrilegi *(m)*
sacrilegious • *adj* sacríleg
sacrilegiously • *adv* sacrílegament
sacrosanct • *adj* sacrosant

sacrum • *n* sacre *(m)*
sad • *adj* trist *(m)*, trista *(f)*, trist, lamentable, deplorable, patètic
saddle • *n* sella *(f)*
saddlebag • *n* alforja *(f)*
sadistic • *adj* sàdic
sadly • *adv* tristament
sadness • *n* tristesa *(f)*
sadomasochistic • *adj* sadomasoquista
safe • *n* caixa forta *(f)* • *adj* segur, salv
safe-conduct • *n* salconduit *(m)*
safety • *n* seguretat *(f)*
saffron • *n* safranera *(f)*, safrà *(m)* • *adj*

safrà
saga • *n* saga *(f)*
sagacious • *adj* sagaç
sagacity • *n* sagacitat *(f)*
sage • *adj* savi • *n* sàlvia *(f)*
sail • *n* vela *(f)* • *v* navegar
sailor • *n* marí *(m)*
saint • *n* sant *(m)*, santa *(f)*
sainthood • *n* santedat *(f)*
salad • *n* amanida *(f)*
salary • *n* salari *(m)*, sou *(m)*
sale • *n* venda *(f)*
salesman • *n* venedor *(m)*
saline • *adj* salí
saliva • *n* saliva *(f)*
salmon • *n* salmó *(m)*
salt • *v* salar • *n* sal *(f)*
salty • *adj* salat
salvation • *n* salvació *(f)*
salve • *n* ungüent *(m)*, pomada *(f)*, bàlsam *(m)*
samarium • *n* samari *(m)*
same • *adj* mateix • *pron* mateix
sample • *n* mostra *(f)*, tast *(m)*
sampling • *n* mostratge *(m)*
sand • *n* sorra *(f)*, arena *(f)*, platja *(f)*
sandal • *n* sandàlia *(f)*
sandbox • *n* sorrera *(f)*
sandpiper • *n* territ *(m)*
sandwich • *n* entrepà *(m)*, sandvitx *(m)*, badall *(m)*
sandy • *adj* sorrenc, vermellós
sap • *n* saba *(f)*
sapling • *n* plançó *(m)*
sapper • *n* sapador
sapphire • *n* safir *(m)*
sarcasm • *n* sarcasme
sarcastic • *adj* sarcàstic
sarcastically • *adv* sarcàsticament
sarcophagus • *n* sarcòfag *(m)*
sartorius • *n* sartori *(m)*
satanic • *adj* satànic
satellite • *n* satèl·lit *(m)*
satiate • *v* saciar
satiety • *n* sacietat *(f)*
satirical • *adj* satíric
satirically • *adv* satíricament
satisfaction • *n* satisfacció *(f)*
satisfactorily • *adv* satisfactòriament
satisfactory • *adj* satisfactori
satisfied • *adj* satisfet
satisfy • *v* satisfer
saturated • *adj* saturat
satyr • *n* sàtir *(m)*
saucepan • *n* cassó *(m)*
sauerkraut • *n* xucrut *(f)*
sauna • *n* sauna *(f)*

sausage • *n* salsitxa *(f)*
savage • *n* salvatge *(f)* • *adj* salvatge
savagely • *adv* salvatgement
save • *v* salvar, desar, estalviar • *n* aturada *(f)*
savor • *v* assaborir
saw • *v* serrar • *n* serra *(f)*
sawdust • *n* serradures
sawmill • *n* serradora
saxophonist • *n* saxofonista *(f)*
say • *v* dir, recitar, declamar
saying • *n* dita *(f)*, proverbi *(m)*
scab • *n* crosta *(f)*
scabbard • *n* beina *(f)*
scaffolding • *n* bastida *(f)*
scalable • *adj* escalable
scales • *n* balança *(m)*
scallion • *n* ceba d'hivern *(f)*
scalp • *n* cuir cabellut *(m)*
scam • *v* estafar • *n* estafa *(f)*, enredada *(f)*
scan • *v* escanejar, escorcollar, escandir
scandal • *n* escàndol *(m)*
scandium • *n* escandi *(m)*
scaphoid • *adj* escafoide
scar • *n* cicatriu *(f)*
scarab • *n* escarabeu *(m)*
scarce • *adj* escàs
scarcity • *n* escassetat *(f)*, escassedat *(f)*, escassesa *(f)*
scare • *v* espantar, espaventar
scarecrow • *n* espantall *(m)*, babarota *(f)*, espantaocells *(m)*
scarf • *n* bufanda *(f)*
scenario • *n* escenari *(m)*
scene • *n* escena *(f)*
scenic • *adj* escènic
scent • *n* esència *(f)*, olfacte *(m)*
schedule • *n* horari *(m)*, programa *(m)*
schist • *n* esquist
schizophrenia • *n* esquizofrènia *(f)*
scholarship • *n* beca *(f)*
school • *n* banc *(m)*, mola de peix *(f)*, escola *(f)*
schoolmistress • *n* mestressa *(f)*
science • *n* ciència *(f)*
scientific • *adj* científic
scientifically • *adv* científicament
scientist • *n* científic *(m)*
scissor • *n* tisora *(f)*
scissors • *n* tisores
sclerometer • *n* escleròmetre *(m)*
scold • *n* renyir
scooter • *n* patinet *(m)*, escúter *(m)*
scope • *n* mira *(f)*
score • *v* marcar • *n* resultat *(m)*, partitura *(f)*
scorer • *n* golejador *(m)*

scorpion • *n* escorpí *(m)*
scratch • *v* rascar, esgarrapar, gratar, arpejar
screech • *n* grinyol
screen • *n* pantalla *(f)*, xarxa *(f)*
screw • *v* collar, fotre, follar • *n* bis *(m)*, cargol *(m)*, hèlice *(f)*
screwdriver • *n* tornavís *(m)*, desengramponador
screwed • *adj* fotut *(m)*, fastiguejat, putejat
script • *n* guió *(m)*
scrotal • *adj* escrotal
scrotum • *n* escrot *(m)*
scruff • *n* clotell *(m)*
scruffy • *adj* malgirbat
scrum • *n* melé *(f)*
scrutinize • *v* escrutar
sculptor • *n* escultor *(m)*, escultora *(f)*
sculptural • *adj* escultural
sculpture • *n* escultura *(f)*
scuttle • *v* barrinar
sea • *n* mar *(f)*
seal • *n* foca *(f)*, segell *(m)* • *v* segellar
seaman • *n* mariner *(m)*
seaplane • *n* hidroavió *(m)*
search • *v* inspeccionar, buscar, cercar
searcher • *n* cercador *(m)*
seascape • *n* marina
season • *v* condimentar, amanir • *n* estació *(f)*
seasonal • *adj* estacional
seat • *n* seu *(f)*
seaweed • *n* algues
sebaceous • *adj* sebaci
sebum • *n* sèu *(m)*
secluded • *adj* retirat
second • *n* segona *(f)*, segon *(m)*, moment *(m)*, instant *(m)* • *adj* segon, segon *(m)*
secondary • *adj* secundari *(m)*, secundària *(f)*
secondhand • *adj* segona mà
secrecy • *n* secretisme *(m)*
secret • *n* secret *(m)* • *adj* secret *(m)*
secrete • *v* secretar
secretin • *n* secretina *(f)*
secretion • *n* secreció *(f)*
secretly • *adv* secretament, cobertament, en secret
sect • *n* secta *(f)*
section • *n* secció *(f)*
secular • *adj* secular, laic
security • *n* seguretat *(f)*
sedative • *n* sedant • *adj* sedant
sedentary • *adj* sedentari
sedition • *n* sedició *(f)*
seductive • *adj* seductor

see • *v* veure • *n* seu *(f)*
seed • *n* llavor *(f)*
seem • *v* semblar, parèixer
segregate • *v* segregar
segregation • *n* segregació *(f)*
seismic • *adj* sísmic
seismograph • *n* sismògraf *(m)*
seismological • *adj* sismològic
seismologist • *n* sismòleg *(m)*
seismology • *n* sismologia *(f)*
seismometer • *n* sismòmetre *(m)*
seize • *v* apoderar-se
seizure • *n* apropiació *(f)*
seldom • *adv* rarament
select • *v* seleccionar
selection • *n* selecció *(f)*
selenium • *n* seleni *(m)*
self-awareness • *n* autognòsia *(f)*
self-control • *n* autocontrol *(m)*
self-criticism • *n* autocrítica *(f)*
self-defense • *n* autodefensa *(f)*
self-destructive • *adj* autodestructiu
self-determination • *n* autodeterminació *(f)*
self-discipline • *n* autodisciplina *(f)*
self-esteem • *n* autoestima *(f)*
self-pollination • *n* autopolůlinització *(f)*
self-sufficient • *adj* autosuficient
selfish • *adj* egoista
sell • *v* vendre
semantic • *adj* semàntic
semantics • *n* semàntica *(f)*
semaphore • *n* semàfor *(m)*
semen • *n* esperma *(f)*
semicircle • *n* semicercle *(m)*
semicolon • *n* punt i coma *(m)*
semiconductor • *n* semiconductor *(m)*
senary • *adj* senari *(m)*, senària *(f)*
senate • *n* senat *(m)*
senator • *n* senador *(m)*, senadora *(f)*
send • *v* enviar, trametre
senile • *adj* senil
senility • *n* senilitat *(f)*
sensational • *adj* sensacional
sensationalism • *n* sensacionalisme *(m)*
sensationalist • *adj* sensacionalista
sense • *v* sentir • *n* sentit *(m)*, sensació *(f)*, significat *(m)*, accepció *(f)*
sensible • *adj* sensat, assenyat
sensibly • *adv* assenyadament
sensory • *adj* sensorial, sensori
sensual • *adj* sensual
sentence • *n* sentència *(f)*, frase *(f)*
sentimental • *adj* sentimental
sentimentally • *adv* sentimentalment
separate • *v* separar • *adj* separat
separately • *adv* separadament

sepia • *n* sèpia *(f)* • *adj* sèpia
sepoy • *n* sipai *(m)*
septic • *adj* sèptic
septum • *n* septe *(m)*
sequence • *n* seqüència *(f)*
serac • *n* serac *(m)*
serene • *adj* serè
series • *n* sèrie *(f)*
serin • *n* gafarró *(m)*
serious • *adj* seriós
seriously • *adv* seriosament
seriousness • *n* serietat *(f)*
serotonin • *n* serotonina *(f)*
serpent • *n* serpent, serp, serpentó *(m)*
serum • *n* sèrum
serve • *v* servir • *n* servei *(m)*
service • *v* servir • *n* servei *(m)*
sesame • *n* sèsam *(m)*
sessile • *adj* sèssil
session • *n* sessió *(f)*
set • *v* posar, determinar, establir, fixar, ajustar, parar, introduir, assignar, pondre's • *n* aparell *(m)*, joc *(m)*, conjunt, grup *(m)*, plató *(m)*, set *(m)* • *adj* preparat, llest, establert
settlement • *n* assentament *(m)*
settler • *n* colon *(m)*
seven • *n* set *(m)*
seventeenth • *n* dissetè *(m)*
seventh • *n* setè *(m)*, sèptim *(m)*, sèptima *(f)* • *adj* setè *(m)*, sèptim *(m)*
severely • *adv* severament
sew • *v* cosir
sewer • *n* claveguera *(f)*
sex • *v* sexar • *n* sexe *(m)*
sexism • *n* sexisme *(m)*
sexist • *n* sexista *(f)* • *adj* sexista
sext • *n* sexta *(f)*
sextodecimo • *n* setzè *(m)*
sexton • *n* sagristà *(m)*
sexual • *adj* sexual
sexually • *adv* sexualment
shade • *n* ombra *(f)*
shadow • *n* ombra *(f)*
shaker • *n* sacsejador *(m)*
shale • *n* esquist *(m)*
shallow • *adj* pla, poc profund, superficial
shaman • *n* xaman *(m)*
shamanism • *n* xamanisme *(m)*
shame • *n* vergonya *(f)*, llàstima *(f)*
shameful • *adj* vergonyós, escadalós
shameless • *adj* desvergonyit
shampoo • *n* xampú *(m)*
shape • *v* formar
share • *v* compartir • *n* escot *(m)*, acció *(f)*
shared • *adj* compartit

shark • *n* tauró *(m)*
sharp • *adj* esmolat
shave • *v* afaitar, rapar, afaitar-se
shawm • *n* bombarda *(f)*
she • *pron* ella
sheaf • *n* garba *(f)*, feix *(m)*
shear • *v* tondre
shears • *n* tisores, cisalla *(f)*
shearwater • *n* baldriga *(f)*
sheath • *v* embeinar • *n* beina *(f)*, embolcall *(m)*
shed • *v* separar, vessar • *n* barraca *(f)*, carraca *(f)*
sheepskin • *n* badana *(f)*
sheet • *n* full *(m)*, escota *(f)*
sheik • *n* xeic
shelf • *n* prestatge *(m)*, estant *(m)*
shell • *n* closca *(f)*, conquilla *(f)*, conxa *(f)*, clovella *(f)*, buc *(m)*, consola *(f)*, terminal *(m)*
shellac • *n* goma laca *(f)*
shepherd • *n* pastor *(m)*
sherry • *n* xerès *(m)*
shield • *n* escut *(m)*
shine • *v* brillar, lluir • *n* brillantor *(f)*, lluentor *(f)*, lluïssor *(f)*
ship • *n* vaixell *(m)*, nau, nau *(f)*
shipwreck • *v* naufragar • *n* naufragi *(m)*
shipwrecked • *adj* nàufrag
shipyard • *n* drassana *(f)*
shirt • *n* camisa *(f)*
shit • *n* merda *(f)*, tifa *(f)*, excrement *(m)*, caca *(f)*, femta *(f)*, cagarro *(m)*, diarrea *(f)*, (una) merda • *adj* de merda • *v* cagar, cagar-se • *interj* merda
shock • *v* xocar • *n* xoc *(m)*
shoe • *v* ferrar • *n* sabata *(f)*, calçat *(m)*
shoemaker • *n* sabater *(m)*
shoot • *v* disparar
shooting • *n* tiroteig *(m)*, afusellament *(m)*
shop • *n* botiga *(f)*, tenda *(f)*
shopkeeper • *n* botiguer
shore • *n* riba *(f)*, vorera *(f)*, vora *(f)*
short • *adj* curt, baix
shortcoming • *n* defecte, mancança
shortcut • *n* drecera *(f)*, accés directe *(m)*, enllaç simbòlic *(m)*
shortly • *adv* aviat, breument, bruscament
shot • *n* cop *(m)*, llançament *(m)*
shotgun • *n* escopeta *(f)*
shoulder • *n* espatlla *(f)*, espatla *(f)*, muscle *(m)*, voral *(m)*, vorera d'emergència *(f)*
shove • *v* empentar, empentejar, espitjar, empènyer • *n* empenta *(f)*
shovel • *n* pala *(f)*

show • *v* mostrar, ensenyar, demostrar • *n* espectacle *(m)*
shower • *v* dutxar-se • *n* dutxa *(f)*
shred • *v* trocejar, tallar, triturar, trinxar
shrew • *n* musaranya *(f)*
shrike • *n* capsigrany *(m)*, capsot *(m)*, botxí *(m)*, escorxador *(m)*, trenca *(f)*
shrimp • *n* gamba *(f)*
shrub • *n* arbust *(m)*
shrug • *n* encongiment d'espatlles
shuffle • *v* mesclar, barrejar, barallar
shutter • *n* porticó *(m)*, finestró *(m)*
shuttlecock • *n* volant *(m)*
shy • *adj* vergonyós
shyly • *adv* tímidament
si • *n* si *(m)*
sibling • *n* germà *(m)*, germana *(f)*
sickle • *n* falç *(f)*
sickly • *adj* malaltís, malaltós, malaltús
side • *n* costat *(m)*
sideline • *n* línia de banda *(f)*
sidewalk • *n* vorera *(f)*
siege • *n* setge *(m)*
siesta • *n* sesta *(f)*, migdiada *(f)*, becada *(f)*
sieve • *v* filtrar, colar • *n* garbell *(m)*, sedàs *(m)*, colador *(m)*
sigh • *v* sospirar • *n* sospir *(m)*
sigma • *n* sigma *(f)*
sign • *n* senyal
signal • *n* senyal *(m)*
signature • *n* signatura *(f)*, quadern *(m)*
significance • *n* significat *(m)*
significant • *adj* significatiu
significantly • *adv* significativament
silence • *n* silenci *(m)*
silent • *adj* callar
silently • *adv* silenciosament
silhouette • *n* silueta *(f)*
silicate • *n* silicat *(m)*
silicon • *n* silici
silicone • *n* silicona *(f)*
silk • *n* seda *(f)*
silkworm • *n* cuc de seda *(m)*
silky • *adj* sedós
sill • *n* ampit *(m)*, llindar
silly • *adj* ximple, ximplet, fava
silo • *n* sitja *(f)*
silt • *n* llim *(m)*
silver • *n* plata *(f)*, argent *(m)* • *adj* plate-jat, argentat
silvery • *adj* argentat
similar • *adj* similar, semblant
similarity • *n* semblança *(f)*, similitud *(f)*
similarly • *adv* semblantment
simple • *adj* simple, senzill
simplex • *adj* símplex

simplification • *n* simplificació *(f)*
simply • *adv* simplement, senzillament
simulacrum • *n* simulacre *(m)*
simulation • *n* simulació *(f)*, fingiment *(m)*, teatre *(m)*, comèdia
simultaneous • *adj* simultani
simultaneously • *adv* simultàniament
sin • *v* pecar • *n* pecat *(m)*
since • *conj* des que, des de que, ja que, com que • *prep* des de
sincere • *adj* sincer
sincerely • *adv* sincerament
sincerity • *n* sinceritat *(f)*
sine • *n* sinus *(m)*
sing • *v* cantar
singable • *adj* cantable
singer • *n* cantant *(f)*, cantor *(m)*, cantaire *(f)*
single • *n* single *(m)*, batada d'una base *(f)* • *adj* simple, escàpol
singles • *n* individuals
singlet • *n* samarreta *(f)*
singular • *n* singular *(m)* • *adj* singular, únic
sink • *v* enfonsar, submergir-se • *n* pica *(f)*, lavabo *(m)*, desaigua *(m)*
sinner • *n* pecador *(m)*
sinus • *n* si *(m)*
sip • *v* xarrupar • *n* glop *(m)*
siren • *n* sirena *(f)*
sirocco • *n* xaloc *(m)*
sister • *n* germana *(f)*, sor *(f)*, infermera *(f)*
sit • *v* seure, asseure's
sit-in • *n* tancada *(f)*
situated • *adj* situat
six • *n* sis *(m)*
sixteenth • *n* setzè *(m)*
sixth • *n* sisè *(m)*, sext *(m)*, sexta *(f)* • *adj* sisè *(m)*, sext *(m)*
sizzle • *v* espurnejar
skate • *v* patinar • *n* patí *(m)*
skateboard • *n* monopatí *(m)*
skating • *n* patinatge *(m)*
skeletal • *adj* esquelètic
skeleton • *n* esquelet *(m)*, estructura *(f)*
skeptic • *n* escèptic *(m)*
skeptical • *adj* escèptic
skepticism • *n* escepticisme
sketch • *n* esbós *(m)*, esbossos, esborrany *(m)*, esquetx *(m)*
skewer • *n* broqueta *(f)*
ski • *n* esquí
skier • *n* esquiador *(m)*
skiing • *n* esquí *(m)*
skill • *n* habilitat *(f)*
skillful • *adj* hàbil *(f)*

skin • *v* escorxar • *n* pell *(f)*
skinner • *n* escorxador *(m)*
skinny • *adj* magre
skirmish • *v* escaramussar • *n* escaramussa *(f)*
skirt • *n* faldilla *(f)*
skull • *n* crani *(m)*
skunk • *n* mofeta *(f)*
sky • *n* cel *(m)*
skylark • *n* alosa *(f)*
skylight • *n* claraboia, lluerna
skyscraper • *n* gratacel *(m)*
slab • *n* placa *(f)*, tauló *(m)*, llosa *(f)*
slam • *v* esmaixar • *n* esmaixada *(f)*
slander • *v* calumniar, injuriar • *n* calúmnia *(f)*, injúria *(f)*
slang • *n* argot *(m)*
slap • *n* bufetada *(f)*
slapdash • *adj* barroer *(m)* • *adv* barroerament
slapstick • *n* fuet *(m)*
slave • *n* esclau *(m)*, esclava *(f)*
slavery • *n* esclavitud *(f)*, esclavatge *(m)*
sledge • *n* trineu *(m)*
sleep • *v* dormir • *n* son *(m)*
sleeper • *n* dormilega *(m)*, travessa *(f)*
sleeping • *n* dormint *(m)*
sleepwalking • *n* somnambulisme *(m)*
sleepy • *adj* somnolent
sleet • *n* aiguaneu *(f)*
sleeve • *n* màniga *(f)*, mànega *(f)*
slice • *n* llesca *(f)*
slide • *n* tobogan *(m)*
slightly • *adv* lleugerament
slim • *adj* prim
slip • *n* engalba *(f)*, relliscada *(f)*, combinació *(f)*
slipper • *n* plantofa *(f)*, sabatilla *(f)*
slippery • *adj* lliscant
slogan • *n* eslògan *(m)*
sloop • *n* sloop *(m)*
slot • *n* màquina escurabutxaques *(f)*
sloth • *n* accídia *(f)*, peresa *(f)*, mandra *(f)*,
peresós *(m)*
slow • *adj* lent
slowly • *adv* lentament
slowness • *n* lentitud *(f)*
slug • *n* llimac *(m)*
sluice • *n* àbac *(m)*
slump • *n* depressió *(m)*
small • *adj* petit
smallpox • *n* verola *(f)*, pigota *(f)*
smash • *n* esmaixada *(f)*
smear • *v* escampar, untar, empastifar
smell • *v* olorar, odorar, ensumar, flairar,
fer olor a • *n* olor *(f)*, flaire *(f)*, olfacte *(m)*
smile • *v* somriure • *n* somrís *(m)*, somri-

ure *(m)*
smiling • *adj* somrient
smith • *n* ferrer *(m)*, ferrera *(f)*
smog • *n* boirum *(m)*
smoke • *v* fumar, fumejar • *n* fum *(m)*
smoker • *n* fumador *(m)*
smooth • *v* allisar • *adj* llis
smother • *v* asfixiar
smug • *adj* ufà, petulant
smuggler • *n* contrabandista
snail • *n* caragol *(m)*
snake • *n* serp *(f)*, serpent *(f)*
snap • *n* esnap *(m)*
sneer • *n* somriure de menyspreu *(m)*,
somriure d'escarni *(m)*
sneeze • *v* esternudar • *n* esternut *(m)*
snipe • *n* becadell *(m)*
sniper • *n* franctirador *(m)*
snippet • *n* fragment
snood • *n* moc *(m)*
snooker • *n* billar *(m)*
snoop • *n* dotoreig *(m)*, dotor *(m)*
snore • *v* roncar
snout • *n* musell, morro *(m)*, nas *(m)*,
nàpia *(f)*
snow • *v* nevar • *n* neu *(f)*, neu
snowball • *n* bola de neu *(f)*
snowman • *n* ninot de neu
so • *adj* això, açò • *adv* tan, així • *interj*
així, doncs • *conj* perquè, així que
soak • *v* amarar, penetrar
soap • *n* sabó *(m)*
sober • *adj* sobri
soccer • *n* futbol *(m)*
sociable • *adj* sociable
social • *adj* social
socialism • *n* socialisme *(m)*
socialist • *n* socialista *(f)* • *adj* socialista
socially • *adv* socialment
society • *n* societat *(f)*
sociological • *adj* sociològic
sociologist • *n* sociòleg *(m)*
sociology • *n* sociologia *(f)*
sock • *n* mitjó *(m)*
sodium • *n* sodi *(m)*
sodomite • *n* sodomita *(m)*
sodomy • *n* sodomia *(f)*
sofa • *n* sofà *(m)*
soft • *adj* tou, suau, dolç, lleuger
softball • *n* softbol *(m)*
softly • *adv* suaument
software • *n* programari *(m)*
soil • *n* sòl *(m)*
sojourn • *n* estada *(f)*
sol • *n* sol *(m)*
solace • *n* consol
soldier • *n* soldat

sole • *adj* sol, solter • *n* planta del peu (f), sola (f)

solemn • *adj* solemne

solemnity • *n* solemnitat (f)

solemnly • *adv* solemnement

solid • *n* sòlid (m) • *adj* sòlid

solidify • *v* solidificar

solidly • *adv* sòlidament

solidus • *n* sòlid (m)

soliloquy • *n* soliloqui (m)

solitaire • *n* Solitari (m) • *adj* solitari

solitary • *n* solitari (m) • *adj* solitari

solitude • *n* solitud (f)

solstice • *n* solstici (m)

soluble • *adj* soluble

solute • *n* solut (m)

solve • *v* resoldre, solucionar

somebody • *pron* algú

something • *pron* alguna cosa, quelcom

sometimes • *adv* a vegades, de vegades

somnambulism • *n* somnambulisme (m)

son • *n* fill (m)

son-in-law • *n* gendre (m)

sonar • *n* sonar (m)

song • *n* cançó (f)

songbook • *n* cançoner (m)

songwriter • *n* compositor de cançons (m), compositora de cançons (f)

sonic • *adj* sònic

sonnet • *n* sonet

soon • *adv* aviat

soot • *n* estalzí, sutge (m), sutja (f)

soothe • *v* calmar

soporific • *n* somnífer (m), hipnòtic (m), soforífic (m), narcòtic (m) • *adj* soporífer, soporífic, narcòtic, somnífer, hipnòtic

soprano • *n* soprano (f)

sorcerer • *n* mag (m), màgic (m), fetiller (m)

sordid • *adj* sòrdid

sore • *adj* adolorit

sorghum • *n* melca (f)

sorrowfully • *adv* apesaradament

sorry • *adj* afligit, llastimós • *interj* perdó, disculpes

sort • *n* tipus (m), gènere (m), classe (f), varietat (f), mena (f), mena • *v* classificar, ordenar, arreglar, reparar

soul • *n* ànima (f)

sound • *adj* sa, sòlid • *v* sonar • *n* so

soundtrack • *n* banda sonora (f)

sour • *adj* àcid, agre

sourly • *adv* agrament

south • *n* sud (m), migdia (m), migjorn (m)

southeast • *n* sud-est (m)

souvenir • *n* record (m)

sovereign • *n* sobirà (m) • *adj* sobirà

sovereignty • *n* sobirania (f)

sow • *n* truja (f), porca (f), verra (f) • *v* sembrar

soy • *n* soia (f), soja (f)

spacecraft • *n* nau espacial

spaceship • *n* nau espacial (f), astronau (f)

spacetime • *n* espai-temps

spacious • *adj* espaiós

spaghetti • *n* espagueti (m), laberint (m)

spam • *n* correu brossa (m)

span • *n* pam (m), període

sparingly • *adv* parcament

spark • *n* espurna (f), guspira (f)

sparrow • *n* pardal (m)

sparse • *adj* dispers, espars, clar, escàs

spasmodic • *adj* espasmòdic

spat • *n* polaina (f)

spatula • *n* espàtula (f)

spawn • *n* fresa (f)

speak • *v* parlar

speaker • *n* parlant (f), altaveu (m)

spear • *n* llança (f)

special • *adj* especial

specialist • *n* especialista (f)

specially • *adv* especialment

specialty • *n* especialitat (f)

specie • *n* espècie (f)

species • *n* espècie (f)

specific • *adj* específic (m)

specifically • *adv* específicament

specify • *v* especificar

spectacles • *n* ulleres

spectacular • *adj* espectacular

spectroscopy • *n* espectroscòpia (f)

spectrum • *n* espectre (m)

speculation • *n* especulació (f)

speculative • *adj* especulatiu

speech • *n* parla (f), discurs (m)

speechless • *adj* bocabadat, emmudit

speed • *n* rapidesa (f), velocitat (f)

speedometer • *n* velocímetre (m)

speedy • *adj* ràpid (m), veloç (m)

spell • *n* encís (m), conjur (m), embruixament (m), encantament (m) • *v* lletrejar

spellbound • *adj* embadalit

spelt • *n* espelta (f)

spend • *v* gastar, passar

sperm • *n* esperma (f)

sphere • *n* esfera (f)

spherical • *adj* esfèric

spherometer • *n* esferòmetre (m)

sphincter • *n* esfínter (m)

sphinx • *n* esfinx (m)

sphygmomanometer • *n* esfigmomanòmetre (m)

spice • *n* espècia *(f)*
spicy • *adj* picant
spider • *n* aranya *(f)*
spigot • *n* tap *(m)*, aixeta *(f)*
spike • *n* urpa *(f)*, espiga
spill • *v* vessar
spin • *n* espín *(m)*, efecte *(m)*
spinach • *n* espinac *(m)*
spindle • *n* fus
spine • *n* espinada *(f)*, raquis *(m)*, llom *(m)*, espina *(f)*
spinel • *n* espinel
spinet • *n* espineta *(f)*
spiral • *n* espiral *(f)*
spire • *n* cuculla, agulla
spirit • *n* esperit *(m)*
spiritual • *adj* espiritual
spirituality • *n* espiritualitat *(f)*
spirometer • *n* espiròmetre *(m)*
spit • *v* escopir
spite • *n* despit
spiteful • *adj* maliciós, rancuniós
splay • *n* esplandit *(m)*
spleen • *n* melsa *(f)*
splendid • *adj* esplèndid
splinter • *n* estella
split • *v* partir, dividir, escindir, repartir, separar • *n* banyes
spoil • *v* espoliar
spoiler • *n* filtració *(f)*
spoilsport • *n* aixafaguitarres
spokesperson • *n* portaveu *(m)*
sponge • *v* esponjar • *n* esponja *(f)*
spongy • *adj* esponjós
spontaneity • *n* espontaneïtat *(f)*
spontaneously • *adv* espontàniament
spoon • *n* cullera *(f)*
spoonerism • *n* contrapet *(m)*
spoonful • *n* cullerada *(f)*
sporadic • *adj* esporàdic
sporadically • *adv* esporàdicament
spore • *n* espora *(f)*
sport • *n* esport *(m)*, deport *(m)*
spot • *n* taca *(f)*
spouse • *n* cònjuge, espòs *(m)*, esposa *(f)*
spout • *n* broc *(m)*, raig *(m)*, brollador *(m)*
sprain • *n* torçada *(f)*
spring • *v* saltar • *n* primavera *(f)*, font, molla *(f)*, ressort *(m)*
sprinkle • *v* ruixar, arruixar
sprinkler • *n* ruixador *(m)*, arruixador *(m)*
sprite • *n* follet *(m)*
sprout • *v* germinar, brollar
spruce • *n* avet roig
spunk • *n* escorreguda *(f)*
spur • *v* esperonar • *n* esperó *(m)*

spurious • *adj* espuri, fals, bastard
spurt • *n* raig
spy • *v* espiar • *n* espia *(f)*
square • *v* quadrar • *n* quadrat *(m)*, plaça *(f)* • *adj* quadrat
squash • *n* esquaix *(m)*
squeeze • *v* esprémer, estrènyer, serrar, apretar
squid • *n* calamars *(m)*, calamar *(m)*
squinch • *n* trompa *(f)*
squire • *n* escuder
squirrel • *n* esquirol *(m)*
stab • *v* apunyalar, acoltellar • *n* punyalada *(f)*, ganivetada *(f)*
stability • *n* estabilitat *(f)*
stable • *n* estable *(m)* • *adj* estable
stadium • *n* estadi *(m)*
staff • *n* bastó *(m)*, pentagrama *(m)*, staff *(m)*, plantilla *(f)*
stage • *n* pas, estadi, fase, etapa *(f)*, escena *(f)*, escenari *(m)*
stagger • *n* titubar, titubejar
stagnant • *adj* estancat *(m)*, estancada *(f)*
stagnation • *n* estancament *(m)*, estacament *(m)*
stain • *n* taca
staircase • *n* escala *(f)*
stairs • *n* escala *(f)*
stake • *n* pal *(m)*, estaca *(f)*
stakeholder • *n* part interessada *(f)*
stalactite • *n* estalactita *(f)*, caramell *(m)*
stalagmite • *n* estalagmita *(f)*
stamen • *n* estam *(m)*
stammer • *v* titubar, titubejar
stamp • *v* estampar, segellar • *n* segell *(m)*
stand • *v* estar dret, posar-se dret, suportar
standard • *n* estàndard, estendard • *adj* estàndard
stapes • *n* estrep *(m)*
staple • *n* grapa *(f)*
stapler • *n* engrapadora *(f)*
star • *n* estrella *(f)*, estel *(m)*
starboard • *n* estribor
starch • *v* emmidonar • *n* midó *(m)*, midó
stare • *v* mirar fixament
starfish • *n* estrella de mar *(f)*
starling • *n* estornell
starry • *adj* estelat
state • *v* declarar • *n* estat *(m)*
static • *adj* estàtic
station • *v* apostar • *n* estació *(f)*
stationary • *adj* estacionari, immòbil
stationery • *n* papereria *(f)*
statue • *n* estàtua *(f)*
stature • *n* estatura *(f)*, talla *(f)*

staunch • *adj* acèrrim

stay • *v* quedar-se, restar

steal • *v* robar • *n* robatori *(m)*

stealth • *n* furtivitat *(f)*

steel • *n* acer *(m)*

steeple • *n* campanar *(m)*

steer • *v* castrar, capar, guiar, dirigir, manejar, dur

steganography • *n* esteganografia *(f)*

stegosaur • *n* estegosaure *(m)*

stele • *n* estela

step • *n* pas *(m)*, esglaó *(m)*, petjada *(f)*

stepbrother • *n* germanastre *(m)*

stepdaughter • *n* fillastra *(f)*

stepfather • *n* padrastre *(m)*

stepmother • *n* madrastra *(f)*

steppe • *n* estepa *(f)*

stepson • *n* fillastre *(m)*

stereotype • *n* estereotip *(m)*

sterile • *adj* estèril

sterilization • *n* esterilització *(f)*

sterilize • *v* esterilitzar

sterling • *n* lliura *(f)*, lliura esterlina *(f)* • *adj* esterlí

stern • *adj* sever • *n* popa *(f)*

sternal • *adj* esternal

steward • *n* administrador *(m)*, representant *(m)*, apoderat *(m)*, hostessa *(f)*, cambrer d'avions *(m)*

stewardess • *n* hostessa *(f)*

stick • *n* garrot *(m)*, bastó *(m)*, barra *(f)*, estic *(m)* • *v* enganxar, apegar

stiff • *adj* rígid, encarcarat

stigmatize • *v* estigmatitzar

still • *adj* quiet • *adv* encara

stillborn • *adj* nascut mort *(m)*

stillness • *n* calma *(f)*

stilt • *n* xanca *(f)*

stimulant • *n* estimulant *(m)*, estimulador *(m)*

stimulation • *n* estimulació *(f)*

stingray • *n* dasyatis

stingy • *adj* garrepa, aferrat

stir • *v* remoure • *n* avalot *(m)*, gatzara *(f)*, cridòria, esvalot *(m)*, aldarull *(m)*, rebombori *(m)*, esvalot

stirrup • *n* estrep *(m)*

stitch • *n* punt *(m)*

stochastic • *adj* estocàstic

stocky • *adj* rabassut

stoical • *adj* estoic

stoke • *v* atiar

stole • *n* estola *(f)*

stomach • *n* estómac *(m)*

stone • *n* pedra *(f)*, roca *(f)* • *adj* petri, pedrenc

stool • *n* tamboret *(m)*

stop • *v* parar, aturar, deixar • *n* parada *(f)*, punt *(m)*

stoppage • *n* aturada *(f)*, bloqueig *(m)*

store • *v* emmagatzemar

stork • *n* cigonya

storm • *n* tempesta *(f)*, temporal *(m)*, tempestat *(f)*

stormy • *adj* tempestuós

stove • *n* estufa *(f)*, cuina *(f)*

straight • *n* escala *(f)*

straighten • *v* adreçar, redreçar

strain • *v* colar

strainer • *n* colador *(m)*

strand • *n* platja *(f)*

strange • *adj* estrany

strangely • *adv* estranyament

stranger • *n* desconegut *(m)*, foraster *(m)*, estranger *(m)*

strangle • *v* estrangular

strangulation • *n* estrangulació *(f)*

strategic • *adj* estratègic

strategically • *adv* estratègicament

strategy • *n* estratègia *(f)*

stratosphere • *n* estratosfera *(f)*

stratum • *n* estrat *(m)*

stratus • *n* estratus *(m)*, estrat *(m)*

straw • *n* palla *(f)*

strawberry • *n* maduixa *(f)*, freula *(f)*, maduixer *(m)*, maduixera *(f)*

stream • *n* corrent, rierol

street • *n* carrer *(m)*

streetlight • *n* farola *(f)*

strength • *n* força *(f)*, fort *(m)*

stress • *v* estressar • *n* tensió *(f)*, estrès *(m)*, accent *(m)*, èmfasi *(m)*

stressed • *adj* estressat, tònic

stretch • *v* estirar

strike • *n* ple *(m)*, vaga *(f)*

striker • *n* vaguista *(f)*

string • *n* corda *(f)*, cordill, cordell *(m)*

striped • *adj* ratllat, llistat

stroke • *n* carícia *(f)*, cop *(m)*

stroll • *v* passejar-se, passejar • *n* passeig *(m)*, passejada *(f)*

strong • *adj* fort • *adv* fort

stronghold • *n* fortalesa *(f)*

strongly • *adv* fort

strontium • *n* estronci

structural • *adj* estructural

structure • *n* estructura *(f)*

struggle • *n* lluita *(f)*

stub • *n* esborrany

stubborn • *adj* tossut

stubbornly • *adv* tossudament

stucco • *n* estuc *(m)*

stuck • *adj* encallat

student • *n* estudiant *(f)*

study • *v* estudiar • *n* estudi *(m)*
stun • *v* atordir, entebenar
stupid • *adj* toix *(m)*, estúpid *(m)*, bèstia *(f)*
stupidity • *n* estupidesa *(f)*
stupidly • *adv* estúpidament
sturdy • *adj* robust
stutter • *v* quequejar, tartamudejar • *n* quequeig *(m)*
subatomic • *adj* subatòmic
subconscious • *n* subconscient *(m)*, subconsciència *(f)* • *adj* subconscient
subcontinent • *n* subcontinent *(m)*
subcutaneous • *adj* subcutani
subject • *adj* subjecte • *n* subjecte *(m)*, matèria *(f)*, assignatura *(f)*, súbdit *(m)*
subjective • *adj* subjectiu
subjectively • *adv* subjectivament
subjectivity • *n* subjectivitat *(f)*
subjugate • *v* subjugar
sublease • *v* sotsarrendar, rellogar • *n* sotsarrendament *(m)*
sublime • *adj* sublim
submarine • *n* submarí *(m)* • *adj* submarí *(m)*
submerge • *v* submergir
submit • *v* sotmetre's, sotmetre, presentar
suborder • *n* subordre *(m)*
subscribe • *v* subscriure's
subsequent • *adj* subsegüent
subsequently • *adv* subseqüentment
subsidize • *v* subvencionar
subsidy • *n* subsidi *(m)*, subvenció *(m)*
subsoil • *n* subsòl *(m)*
substance • *n* substància *(f)*
substitute • *v* substituir, canviar • *n* substitut *(m)*
substrate • *n* substrat *(m)*
substratum • *n* substrat *(m)*
subterranean • *adj* subterrani
subtitle • *n* subtítol *(m)*, subtítols
subtle • *adj* subtil
subtlety • *n* subtilesa *(f)*
subtly • *adv* subtilment
subtraction • *n* sostracció *(f)*, subtracció *(f)*
suburb • *n* suburbi *(m)*
suburban • *n* suburbà
subway • *n* metro *(m)*
success • *n* èxit *(m)*
successful • *adj* exitós
successive • *adj* successiu
successively • *adv* successivament
succinct • *adj* succint
succinctly • *adv* succintament
succor • *n* socors

succubus • *n* súcub *(m)*, súcube *(m)*
succulent • *adj* suculent
suck • *v* xuclar
sucker • *n* tany *(m)*
suckle • *v* alletar
sucrose • *n* sacarosa *(f)*
sudden • *adj* sobtat
suddenly • *adv* de sobte, sobtadament, tot d'una
suffer • *v* sofrir, patir, empitjorar
suffering • *n* patiment *(m)*
sufficient • *adj* suficient
sufficiently • *adv* suficientment
suffocate • *v* ofagar, sufocar, ofegar-se, ofegar
sugar • *n* sucre *(m)*, ploma *(f)*
suggestion • *n* suggeriment *(m)*, suggestió *(f)*
suicide • *n* suïcidi *(m)*
suit • *n* vestit *(m)*
suitable • *adj* apropiat
sulfur • *n* sofre *(m)*
sultry • *adj* xafogós *(m)*, xafogosa *(f)*, tòrrid *(m)*, calent *(m)*
sumac • *n* sumac *(m)*
summarily • *adv* sumàriament, breument
summarize • *v* resumir, recapitular
summary • *n* resum *(m)*, sumari *(m)* • *adj* sumari
summer • *v* estiuejar • *n* estiu *(m)*
summit • *n* cim *(m)*, cimera *(f)*
summon • *v* cridar, citar
sumptuous • *adj* sumptuós
sun • *n* sol *(m)*
sundial • *n* rellotge de sol *(m)*
sunfish • *n* centràrquid *(m)*, bot, peix lluna, mola
sunflower • *n* gira-sol *(m)*, mira-sol *(m)*
sunglasses • *n* ulleres de sol
sunny • *adj* asolellat, radiant
sunrise • *n* sortida de sol *(f)*
sunset • *n* posta de sol *(f)*
sunshade • *n* para-sol *(m)*
superb • *adj* soberg
superego • *n* superjò *(m)*, superego *(m)*
superficial • *adj* superficial
superficially • *adv* superficialment
superfluous • *adj* superflu
superfluously • *adv* supèrfluament
superior • *adj* superior
superiority • *n* superioritat *(f)*
superlative • *adj* superlatiu
supermarket • *n* supermercat *(m)*
supernatural • *adj* sobrenatural
supersede • *v* substituir, reemplaçar
superstition • *n* superstició *(f)*
superstitious • *adj* supersticiós

superstitiously • *adv* supersticiosament
supper • *v* sopar • *n* sopar *(m)*
supplement • *v* suplementar, complementar
supplementary • *adj* suplementari
supply • *v* fornir, subministrar, proveir
support • *v* sostenir, recolzar
suppose • *v* suposar
suppository • *n* supositori *(m)*
supremacy • *n* supremacia *(f)*
supreme • *adj* suprem
sure • *adj* segur
surely • *adv* segurament
surface • *n* superfície *(f)*
surfboard • *n* planxa de surf *(f)*
surfer • *n* surfista *(f)*
surgeon • *n* cirurgià
surgery • *n* cirurgia *(f)*, operació *(f)*, quiròfan *(m)*
surgical • *adj* quirúrgic
surgically • *adv* quirúrgicament
surname • *n* cognom *(m)*
surplus • *n* superàvit *(m)*
surprise • *v* sorprendre • *n* sorpresa *(f)*
surprising • *adj* sorprenent
surprisingly • *adv* sorprenentment
surrealism • *n* surrealisme *(m)*
surrogate • *n* suplent *(m)*, substitut *(m)*
surround • *v* circumdar, rodejar, envoltar, voltar
surrounding • *adj* circumdant
surveyor • *n* agrimensor *(f)*
survive • *v* sobreviure
survivor • *n* supervivent *(f)*
susceptibility • *n* susceptibilitat *(f)*
susceptible • *adj* susceptible
sushi • *n* sushi
suspect • *v* sospitar • *adj* sospitós
suspicion • *n* sospita *(f)*
suspicious • *adj* sospitós, suspicaç
suspiciously • *adv* sospitosament
sustain • *v* sostenir
sustainable • *adj* sostenible
swallow • *v* engolir, enviar • *n* engoliment, oreneta *(f)*
swamp • *n* pantà *(m)*
swan • *n* cigne *(m)*
swarm • *n* eixam *(m)*
swastika • *n* esvàstica *(f)*, creu gammada *(f)*
swear • *v* jurar
sweat • *n* suor *(f)* • *v* suar
sweatshirt • *n* dessuadora *(f)*
sweep • *v* escombrar
sweeper • *n* defensa lliure *(f)*
sweet • *n* dolç *(m)*, llaminadura *(f)* • *adj* dolç, dolç *(m)*, ensucrat *(m)* • *adv* dolçament

sweeten • *v* endolcir
sweetly • *adv* dolçament
sweetness • *n* dolçor *(f)*
sweets • *n* caramels, llaminadures, dulces
swell • *v* inflar-se, rebotir, unflar-se • *adj* excelůlent *(f)*
swift • *n* falciot *(m)* • *adj* ràpid
swim • *v* nedar
swimmer • *n* nedador *(m)*, nedadora *(f)*
swimming • *n* natació *(f)*
swimsuit • *n* vestit de bany *(m)*, banyador *(m)*
swing • *v* engronsar, balancejar • *n* gronxador *(m)*
swirl • *n* remolí
switch • *n* interruptor *(m)*, agulla *(f)*, opció *(f)*
sword • *n* espasa *(f)*
swordfish • *n* peix espasa *(m)*
swordsman • *n* espadatxí *(m)*
syllabic • *adj* silůlàbic
syllable • *n* sílůlaba *(f)*
syllogism • *n* silůlogisme *(m)*
symbiosis • *n* simbiosi *(f)*
symbiotic • *adj* simbiòtic
symbol • *n* símbol *(m)*
symbolic • *adj* simbòlic
symbolically • *adv* simbòlicament
symbolism • *n* simbolisme *(m)*
symbolize • *v* simbolitzar
symmetrical • *adj* simètric
symmetrically • *adv* simètricament
symmetry • *n* simetria *(f)*
sympathetic • *adj* simpàtic
sympathy • *n* compassió *(f)*, empatia *(f)*, simpatia *(f)*
symptom • *n* símptoma *(m)*
symptomatic • *adj* simptomàtic
synagogue • *n* sinagoga *(f)*
synapse • *n* sinapsi *(f)*
synchronize • *v* sincronitzar
synclinal • *n* sinclinal *(m)*
syndrome • *n* síndrome *(f)*
synecdoche • *n* sinècdoque *(f)*
synod • *n* sínode *(m)*
synonym • *n* sinònim *(m)*
synonymous • *adj* sinònim
synopsis • *n* sinopsi *(f)*
syntactic • *adj* sintàctic
syntactically • *adv* sintàcticament
syntax • *n* sintaxi *(f)*
synthesis • *n* síntesi *(f)*
synthesizer • *n* sintetitzador *(m)*
syringe • *n* xeringa *(f)*
syrup • *n* xarop *(m)*

system • *n* sistema *(m)*
systematic • *adj* sistemàtic

systematically • *adv* sistemàticament

T

table • *n* taula *(f)*
tablespoon • *n* cullera de sopa *(f)*, cullerada *(f)*
taboo • *n* tabú • *adj* tabú
tabor • *n* tabalet *(m)*
tabular • *adj* tabular *(f)*
tachometer • *n* tacòmetre *(m)*, comptarevolucions *(m)*, comptavoltes *(m)*
tachymeter • *n* taquímetre *(m)*
tacit • *adj* tàcit
tacitly • *adv* tàcitament
taciturn • *adj* taciturn
tackle • *v* placar • *n* entrada *(f)*, placatge *(m)*
tactful • *adj* discret
tactic • *n* tàctica *(f)*
tactician • *n* estrateg *(m)*, estratega *(f)*
tactile • *adj* tàctil
tactless • *adj* indiscret
tadpole • *n* capgròs *(m)*, cullerot *(m)*
tag • *v* etiquetar • *n* etiqueta *(f)*, tocar i parar
taiga • *n* taigà
tail • *n* cua *(f)*, natja *(f)*
tailor • *n* sastre *(m)*, sastressa *(f)*, tallahams *(m)*
take • *v* agafar, prendre, violar, forçar, portar, escollir • *n* presa
talc • *n* talc *(m)*
talent • *n* talent *(m)*
talented • *adj* talentós
talk • *v* parlar, conversar
tallow • *n* sèu
talon • *n* urpa *(f)*
talus • *n* talús *(m)*
tambourine • *n* pandereta *(f)*
tame • *v* domar, amansir • *adj* mans
tamer • *n* domador *(m)*
tampon • *v* tamponar
tangent • *n* tangent *(f)*
tangible • *adj* tangible
tango • *n* tango *(m)*
tank • *n* tanc *(m)*, dipòsit *(m)*
tanned • *adj* bronzejat
tantalize • *v* tantalitzar
tantalum • *n* tàntal *(m)*
tantamount • *adj* equivalent
tantrum • *n* enrabiada *(f)*, rebequeria *(f)*
tar • *v* enquitranar • *n* quitrà *(m)*
tarsal • *adj* tarsal, tarsià

tarsier • *n* tarser
tarsus • *n* tars *(m)*
tart • *n* puta, bagassa, bandarra, marcolfa, marfanta
taste • *v* tastar, gustar • *n* gust, sabor, tast
tatter • *n* drap *(m)*
tattoo • *v* tatuar • *n* tatuatge *(m)*
tau • *n* tau *(f)*
tauon • *n* tauó *(m)*
taut • *adj* tens, tibant
tax • *n* impost *(m)*, taxa *(f)*
taxi • *n* taxi *(m)*
taxidermy • *n* taxidèrmia *(f)*
taximeter • *n* taxímetre *(m)*
taxonomy • *n* taxonomia *(f)*
tea • *n* te *(m)*
teach • *v* ensenyar
teacher • *n* ensenyant *(f)*
teaching • *n* ensenyament *(m)*
teakettle • *n* bullidor *(m)*, tetera *(f)*
teal • *n* xarxet comú • *adj* xarxet
team • *n* equip *(m)*
tear • *v* estripar, esquinçar, esgarrar • *n* llàgrima *(f)*
tease • *v* pentinar
technetium • *n* tecneci
technical • *adj* tècnic
technically • *adv* tècnicament
technocracy • *n* tecnocràcia *(f)*
technological • *adj* tecnològic
technologically • *adv* tecnològicament
technology • *n* tecnologia *(f)*
tectonic • *adj* tectònic
tedious • *adj* tediós
teeter • *v* titubejar
telegraphy • *n* telegrafia *(f)*
telekinesis • *n* telecinesi *(f)*
teleology • *n* teleologia *(f)*
telepathic • *adj* telepàtic
telepathy • *n* telepatia
telephone • *v* telefonar, trucar, cridar • *n* telèfon *(m)*
telescope • *n* telescopi *(m)*
telescopic • *adj* telescòpic
television • *n* televisió *(f)*, televisor *(m)*
tell • *v* dir, explicar
telltale • *adj* revelador *(m)*
tellurium • *n* telluri
telophase • *n* telofase *(f)*
temper • *n* humor *(m)*, tremp *(m)*

temperance • *n* temperança
temperate • *adj* temperat
temperature • *n* temperatura *(f)*, febre *(f)*
tempest • *v* tempestejar • *n* tempesta *(f)*
template • *n* plantilla *(f)*
temple • *n* temple *(m)*
temporal • *adj* temporal *(f)*, temporal *(m)*
• *n* temporal *(m)*
temporarily • *adv* temporalment
temporary • *n* eventual • *adj* temporal
tempt • *v* temptar
temptation • *n* temptació *(f)*
tempter • *n* temptador *(m)*, temptadora
(f), seductor *(m)*
tempting • *adj* temptador *(m)*, temptadora *(f)*
ten • *n* deu *(m)*
tenacious • *adj* tenaç
tenant • *n* llogater *(m)*, inquilí *(m)*
tendency • *n* tendència *(f)*
tendentious • *adj* tendenciós
tendentiously • *adv* tendenciosament
tender • *adj* tendre
tenderly • *adv* tendrament
tendon • *n* tendó *(m)*
tennis • *n* tennis *(m)*
tense • *n* temps • *v* tesar • *adj* tens
tent • *n* tenda *(f)*
tentacle • *n* tentacle *(m)*
tenth • *adj* desè *(m)*, dècim *(m)*
tenuous • *adj* tènue *(f)*
tepid • *adj* tebi
tequila • *n* tequila *(m)*
terbium • *n* terbi *(m)*
term • *n* terme *(m)*
terminal • *n* terminal • *adj* terminal
terminology • *n* terminologia *(f)*
termite • *n* tèrmit *(m)*
terrace • *n* terrassa *(f)*
terrestrial • *adj* terrestre
terrible • *adj* terrible
terribly • *adv* terriblement
territorial • *adj* territorial
territory • *n* territori *(m)*
terror • *n* terror *(f)*
terrorism • *n* terrorisme *(m)*
terrorist • *n* terrorista *(f)* • *adj* terrorista
tesla • *n* tesla *(m)*
tessellation • *n* tessel·lació *(f)*
test • *v* provar
testicular • *adj* testicular
tether • *n* amarra *(f)*
tetragon • *n* tetràgon *(m)*
tetrahedron • *n* tetràedre *(m)*, tetraedre
(m)
tetralogy • *n* tetralogia *(f)*
tetrameter • *n* tetrámetro *(m)*

textbook • *n* llibre de text *(m)*, llibre de
classe *(m)*
textual • *adj* textual
texture • *n* textura *(f)*
thalamus • *n* tàlem *(m)*
thallium • *n* tal·li *(m)*
than • *prep* que
thanatophobia • *n* tanatofòbia *(f)*
thank • *v* agrair
thankful • *adj* agraït
thankless • *adj* ingrat, desagraït
thanks • *interj* gràcies, mercès, merci
that • *conj* que • *pron* açò, això, allò
the • *art* el *(m)*, lo *(m)*, la *(f)*, els, les, es *(m)*,
so *(m)*, sa *(f)*, es, sos, ets, ses
theater • *n* teatre *(m)*
theatrical • *adj* teatral
theft • *n* robatori *(m)*
them • *pron* els *(m)*, les *(f)*, els
themselves • *pron* es, mateix
then • *adv* llavors, després, mentrestant,
al mateix temps
theocracy • *n* teocràcia *(f)*
theocratic • *adj* teocràtic
theologian • *n* teòleg *(m)*
theological • *adj* teològic
theology • *n* teologia *(f)*
theorbo • *n* tiorba *(f)*
theorem • *n* teorema *(m)*
theoretical • *adj* teòric
theoretically • *adv* teòricament, en teoria
theorize • *v* teoritzar
theory • *n* teoria *(f)*
therapeutic • *adj* terapèutic
therapist • *n* terapeuta *(f)*
therapy • *n* teràpia *(f)*
there • *adv* allà, allí
therefore • *adv* per tant, per això
thereof • *adv* en
thermodynamic • *adj* termodinàmic
thermoelectric • *adj* termoelèctric
thermoelectricity • *n* termoelectricitat *(f)*
thermometer • *n* termòmetre *(m)*
thermosphere • *n* termosfera *(f)*
thesaurus • *n* diccionari de sinònims,
tesaurus *(m)*
thesis • *n* tesi *(f)*, tesi doctoral *(f)*
theta • *n* theta *(f)*
they • *pron* ells, elles
thief • *n* lladre *(m)*
thigh • *n* cuixa *(f)*
thimble • *n* didal *(m)*
thin • *v* aprimar, aprimar-se
thing • *n* cosa *(f)*
think • *v* pensar
third • *n* tercer, tercer *(m)*, tercera *(f)* • *adj*
tercer

thirdly • *adv* tercer, tercerament
thirst • *n* set *(f)*, ambició *(f)*
thirsty • *adj* assedegat
this • *pron* això *(n)*, aquest *(m)*, aquesta *(f)*
thistle • *n* card *(m)*
thorax • *n* tòrax *(m)*
thorium • *n* tori *(m)*
thorn • *n* aculi, espina, eculi, agulló, fibló
thorough • *adj* minuciós
thou • *pron* tu
thought • *n* pensament *(m)*
thoughtful • *adj* pensarós, atent
thousandth • *adj* milůlèsim *(m)*, milè *(m)*, 1000è *(m)*, 1000a *(f)*
thrall • *n* esclau *(m)*
thread • *v* enfilar • *n* fil *(m)*, fil conductor *(m)*, tema *(m)*
threat • *n* amenaça *(f)*
threaten • *v* amenaçar
threatening • *adj* amenaçador
three • *n* tres *(m)*
three-dimensional • *adj* tridimensional
thresh • *v* trillar
threshold • *n* llindar *(m)*
thrice • *adv* tres vegada, tres volta, tres cop
thrifty • *adj* estalviador
throat • *n* gola *(f)*
throne • *n* tron *(m)*
through • *prep* mitjançant
throughout • *prep* al llarg de
throw • *v* llançar, tirar
throw-in • *n* servei *(m)*
thrush • *n* tord *(m)*
thulium • *n* tuli *(m)*
thumb • *n* polze *(m)*
thunder • *v* tronar • *n* tro *(m)*
thunderstorm • *n* tempesta *(f)*
thus • *adv* així
thwart • *v* frustrar, desbaratar
thyme • *n* farigola *(f)*
tic • *n* tic *(m)*
tick • *n* paparra *(f)*
tidal • *adj* mareal
tide • *n* marea *(f)*
tidy • *adj* endreçat
tie • *n* empat *(m)*, lligam *(m)*, lligadura *(f)* • *v* fermar, lligar, ennuar
tierce • *n* tercer *(m)*
tiger • *n* tigre *(m)*
tigress • *n* tigressa *(f)*, tigra
tilde • *n* titlla *(f)*
tile • *v* enrajolar, teular • *n* teula *(f)*, rajola *(f)*
tilt • *v* inclinar
timber • *n* biga *(f)*
time • *n* temps *(m)*, pena *(f)*, hora *(f)*, veg-ada *(f)*, cop *(m)*
time-out • *n* temps mort *(m)*, téntol *(m)*
timely • *adj* oportú
timid • *adj* tímid
tin • *n* estany *(m)*
tinamou • *n* tinamú *(m)*
tiny • *adj* minúscul
tip • *n* punta *(f)*, punxa *(f)*, propina *(f)*, indici *(m)*
tire • *v* cansar-se, fatigar-se, cansar, fatigar, avorrir-se, adornar, guarnir
tired • *adj* cansat *(m)*, cansada *(f)*
tiresome • *adj* empipador
tissue • *n* teixit *(m)*
titan • *n* tità *(m)*
titanic • *adj* titànic
titanium • *n* titani *(m)*
tithe • *n* delme *(m)*
title • *n* títol *(m)*
titubate • *v* titubar, titubejar
to • *prep* a, cap a
toad • *n* gripau *(m)*
toadstool • *n* bolet verinós
toast • *v* torrar, brindar • *n* torrada *(f)*, brindis *(m)*
tobacco • *n* tabac *(m)*
toccata • *n* tocata *(f)*
today • *n* avui, hui *(m)* • *adv* avui, avui en dia, avui dia
toe • *n* dit del peu *(m)*, dit *(m)*
together • *adv* junt
toil • *n* treball
toilet • *n* vàter *(m)*, escusat *(m)*, lavabo *(m)*
tolerable • *adj* tolerable
tolerant • *adj* tolerant
tolerate • *v* tolerar
tom • *n* gat *(m)*, mascle *(m)*
tomato • *n* tomaquera *(f)*, tomàquet *(m)*
tomb • *n* tomba *(f)*
tome • *n* tom *(m)*
tomorrow • *n* demà *(m)* • *adv* demà
tone • *n* to *(m)*, to
tone-deaf • *adj* dur d'orella
toner • *n* tòner *(m)*
tongue • *n* llengua *(f)*
tonight • *n* anit • *adv* anit
tonsil • *n* amígdala *(f)*
tonsillitis • *n* tonsilito
tontine • *n* tontina *(f)*
too • *adv* també, massa
tool • *v* equipar • *n* eina *(f)*
toolbox • *n* caixa d'eines *(f)*
tooth • *n* dent *(f)*
toothbrush • *n* raspallet de les dents *(m)*
top • *n* baldufa *(f)*, cofa *(f)*
topaz • *n* topazi *(m)*

topple • *v* tombar, enderrocar, vinclar
topspin • *n* efecte de rodolament *(m)*
torch • *n* torxa *(f)*, llanterna *(f)*
torment • *v* turmentar • *n* turment *(m)*
tormentor • *n* turmentador *(m)*
tornado • *n* tornado *(m)*
torpedo • *v* torpedinar • *n* torpede *(m)*
torrent • *n* torrent *(m)*, riera *(f)*
torrential • *adj* torrencial
torso • *n* tors *(m)*
tortoise • *n* tortuga *(f)*
torture • *v* torturar • *n* tortura *(f)*
torturer • *n* torturador *(m)*
tot • *n* infant *(m)*, glop *(m)*
total • *n* total *(m)*, suma *(f)*
totalitarian • *adj* totalitari
totally • *adv* totalment
touch • *v* tocar
tourism • *n* turisme *(m)*
tournament • *n* torneig *(m)*
tourniquet • *n* torniquet *(m)*
tow • *v* remolcar
toward • *prep* cap a, sobre, en relació a, per, per a
towel • *n* tovallola *(f)*
tower • *n* torre *(f)*, la torre, casa de déu
town • *n* poble *(m)*
toxic • *adj* tòxic, verinós
toxicity • *n* toxicitat *(f)*
toy • *n* joguina *(f)*, joguet *(m)*
trachea • *n* tràquea *(f)*
tracheal • *adj* traqueal
tracheitis • *n* traqueïtis *(f)*
trachoma • *n* tracoma *(m)*
tract • *n* extensió *(f)*, tracte *(m)*, fullet *(m)*, tractat *(m)*
tractable • *adj* tractable *(f)*
tractor • *n* tractor *(m)*
tradition • *n* tradició *(f)*
traditional • *adj* tradicional
traditionally • *adv* tradicionalment
traffic • *n* tràfic *(m)*
tragedy • *n* tragèdia *(f)*
tragic • *adj* tràgic
tragicomic • *adj* tragicòmic
trail • *v* arrossegar • *n* rastre *(m)*, pista *(f)*, corriol *(m)*
train • *v* entrenar • *n* tren *(m)*
trainer • *n* entrenador *(m)*
training • *n* entrenament *(m)*
traitor • *v* trair • *n* traïdor *(m)* • *adj* traïdor
traitorous • *adj* traïdor
trajectory • *n* trajectòria *(f)*
tram • *n* tramvia *(m)*
tramp • *n* rodamón *(m)*
transalpine • *adj* transalpí
transatlantic • *adj* transatlàntic

transcendentally • *adv* transcendentalment
transcription • *n* transcripció *(f)*
transept • *n* creuer *(m)*, transsepte *(m)*
transform • *v* transformar
transformation • *n* transformació *(f)*
transistor • *n* transistor *(m)*
transition • *n* transició *(f)*
transitional • *adj* transitori
transitive • *adj* transitiu
transitively • *adv* transitivament
transitory • *adj* transitori
translate • *v* traduir
translation • *n* traducció *(f)*
translator • *n* traductor
transliteration • *n* transliteració *(f)*
translucent • *adj* translúcid
transmitter • *n* transmissor *(m)*
transparent • *adj* transparent
transparently • *adv* transparentment
transplant • *v* trasplantar
transport • *v* transportar, deportar • *n* transport *(m)*, deportat *(m)*
transpose • *n* transportar
transsexual • *adj* transexual
transverse • *adj* transversal
trapdoor • *n* trapa *(f)*, porta del darrere *(f)*
trapeze • *n* trapezi *(m)*
trapezium • *n* trapezi *(m)*
trapezoid • *n* trapezi *(m)*, trapezoide *(m)*
traumatic • *adj* traumàtic
travel • *v* viatjar, transitar, fer passes • *n* viatjar
tread • *v* trepitjar • *n* trepitjada *(f)*, dibuix *(f)*
treason • *n* traïció *(f)*
treasure • *n* tresor *(m)*, tesor *(m)*
treatment • *n* tractament *(m)*
trebuchet • *n* trabuquet *(m)*
tree • *n* arbre *(m)*
tremble • *v* tremolar • *n* tremolor
tremulous • *adj* tremolós
trench • *n* trinxera *(f)*
trencher • *n* tallador *(m)*
trestle • *n* cavallet *(m)*
triangle • *n* triangle *(m)*
triangulation • *n* triangulació *(f)*
tribal • *adj* tribal
tribe • *n* tribu *(f)*
tribune • *n* tribú *(m)*, tribuna *(f)*
trichotillomania • *n* tricotilomanía
trick • *v* enganyar
tricycle • *n* tricicle *(m)*
trident • *n* trident *(m)*
trifle • *n* fotesa *(f)*
trifling • *adj* insignificant
trigger • *n* gallet *(m)*

triglyceride • *n* triglicèrid *(m)*
trigon • *n* trígon *(m)*
trigonometric • *adj* trigonomètric
trigonometry • *n* trigonometria *(f)*
trill • *n* trinat *(m)*
trilogy • *n* trilogia *(f)*
trimaran • *n* trimarà *(m)*
trimer • *n* trímer *(m)*
trimester • *n* trimestre *(m)*
trip • *v* entrebancar-se
tripartite • *adj* tripartit
tripe • *n* butza *(f)*, butzes
triple • *v* triplicar • *n* batada triple *(f)*, terna • *adj* triple, ternari
triptych • *n* tríptic *(m)*
trisect • *v* trisecar
triumphant • *adj* triomfant, triomfador
triumvirate • *n* triumvirat *(m)*
trivial • *adj* trivial, banal
troika • *n* troica *(f)*
trombone • *n* trombó *(m)*
troop • *n* colla *(f)*, tropa *(f)*, soldats *(m)*
trophy • *n* trofeu *(m)*
tropopause • *n* tropopausa *(f)*
troposphere • *n* troposfera *(f)*
troubadour • *n* trobador *(m)*, trobadora *(f)*
trough • *n* cóm
trout • *n* truita *(f)*
trowel • *n* paleta *(f)*, desplantador *(m)*
truancy • *n* absentisme
truck • *n* camió *(m)*
true • *adj* veritable
truffle • *n* tòfona
truism • *n* obvietat *(f)*, truisme *(m)*, banalitat *(f)*, lloc comú *(m)*, tòpic *(m)*, clixé *(m)*
truly • *adv* veritablement
trump • *v* trumfar
trumpet • *n* trompeta *(f)*
trumpeter • *n* trompetista *(f)*, trompeter *(m)*, trompeta *(f)*
trunk • *n* trompa *(f)*, portaequipatge *(m)*, maleter *(m)*
trust • *n* confiança *(f)*
trustworthy • *adj* fidedigne
truth • *n* veritat *(f)*
try • *v* intentar, tractar de, provar, esforçar-se, tastar, jutjar • *n* assaig *(m)*
tryptophan • *n* triptòfan *(m)*
tsar • *n* tsar *(m)*
tuba • *n* tuba *(f)*
tube • *n* tub *(m)*

tuber • *n* tubercle
tuberculosis • *n* tuberculosi *(f)*
tugboat • *n* remolcador *(m)*
tulip • *n* tulipa *(f)*
tumor • *n* tumor *(m)*
tuna • *n* tonyina *(f)*
tune • *v* afinar • *n* melodia *(f)*, tonada *(f)*
tungsten • *n* tungstè *(m)*
tunic • *n* túnica *(f)*
turban • *n* turbant *(m)*
turbojet • *n* turbojet *(m)*
turd • *n* cagarro *(m)*
turf • *n* gespa
turkey • *n* gall dindi *(m)*, indiot *(m)*, polla d'índia *(f)*
turmeric • *n* cúrcuma *(f)*
turn • *v* girar • *n* torn *(m)*
turnover • *n* pèrdua de possessió *(f)*
turnstile • *n* torniquet
turpentine • *n* aiguarràs *(m)*
turquoise • *n* turquesa *(f)* • *adj* turquesa
turtle • *n* tortuga *(f)*
tusk • *n* ullal *(m)*
tutorial • *n* tutoria *(f)*, tutorial *(m)*
tweet • *v* piular • *n* piulada *(f)*
twelfth • *n* dotzè *(m)* • *adj* dotzè *(m)*, dotzena *(f)*
twentieth • *n* vintè *(m)* • *adj* vintè *(m)*, vigèsim *(m)*
twenty-first • *n* vint-i-unè *(m)* • *adj* vint-i-unè *(m)*
twenty-second • *n* vint-i-dosè *(m)* • *adj* vint-i-dosè
twice • *adv* dos cops, dues vegades
twilight • *n* crepuscle *(m)*
twin • *n* bessó *(m)*, bessó
two • *n* dos *(m)*
tympanum • *n* timpà *(m)*
type • *v* teclejar • *n* tipus *(m)*
typewriter • *n* màquina d'escriure *(f)*
typhoon • *n* tifó *(m)*
typhus • *n* tifus *(m)*
typical • *adj* típic
typically • *adv* típicament
typographical • *adj* tipogràfic
tyrannical • *adj* tirànic
tyrannize • *v* tiranitzar
tyranny • *n* tirania *(f)*
tyrant • *n* tirà *(m)*
tyre • *n* neumàtic *(m)*, pneumàtic *(m)*
tyrosine • *n* tirosina *(f)*

U

u • *n* u *(f)*
ubiquitous • *adj* ubic
udder • *n* braguer *(m)*, mamella *(f)*
ugliness • *n* lletgesa *(f)*, lletjor *(f)*
ugly • *adj* lleig
ukase • *n* ucàs *(m)*
ulna • *n* cúbit *(m)*, ulna *(f)*
ultimately • *adv* finalment
ultraviolet • *n* ultraviolat *(m)* • *adj* ultra-violat
umbilical • *adj* umbilical
umbrella • *n* paraigua *(m)*, para-sol *(m)*, ombrelůla *(f)*
unable • *adj* incapaç
unacceptability • *n* inacceptabilitat *(f)*
unacceptable • *adj* inacceptable
unacceptably • *adv* inacceptablement
unambiguous • *adj* inequívoc
unambiguously • *adv* inequívocament
unanimous • *adj* unànime
unanimously • *adv* unànimement
unarmed • *adj* desarmat
unavailable • *adj* indisponible
unavoidable • *adj* inevitable
unbearable • *adj* insuportable
unbeatable • *adj* imbatible
unbeaten • *adj* invicte
unbelievably • *adv* increïblement
unborn • *adj* nonat
unbroken • *adj* sencer, continu
uncertain • *adj* incert
uncertainly • *adv* incertament
unchain • *v* desencadenar
uncle • *n* oncle *(m)*, tio *(m)*
unclean • *adj* brut, impur
unclothed • *adj* desvestit
uncomfortable • *adj* incòmode
uncomfortably • *adv* incòmodament
uncompromising • *adj* intransigent
unconditional • *adj* incondicional
unconscious • *n* inconscient *(m)* • *adj* in-conscient
unconstitutional • *adj* inconstitucional
unconvincing • *adj* increïble
uncourteous • *adj* descortès
undefined • *adj* indefinit
undemocratic • *adj* antidemocràtic
undeniable • *adj* innegable
under • *adv* sota • *prep* sota
underestimate • *v* subestimar
underground • *adj* subterrani
underlying • *adj* subjacent
underneath • *adv* sota • *prep* sota
underpants • *n* calçotets, calçons blancs, bragues
understand • *v* entendre, comprendre
understanding • *adj* comprensiu

undertake • *v* emprendre
undertow • *n* contracorrent *(m)*
underwear • *n* roba interior *(f)*
undesirable • *adj* indesitjable
undine • *n* ondina *(f)*
undo • *v* desfer
undoubtedly • *adv* indubtablement
unduly • *adv* indegudament
undying • *adj* etern
uneasy • *adj* difícil, complicat
unemployed • *adj* aturat
unemployment • *n* atur *(m)*, parada forçosa *(f)*, manca de treball *(f)*
unequal • *adj* desigual
unequivocal • *adj* inequívoc
uneven • *adj* desigual, rugós
unevenly • *adv* desigualment
unexpected • *adj* inesperat
unexpectedly • *adv* inesperadament
unfair • *adj* injust
unfaithful • *adj* infidel
unfaithfully • *adv* infidelment
unfinished • *adj* inacabat, inconclús
unforeseen • *adj* imprevist
unforgettable • *adj* inoblidable
unfortunate • *adj* desafortunat
unfortunately • *adv* malauradament
unfounded • *adj* infundat
unfriendly • *adj* antipàtic, hostil
ungainly • *adj* desmanyotat
ungrammatical • *adj* agramatical
unhappy • *adj* infeliç
unhealthy • *adj* insalubre
unicellular • *adj* unicelůlular
unicorn • *n* unicorn *(m)*
unilateral • *adj* unilateral
unilaterally • *adv* unilateralment
unimaginable • *adj* inimaginable
uninhabitable • *adj* inhabitable
unintelligent • *adj* inintelůligent
unintelligently • *adv* inintelůligentment
unintelligibility • *n* inintelůligibilitat *(f)*
unintelligible • *adj* inintelůligible
unintelligibly • *adv* inintelůligiblement
unintentional • *adj* involuntari
unintentionally • *adv* involuntàriament
uninterrupted • *adj* ininterromput
uninterruptedly • *adv* ininterrompuda-ment
unique • *adj* únic
uniquely • *adv* únicament, singularment
unisex • *adj* unisex
unit • *n* unitat *(f)*
unitarian • *adj* unitari
unitary • *adj* unitari
unite • *v* unir
unity • *n* unitat *(f)*

universe • *n* univers *(m)*
university • *n* universitat *(f)*
unjust • *adj* injust
unjustifiable • *adj* injustificable
unjustly • *adv* injustament
unknown • *adj* desconegut
unless • *conj* a menys que, llevat que, tret que, fora que
unlikely • *adj* improbable
unlimited • *adj* il·limitat
unload • *v* descarregar
unlucky • *adj* desafortunat, malaurat, infortunat
unmarried • *adj* solter
unmask • *v* desemmarcar, desemmarcar-se
unnecessarily • *adv* innecessàriament
unnecessary • *adj* innecessari
unnoticed • *adj* desapercebut
unpleasant • *adj* desagradable
unpopularity • *n* impopularitat *(f)*
unpredictable • *adj* imprevisible
unproductive • *adj* improductiu
unpublished • *adj* inèdit
unquestionable • *adj* inqüestionable
unquestionably • *adv* indubtablement
unrecognizable • *adj* irreconeixible
unremitting • *adj* incessant
unrestrainedly • *adv* desenfrenadament
unsafe • *adj* insegur
unsatisfactory • *adj* insatisfactori
unscathed • *adj* incòlume
unselfish • *adj* desinteressat
unstable • *adj* inestable
unstoppable • *adj* imparable
unsuitable • *adj* inadequat
unsustainable • *adj* insostenible
unthinkable • *adj* impensable
untidy • *adj* desendreçat, desordenat
untie • *v* deslligar
until • *prep* fins
unusual • *adj* inusual
unwieldy • *adj* farragós *(m)*
unwilling • *adj* reaci
unwise • *adj* imprudent
unworthy • *adj* indigne

up • *adv* amunt • *prep* dalt
update • *v* actualitzar • *n* actualització *(f)*
uphill • *adv* costa amunt
upper • *adj* superior, alt
upright • *adj* dret, recte • *adv* dempeus
uproar • *n* brogit *(m)*, avalot *(m)*, gatara *(f)*, cridòria *(f)*, aldarull *(m)*, rebombori *(m)*
upset • *adj* molest, trasbalsat, disgustat
upsilon • *n* ípsilon *(f)*
uracil • *n* uracil *(m)*
uranium • *n* urani
urban • *adj* urbà
urea • *n* urea *(f)*
urethra • *n* uretra *(f)*
urgent • *adj* urgent
urgently • *adv* urgentment
uric • *adj* úric
urinary • *adj* urinari
urine • *n* orina *(f)*
urologist • *n* uròleg *(m)*
urology • *n* urologia *(f)*
use • *n* ús *(m)* • *v* fer servir, usar, utilitzar
useful • *adj* útil
usefully • *adv* útilment
usefulness • *n* utilitat *(f)*
useless • *adj* inútil *(f)*
user • *n* usuari *(m)*
usher • *n* uixer
usual • *adj* usual
usually • *adv* normalment
usurp • *v* usurpar
utensil • *n* utensili *(m)*
uterine • *adj* uterí
utilitarian • *n* utilitari *(m)*, utilitària *(f)* • *adj* utilitari
utopia • *n* utopia *(f)*
utopian • *adj* utòpic
utter • *adj* absolut *(m)*, total *(f)*, incondicional *(f)* • *v* dir, pronunciar, emetre, balbucejar, balbotejar
utterance • *n* articulació *(f)*, expressió *(f)*, pronunciació *(f)*, discurs *(m)*, enunciat *(m)*, eloqüència *(f)*, parla *(f)*
uvula • *n* úvula *(f)*

V

vacant • *adj* vacant, vacu
vaccine • *n* vacuna *(f)*, vaccí *(m)*
vacillate • *v* vacil·lar
vacillation • *n* vacil·lació *(f)*
vacuum • *n* buit *(m)*
vagina • *n* vagina, vagina *(f)*

vague • *adj* vague
vaguely • *adv* vagament
vagueness • *n* vaguetat *(f)*
vain • *adj* vanitós, va
vainly • *adv* vanament
valediction • *n* comiat *(m)*, despedida *(f)*

valiant • *adj* valent
valid • *adj* vàlid
valkyrie • *n* valquíria
valley • *n* vall *(f)*
valuable • *adj* valuós
value • *n* valor
valve • *n* vàlvula *(f)*
vampire • *n* vampir
van • *n* furgoneta *(f)*
vanadinite • *n* vanadinita
vanadium • *n* vanadi *(m)*
vandal • *n* vàndal *(f)* • *adj* vàndal *(f)*
vandalism • *n* vandalisme *(m)*
vane • *n* aspa *(f)*
vanity • *n* vanitat *(f)*
vapor • *n* vapor *(m)*
variable • *n* variable *(f)* • *adj* variable
variably • *adv* variablement
variation • *n* variació *(f)*
variety • *n* varietat *(f)*
various • *adj* varis
varmint • *n* feristela *(f)*, escurçó *(m)*
varnish • *n* vernís *(m)*
vascular • *adj* vascular
vase • *n* gerro *(m)*, florera *(f)*
vasectomy • *n* vasectomia *(f)*
vault • *n* volta *(f)*
vector • *n* vector *(m)*
vegan • *n* vegà • *adj* vegà
vegetable • *n* vegetal *(m)*, verdura *(f)*, hortalissa *(f)*, llegum *(m)* • *adj* vegetal
vegetarian • *n* vegetarià *(m)*, vegetariana *(f)* • *adj* vegetarià
vegetarianism • *n* vegetarianisme *(m)*
vegetation • *n* vegetació *(f)*
vehicle • *n* vehicle *(m)*
vein • *n* vena *(f)*
velar • *n* velar
velleity • *n* velŭleïtat *(f)*
velocity • *n* velocitat *(f)*
velvet • *n* vellut *(m)*
velvety • *adj* vellutat
vendor • *n* venedor
venom • *n* verí *(m)*, malvolença *(f)*
venomous • *adj* verinós
venture • *v* arriscar
venue • *n* local *(m)*, seu *(f)*, escena *(f)*, jurisdicció *(f)*
verb • *n* verb
verbal • *adj* verbal
verbatim • *adv* mot a mot
verbose • *adj* verbós
verification • *n* verificació *(f)*
vermouth • *n* vermut *(m)*
versatile • *adj* versàtil
versatility • *n* versatilitat *(f)*
versus • *prep* en comparació amb

vertebra • *n* vèrtebra *(f)*
vertebrate • *n* vertebrat • *adj* vertebrat
vertex • *n* vèrtex *(m)*
vertical • *adj* vertical
vertically • *adv* verticalment
very • *adv* molt
vesicle • *n* vesícula *(f)*
vest • *n* armilla *(f)*, samarreta *(f)*
vestige • *n* vestigi *(m)*
vestigial • *adj* vestigial
vetch • *n* veça *(f)*
vexatious • *adj* vexatori
viable • *adj* viable
vial • *n* fiola *(f)*
vibraphone • *n* vibràfon
vibrato • *n* vibrato *(m)*
vice • *n* vici *(m)*
viceroy • *n* virrei *(m)*
victim • *n* víctima *(f)*
victorious • *adj* victoriós
victoriously • *adv* victoriosament
victory • *n* victòria *(f)*
vicuna • *n* vicunya *(m)*
vie • *v* rivalitzar
view • *v* veure • *n* vista *(f)*, parer *(m)*
vigil • *n* vetlla *(f)*, vigília *(f)*
vigilance • *n* vigilància *(f)*
vigilant • *adj* vigilant
vigilantly • *adv* vigilantment
vigorously • *adv* vigorosament
vile • *adj* vil
village • *n* poble *(m)*
vincible • *adj* vencible
vine • *n* vinya
vinegar • *n* vinagre *(m)*
vineyard • *n* vinya *(f)*
vintage • *n* verema *(f)*, collita *(f)*
viola • *n* viola *(f)*
violence • *n* violència *(f)*
violent • *adj* violent
violently • *adv* violentament
violet • *n* violeta • *adj* violeta
violin • *n* violí *(m)*
violinist • *n* violinista *(f)*
viper • *n* escurçó
viral • *adj* víric, viral
virgin • *n* verge • *adj* verge
virginal • *n* virginal *(m)*
virginity • *n* virginitat *(f)*
virile • *adj* viril, masculí
virility • *n* virilitat *(f)*
virology • *n* virologia
virtual • *adj* virtual
virtually • *adv* virtualment
virtue • *n* virtut *(f)*
virtuosity • *n* virtuosisme *(m)*
virtuoso • *n* virtuós *(m)*, virtuosa *(f)*

virtuous • *adj* virtuós
virtuously • *adv* virtuosament
virulent • *adj* virulent
virulently • *adv* virulentament
virus • *n* virus *(m)*
visa • *n* visat *(m)*
viscera • *n* víscera *(f)*
viscometer • *n* viscosímetre *(m)*
viscosity • *n* viscositat *(f)*
viscount • *n* vescomte *(m)*
viscous • *adj* viscós
vise • *n* cargol de banc *(m)*
visibility • *n* visibilitat *(f)*
visible • *adj* visible
visibly • *adv* visiblement
vision • *n* vista *(f)*, visió *(f)*
visual • *adj* visual
vital • *adj* vital *(f)*
vitalism • *n* vitalisme *(m)*
vitality • *n* vitalitat *(f)*
vitamin • *n* vitamina *(f)*
vivacious • *adj* vivaç *(f)*
vivaciously • *adv* vivaçment
vivacity • *n* vivacitat *(f)*
vivid • *adj* vívid
viviparous • *adj* vivípar
vixen • *n* guineu femella *(f)*, guilla *(f)*
vizier • *n* visir *(m)*
vocal • *adj* vocal
vocally • *adv* vocalment

vociferate • *v* vociferar
vociferation • *n* vociferació *(f)*
vodka • *n* vodka *(f)*
voice • *n* veu *(f)*, sonor *(m)*, vot *(m)*
void • *n* buit *(m)*
volcanic • *adj* volcànic
volcano • *n* volcà *(m)*
volcanology • *n* vulcanologia *(f)*
vole • *n* talpó *(m)*
volley • *n* volea *(f)*
volleyball • *n* voleibol *(m)*, vòlei *(m)*
volume • *n* volum *(m)*
voluntarily • *adv* voluntàriament
voluntary • *adj* voluntari
voluptuous • *adj* voluptuós
vomit • *v* vomitar • *n* vòmit *(m)*
voodoo • *n* vodú *(m)*, vudú *(m)*
vortex • *n* remolí *(m)*, vòrtex
vote • *v* votar • *n* vot *(m)*
voter • *n* votant
vow • *v* jurar • *n* vot *(m)*
vowel • *n* vocal *(f)*
voyage • *n* viatge *(m)*
voyeurism • *n* voyeurisme *(m)*
vulcanization • *n* vulcanització *(f)*
vulgar • *adj* vulgar *(f)*, vulgar
vulnerability • *n* vulnerabilitat *(f)*
vulture • *n* voltor *(m)*
vulva • *n* vulva *(f)*, cony *(m)*

W

wafer • *n* neula *(f)*
wage • *n* salari *(m)*, sou *(m)*, paga *(f)*, honorari *(m)*, estipendi *(m)*, remuneració *(f)*, retribució *(f)*
wagon • *n* carro *(m)*, cotxe *(m)*, cotxet *(m)*
waist • *n* cintura *(f)*
waistcoat • *n* armilla *(f)*
wait • *v* esperar, esperar-se
waitress • *n* cambrera
walk • *v* caminar • *n* passejada *(m)*, passejada *(f)*, passeig *(m)*
wall • *v* emmurallar, murar • *n* mur *(m)*, muralla *(f)*, paret *(f)*, embà *(m)*
wallaby • *n* ualabi *(m)*
wallet • *n* bitlletera *(f)*, cartera *(f)*
wallflower • *n* violer groc, viola groca
wallpaper • *n* paper pintat, paper d'empaperar
walnut • *n* noguera *(f)*
walrus • *n* morsa *(f)*
wander • *v* vagar
wanderer • *n* rodamón *(m)*

want • *v* voler
war • *v* guerrejar • *n* guerra *(f)*
warbler • *n* bosquerola *(f)*
wardrobe • *n* armari *(m)*
warlike • *adj* belŭligerant, belŭlicós
warlock • *n* bruixot *(m)*
warm • *adj* calent, càlid
warn • *v* advertir, avisar
warp • *v* deformar, torçar
warrior • *n* guerrer *(m)*
warship • *n* vaixell de guerra *(m)*
wart • *n* berruga *(f)*
warthog • *n* facoquer *(m)*
wary • *adj* cautelós
wash • *v* rentar, llavar
washable • *adj* rentable
washbasin • *n* lavabo *(m)*, pica *(f)*
washstand • *n* rentamans *(m)*
wasp • *n* vespa *(f)*
watch • *n* rellotge *(m)*, guarda *(f)*, guardià *(m)* • *v* mirar
watchmaker • *n* rellotger *(m)*, rellotgera

(f)
watchtower • *n* talaia *(f)*
water • *n* aigua *(f)*, aigües
watercress • *n* creixen *(m)*
watermark • *n* filigrana *(f)*, marca d'aigua *(f)*
watermelon • *n* sindriera *(f)*, síndria *(f)*
waterproof • *adj* submergible, impermeable
waterproofing • *n* impermeabilització *(f)*
watt • *n* watt *(m)*
wattle • *n* barballera *(f)*
wave • *v* saludar
wax • *v* encerar, tornar-se, créixer • *n* cera *(f)* • *adj* cerós
waxwing • *n* ocell sedós *(m)*
way • *n* via *(f)*, camí *(m)*, manera *(f)*, mitjà *(m)*
we • *pron* nosaltres
weak • *adj* feble, dèbil
weaken • *v* debilitar, afeblir, debilitar-se, afeblir-se
weakly • *adv* dèbilment
weakness • *n* debilitat *(f)*, feblesa *(f)*
weapon • *n* arma *(f)*
wear • *v* portar
wearily • *adv* cansadament
weather • *n* temps *(m)*
weave • *v* teixir
web • *n* xarxa *(f)*, membrana *(f)*
wedding • *n* boda *(f)*, casament *(m)*
wedge • *n* falca *(f)*, tascó *(f)*
weed • *n* mala herba *(f)*
week • *n* setmana *(f)*
weekday • *n* dia feiner, dia laborable
weekend • *n* cap de setmana *(m)*
weekly • *adj* setmanal • *adv* setmanalment, setmanal
weep • *v* plorar
weevil • *n* morrut *(m)*
weigh • *v* pesar
weightlifter • *n* halterofilista *(f)*
weightlifting • *n* halterofília *(f)*
weird • *adj* rar, estrany
welcome • *v* donar la benvinguda, acollir • *n* benvinguda *(f)* • *adj* benvingut • *interj* benvingut *(m)*, benvinguda *(f)*, benvinguts, benvingudes
welcoming • *adj* acollidor
weld • *v* soldar
welder • *n* soldador *(m)*
well • *adv* bé, ben • *interj* bé • *n* pou *(m)*
well-being • *n* benestar *(m)*, benanança *(f)*
wench • *n* mossa *(f)*
werewolf • *n* home llop *(m)*
west • *n* oest *(m)*, ponent *(m)*

western • *adj* occidental
wet • *v* mullar, mullar-se • *adj* moll
wetland • *n* marjal *(f)*, aiguamoll *(m)*
whale • *n* balena *(f)*
whaler • *n* balener *(m)*
what • *adv* que • *pron* què
whatever • *interj* el que tu diguis
wheat • *n* blat *(m)*
wheel • *v* rodar, voltar • *n* roda *(f)*, roda de timó *(f)*, peix gros *(m)*
wheelbarrow • *n* carretó *(m)*
wheelchair • *n* cadira de rodes *(f)*
when • *adv* quan
where • *adv* on • *conj* on
wherever • *adv* onsevulla • *conj* onsevulga, onsevol, onsevulla
whet • *v* afilar
while • *n* estona *(f)* • *conj* mentre, malgrat
whilst • *conj* mentre que
whim • *n* antull *(m)*, capritx *(m)*, caprici *(m)*
whip • *v* assotar, fuetejar • *n* fuet *(m)*
whirlpool • *n* remolí
whirlwind • *n* terbolí *(m)*
whisk • *n* batedora *(f)*
whisker • *n* vibrissa *(f)*, bigoti *(m)*
whiskey • *n* whisky *(m)*
whisper • *v* xiuxiuejar • *n* xiuxiueig
whistle • *v* xiular • *n* xiulet *(m)*, xiulo *(m)*, xiulada *(f)*
white • *n* blanc *(m)* • *adj* blanc
whiteness • *n* blancor *(f)*, blancúria *(f)*, albor *(f)*
whitewash • *n* blanquejat *(m)*
whiting • *n* merlà *(m)*
whitish • *adj* blanquinós
who • *pron* qui
whoa • *interj* xo
whole • *n* tot, totalitat • *adj* tot *(m)*
wholesale • *n* a l'engròs
whore • *n* puta
whose • *pron* qui, qual
why • *n* perquè *(m)* • *adv* per què
wick • *n* ble *(m)*
wicker • *n* vímet *(m)*
wide • *adj* ample
widow • *n* vidu *(f)*
widower • *n* vidu *(m)*
wife • *n* dona *(f)*, muller *(f)*
wild • *adj* salvatge
will • *v* llegar, desitjar • *n* voluntat *(f)*, testament *(m)*
willing • *adj* disposat
willingly • *adv* gustosament
willow • *n* salze
wilt • *v* mustiar, pansir
win • *n* victòria *(f)*

winch • *n* cabrestant
wind • *n* vent *(m)*
windmill • *n* molí de vent *(m)*
window • *n* finestra *(f)*
windowsill • *n* ampit *(m)*
wine • *n* vi *(m)*
wineskin • *n* bot *(m)*
wing • *n* ala *(f)*, banda *(f)*, aler *(m)*, lateral
winger • *n* extrem, volant, ala, aler
wink • *v* fer l'ullet, picar l'ullet
winner • *n* guanyador *(m)*, guanyadora *(f)*
winter • *v* hivernar • *n* hivern *(m)*
wipe • *v* eixugar
wire • *n* filferro *(m)*, fil d'aram *(m)*, cable *(m)*
wireless • *n* ràdio *(f)* • *adj* sense fil
wisdom • *n* saviesa *(f)*, saviesa
wise • *adj* savi
wisely • *adv* sàviament
wisent • *n* bisó europeu
wish • *v* desitjar • *n* desig *(m)*
wit • *n* ment *(f)*, enteniment *(m)*, divertit
witch • *n* bruixa *(f)*
witch-hunt • *n* caça de bruixes *(f)*
witchcraft • *n* bruixeria *(f)*
with • *prep* amb
wither • *v* pansir, marcir, musteir, mustiar
within • *prep* en, dins
without • *prep* sense
witless • *adj* desentenimentat
witness • *v* provar, veure, contemplar, testificar • *n* testimoni *(m)*, testimoniatge *(m)*, atestat *(m)*, prova *(f)*, evidència *(f)*
wittol • *n* marit còmode *(m)*, cabró *(m)*
wizard • *n* mag *(m)*, màgic *(m)*, fetiller *(m)*
wolf • *n* llop *(m)*
wolverine • *n* golut *(m)*
woman • *n* dona *(f)*
womb • *n* úter *(m)*, matriu *(f)*
wonder • *v* sorprendre's, estorat *(m)*, preguntar-se • *n* meravella *(f)*
wonderful • *adj* meravellós

wonderfully • *adv* meravellosament
woodcock • *n* becada *(f)*
wooded • *adj* boscós
wooden • *adj* ligni *(m)*
woodlouse • *n* porquet de Sant Antoni
woodpecker • *n* picot *(m)*
woof • *v* bordar • *n* bof, buf
wool • *n* llana *(f)*
woolly • *adj* llanós
word • *v* redactar • *n* paraula *(f)*, mot *(m)*
work • *n* treball *(m)*
worker • *n* treballador *(m)*, treballadora *(f)*, obrer *(m)*
workshop • *n* taller *(m)*, seminari *(m)*
world • *n* món *(m)*, terra *(f)*
worldly • *adj* mundà
worldwide • *adj* mundial • *adv* mundialment
worm • *n* cuc *(m)*
wormwood • *n* donzell *(m)*
worried • *adj* preocupat *(m)*, preocupada *(f)*
worry • *v* preocupar, amoinar, preocupar-se, amoinar-se • *n* preocupació, angoixa
worrying • *adj* preocupant
worse • *adj* pitjor
worsening • *n* empitjorament *(m)*
worship • *v* adorar, venerar • *n* adoració *(f)*, culte *(m)*, veneració *(f)*
worth • *n* valor *(m)*
worthily • *adv* dignament
worthy • *adj* digne
wound • *v* ferir
wrap • *v* embolicar
wreck • *n* ruïna *(f)*
wrestler • *n* lluitador *(m)*, lluitadora *(f)*
wrist • *n* canell *(m)*
write • *v* escriure
writer • *n* escriptor *(m)*
written • *adj* escrit
wrongdoer • *n* malfactor *(m)*
wrongly • *adv* erròniament
wrought • *adj* treballat
wyvern • *n* víbria *(f)*, vibra *(f)*

X

xebec • *n* xabec *(m)*
xenon • *n* xenó *(m)*
xenophobia • *n* xenofòbia *(f)*
xenophobic • *adj* xenòfob *(m)*, xenòfoba *(f)*
xerography • *n* xerografia *(f)*

xerox • *v* fotocopiar
xi • *n* ksi *(f)*
xylem • *n* xilema *(m)*
xylophone • *n* xilòfon *(m)*

Y

yacht • *n* iot *(m)*
yak • *n* iac *(m)*
yam • *n* nyam *(m)*
yard • *n* iarda *(f)*
yarn • *n* fil *(m)*
yarrow • *n* milfulles *(f)*
yawn • *v* badallar • *n* badall *(m)*
yeah • *adv* sí
year • *n* any *(m)*
yearbook • *n* anuari
yearly • *adj* anual • *adv* anualment
yearning • *n* anhel *(m)*
yeast • *n* llevat *(m)*
yellow • *n* groc *(m)* • *adj* groc, covard
yellowness • *n* grogor *(f)*
yesterday • *n* ahir, dia d'ahir *(m)* • *adv* ahir
yesteryear • *n* antany
yet • *adv* encara • *conj* tanmateix, no obstant això

yew • *n* teix, teixeda *(f)*
yield • *v* cedir
yo-yo • *n* io-io *(m)*
yodh • *n* iod *(f)*
yoga • *n* ioga *(m)*
yogurt • *n* iogurt *(m)*
yoke • *v* junyir, júnyer, enjovar • *n* jou *(m)*, coble *(m)*
yolk • *n* rovell *(m)*
yonder • *adv* allà
you • *pron* vosaltres, vostès, vós, tu, vostè, hom, u
young • *adj* jove *(f)*
yourself • *pron* et, mateix
youth • *n* joventut *(f)*, abril *(m)*, jove *(f)*
ytterbium • *n* iterbi
yttrium • *n* itri
yuck • *interj* ecs
yum • *adj* nyam

Z

zap • *v* fer zàping *(m)* • *n* fiblada
zeal • *n* zel *(m)*
zebra • *n* zebra *(f)*
zee • *n* zeta *(f)*
zero • *v* posar a zero • *n* zero, zero *(m)*, res, zero a l'esquerra
zeta • *n* zeta *(f)*
zeugma • *n* zeugma *(m)*
zigzag • *v* zigzaguejar • *n* ziga-zaga *(f)*, zig-zag *(m)*
zinc • *n* zinc
zip • *n* codi postal *(m)*

zirconium • *n* zirconi
zither • *n* cítara *(f)*
zoanthropy • *n* zoantropia *(f)*
zodiac • *n* zodíac *(m)*
zombie • *n* zombi *(f)*
zone • *n* zona *(f)*
zoo • *n* zoològic *(m)*
zoological • *adj* zoològic
zoologist • *n* zoòleg *(m)*
zoology • *n* zoologia *(f)*
zoospore • *n* zoòspora *(f)*

CATALAN-ENGLISH

A

a • *n* a • *prep* at, to
àbac • *n* abacus, chessboard, sluice
abacà • *n* abaca
abacial • *adj* abbatial
abadessa • *n* abbess
abadia • *n* abbacy, abbey, rectory
abaixament • *n* lowering
abaixar • *v* lower
abandonar • *v* abandon
abandonat • *adj* abandoned
abans • *adv* before • *prep* before
abassegar • *v* hoard
abat • *n* abbot
abdicació • *n* abdication
abdomen • *n* abdomen, belly
abdominal • *adj* abdominal
abecedari • *n* abecedary, alphabet
abella • *n* bee
abeller • *n* beekeeper
abellir • *v* appeal
aberració • *n* aberration
aberrant • *adj* aberrant
abeurador • *n* drinker
abiogènesi • *n* abiogenesis
abisme • *n* abyss
abjectament • *adv* abjectly
abjecte • *adj* base
abocador • *n* landfill
abocar • *v* lean
abolir • *v* abolish
abominable • *adj* abominable
abominar • *v* abominate
aborigen • *adj* aboriginal
abortiu • *n* abortive • *adj* abortive
abortiva • *adj* abortive
abraçada • *n* embrace, hug
abraçar • *v* embrace, fathom, hug
abrasió • *n* abrasion
abrasiu • *adj* abrasive
abreujat • *adj* abridged
abreviatura • *n* abbreviation
abric • *n* coat, overcoat, paletot
abril • *n* youth
abrogar • *v* abrogate
abruptament • *adv* abruptly
abrupte • *adj* abrupt
abscissa • *n* abscissa
abscondir • *v* abscond
absència • *n* absence
absent • *adj* absent
absenta • *n* absinthe
absentar • *v* absent
absentisme • *n* truancy
absis • *n* apse

absolut • *adj* absolute, implicit, utter
absolutament • *adv* absolutely
absolutista • *adj* absolutist
absorbent • *n* absorbent • *adj* absorbent
absorbir • *v* absorb
absort • *adj* engrossed
abstemi • *adj* abstemious
abstenció • *n* abstention
abstersió • *n* abstersion
abstersiu • *adj* abstersive
abstracció • *n* abstract, abstraction
abstraccionisme • *n* abstractionism
abstraccionista • *n* abstractionist • *adj* abstractionist
abstracte • *adj* abstract
absurd • *adj* absurd
absurdament • *adv* absurdly
abúlia • *n* abulia
abúlic • *adj* abulic
abundant • *adj* abundant
abundantment • *adv* abundantly
abusiu • *adj* abusive
abusivament • *adv* abusively
acabar • *v* end, finish
acabat • *adv* after
acàcia • *n* acacia
acadèmic • *n* academic, academician • *adj* academic
acadèmicament • *adv* academically
acant • *n* acanthus
acaparar • *v* hoard
àcar • *n* mite
acariciar • *v* fondle
acaronar • *v* fondle
acceleració • *n* acceleration
accelerar • *v* accelerate, hurry
acceleròmetre • *n* accelerometer
accent • *n* accent, stress
accentuar • *v* accent, accentuate
accepció • *n* sense
acceptabilitat • *n* acceptability
acceptable • *adj* acceptable
acceptablement • *adv* acceptably
acceptant • *n* acceptor
acceptar • *v* accept
accessible • *adj* accessible
accident • *n* accident, accidental
accidental • *adj* accidental
accidentalment • *adv* accidentally
accídia • *n* sloth
acció • *n* action, share
acer • *n* steel
acerola • *n* acerola
acèrrim • *adj* staunch

acetàbul • *n* acetabulum
acetamida • *n* acetamide
acetat • *n* acetate
acetona • *n* acetone
ací • *adv* here
acíclic • *adj* acyclic
àcid • *n* acid • *adj* acid, acidic, sour
acidificar • *v* acidify
acidimetria • *n* acidimetry
aclarir-se • *v* clear
açò • *adj* so • *pron* that
acòlit • *n* acolyte
acollidor • *adj* cosy, welcoming
acollir • *v* welcome
acolorir • *v* color
acoltellar • *v* knife, stab
acomiadar • *v* dismiss, fire, sack
acompanyament • *n* accompaniment
acompanyant • *n* companion
acompanyar • *v* accompany
acomplir • *v* achieve
acònit • *n* aconite
aconseguir • *v* achieve, attain, get
aconsellable • *adj* advisable
acord • *n* agreement, arrangement
acordió • *n* accordion
acordionista • *n* accordionist
acostumat • *adj* accustomed
acreció • *n* accretion
acrílic • *adj* acrylic
acròbata • *n* acrobat
acrofòbia • *n* acrophobia
acromàtic • *adj* achromatic
acromi • *n* acromion
acrònim • *n* acronym
acròpolis • *n* acropolis
acròstic • *n* acrostic
acta • *n* deed
acte • *n* act, deed
actini • *n* actinium
actinòmetre • *n* actinometer
actitud • *n* attitude
activament • *adv* actively
activisme • *n* activism
activitat • *n* activity
actor • *n* actor
actriu • *n* actor, actress
actuació • *n* performance
actual • *adj* current, present
actualització • *n* update
actualitzar • *v* update
actualment • *adv* currently, nowadays
actuar • *v* act, play
actuari • *n* actuary
acubar-se • *v* faint
acudit • *n* joke
aculi • *n* thorn

aculturació • *n* acculturation
acúmetre • *n* audiometer
acupuntura • *n* acupuncture
acuradament • *adv* accurately, carefully
acurat • *adj* painstaking
acusació • *n* accusation
acusar • *v* accuse
acusatiu • *n* accusative • *adj* accusative
acústic • *adj* acoustic
acústica • *n* acoustics
adaptable • *adj* adaptable
adaptació • *n* adaptation
adaptador • *n* adapter
adaptatiu • *adj* adaptive
addició • *n* addition
addicional • *adj* additional
addicionalment • *adv* additionally
addicte • *n* addict
addictiu • *adj* addictive
additiu • *n* additive
adenoide • *n* adenoid
adequadament • *adv* adequately
adequat • *adj* adequate, fit, proper
adéu • *interj* bye, farewell, goodbye • *n* farewell
adéu-siau • *interj* goodbye
adherent • *adj* adherent
adherir • *v* adhere
adhesiu • *adj* adherent, adhesive • *n* adhesive
adiabàtic • *adj* adiabatic
adjacència • *n* adjacency
adjacent • *adj* adjacent
adjectiu • *adj* adjectival, adjective • *n* adjective
adjectivament • *adv* adjectivally
adjudicar • *v* adjudicate
adlàter • *n* minion
administració • *n* management
administrador • *n* administrator, steward
administradora • *n* administrator
administrar • *v* administer
administratiu • *adj* administrative
administrativament • *adv* administratively
admirable • *adj* admirable
admirablement • *adv* admirably
admirar • *v* admire
admissible • *adj* admissible
admissió • *n* admission
adob • *n* dung, fertilizer
adoctrinament • *n* indoctrination
adolescència • *n* adolescence
adolescent • *n* adolescent • *adj* adolescent
adolorit • *adj* sore
adonar-se • *v* notice, realize

adoptiu • *adj* adoptive
adorable • *adj* adorable
adorablement • *adv* adorably
adoració • *n* worship
adorar • *v* worship
adormit • *adj* asleep
adornar • *v* tire
adquirible • *adj* acquirable
adquirir • *v* acquire
adquisició • *n* acquisition
adreça • *n* address
adreçar • *v* address, direct, straighten
adrenalina • *n* adrenaline
adulació • *n* adulation
adult • *n* adult
adúlter • *n* adulterer
adulteri • *n* adultery
advecció • *n* advection
adventici • *adj* adventitious
adverbi • *n* adverb
adverbial • *adj* adverbial
adverbialment • *adv* adverbially
adversitat • *n* adversity
advertir • *v* warn
advocada • *n* lawyer
advocat • *n* attorney, lawyer
aeri • *adj* aerial
aeròbic • *adj* aerobic
aerodinàmi • *adj* aerodynamic
aerodinàmica • *n* aerodynamics
aeròdrom • *n* aerodrome
aerolliscador • *n* hovercraft
aeròmetre • *n* aerometer
aeronau • *n* aircraft
aeronàutica • *n* aeronautics
aeroport • *n* airport
aerosfera • *n* atmosphere
aerosol • *n* aerosol
afaitar • *v* shave
afaitar-se • *v* shave
afalagador • *adj* flattering
afamat • *adj* hungry
afàsia • *n* aphasia
afeblir • *v* weaken
afeblir-se • *v* weaken
afecció • *n* affection
afectar • *v* affect
afecte • *n* affect, affection, endearment
afectuós • *adj* affectionate
afegir • *v* add
afegir-se • *v* join
aferrat • *adj* stingy
afilar • *v* whet
afinar • *v* tune
afirmació • *n* affirmation, assertion
afirmativament • *adv* affirmatively
afligit • *adj* sorry

aflorament • *n* outcrop
afluixar • *v* loose, relax
afores • *n* outskirt
aforisme • *n* aphorism
afortunadament • *adv* fortunately, happily
afortunat • *adj* happy, lucky
afusellament • *n* shooting
agafar • *v* grip, take
àgata • *n* agate
agència • *n* agency
agenda • *n* calendar, planner
agent • *n* agent
àgil • *adj* agile, nimble
agilitat • *n* agility
àgilment • *adv* agilely
agnòsia • *n* agnosia
agnosticisme • *n* agnosticism
agobiar • *v* overwhelm
agonitzar • *v* agonize
àgora • *n* agora
agorafòbia • *n* agoraphobia
agosarat • *adj* bold, daring
agradable • *adj* agreeable, pleasant
agradablement • *adv* agreeably, pleasantly
agradar • *v* like, please
agraïment • *n* acknowledgement, gratefulness
agrair • *v* thank
agraït • *adj* grateful, thankful
agramatical • *adj* ungrammatical
agrament • *adv* sourly
agrassó • *n* gooseberry
agre • *adj* sour
agressiu • *adj* aggressive
agressivament • *adv* aggressively
agressivitat • *n* aggressiveness
agrícola • *adj* agricultural, agriculturist
agricultor • *n* agriculturist
agricultora • *n* agriculturist
agricultura • *n* agriculture
agrimensor • *n* surveyor
agró • *n* egret, heron
agrupar • *v* collect
aguaitar • *v* lurk, prowl
aguantar • *v* hold
àguila • *n* eagle
aguilenc • *adj* aquiline
agulla • *n* agility, hand, needle, spire, switch
agulló • *n* thorn
agut • *adj* acute
ahir • *n* yesterday • *adv* yesterday
aidar • *v* help
aigua • *n* water
aiguafort • *n* etching

aiguamoll • *n* marsh, wetland
aiguaneu • *n* sleet
aiguarràs • *n* turpentine
aiguatinta • *n* aquatint
aigües • *n* water
aïllacionisme • *n* isolationism
aïllament • *n* isolation
aïllar • *v* insulate, isolate
aïllat • *adj* insular, isolated
aïnada • *n* neigh
aïnar • *v* neigh
aire • *n* air
airejós • *adj* breezy
airós • *adj* breezy
airosament • *adv* breezily
aixa • *n* adze
aixada • *n* hoe, mattock
aixafaguitarres • *n* spoilsport
aixecar • *v* heighten
aixella • *n* armpit
aixeta • *n* spigot
així • *adv* so, thus • *interj* so
això • *adj* so • *pron* that, this
ajornar • *v* adjourn, postpone
ajuda • *n* help
ajudador • *n* helper
ajudant • *n* helper
ajudar • *v* help
ajuntar • *v* collect
ajuntar-se • *v* coalesce
ajust • *n* adjustment
ajustable • *adj* adjustable
ajustar • *v* set
ajustment • *n* adjustment
alŭlegar • *v* allege
alŭlegoria • *n* allegory
alŭlegòric • *adj* allegorical
alŭlegòricament • *adv* allegorically
alŭlel • *n* allele
alŭleluia • *interj* hallelujah
alŭlèrgia • *n* allergy
alŭlèrgic • *adj* allergic
alŭligàtor • *n* alligator
alŭliteració • *n* alliteration
alŭlòcton • *adj* allochthonous
alŭlot • *n* boy
alŭlota • *n* girl
alŭlucinació • *n* hallucination
alŭlucinogen • *n* hallucinogen, hallucinogenic • *adj* hallucinogenic
alŭlusió • *n* allusion
alŭlusiu • *adj* allusive
alŭluvial • *adj* alluvial
alŭluvió • *n* alluvial, alluvium
ala • *n* forward, wing, winger
alabarda • *n* halberd
alabarder • *n* halberdier

alabastre • *n* alabaster
alabastrí • *adj* alabaster
alambí • *n* alembic
alarma • *n* alarm
alarmant • *adj* alarming
alarmar • *v* alarm
alarmisme • *n* alarmism
alba • *n* dawn, daybreak
albada • *n* dawn
albatros • *n* albatross
albedo • *n* albedo
àlber • *n* poplar
albercoc • *n* apricot
albercoquer • *n* apricot
alberg • *n* hostel
albergínia • *n* eggplant
alberginiera • *n* eggplant
albí • *n* albino • *adj* albino
albita • *n* albite
albor • *n* whiteness
albors • *n* dawn
àlbum • *n* book
albumen • *n* albumen
alçada • *n* altitude
alcalde • *n* mayor
alcalimetria • *n* alkalimetry
alcaloide • *n* alkaloid
alçar • *v* lift
alcàsser • *n* alcazar
alçat • *n* elevation
alció • *n* halcyon, kingfisher
alcohol • *n* alcohol
alcohòlic • *n* alcoholic • *adj* alcoholic
alcoholisme • *n* alcoholism
aldarull • *n* brouhaha, commotion, fuss,
hubbub, mayhem, ruckus, stir, uproar
alè • *n* breath
aleatori • *adj* random
aleatòriament • *adv* randomly
alegre • *adj* glad, happy
alegrement • *adv* happily
alegria • *n* glee, joy
alemanda • *n* allemande
alemanya • *n* allemande
alena • *n* awl
alenar • *v* breathe
aler • *n* forward, wing, winger
alerta • *n* alert
alertar • *v* alert
aleta • *n* fin
aleví • *n* fry
alfa • *n* alpha
alfàbega • *n* basil
alfabet • *n* alphabet • *adj* literate
alfabètic • *adj* alphabetical
alfabèticament • *adv* alphabetically
alfàbrega • *n* basil

alfanumèric • *adj* alphanumeric
alfil • *n* bishop
alforja • *n* saddlebag
algaravia • *n* claptrap
àlgebra • *n* algebra
algebraic • *adj* algebraic
algebraicament • *adv* algebraically
algèbricament • *adv* algebraically
algorisme • *n* algorithm
algú • *pron* somebody
algues • *n* seaweed
algun • *pron* any
aliança • *n* alliance
aliatge • *n* alloy
aliè • *adj* alien
alié • *adj* alien
alienació • *n* alienation
alienar • *v* alienate
alifàtic • *adj* aliphatic
àliga • *n* eagle
aligot • *n* buzzard, hawk
aliment • *n* food, foodstuff
alimentador • *adj* nutritious
alimentar • *v* feed
alimentós • *adj* nutritious
all • *n* clove, garlic
allà • *adv* there, yonder
allau • *n* avalanche
alletar • *v* nurse, suckle
alleugerir • *v* lighten
alleujament • *n* relief
alleujar • *v* lighten
alleujat • *adj* relieved
allí • *adv* there
alliberació • *n* liberation
alliberament • *n* liberation, release
alliberar • *v* free, liberate, loose, release
alliberat • *n* release
allioli • *n* aioli
allisar • *v* smooth
allistar • *v* list
allitar-se • *v* bed
allò • *pron* that
allotjar • *v* host, house
allunyar • *v* distance
almanac • *n* almanac
almirall • *n* admiral
almoina • *n* alms
alopècia • *n* alopecia
alosa • *n* lark, skylark
alou • *n* allodium
alpaca • *n* alpaca
alpí • *adj* alpine
alpinista • *n* mountaineer
alquímia • *n* alchemy
alquimista • *n* alchemist
alt • *adj* high, loud, upper

altament • *adv* highly
altar • *n* altar
altaveu • *n* loudspeaker, speaker
alteració • *n* alteration
alterar • *v* alter
alternatiu • *adj* alternative
alternativament • *adv* alternatively
altímetre • *n* altimeter
altitud • *n* altitude
altrament • *adv* otherwise
altre • *adj* else
altres • *n* others
altruisme • *n* altruism
altruista • *n* altruist • *adj* altruistic
alvèol • *n* alveolus
alvocat • *n* avocado
alvocater • *n* avocado
amable • *adj* kind, lovable
amablement • *adv* kindly
amagar • *v* abscond, hide, occult
amagat • *adj* hidden, occult
amanida • *n* salad
amanir • *v* season
amansir • *v* tame
amant • *n* lover
amarant • *n* amaranth
amarar • *v* soak
amarg • *adj* bitter
amargament • *adv* bitterly
amarilŭlis • *n* amaryllis
amarra • *n* tether
amassar • *v* knead
amazona • *n* amazon
amb • *prep* with
ambaixada • *n* embassy
ambaixador • *n* ambassador
ambició • *n* thirst
ambiciós • *adj* ambitious
ambiciosament • *adv* ambitiously
ambidextre • *adj* ambidextrous
ambient • *n* ambient, atmosphere, environment • *adj* ambient
ambiental • *adj* environmental
ambientalment • *adv* environmentally
ambigu • *adj* ambiguous
ambiguament • *adv* ambiguously
ambigüitat • *n* ambiguity
àmbit • *n* compass
ambliopia • *n* amblyopia
ambó • *n* ambo
ambre • *n* amber
ambulància • *n* ambulance
ambulatori • *adj* ambulatory
amén • *interj* amen
amenaça • *n* threat
amenaçador • *adj* threatening
amenaçar • *v* jeopardize, threaten

amenitat • *n* amenity
americi • *n* americium
ametlla • *n* almond
ametller • *n* almond
amfibi • *n* amphibian • *adj* amphibious
amfiteatre • *n* amphitheater
amfitrió • *n* host
amfitriona • *n* host
àmfora • *n* amphora
amiant • *n* asbestos
amic • *n* boyfriend, friend
amidar • *v* measure
amiga • *n* friend, girlfriend
amigable • *adj* amicable
amigablement • *adv* amicably
amígdala • *n* amygdala, tonsil
amilasa • *n* amylase
amistançada • *n* mistress
amistançat • *n* lover
amistat • *n* friendship, kith
amistós • *adj* friendly
amnèsia • *n* amnesia
amni • *n* amnion
àmnic • *adj* amniotic
amniòtic • *adj* amniotic
amoinar • *v* worry
amoinar-se • *v* worry
amollar • *v* release
amoni • *n* ammonium
amor • *n* love
amorf • *adj* amorphous
amorós • *adj* amorous, loving
amorosament • *adv* amorously
ampere • *n* ampere
amperímetre • *n* ammeter
amperòmetre • *n* ammeter
ampit • *n* parapet, sill, windowsill
ample • *adj* wide
amplitud • *n* amplitude
ampolla • *n* bottle
amprar • *v* borrow
amputació • *n* amputation
amputar • *v* amputate
amulet • *n* charm
amunt • *adv* up
anacard • *n* cashew
anacronisme • *n* anachronism
anacrusi • *n* anacrusis
anàdrom • *adj* anadromous
anafòric • *adj* anaphoric
anafrodisíac • *n* antaphrodisiac • *adj* antaphrodisiac
anafrodisíaca • *n* antaphrodisiac
anagrama • *n* anagram
anal • *adj* anal
analfabet • *n* illiterate • *adj* illiterate
analfabetisme • *n* illiteracy

analgèsia • *n* analgesia
analgèsic • *n* analgesic, anodyne • *adj* analgesic
anàlgia • *n* analgesia
anàlisi • *n* analysis
analític • *adj* analytic
analíticament • *adv* analytically
analitzar • *v* analyze, parse
anàlogament • *adv* analogously
analogia • *n* analogy
anamòrfic • *adj* anamorphic
anamòrfica • *adj* anamorphic
ananàs • *n* pineapple
anapest • *n* anapest
anar • *v* go
anar-se • *v* go
anarquia • *n* anarchy
anàrquic • *adj* anarchic
anàrquicament • *adv* anarchically
anarquisme • *n* anarchism
anastomosi • *n* anastomosis
anatomia • *n* anatomy
anatòmic • *adj* anatomical
anatòmicament • *adv* anatomically
ancestral • *adj* ancestral
ancià • *adj* elderly
ancian • *n* elder
àncora • *n* anchor
ancorar • *v* anchor
andana • *n* platform
androgin • *adj* androgynous
ànec • *n* duck
anecdotari • *adj* anecdotal
anecdòtic • *adj* anecdotal
aneguet • *n* duckling
anèl·lid • *n* annelid
anell • *n* annulus, ring
anella • *n* ring
anèmia • *n* anemia
anèmic • *adj* anemic
anemòmetre • *n* anemometer
anet • *n* dill
aneurisma • *n* aneurysm
àngel • *n* angel
angèlic • *adj* angelic
angelical • *adj* angelic
angèlicament • *adv* angelically
angiografia • *n* angiography
angle • *n* angle
anglès • *n* creditor
angoixa • *n* worry
angost • *adj* narrow
anguila • *n* eel
anhel • *n* yearning
ànim • *n* mood
ànima • *n* soul
animació • *n* animation

animadversió • *n* animadversion
animal • *n* animal • *adj* animal, beastly
animàlcul • *n* animalcule
animar • *v* animate
animat • *adj* animate, animated
anime • *n* anime
animisme • *n* animism
anís • *n* anise
anit • *n* tonight • *adv* tonight
anivellat • *adj* level
aniversari • *n* birthday
annato • *n* annatto
annex • *n* annex
annexar • *v* annex
ànode • *n* anode
anodí • *adj* anodyne
anòmal • *adj* anomalous
anomenar • *v* name
anònim • *adj* anonymous
anònimament • *adv* anonymously
anorèxia • *n* anorexia
anorèxica • *n* anorexic
anormal • *adj* abnormal
anormalitat • *n* abnormality
anormalment • *adv* abnormally
anortita • *n* anorthite
anotació • *n* observation
anotar • *v* book
ànsia • *n* craving
ansiar • *v* crave
ansietat • *n* anxiety
ansiós • *adj* anxious
ansiosament • *adv* anxiously
ant • *n* moose
antagonisme • *n* antagonism
antagonista • *n* antagonist • *adj* antagonistic
antany • *n* yesteryear
antecedent • *n* antecedent
antecedents • *n* background
antecessor • *n* predecessor
antediluvià • *adj* antediluvian
antefixa • *n* antefix
antena • *n* aerial, antenna
antenupcial • *adj* prenuptial
antepenúltim • *adj* antepenultimate
anterior • *adj* previous
anteriorment • *adv* previously
antiàcid • *n* antacid • *adj* antacid
antiàcida • *adj* antacid
antiadherent • *adj* nonstick
antiafrodisíac • *n* antaphrodisiac
antiafrodisíaca • *n* antaphrodisiac
antibacterià • *n* antibacterial • *adj* antibacterial
antibales • *adj* bulletproof
antibiòtic • *n* antibiotic • *adj* antibiotic

antic • *adj* ancient, antique, old • *n* antique
anticicló • *n* anticyclone
anticonceptiu • *n* contraceptive • *adj* contraceptive
anticòs • *n* antibody
anticrist • *n* antichrist
antidemocràtic • *adj* undemocratic
antidepressiu • *n* antidepressant • *adj* antidepressant
antídot • *n* antidote
antífona • *n* antiphony
antigament • *adv* anciently
antiheroi • *n* antihero
antihistamínic • *n* antihistamine
antiinflamatori • *n* antiphlogistic • *adj* antiphlogistic
antílop • *n* antelope
antimoni • *n* antimony
antineutró • *n* antineutron
antioxidant • *n* antioxidant • *adj* antioxidant
antiparal·lel • *adj* antiparallel
antipartícula • *n* antiparticle
antipàtic • *adj* unfriendly
antípoda • *n* antipodean • *adj* antipodean
antiprotó • *n* antiproton
antiquat • *adj* antiquated, antique
antisèptic • *n* antiseptic • *adj* antiseptic
antitanc • *adj* antitank
antitèticament • *adv* antithetically
antivíric • *adj* antiviral
antivirus • *adj* antiviral
antònim • *n* antonym • *adj* antonymous
antonímia • *n* antonymy
antonomàsia • *n* antonomasia
àntrax • *n* anthrax
antre • *n* antrum
antropocèntric • *adj* anthropocentric
antropocentrisme • *n* anthropocentrism
antropofàgia • *n* cannibalism
antropofòbia • *n* homophobia
antropoide • *n* anthropoid • *adj* anthropoid
antropòleg • *n* anthropologist
antropologia • *n* anthropology
antropometria • *n* anthropometry
antropomorf • *adj* anthropomorphic
antropomòrfic • *adj* anthropomorphic
antropomorfisme • *n* anthropomorphism
antull • *n* impulse, whim
anual • *adj* annual, yearly
anualment • *adv* annually, yearly
anuari • *n* annual, yearbook
anular • *adj* annular
anunci • *n* advertisement, commercial
anunciador • *n* harbinger

anunciar • *v* announce, harbinger
anus • *n* anus
anvers • *n* obverse • *adj* obverse
any • *n* year
anyal • *adj* annual
anyell • *n* lamb
aorta • *n* aorta
apagar • *v* extinguish
apaïsat • *n* landscape
aparèixer • *v* appear
aparell • *n* bond, rig, set
aparença • *n* appearance
aparent • *adj* apparent
aparentment • *adv* apparently
aparició • *n* appearance
apartador • *n* bypass
apartheid • *n* apartheid
apassionadament • *adv* passionately
apassionat • *adj* passionate
àpat • *n* meal
apatia • *n* apathy
apàtic • *adj* apathetic, listless
apàticament • *adv* apathetically
apatita • *n* apatite
apegar • *v* stick
apendicectomia • *n* appendectomy
apèndix • *n* appendix
apesaradament • *adv* sorrowfully
apetitós • *adj* appetizing
àpex • *n* apex
api • *n* celery
apiari • *n* apiary
apicultor • *n* beekeeper
aplaudiment • *n* applause, clap
aplaudir • *v* clap
aplegar • *v* collect
aplicat • *adj* applied
apocalipsi • *n* apocalypse
apocalíptic • *adj* apocalyptic
apocàrpic • *adj* apocarpous
apòcrif • *adj* apocryphal
apoderar-se • *v* seize
apoderat • *n* steward
apòfisi • *n* apophysis
apogeu • *n* apogee
apògraf • *n* apograph
apologètic • *adj* apologetic
apologèticament • *adv* apologetically
apologitzar • *v* apologize
aponeurosi • *n* aponeurosis
aposento • *n* room
aposta • *n* bet
apostar • *v* bet, station
apostatar • *v* apostatize
apòstol • *n* apostle
apòstrof • *n* apostrophe
apòstrofe • *n* apostrophe

apotegma • *n* apothegm
apreciable • *adj* considerable
apreciablement • *adv* appreciably
aprehendre • *v* apprehend
aprendre • *v* learn
aprenent • *n* learner
aprenentatge • *n* apprenticeship, learning
aprensiu • *adj* apprehensive
apressar • *v* hurry
apretar • *v* squeeze
aprimar • *v* thin
aprimar-se • *v* thin
apropar • *v* near
apropiació • *n* seizure
apropiadament • *adv* accordingly, appropriately
apropiat • *adj* suitable
aprovació • *n* go
aprovar • *v* approve, pass
aproximadament • *adv* approximately
aproximar • *v* near
aproximar-se • *v* approach
aproximat • *adj* approximate, rough
apte • *adj* fit
apuntador • *n* pointer
apuntar • *v* aim
apunyalar • *v* fist, knife, stab
aquàtic • *adj* aquatic
aqüeducte • *n* aqueduct
aqueni • *n* achene
aquest • *pron* this
aquesta • *pron* this
aquí • *adv* here
aqüífer • *n* aquifer
aquilí • *adj* aquiline
aquirit • *adj* adventitious
ara • *n* now • *adv* now • *interj* now • *conj* now
arabesc • *n* arabesque
aràcnid • *n* arachnid
arada • *n* plough
aram • *n* copper
aranger • *n* grapefruit
aranja • *n* grapefruit
aranya • *n* spider
arbitrari • *adj* arbitrary
àrbitre • *n* judge
arbre • *n* tree
arbust • *n* bush, shrub
arc • *n* arc, arch, bow
arcà • *adj* arcane
arcada • *n* arcade
arcaic • *adj* archaic
arcàngel • *n* archangel
ardent • *adj* ablaze, burning
ardiaca • *n* archdeacon

ardu • *adj* arduous
àrea • *n* area, compass
arena • *n* sand
areng • *n* herring
arèola • *n* areola
argent • *n* argent, silver
argentat • *adj* silver, silvery
argentita • *n* argentite
argila • *n* clay
arginina • *n* arginine
argó • *n* argon
argot • *n* cant, jargon, slang
arguïble • *adj* arguable
argument • *n* argument, plot
argumentació • *n* argument
àrid • *adj* arid
aristocràcia • *n* aristocracy
aristòcrata • *n* aristocrat
aristocràtic • *adj* aristocratic
aristocràticament • *adv* aristocratically
aritmètica • *n* arithmetic
aritmèticament • *adv* arithmetically
arítmia • *n* arrhythmia
arítmic • *adj* arrhythmic
arlequí • *n* harlequin
arma • *n* arm, weapon
armadillo • *n* armadillo
armadura • *n* armor
armar • *v* arm
armari • *n* cabinet, cupboard, locker, wardrobe
armat • *adj* armed
armilla • *n* vest, waistcoat
arna • *n* beehive, dandruff, moth
arner • *n* kingfisher
arnès • *n* armor, harness
aromàtic • *adj* aromatic
arpa • *n* harp
arpejar • *v* scratch
arpella • *n* harrier
arpó • *n* harpoon
arponar • *v* harpoon
arponer • *n* harpooner
arquebisbe • *n* archbishop
arquejar • *v* arch
arqueòleg • *n* archaeologist
arqueologia • *n* archaeology
arqueològic • *adj* archaeological
arquer • *n* archer
arquetip • *n* archetype
arquetípic • *adj* archetypal
arquitecte • *n* architect
arquitectònic • *adj* architectural
arquitectura • *n* architecture
arquitrau • *n* architrave
arracada • *n* earring

arraconar • *v* corner
arrambar-se • *v* lean
arrangement • *n* arrangement
arrauxat • *adj* rash
arravatament • *n* rapture
arreglada • *n* arrangement
arreglar • *v* arrange, array, clean, fix, sort
arrel • *n* race, root
arrencada • *n* bootstrap
arrenjar • *v* arrange
arreplegar • *v* collect
arrest • *n* arrest
arribar • *v* arrive, get
arriscar • *v* imperil, risk, venture
arriscar-se • *v* chance
arrissat • *adj* curly, fuzzy
arrodonit • *adj* rounded
arrogància • *n* arrogance
arrogant • *adj* arrogant, haughty, proud
arrogantment • *adv* arrogantly
arròs • *n* rice
arrossegar • *v* drag, grovel, trail
arrossegar-se • *v* crawl
arruixador • *n* sprinkler
arruixar • *v* sprinkle
arsenal • *n* magazine
arsènic • *n* arsenic
artefacte • *n* artifact
artell • *n* knuckle
artèria • *n* artery
arterial • *adj* arterial
arteriola • *n* arteriole
artesà • *n* artisan, craftsman
article • *n* article, paper
articulació • *n* articulation, joint, utterance
articuladament • *adv* articulately
articulat • *adj* articulate
artificial • *adj* artificial, contrived, false
artificialment • *adv* artificially
artiller • *n* artilleryman, gunner
artilleria • *n* artillery, ordnance
artista • *n* artist
artístic • *adj* artistic
artísticament • *adv* artistically
artrític • *adj* arthritic
artritis • *n* arthritis
artròpode • *n* arthropod
arxidiaca • *n* archdeacon
arxiduc • *n* archduke
arxiduquessa • *n* archduchess
arxillaüt • *n* archlute
arxipèlag • *n* archipelago
arxiu • *n* archive, file
as • *n* ace
asbest • *n* asbestos
ascendència • *n* ancestry

ascendir • *v* ascend
ascensió • *n* ascension
ascensor • *n* lift
ascites • *n* ascites
ascla • *n* flake
ase • *n* donkey
asexualitat • *n* asexuality
asfalt • *n* asphalt
asfixiar • *v* smother
asil • *n* asylum
asimètric • *adj* asymmetrical
asimètricament • *adv* asymmetrically
asimptomàtic • *adj* asymptomatic
asímptota • *n* asymptote
asma • *n* asthma
asmàtic • *adj* asthmatic
asolellat • *adj* sunny
aspa • *n* vane
aspirar • *v* inhale
aspirina • *n* aspirin
aspra • *adj* acrimonious
aspre • *adj* acrimonious, harsh, rough
assaborir • *v* savor
assaig • *n* rehearsal, try
assajar • *v* rehearse
assassí • *n* assassin, murderer • *adj* murderous
assassinar • *v* assassinate, murder
assassinat • *n* assassination, kill, murder
assecadora • *n* dryer
assedegat • *adj* parched, thirsty
assegurança • *n* insurance
assemblea • *n* assembly
assentament • *n* settlement
assenyadament • *adv* sensibly
assenyat • *adj* sensible
asserció • *n* assertion
assertiu • *adj* assertive
assertivitat • *n* assertiveness
assetjar • *v* besiege, molest
asseureś • *v* sit
asseveració • *n* asseveration
assíduament • *adv* assiduously
assignar • *v* set
assignatura • *n* subject
assimilar • *v* assimilate
assistència • *n* assist, assistance
assistente • *n* assistant
assistir • *v* attend
associació • *n* association
associar • *v* associate
associat • *n* associate
associatiu • *adj* associative
assolible • *adj* achievable
assossegat • *adj* peaceful
assotar • *v* whip
àstat • *n* astatine

astenosfera • *n* asthenosphere
asterisc • *n* asterisk
asteroide • *n* asteroid
asticot • *n* maggot
astigmatisme • *n* astigmatism
astor • *n* goshawk
astràgal • *n* anklebone, astragalus
astrofísic • *adj* astrophysical • *n* astrophysicist
astrofísica • *n* astrophysics
astrologia • *n* astrology
astrològic • *adj* astrological
astronau • *n* spaceship
astronauta • *n* astronaut
astrònom • *n* astronomer
astrònoma • *n* astronomer
astronomia • *n* astronomy
astronòmicament • *adv* astronomically
astut • *adj* astute, cunning
astutament • *adv* astutely
atac • *n* attack
atacant • *n* attacker, forward
atacar • *v* attack
ataràxia • *n* ataraxia
ataronjat • *adj* orange
atàxia • *n* ataxia
ateisme • *n* atheism
ateístic • *adj* atheistic
atemorit • *adj* frightened
atenció • *n* attention
atendre • *v* attend
atent • *adj* attentive, thoughtful
atentament • *adv* attentively
atenuar • *v* attenuate, palliate
aterrar • *v* land
atestat • *n* witness
ateu • *n* atheist • *adj* atheistic
atiar • *v* stoke
àtic • *n* attic, penthouse
atípic • *adj* atypical
atles • *n* atlas
atleta • *n* athlete
atmosfera • *n* atmosphere
atmosfèric • *adj* atmospheric
atol • *n* atoll
àtom • *n* atom
atòmic • *adj* atomic
atordir • *v* stun
atordit • *adj* dazed
atracar • *v* land
atracció • *n* attraction
atractiu • *adj* attractive
atri • *n* atrium
atroç • *adj* atrocious
atrocitat • *n* atrocity, outrage
atròfia • *n* atrophy
atrofiar • *v* atrophy

atur • *n* unemployment
aturada • *n* save, stoppage
aturar • *v* quit, stop
aturat • *adj* idle, unemployed
atzabeja • *n* jet
atzagaia • *n* assegai
atzar • *n* chance
atzarós • *adj* hazardous
atzur • *n* azure • *adj* azure
au • *n* bird, hen • *interj* ouch
audaç • *adj* audacious, brave
audàcia • *n* bottle
àudio • *adj* audio
audiòmetre • *n* audiometer
audiometria • *n* audiometry
audiovisual • *adj* audiovisual
auditoria • *n* audit
augita • *n* augite
augment • *n* increase
augmentar • *v* augment, increase
aura • *n* aura
aurèola • *n* aureole
aurícula • *n* pinna
aurífer • *adj* auriferous
aurora • *n* aurora, dawn
austerament • *adv* austerely
australopitecí • *adj* australopithecine
autèntic • *adj* authentic
autenticació • *n* authentication
autènticament • *adv* authentically
autenticitat • *n* authenticity
autisme • *n* autism
autista • *n* autistic • *adj* autistic
auto • *n* machine
autobiògraf • *n* autobiographer
autobiografia • *n* autobiography
autobiogràfic • *adj* autobiographical
autobús • *n* bus
autocar • *n* coach
autocontrol • *n* self-control
autòcrata • *n* autocrat
autocràtic • *adj* autocratic
autocràticament • *adv* autocratically
autocrítica • *n* self-criticism
autodefensa • *n* self-defense
autodestructiu • *adj* self-destructive
autodeterminació • *n* self-determination
autodisciplina • *n* self-discipline
autoerotisme • *n* autoeroticism
autoestima • *n* self-esteem
autogàmia • *n* autogamy
autogènesi • *n* abiogenesis
autognòsia • *n* self-awareness
autògraf • *n* autograph
autografiar • *v* autograph
autoimmune • *adj* autoimmune
autoimmunitat • *n* autoimmunity

autòlisi • *n* autolysis
automàtic • *adj* automatic
automàticament • *adv* automatically
automatisme • *n* automatism
automatització • *n* automation
automòbil • *n* automobile, car, machine
autònom • *adj* autonomous
autonomia • *n* autonomy
autonomy • *n* autonomy
autopolůlinització • *n* self-pollination
autòpsia • *n* autopsy
autor • *n* author
autora • *n* author
autoritari • *adj* authoritarian
autoritàriament • *adv* authoritatively
autorització • *n* permission
autoritzar • *v* authorize
autosuficient • *adj* self-sufficient
autosuggestió • *n* affirmation
autumnal • *adj* autumnal
auxiliar • *adj* ancillary, assistant, auxiliary
avall • *adv* down
avalot • *n* brouhaha, commotion, hubbub, mayhem, stir, uproar
avaluació • *n* appraisal
avaluar • *v* assess
avantatge • *n* advantage
avantatjós • *adj* advantageous
avantbraç • *n* forearm
avantguarda • *n* forefront
avantpaís • *n* foreland
avantpassat • *n* ancestor
avar • *adj* greedy
avaria • *n* flat
avarícia • *n* avarice, greed
avariciós • *adj* avaricious, greedy
avariciosament • *adv* avariciously
avellana • *n* hazelnut
avellaner • *n* hazel
aventura • *n* adventure
aventurer • *n* adventurer • *adj* adventurous
avergonyida • *adj* embarrassed
avergonyiment • *n* embarrassment
avergonyit • *adj* ashamed, embarrassed
aversió • *n* aversion, loathing
avet • *n* fir
avi • *n* grandfather
àvia • *n* crone, grandmother
aviari • *adj* avian • *n* aviary
aviat • *adv* early, shortly, soon
àvid • *adj* greedy
àvidament • *adv* avidly
avidesa • *n* avarice
avinguda • *n* avenue
avió • *n* airplane

aviram • *n* poultry
avisar • *v* warn
avitarda • *n* bustard
avorrir • *v* abhor, bore
avorrir-se • *v* tire
avorrit • *adj* bored, boring, humdrum
avort • *n* abortion
avortament • *n* abort, abortion
avortar • *v* abort
avortiu • *adj* abortive
avortiva • *adj* abortive
avui • *n* today • *adv* today

axilůla • *n* armpit
axilůlar • *adj* axillary
axioma • *n* axiom
axiomàtic • *adj* axiomatic
axiomàticament • *adv* axiomatically
axis • *n* axis
axó • *n* axon
àxon • *n* axon
azalea • *n* azalea
azimut • *n* azimuth

B

babaiana • *n* butterfly
babarota • *n* scarecrow
babau • *n* nincompoop
babor • *n* larboard
babuí • *n* baboon
bac • *n* ferry
bacallà • *n* cod
bacanal • *n* bacchanal • *adj* bacchanal
bacarà • *n* baccarat
backgammon • *n* backgammon
baclaua • *n* baklava
bacterià • *adj* bacterial
bacteriòleg • *n* bacteriologist
bacteriologia • *n* bacteriology
bacteriològic • *adj* bacteriological
badall • *n* crack, sandwich, yawn
badallar • *v* yawn
badana • *n* sheepskin
badia • *n* bay
bàdminton • *n* badminton
bagassa • *n* tart
bagatelůla • *n* bagatelle
bagatge • *n* background, luggage
bai • *n* bay
baia • *n* berry
baioneta • *n* bayonet
baix • *adj* base, down, low, short • *adv* low
baixada • *n* descent
baixar • *v* lower
baixó • *n* bassoonist
bajanada • *n* nonsense
bala • *n* bullet, marble
baladre • *n* oleander
balalaica • *n* balalaika
balanç • *n* balance
balança • *n* balance, scales
balancejar • *v* swing
balbotejar • *v* utter
balbucejar • *v* utter

balcó • *n* balcony
baldriga • *n* shearwater
baldufa • *n* top
balena • *n* whale
balener • *n* whaler
balístic • *adj* ballistic
balística • *n* ballistics
ball • *n* dance
ballador • *n* dancer
ballar • *v* dance
ballarí • *n* dancer
ballarina • *n* ballerina
ballaruga • *n* fidget
ballesta • *n* crossbow
baló • *n* balloon
bàlsam • *n* salve
bambú • *n* bamboo
banal • *adj* banal, trivial
banalitat • *n* truism
banana • *n* banana
banc • *n* bank, bench, school
banda • *n* crew, wing
bandada • *n* flock
bandarra • *n* tart
bandejament • *n* exile
bandejar • *v* banish, exile
bandejat • *n* exile
bandera • *n* banner, flag
banderilla • *n* banderilla
banderola • *n* banner
banjo • *n* banjo
banner • *n* banner
banquer • *n* banker
banqueta • *n* bench
banquisa • *n* floe
banús • *n* ebony, persimmon
bany • *n* bath, bathroom
banya • *n* horn
banyador • *n* swimsuit
banyes • *n* split

baptismal • *adj* baptismal
baptisme • *n* baptism
baptista • *n* baptist
bar • *n* pub
baralla • *n* deck, quarrel
barallar • *v* shuffle
barallar-se • *v* fight, quarrel
barat • *adj* inexpensive
barb • *n* barbel
barba • *n* beard
barbacana • *n* barbican
barballera • *n* wattle
bàrbar • *n* barbarian • *adj* barbarian
barbar • *v* beard
bari • *n* barium
barió • *n* baryon
baríton • *n* baritone
bàrman • *n* bartender
barnús • *n* bathrobe
baró • *n* baron
baròmetre • *n* barometer
baromètric • *adj* barometric
baronessa • *n* baroness
baronia • *n* barony
baronial • *adj* baronial
barra • *n* stick
barraca • *n* shed
barratgina • *n* dragonfly
barrejar • *v* mix, shuffle
barret • *n* hat
barri • *n* neighborhood
barril • *n* drum, keg
barrina • *n* auger
barrinar • *v* bore, ream, scuttle
barroer • *adj* slapdash
barroerament • *adv* slapdash
basalt • *n* basalt
basament • *n* base
basar • *v* base • *n* bazaar
basarda • *n* fear
base • *n* base
bàsic • *adj* basic • *n* primary
bàsicament • *adv* basically
basílica • *n* basilica
basilisc • *n* basilisk
bàsquet • *n* basket, basketball
basquetbol • *n* basketball
bassa • *n* pond
bassiot • *n* puddle
bast • *adj* coarse, rude
basta • *adj* coarse
bastant • *adv* quite, rather
bastard • *n* bastard • *adj* bastard, spurious
bastida • *n* scaffolding
bastió • *n* bastion
bastó • *n* club, staff, stick

bastonejar • *v* club
bastonet • *n* chopstick
bat • *n* bat
batall • *n* clapper
batalla • *n* battle, combat
batallar • *v* battle
batedor • *n* batter
batedora • *n* mixer, whisk
batejar • *v* baptize
bateria • *n* battery
batidora • *n* blender
bàtik • *n* batik
batímetre • *n* bathometer
batimetria • *n* bathymetry
batimètric • *adj* bathymetric
batiscaf • *n* bathyscaphe
batisfera • *n* bathysphere
batòmetre • *n* bathometer
batre • *v* duel, hit, knock
batut • *n* batter
batuta • *n* baton
baula • *n* link
bauprès • *n* bowsprit
bavejar • *v* drivel
be • *n* bee
bé • *adv* well • *interj* well
bear • *n* bear
bebè • *n* baby
bec • *n* beak, bill, nib
beca • *n* scholarship
becada • *n* siesta, woodcock
becadell • *n* snipe
becaina • *n* nap
beceroles • *n* abecedary
becut • *n* curlew
bedoll • *n* birch
beduí • *n* bedouin
beguda • *n* drink
beina • *n* scabbard, sheath
beisbol • *n* baseball
bel • *n* baa
belůlicós • *adj* warlike
belůligerant • *adj* warlike
belar • *v* baa
bell • *adj* beautiful, fair
bella • *adj* beautiful
bellament • *adv* beautifully
bellesa • *n* beauty
belluguet • *n* fidget
bemoll • *n* flat
ben • *adv* well
benanança • *n* well-being
benèfic • *adj* benevolent
benefici • *n* advantage, benefit
beneficiar • *v* benefit
beneficiós • *adj* beneficial
beneir • *v* bless

beneit • *n* fool, nincompoop
benestar • *n* well-being
benèvolament • *adv* benevolently
benevolència • *n* benevolence
benevolent • *adj* benevolent
benfactor • *n* benefactor
benjamí • *n* baby
béns • *n* estate, goods
benvinguda • *n* welcome • *interj* welcome
benvingudes • *interj* welcome
benvingut • *adj* welcome • *interj* welcome
benvinguts • *interj* welcome
benvolgut • *adj* dear
benzè • *n* benzene
benzina • *n* gasoline, oil
bergantí • *n* brig
beril • *n* beryl
berilůli • *n* beryllium
berkeli • *n* berkelium
berruga • *n* wart
bes • *n* kiss
besada • *n* kiss
besant • *n* bezant
besar • *v* kiss
bescoll • *n* nape
besoncle • *n* great-uncle
bessó • *n* essence, meat, twin
bèstia • *n* animal, beast • *adj* irrational, stupid
bestial • *adj* beastly
bestialitat • *n* bestiality
bestiar • *n* cattle, livestock
bestiari • *n* bestiary
bestiesa • *n* nonsense
beta • *n* beta
bètel • *n* betel
beure • *v* drink
bevedor • *n* drinker
bevedora • *n* drinker
biaix • *n* bias
bíblic • *adj* biblical
bibliografia • *n* bibliography
bibliogràfic • *adj* bibliographic
biblioteca • *n* library
bibliotecari • *n* librarian
bicameral • *adj* bicameral
bici • *n* bike
bicicleta • *n* bicycle
bifaç • *n* biface
bifurcació • *n* fork
biga • *n* timber
bigàmia • *n* bigamy
bigoti • *n* moustache, whisker
bilabial • *adj* bilabial
bilateral • *adj* bilateral

bilingüe • *adj* bilingual
bilis • *n* bile
billar • *n* billiards, snooker
bimestral • *adv* bimonthly
bimolecular • *adj* bimolecular
binari • *adj* binary
bingo • *n* bingo
binocles • *n* binoculars
binomi • *n* binomial
biodegradable • *adj* biodegradable
biogènesi • *n* biogenesis
biògraf • *n* biographer
biografia • *n* biography
biòleg • *n* biologist
biòloga • *n* biologist
biologia • *n* biology
biològic • *adj* biological
bioluminescència • *n* bioluminescence
biomedicina • *n* biomedicine
bioquímic • *adj* biochemical
bioquímica • *n* biochemistry
bioremediació • *n* bioremediation
biòtic • *adj* biotic
biotita • *n* biotite
bipolar • *adj* bipolar
biquini • *n* bikini
birra • *n* beer
bis • *n* screw
bisbat • *n* bishopric
bisbe • *n* bishop
bisexual • *n* bisexual • *adj* bisexual
bismut • *n* bismuth
bisó • *n* buffalo
bistrot • *n* bistro
bitllaire • *n* bowler
bitlles • *n* bowling
bitlletera • *n* wallet
blanc • *n* white • *adj* white
blancor • *n* whiteness
blancúria • *n* whiteness
blanquejat • *n* whitewash
blanquinós • *adj* whitish
blasfèmia • *n* blasphemy
blat • *n* wheat
blau • *n* blue, bruise • *adj* blue
blauet • *n* halcyon, kingfisher
blavenc • *adj* bluish
blavís • *adj* bluish
blavor • *n* blueness
blavós • *adj* bluish
ble • *n* lock, wick
bleda • *n* chard
blefaritis • *n* blepharitis
blindat • *adj* armored
bloc • *n* block, boulder
blocar • *v* block
bloqueig • *n* block, blockade, stoppage

bloquejar • *v* block, blockade, hang
bloquejar-se • *v* hang
bo • *adj* good • *n* good
boa • *n* boa
boà • *n* boa
boc • *n* buck
boca • *n* mouth
bocabadat • *adj* speechless
boccia • *n* bocce
bocí • *n* mouthful
boda • *n* marriage, wedding
bof • *n* woof
bogeria • *n* craziness, insanity
boia • *n* buoy
boicot • *n* boycott
boicotejar • *v* boycott
boig • *adj* certifiable, crazy, gaga, mad
boira • *n* fog, mist
boirum • *n* smog
boix • *n* box, boxwood
boja • *adj* mad
bojament • *adv* madly
bol • *n* bowl
bola • *n* ball
bolcall • *n* diaper
bolcalls • *n* diaper
bolet • *n* mushroom
bolig • *n* jack
bolígraf • *n* pen
bolòmetre • *n* bolometer
bolquer • *n* diaper
bolquers • *n* diaper
bomba • *n* bomb
bombar • *v* lob
bombarda • *n* bombard, shawm
bombardejar • *v* bomb, bombard
bombó • *n* chocolate
bombolla • *n* bubble
bon • *adj* good
bona • *n* good
bondat • *n* goodness, kindness
bonesa • *n* goodness
bongo • *n* bongo
bonic • *adj* beautiful, pretty
bonica • *adj* beautiful
bony • *n* bonk
boom • *n* boom
bor • *n* boron
bòrax • *n* borax
bord • *n* bastard • *adj* bastard
bordar • *v* bark, woof
bordejar • *v* circumvent
bòric • *adj* boric
borinot • *n* bumblebee
borni • *adj* one-eyed
bornita • *n* bornite
borratja • *n* borage

borratxera • *n* drunkenness
borratxo • *n* drunk, drunkard • *adj* drunk
borró • *n* bud
borrós • *adj* blurred, fuzzy
bosc • *n* forest
boscós • *adj* forested, wooded
bosó • *n* boson
bosquerola • *n* warbler
bossa • *n* bag
bot • *n* dinghy, sunfish, wineskin
bota • *n* boot
bóta • *n* barrel, cask, keg
botànic • *adj* botanical • *n* botanist
botànica • *n* botany
botella • *n* bottle
boter • *n* cooper
botí • *n* prize
botiga • *n* shop
botiguer • *n* kingfisher, shopkeeper
botó • *n* button
botonar • *v* button
botre • *v* bounce
botxí • *n* executioner, shrike
botxina • *n* executioner
botzina • *n* klaxon
bou • *n* ox
boutique • *n* boutique
boví • *adj* bovine
bovo • *n* nincompoop
boxa • *n* boxing
boxador • *n* boxer
boxar • *v* box
boxejador • *n* boxer
boxejar • *v* box
braç • *n* arm
braça • *n* fathom
braçalet • *n* bracelet
bràctea • *n* bract
bradicàrdia • *n* bradycardia
braguer • *n* udder
bragues • *n* pants, underpants
braille • *n* braille
bram • *n* bray
bramar • *v* bray
branca • *n* branch
brandar • *v* brandish
brandejar • *v* brandish
brandi • *n* brandy
brànquia • *n* gill
brasa • *n* ember
bravesa • *n* bravery
bravor • *n* bravery
bravura • *n* bravery
brema • *n* bream
bresca • *n* honeycomb
bressar • *v* cradle
bressol • *n* cradle

bressolar • *v* cradle
breu • *adj* brief
breument • *adv* briefly, shortly, summarily
bric • *n* carton
bricbarca • *n* barque, corvette
brida • *n* bridle
bridge • *n* bridge
brillant • *adj* bright, brilliant
brillantment • *adv* brilliantly
brillantor • *n* shine
brillar • *v* shine
brindar • *v* toast
brindis • *n* toast
brioix • *n* bun
brisa • *n* breeze
broc • *n* neck, spout
brodar • *v* embroider
brodat • *n* embroidery
brogit • *n* brouhaha, fuss, hubbub, uproar
brollador • *n* spout
brollar • *v* sprout
brom • *n* bromine
broma • *n* joke
bronqui • *n* bronchus
bronquíol • *n* bronchiole
bronze • *n* bronze • *adj* bronze
bronzejat • *adj* tanned
broqueta • *n* skewer
bròquil • *n* broccoli
brot • *n* bud
brou • *n* bouillon, broth
bru • *adj* dark-skinned
bruguerola • *n* ling
bruixa • *n* cow, witch
bruixeria • *n* witchcraft
brúixola • *n* compass
bruixot • *n* warlock
brunyidor • *n* burnisher
bruscament • *adv* shortly
brut • *adj* coarse, dirty, nasty, unclean
bruta • *adj* coarse
brutal • *adj* brutal
brutícia • *n* dirtiness, grime
bu • *interj* boo
bua • *n* badness, pimple
buba • *n* pimple, pox
bubó • *n* bubo
bubònic • *adj* bubonic

buc • *n* abdomen, bed, beehive, belly, body, bodywork, cuirass, fuselage, hull, riverbed, shell
bucal • *adj* oral
bucle • *n* loop
bucòlic • *adj* bucolic
budell • *n* intestine
buf • *n* woof
bufador • *n* blowtorch
búfal • *n* buffalo
bufanda • *n* scarf
bufar • *v* blow
bufeta • *n* bladder
bufetada • *n* slap
bufó • *adj* cute
buidar • *v* empty
buidesa • *n* emptiness
buidor • *n* emptiness
buirac • *n* pincushion, quiver
buit • *adj* empty • *n* vacuum, void
bulb • *n* bulb
bullent • *adj* boiling
bullidor • *n* teakettle
bullir • *v* boil
bumerang • *n* boomerang
búnquer • *n* bunker
bureta • *n* burette
burgès • *adj* bourgeois
burgesia • *n* bourgeoisie
burí • *n* burin
burilla • *n* butt
burlar • *v* circumvent
burleria • *n* jeer
burocràcia • *n* bureaucracy
burocràtic • *adj* bureaucratic
burra • *n* donkey
burro • *n* donkey
bus • *n* bus, diver
busca • *n* hand
buscar • *v* look, search
bust • *n* bust
butlla • *n* bull
butxaca • *n* pocket
butxacada • *n* pocketful
butza • *n* chick, chicken, cockerel, paunch, tripe
butzes • *n* tripe
bypass • *n* bypass

C

ca • *n* dog
cabal • *n* flow
cabaret • *n* cabaret
cabell • *n* hair
cabina • *n* car, cockpit
cable • *n* cable, cord, wire
cablejar • *v* cable
cabotejar • *v* head
cabra • *n* crab, goat
cabrejar • *v* anger
cabrestant • *n* winch
cabrit • *n* kid
cabró • *n* wittol
caça • *n* hunt
caca • *n* shit
caçador • *n* hunter
caçamines • *n* minesweeper
caçar • *v* hunt
cacau • *n* cacao
cacauet • *n* peanut
cacera • *n* hunt
cactus • *n* cactus
cadascú • *pron* everyone
cadastral • *adj* cadastral
cadàver • *n* cadaver, corpse
cadavèric • *adj* cadaveric, cadaverous
cadena • *n* chain
cadenat • *n* lock, padlock
cadència • *n* cadence
cadernera • *n* goldfinch
cadi • *n* caddie, caddy
cadira • *n* chair
cadmi • *n* cadmium
caduc • *adj* deciduous
cafè • *n* coffee • *adj* coffee
cafeïna • *n* caffeine
cafeteria • *n* cafeteria
cagar • *v* poop, shit
cagar-la • *v* fuck
cagar-se • *v* shit
cagarro • *n* shit, turd
cagondena • *interj* damn
caiac • *n* kayak
caiguda • *n* borrow, decline, fall
caixa • *n* box, case
calûlígraf • *n* calligrapher
calûligrafia • *n* calligraphy
calûligràfic • *adj* calligraphic
cala • *n* cove, creek
calabós • *n* brig, cell, dungeon
calaix • *n* drawer
calaixera • *n* cupboard
calamar • *n* squid
calamars • *n* squid
calamarsa • *n* hail
calat • *n* draught
calaza • *n* chalaza

calb • *adj* bald
calbesa • *n* baldness
calc • *n* calque
calcani • *adj* calcaneal
calçat • *n* shoe
calces • *n* pantaloons
calci • *n* calcium
calcinar • *v* calcine
calcita • *n* calcite
calçons • *n* breeches, pants
calcopirita • *n* chalcopyrite
calçotets • *n* pants, underpants
càlcul • *n* calculation, calculus
calculable • *adj* calculable
calculador • *n* computer
calculadora • *n* calculator
calcular • *v* calculate
caldera • *n* kettle
caldre • *v* need
calefacció • *n* heating
calendari • *n* calendar, forecast
calendàriu • *n* calendar
calent • *adj* horny, hot, sultry, warm
calibrador • *n* calipers
calibratge • *n* calibration
càlid • *adj* warm
calidoscopi • *n* kaleidoscope
califa • *n* caliph
californi • *n* californium
callar • *adj* silent
calm • *adj* calm
calma • *n* calm, stillness
calmant • *n* anodyne
calmar • *v* calm, quiet, soothe
calmat • *adj* easygoing
calmosament • *adv* calmly
calor • *n* heat
calorímetre • *n* calorimeter
calorimetria • *n* calorimetry
calorimètric • *adj* calorimetric
calúmnia • *n* slander
calumniar • *v* slander
calvície • *n* baldness
calze • *n* calyx, chalice, goblet
cama • *n* leg
camaleó • *n* chameleon
camarada • *n* comrade
camaraderia • *n* camaraderie
camarot • *n* berth
cambra • *n* bedroom, chamber, room
cambrera • *n* waitress
camell • *n* camel
càmera • *n* camera
cameràman • *n* cameraman
camerí • *adj* platyrrhine
càmfora • *n* camphor
camí • *n* path, road, way

caminada • *n* hike
caminar • *v* walk
camió • *n* truck
camisa • *n* shirt
camp • *n* country, field, ground
campana • *n* bell
campanar • *n* steeple
campanya • *n* campaign
camperol • *n* peasant
campestre • *adj* country
campionat • *n* championship
campus • *n* campus
canadella • *n* cruet
canal • *n* canal, gutter
canana • *n* bandoleer
canari • *n* canary
cancelůlació • *n* cancellation
càncer • *n* cancer
cancerós • *adj* cancerous
cançó • *n* song
cançoner • *n* songbook
candela • *n* candle
candeler • *n* candlestick
candidat • *n* candidate
canell • *n* wrist
canella • *n* cinnamon • *adj* cinnamon
caneller • *n* cinnamon
canelobre • *n* candelabrum
cànem • *n* cannabis, hemp
cangur • *n* babysitter, kangaroo
caní • *adj* canine
caníbal • *n* cannibal
canibalisme • *n* cannibalism
canitx • *n* poodle
canó • *n* barrel, cannon, gun
canoa • *n* canoe
canonera • *n* gunboat
canonitzar • *v* canonize
cansada • *adj* tired
cansadament • *adv* wearily
cansalada • *n* bacon
cansar • *v* tire
cansar-se • *v* tire
cansat • *adj* tired
cantable • *adj* singable
cantaire • *n* singer
cantant • *n* singer
cantar • *v* sing
cantera • *n* quarry
canterano • *n* cupboard
cantonada • *n* angle
cantor • *n* singer
canvi • *n* change
canviar • *v* change, substitute
canya • *n* cane, reed
canyella • *n* cinnamon • *adj* cinnamon
canyeller • *n* cinnamon

caoba • *n* mahogany
caos • *n* chaos
caòtic • *adj* chaotic
caòticament • *adv* chaotically
cap • *n* cape, chief, head • *adj* head • *pron* none
capa • *n* bed, cape, cloak, layer
capaç • *adj* capable, proficient
capacitat • *n* capacity
capar • *v* steer
capçada • *n* crown
capejada • *n* nod
capejar • *v* nod
capell • *n* hat
capella • *n* chapel
capfoguer • *n* andiron
capgròs • *n* tadpole
capibara • *n* capybara
capilůlar • *n* capillary
capità • *n* captain
capital • *n* capital • *adj* capital
capitalisme • *n* capitalism
capitalista • *adj* capitalist
capitell • *n* capital
capítol • *n* chapter
caplletra • *n* initial
capó • *n* bonnet
capoll • *n* cocoon
caporal • *n* corporal
caprici • *n* caprice, impulse, whim
capritx • *n* caprice, impulse, whim
capsa • *n* box, case
capsigrany • *n* shrike
capsot • *n* shrike
càpsula • *n* capsule
captaire • *n* beggar
captura • *n* capture
capturar • *v* capture
caput • *adj* kaput
caputxa • *n* hood
caputxina • *n* nasturtium
capvespre • *n* dusk, nightfall
caqui • *n* kaki, khaki
caquier • *n* persimmon
car • *conj* because • *adj* dear, expensive
cara • *n* face, front
carabassa • *adj* orange • *n* pumpkin
carabassera • *n* pumpkin
caracal • *n* caracal
caràcter • *n* character, letter
característic • *adj* characteristic
característica • *n* characteristic
característicament • *adv* characteristically
caracteritzar • *v* characterize
caragol • *n* snail
carall • *n* dick

caramel • *n* candy, caramel, fudge
caramell • *n* icicle, stalactite
caramels • *n* sweets
carament • *adv* expensively
caravelůla • *n* caravel
carbassa • *n* pumpkin
carbassera • *n* pumpkin
carbó • *n* carbon, coal
carbohidrat • *n* carbohydrate
carbonera • *n* bunker
carboni • *n* carbon
carbur • *n* carbide
carburador • *n* carburetor
carburant • *n* fuel
carcaix • *n* quiver
card • *n* thistle
cardar • *v* fuck
cardíac • *adj* cardiac
càrdies • *n* cardia
càrdigan • *n* cardigan
cardinal • *adj* cardinal
cardiòleg • *n* cardiologist
cardiologia • *n* cardiology
cardiomiopatia • *n* cardiomyopathy
cardiovascular • *adj* cardiovascular
careta • *n* mask
carga • *n* burden
cargol • *n* screw
cariàtide • *n* caryatid
caricatura • *n* cartoon
caricaturista • *n* caricaturist
carícia • *v* caress • *n* stroke
càries • *n* cavity
carilló • *n* carillon, glockenspiel
carismàtic • *adj* charismatic
carmesí • *n* crimson
carmí • *n* carmine
carn • *n* flesh, meat
carnal • *adj* carnal
carnatge • *n* carnage
carnaval • *n* carnival
carnestoltes • *n* carnival
carnisser • *n* butcher
carnissera • *n* butcher
carnívor • *n* carnivore • *adj* carnivorous
carnós • *adj* fleshy
carnotita • *n* carnotite
carotè • *n* carotene
caròtide • *n* carotid
carpa • *n* carp
carpí • *n* hornbeam
carpià • *adj* carpal
carraca • *n* shed
carranc • *n* crab
càrrega • *n* burden, cargo, charge
carregador • *n* magazine
carregar • *v* load

carrer • *n* fairway, street
carrera • *n* career, ladder, run
carreró • *n* alley
carretera • *n* road
carretó • *n* wheelbarrow
carreu • *n* ashlar
carreuada • *n* ashlar
carril • *n* rail
carro • *n* chariot, wagon
carrossa • *n* chariot
carrossí • *n* gig
carruatge • *n* carriage, chariot
carrussel • *n* roundabout
carta • *n* letter
cartell • *n* poster
carter • *n* mailman
cartera • *n* briefcase, wallet
carterista • *n* pickpocket
cartílag • *n* cartilage
cartó • *n* cartoon
cartògraf • *n* cartographer
cartografia • *n* cartography
cartogràfic • *adj* cartographic
cartonet • *n* paperboard
cartutx • *n* cartridge
carxofa • *n* artichoke
carxofera • *n* artichoke
cas • *n* case
casa • *n* home, house
casaca • *n* coat
casament • *n* marriage, wedding
casar • *v* marry
casar-se • *v* marry
casat • *adj* married
casc • *n* helmet
casera • *n* beehive, housekeeper
caserna • *n* barrack, base
caspa • *n* dandruff
casserola • *n* casserole
casset • *n* cassette
cassetó • *n* coffer
cassó • *n* saucepan
castament • *adv* chastely
castany • *n* chestnut • *adj* chestnut
castanya • *n* chestnut
castanyetes • *n* castanet
castanyoles • *n* castanet
castedat • *n* chastity
castell • *n* castle, forecastle
castellà • *n* lord
càstig • *n* penalty, punishment
castigar • *v* punish
càsting • *n* casting
castor • *n* beaver
castració • *n* castration
castrar • *v* castrate, steer
casual • *adj* casual

catacumba • *n* catacomb
catàleg • *n* catalogue
catàlisi • *n* catalysis
catalític • *adj* catalytic
catapulta • *n* catapult
catapultar • *v* catapult
catàstrofe • *n* catastrophe
catastròfic • *adj* catastrophic
catecisme • *n* catechism
catecumen • *n* catechumen
catedral • *n* cathedral
categoria • *n* category
categòric • *adj* categorical
categòricament • *adv* categorically
catifa • *n* carpet
catió • *n* cation
càtode • *n* cathode
catorzè • *adj* fourteenth
catúfol • *n* bucket
catxap • *n* bunny
cau • *n* burrow, den, joint
caure • *v* fall
causa • *n* case, cause
causal • *adj* causal
causalitat • *n* causality
càustic • *adj* caustic
cautelós • *adj* careful, cautious, wary
cautelosament • *adv* cautiously
cauterització • *n* cauterization
cauteritzar • *v* cauterize
cautxú • *n* rubber
cavalcar • *v* ride
cavall • *n* horse, knight
cavalla • *n* mackerel
cavaller • *n* knight
cavalleria • *n* cavalry
cavallet • *n* easel, trestle
cavallets • *n* roundabout
cavar • *v* dig
cavernícola • *n* caveman
caviar • *n* caviar
cavitat • *n* cavity
ceba • *n* onion
cec • *adj* blind • *n* caecum
cedir • *v* yield
cedre • *n* cedar
cegament • *adv* blindly
cegar • *v* blind
ceguesa • *n* blindness
cel • *n* heaven, sky
celŭla • *n* cell
cèlŭlula • *n* cell
celŭlular • *adj* cellular
celŭlulosa • *n* cellulose
celebració • *n* celebration
celebrar • *v* celebrate
cèlebre • *adj* famous

celebritat • *n* celebrity
celesta • *n* celesta
celibat • *n* celibacy
cella • *n* eyebrow
cement • *n* cementum
cendra • *n* ash
cendre • *n* ash
cenotafi • *n* cenotaph
cens • *n* census
centau • *n* cent
centaure • *n* centaur
centèsim • *n* hundredth • *adj* hundredth
cèntim • *n* cent
centímetre • *n* inch
centpeus • *n* centipede
central • *n* center, headquarters • *adj* central
centralitzar • *v* centralize
centralment • *adv* centrally
centràrquid • *n* sunfish
centre • *n* nexus
centrípet • *adj* centripetal
cents • *n* hundreds
centúria • *n* century
cera • *n* wax
ceràmica • *n* ceramic
cercador • *n* searcher
cercar • *v* look, search
cercle • *n* circle, ring
cèrcol • *n* hoop, ring
cerebel • *n* cerebellum
cerebral • *adj* cerebral
cerfull • *n* chervil
ceri • *n* cerium
cerimònia • *n* ceremony
cerimonial • *adj* ceremonial
cerós • *adj* wax
cert • *adj* certain
certament • *adv* certainly
certificable • *adj* certifiable
certificació • *n* certification
certificat • *n* certificate
cerussita • *n* cerussite
cervatell • *n* fawn
cervell • *n* brain, noodle
cervesa • *n* beer
cèrvix • *n* cervix
cérvol • *n* buck, deer
cesura • *n* caesura
cetosa • *n* ketose
ciborg • *n* cyborg
cicatriu • *n* scar
cicle • *n* cycle, loop
cíclic • *adj* cyclic
ciclisme • *n* cycling
ciclista • *n* cyclist
cicló • *n* cyclone

ciclomotor • *n* moped
ciclònic • *adj* cyclonic
ciclop • *n* cyclops
cicuta • *n* hemlock
ciència • *n* science
científic • *adj* scientific • *n* scientist
científicament • *adv* scientifically
cigala • *n* cicada
cigar • *n* cigar
cigarret • *n* cigarette
cigne • *n* swan
cigonya • *n* stork
cigró • *n* chickpea
cigronera • *n* chickpea
ciliat • *n* ciliate • *adj* ciliated
cilindre • *n* cylinder
cilíndric • *adj* cylindrical
cim • *n* peak, summit
ciment • *n* cement
cimera • *n* summit
cinabri • *n* cinnabar
cinc • *n* five
cinema • *n* cinema, picture
cinètic • *adj* kinetic
cínicament • *adv* cynically
cinisme • *n* cynicism
cinquantè • *n* fiftieth • *adj* fiftieth
cinquè • *n* fifth • *adj* fifth
cinta • *n* ribbon
cintura • *n* waist
cinturó • *n* belt
circ • *n* circus
circa • *prep* circa
circular • *adj* circular
circularment • *adv* circularly
circulatori • *adj* circulatory
circumcidar • *v* circumcise
circumcisió • *n* circumcision
circumdant • *adj* surrounding
circumdar • *v* surround
circumferència • *n* circumference
circumnavegació • *n* circumnavigation
circumnavegar • *v* circumnavigate
circumscripció • *n* constituency
circumspecte • *adj* circumspect
circumvalació • *n* circumvention
circumvalar • *v* circumvent
circumvolució • *n* convolution, gyrus
cirera • *n* cherry
cirerer • *n* cherry
cirrus • *n* cirrus
cirurgià • *n* surgeon
cirurgia • *n* surgery
cisalla • *n* shears
cisell • *n* chisel
cisteïna • *n* cysteine
cistell • *n* basket

cistella • *n* basket
cisterna • *n* cistern
cita • *n* appointment, date
citació • *n* quote
citar • *v* summon
cítara • *n* zither
citologia • *n* cytology
citoplasma • *n* cytoplasm
ciuró • *n* chickpea
ciutadà • *n* citizen
ciutadania • *n* citizenship
ciutadella • *n* citadel
ciutat • *n* city
civada • *n* oat
cívic • *adj* civic
civil • *adj* civil
civilitat • *n* civility
civilització • *n* civilization
civilment • *adv* civilly
claca • *n* claque
cladodi • *n* cladode
clam • *n* clamor
clàmide • *n* chlamys
clamor • *n* clamor
claqueta • *n* clapperboard
clar • *adj* bright, brilliant, clear, light, sparse • *n* glade
clara • *n* albumen
claraboia • *n* skylight
clarament • *adv* clearly
clarejar • *v* dawn
clarí • *n* bugle
clariana • *n* clearing
clarinet • *n* clarinet
clarividència • *n* clairvoyance
classe • *n* class, kind, sort
classicisme • *n* classicism
classificació • *n* classification
classificar • *v* sort
clatell • *n* nape
clau • *n* clef, code, fuck, key, nail • *adj* key
claustre • *n* cloister
claustrofòbia • *n* claustrophobia
claustrofòbic • *adj* claustrophobic
clausura • *n* closure
clavar • *v* hammer, nail
clavecí • *n* harpsichord
clavecinista • *n* harpsichordist
claveguera • *n* sewer
clavicèmbal • *n* harpsichord
clavicordi • *n* clavichord
clavícula • *n* clavicle
clavilla • *n* plug
clàxon • *n* horn
claxon • *n* klaxon
cleptomania • *n* kleptomania
clergue • *n* clergyman

clic • *n* click
clicar • *v* click
client • *n* client, customer
climàtic • *adj* climatic
climatologia • *n* climatology
clímax • *n* climax
clinòmetre • *n* clinometer
clítoris • *n* clitoris
clixé • *n* truism
clofolla • *n* husk
cloïssa • *n* clam
clon • *n* clone
clonar • *v* clone
cloquejar • *v* cluck
clor • *n* chlorine
clorat • *n* chlorate
clorofilůla • *n* chlorophyll
closca • *n* eggshell, husk, rind, shell
clotell • *n* scruff
cloure • *v* close
clovella • *n* husk, shell
club • *n* club
coala • *n* koala
coartada • *n* alibi
cobalt • *n* cobalt
cobdícia • *n* avarice, greed
cobdiciós • *adj* greedy
cobejós • *adj* greedy
cobert • *adj* covered
coberta • *n* deck
cobertament • *adv* secretly
cobertura • *n* coat
coble • *n* yoke
cobrar • *v* earn
cobrir • *v* coat
coca • *n* cookie
còccix • *n* coccyx
còclea • *n* cochlea
coclear • *adj* cochlear
coco • *n* coconut
cocodril • *n* crocodile
còctel • *n* cocktail
codi • *n* code
còdol • *n* cobblestone, pebble
codony • *n* quince
codonyer • *n* quince
coerció • *n* coercion
coet • *n* rocket
coexistència • *n* coexistence
coexistir • *v* coexist
cofa • *n* top
cofre • *n* coffer
cofret • *n* casket
cognom • *n* surname
cogombre • *n* cucumber
cogombrera • *n* cucumber
cogombret • *n* gherkin

coherent • *adj* coherent
coherentment • *adv* coherently
cohesiu • *adj* cohesive
cohort • *n* cohort
coincidir • *v* match
coiot • *n* coyote
coïssor • *n* chafe
coix • *adj* lame
coixejar • *v* limp
coixesa • *n* limp
coixí • *n* bag, cushion, pillow
col • *n* cabbage
colůlaboració • *n* collaboration
colůlecció • *n* collection
colůleccionador • *n* collector
colůleccionar • *v* collect
colůleccionista • *n* collector
colůlectiu • *adj* collective
colůlectivament • *adv* collectively
colůlega • *n* bud, colleague
colůlegial • *adj* collegial
colůlegiat • *adj* collegiate
colůlisonador • *n* collider
colůlocar • *v* place
colůloide • *n* colloid
colůloquial • *adj* colloquial
cola • *n* cola
colador • *n* sieve, strainer
colar • *v* sieve, strain
colcar • *v* ride
còlera • *n* anger, cholera
colèric • *adj* choleric
colibrí • *n* hummingbird
coliflor • *n* cauliflower
coll • *n* collar, neck
colla • *n* crew, troop
collador • *n* heddle
collage • *n* collage
collar • *v* collar, screw • *n* collar, necklace
collaret • *n* necklace
collera • *n* collar
collita • *n* vintage
collonades • *n* bullshit
colloqui • *n* colloquy
colom • *n* dove, pigeon
còlon • *n* colon
colon • *n* colonist, settler
colònia • *n* cologne, colony
colonial • *adj* colonial
colonialisme • *n* colonialism
colonització • *n* colonization
colonitzador • *n* colonist
color • *n* color, coral
coloret • *n* blush
colorímetre • *n* colorimeter
colós • *n* colossus
colpejar • *v* hit, knock

coltell • *n* knife
columna • *n* column
columnata • *n* colonnade
colxa • *n* bedspread
colze • *n* elbow
cóm • *n* trough
com • *conj* as • *prep* as, like • *adv* how, like
coma • *n* coma, comma
comanda • *n* order
comandar • *v* head
comarca • *n* county, district
combat • *n* combat, fight
combatent • *n* combatant
combatiu • *adj* combative
combatre • *v* combat, fight
combinació • *n* combination, slip
combustible • *n* combustible, fuel • *adj* combustible, inflammable
comèdia • *n* comedy, simulation
començament • *n* beginning, outset
començar • *v* begin, commence
comentar • *v* comment
comentari • *n* comment, commentary, observation
comerç • *n* commerce
comercial • *adj* commercial
comercialment • *adv* commercially
comerciar • *v* deal
comestible • *adj* edible
cometa • *n* comet
comí • *n* cumin
comiat • *n* leave, valediction
comicis • *n* comitia
commoció • *n* commotion, ruckus
commovedor • *adj* pathetic
commutar • *v* commute
còmodament • *adv* comfortably
còmode • *adj* comfortable
comodí • *n* joker
comoditat • *n* amenity
company • *n* colleague
companyia • *n* company
comparable • *adj* comparable
comparació • *n* comparison
comparar • *v* check
comparatiu • *n* comparative • *adj* comparative
comparativament • *adv* comparatively
compartir • *v* share
compartit • *adj* shared
compassió • *n* compassion, sympathy
compassiu • *adj* compassionate
compatible • *adj* compatible
compendi • *n* compendium
compensació • *n* compensation, remuneration
compensar • *v* balance

competència • *n* competence, competition, proficiency
competentment • *adv* competently
competició • *n* competition
competir • *v* compete
competitiu • *adj* competitive
complaent • *adj* complacent
complanta • *n* dirge
complaure • *v* please
complementar • *v* complement, supplement
complementari • *adj* complementary
complet • *adj* complete, full
completa • *adj* complete
completament • *adv* altogether, completely, fully, outright, quite
complex • *n* complex • *adj* complex
complexitat • *n* complexity
complicat • *adj* complicated, convoluted, hard, uneasy
còmplice • *n* accomplice
complir • *v* complete, fulfill
complot • *n* plot
comportament • *n* behavior, demeanor
comportar • *v* act
compositor • *n* composer
compositora • *n* composer
comprar • *v* buy, deal
comprendre • *v* fathom, get, grasp, understand
comprensible • *adj* comprehensible
comprensió • *n* comprehension
comprensiu • *adj* understanding
comprensivament • *adv* comprehensively
compressió • *n* compression
compromís • *n* appointment, compromise
comprovar • *v* check
compta-revolucions • *n* tachometer
comptabilitat • *n* accountancy
comptador • *n* counter
comptaquilòmetres • *n* clock, odometer
comptar • *v* count, number
comptatge • *n* count
comptavoltes • *n* counter, tachometer
compte • *n* care, count
computacional • *adj* computational
computador • *n* computer
computar • *v* compute
comtat • *n* county
comte • *n* count
comtessa • *n* countess
comú • *adj* common
comuna • *n* common, latrine • *adj* common
comunament • *adv* commonly

comunisme • *n* communism
comunista • *n* communist
comunitat • *n* community
con • *n* cone
conca • *n* basin
còncau • *adj* concave
concavitat • *n* concavity
concebre • *v* beget
concentració • *n* concentration
concentrar • *v* concentrate
concepció • *n* conception
concepte • *n* concept
conceptual • *adj* conceptual
conceptuosament • *adv* conceptually
concertina • *n* concertina
concís • *adj* brief, concise
concisament • *adv* concisely
conclau • *n* conclave
conclave • *n* conclave
concloent • *adj* conclusive
concloure • *v* conclude
conclusió • *n* conclusion
conclusivament • *adv* conclusively
concordança • *n* agreement, concordance
concordar • *v* match
concreció • *n* concretion
concret • *adj* concrete
concurrent • *adj* concurrent
concurrentment • *adv* concurrently
concursant • *n* contestant
condemnar • *v* condemn
condensador • *n* capacitor
condescendent • *adj* condescending
condició • *n* condition
condicional • *n* conditional • *adj* conditional
condicionalment • *adv* conditionally
condicionament • *n* conditioning
condicionar • *v* condition
còndil • *n* condyle
condimentar • *v* season
condó • *n* condom, rubber
condom • *n* condom
còndor • *n* condor
conducció • *n* dribble
conducta • *n* behavior, conduct, demeanor
conducte • *n* conduit
conductor • *n* driver
conduir • *v* dribble, drive, lead
coneguda • *n* friend
conegut • *n* acquaintance, friend, kith • *adj* known
coneixement • *n* judgment, knowledge
coneixements • *n* knowledge
conèixer • *v* meet
confederació • *n* confederacy

confiança • *n* confidence, trust
confiat • *adj* confident
confidencialment • *adv* confidentially
confidentment • *adv* confidently
configuració • *n* configuration
confiscar • *v* confiscate
conflagració • *n* conflagration
conflicte • *n* conflict
confondreś • *v* boggle
conformitat • *n* conformity
confraternització • *n* fraternization
confús • *adj* confused, confusing
confusió • *n* confusion
conga • *n* conga
congelar • *v* freeze
congènit • *adj* congenital
congost • *n* canyon
congregar • *v* congregate
congressista • *n* congressman
conífera • *n* conifer
coniforme • *adj* coniform
conill • *n* rabbit
conill! • *interj* hello
conillet • *n* beaver, bunny
conilleta • *n* bunny
conjetura • *n* guess
conjugació • *n* conjugation
conjugalment • *adv* conjugally
conjugar • *v* conjugate
cònjuge • *n* spouse
conjunció • *n* conjunction
conjunt • *adj* joint • *n* set
conjuntament • *adv* jointly
conjuntiva • *n* conjunctiva
conjur • *n* spell
connotació • *n* connotation
connotar • *v* connote
connotatiu • *adj* connotative
conquilla • *n* shell
conquistar • *v* conquer
conrear • *v* cultivate
consagrar • *v* devote
consciència • *n* awareness
conscient • *adj* aware, conscious
conscientment • *adv* consciously
consecutiu • *adj* consecutive
consecutivament • *adv* consecutively
consell • *n* advice, council
consentiment • *n* consent
conseqüència • *n* consequence
conseqüentment • *adv* consequently
conserge • *n* caretaker
conserva • *n* pickle
conservador • *adj* conservative
conservadorisme • *n* conservatism
considerable • *adj* considerable
consideradament • *adv* considerately

considerat • *adj* considerate
consistència • *n* consistency
consistent • *adj* consistent
consistentment • *adv* consistently
consol • *n* relief, solace
consola • *n* shell
consolador • *n* dildo
consolat • *n* consulate
consolidar • *v* consolidate
consonant • *n* consonant • *adj* consonant
conspícuament • *adv* conspicuously
conspiració • *n* plot
conspirar • *v* plot
constanment • *adv* constantly
constant • *n* constant • *adj* constant
constantment • *adv* constantly
constel·lació • *n* constellation
consternació • *n* concern
constipat • *n* cold
constitució • *n* frame
constitucional • *adj* constitutional
constitucionalisme • *n* constitutionalism
constituent • *adj* constituent
construcció • *n* building
constructiu • *adj* constructive
constructivisme • *n* constructivism
construir • *v* build
construït • *v* built
consuetudinàriament • *adv* customarily
consular • *adj* consular
consulta • *n* appointment
consum • *n* consumption
consumidor • *n* consumer
contagiós • *adj* contagious
contaminació • *n* contamination, pollution
contaminant • *n* pollutant
contaminar • *v* contaminate, defile
contemplar • *v* witness
contemporani • *n* contemporary • *adj* contemporary
contenciós • *adj* contentious
contenidor • *n* container
contenir • *v* contain
content • *adj* content, happy, pleased
contigu • *adj* contiguous
contigüitat • *n* contiguity
continent • *n* continent, mainland
contingut • *n* content
continu • *adj* continuous, unbroken
continuadament • *adv* continually
contínuament • *adv* continuously
continuar • *v* continue, keep
continuïtat • *n* continuity
contorsionista • *n* contortionist
contra • *prep* against • *n* con
contraban • *n* bootleg

contrabandista • *n* smuggler
contracció • *n* contraction
contracorrent • *n* undertow
contractar • *v* hire
contracte • *n* agreement, contract
contradicció • *n* contradiction
contradictori • *adj* contradictory
contradictòriament • *adv* contradictorily
contradir • *v* contradict
contraespionatge • *n* counterespionage
contrafagot • *n* contrabassoon
contrafort • *n* buttress
contraoferta • *n* counteroffer
contrapet • *n* spoonerism
contraproduent • *adj* counterproductive
contrarevolució • *n* counterrevolution
contrarevolucionari • *n* counterrevolutionary • *adj* counterrevolutionary
contrari • *n* opposite
contràriament • *adv* contrarily
contrasenya • *n* password
contratenor • *n* countertenor
contreure • *v* contract
contribució • *n* contribution
contrit • *adj* contrite
control • *n* control
controlable • *adj* controllable
controlar • *v* control
controvertit • *adj* contentious, controversial
contumeliós • *adj* contumelious
contusió • *n* contusion
convecció • *n* convection
convèncer • *v* convince
convenció • *n* convention
convencional • *adj* conventional, formal
convencionalisme • *n* conventionalism
convençut • *adj* convinced
conveni • *n* agreement
conveniència • *n* convenience
convenient • *adj* convenient
convenientment • *adv* conveniently
convergència • *n* convergence
convergent • *adj* convergent
conversa • *n* conversation
conversació • *n* conversation
conversar • *v* talk
convertible • *adj* convertible
convertir • *v* convert
convex • *adj* convex
convexitat • *n* convexity
convidar • *v* invite
convidat • *n* guest
convincent • *adj* compelling, convincing
convulsió • *n* convulsion
conxa • *n* shell
cony • *n* cunt, pussy, vulva

conyac • *n* brandy, cognac
cooperar • *v* cooperate
cooperatiu • *adj* cooperative
cooperativa • *n* cooperative
cop • *n* belt, hit, knock, shot, stroke, time
copa • *n* cup
copçar • *v* devise
còpia • *n* copy, mirror
copiar • *v* copy, mirror
copilot • *n* copilot
copra • *n* copra
copròlit • *n* coprolite
coquetament • *adv* coquettishly
cor • *n* heart
coral • *adj* choral
coralůlí • *n* coral • *adj* coral
corall • *n* coral
coratge • *n* bottle, courage
coratjós • *adj* brave, courageous
coratjosament • *adv* bravely
corb • *n* crow, raven
corba • *n* bow, curve
corbar • *v* bow
corbata • *n* necktie
corbes • *n* curve
corbeta • *n* corvette
corda • *n* cord, rope, string
cordam • *n* rigging
cordell • *n* string
corder • *n* lamb
cordill • *n* cord, string
cordó • *n* lace
cordòfon • *n* chordophone
corea • *n* chorea
coreògraf • *n* choreographer
coreografia • *n* choreography
coreogràfic • *adj* choreographic
corn • *n* horn
cornamusa • *n* bagpipes
corneal • *adj* corneal
corneta • *n* bugler, cornet
corni • *adj* horny
còrnia • *n* cornea
corniol • *n* columbine
cornisa • *n* cornice
cornut • *n* cuckold
coroide • *n* choroid
corona • *n* crown, ring
coronació • *n* coronation
coronar • *v* king
coronel • *n* colonel
corporal • *adj* corporal, personal • *n* corporal
corpori • *adj* corporeal
corpus • *n* corpus
correcció • *n* correction, remedy
correctament • *adv* correctly

correcte • *adj* correct
correctiu • *n* remedy
corredor • *n* aisle, runner
corregible • *adj* correctable
corregir • *v* correct
corrent • *n* current, draught, stream
correntia • *n* draught
corrents • *adv* quick
córrer • *v* run • *n* run
correspondència • *n* correspondence
correspondre • *v* match
corresponent • *adj* corresponding
corretja • *n* belt, leash
corriol • *n* plover, trail
corroir • *v* corrode
corrompre • *v* corrupt
corrosió • *n* corrosion
corrosiu • *adj* corrosive
corrupció • *n* corruption
corruptament • *adv* corruptly
corrupte • *adj* corrupt
corruptible • *adj* corruptible
corsari • *n* corsair
corsària • *n* corsair
cort • *n* court
cortejar • *v* court
cortès • *adj* courteous, polite
cortesament • *adv* courteously, politely
cortesia • *n* courtesy, kindness
còrtex • *n* cortex
cortina • *n* curtain
cortisona • *n* cortisone
còrvid • *n* crow
corxera • *n* quaver
cos • *n* body, field
cosa • *n* thing
cosí • *n* cousin
cosina • *n* cousin
cosinus • *n* cosine
cosir • *v* sew
cosmètic • *n* cosmetic
cosmètica • *n* cosmetics
còsmic • *adj* cosmic
cosmogonia • *n* cosmogony
cosmòleg • *n* cosmologist
cosmologia • *n* cosmology
cosmopolita • *n* cosmopolitan • *adj* cosmopolitan
cosmos • *n* cosmos
cost • *n* charge, cost
costa • *n* coast
costal • *adj* coastal
costaner • *adj* coastal
costar • *v* cost
costat • *n* side
costella • *n* rib
coster • *adj* coastal

costós • *adj* costly
costosament • *adv* expensively
costum • *n* custom, habit
cotó • *n* cotton • *adj* cotton
cotxe • *n* car, carriage, wagon
cotxer • *n* coachman
cotxet • *n* wagon
cotxinilla • *n* cochineal
coulomb • *n* coulomb
coure • *v* chafe, cook, fire • *n* copper
coureś • *v* cook
courenc • *adj* copper
cova • *n* cave
covament • *n* incubation
covard • *n* coward • *adj* cowardly, yellow
covardament • *adv* cowardly
covardia • *n* cowardice
covariància • *n* covariance
cranc • *n* crab
crani • *n* skull
cranial • *adj* cranial
cras • *adj* crass
creació • *n* creation
creacionisme • *n* creationism
creador • *n* creator
crear • *v* create
creatiu • *n* creative • *adj* creative
creativitat • *n* creativity
creditor • *n* creditor
crèdul • *adj* credulous
creença • *n* belief
creïble • *adj* credible
creïblement • *adv* believably
creient • *n* believer
creïlla • *n* potato
creixen • *n* watercress
creixent • *adj* growing, rising
créixer • *v* grow, wax
crema • *n* custard
cremada • *n* burn
cremant • *adj* ablaze
cremar • *v* burn
cremós • *adj* creamy
crepuscle • *n* crepuscule, dusk, twilight
crepuscular • *adj* crepuscular
creta • *n* chalk
cretí • *adj* cretinous
creu • *n* cross
creuer • *n* cruise, cruiser, transept
creure • *v* believe
criada • *n* maid
criar • *v* breed, foster
criat • *n* menial
crida • *n* call
cridaner • *adj* loud
cridar • *v* call, summon, telephone
cridòria • *n* brouhaha, fuss, hubbub, stir,

uproar
crim • *n* crime
criminal • *n* criminal • *adj* criminal
criminalment • *adv* criminally
criminòleg • *n* criminologist
criminologia • *n* criminology
criogènic • *adj* cryogenic
crioll • *n* creole
criptó • *n* krypton
criquet • *n* cricket
crisàlide • *n* chrysalis
crisantem • *n* chrysanthemum
crisi • *n* crisis
crisoberil • *n* chrysoberyl
crisòtil • *n* chrysotile
crispeta • *n* popcorn
cristalŭlí • *adj* crystalline
cristalŭlitzar • *v* crystallize
cristall • *n* crystal
cristalleria • *n* glassworks
crit • *n* call
criteri • *n* criterion
crític • *n* critic • *adj* critical
críticament • *adv* critically
criticar • *v* harsh
croada • *n* crusade
crom • *n* chromium
cromlec • *n* cromlech
cromosfera • *n* chromosphere
cromosoma • *n* chromosome
cromosòmic • *adj* chromosomal
crònic • *adj* chronic
crònicament • *adv* chronically
cronograma • *n* chronogram
cronòleg • *n* chronologist
cronologia • *n* chronology
cronològic • *adj* chronological
cronològicament • *adv* chronologically
cronologista • *n* chronologist
cronometrar • *v* clock
cronòmetre • *n* chronometer
croqueta • *n* croquette
crossa • *n* crutch
crosta • *n* crust, rind, scab
crostó • *n* heel
cru • *adj* crude, rare, raw
crucial • *adj* crucial
crucificar • *v* crucify
crucifix • *n* crucifix
cruciforme • *adj* cruciform
cruel • *adj* cruel, outrageous
cruelment • *adv* cruelly
crueltat • *n* cruelty
cruentament • *adv* bloodily
cruïlla • *n* crossroads
crustaci • *n* crustacean
cua • *n* tail

cub • *n* block, cube
cubell • *n* bucket
cubellada • *n* bucket
cúbic • *adj* cubic
cubisme • *n* cubism
cúbit • *n* ulna
cuboide • *adj* cuboid
cuc • *n* worm
cuca • *n* bug
cuculla • *n* spire
cucut • *n* cuckoo
cuina • *n* cuisine, kitchen, stove
cuinar • *v* cook
cuiner • *n* cook
cuir • *n* leather
cuirassa • *n* cuirass
cuirassat • *n* battleship, ironclad
cuixa • *n* thigh
cul • *n* ass, bottom
culinari • *adj* culinary
cullera • *n* spoon
cullerada • *n* spoonful, tablespoon
cullerot • *n* ladle, tadpole
culpa • *n* blame, fault, guilt
culpabilitat • *n* guilt
culpable • *adj* blameworthy, culpable, guilty
culpar • *v* blame
culte • *n* worship

cultivable • *adj* arable
cultivar • *v* cultivate, foster, grow
cultura • *n* culture
cultural • *adj* cultural
culturisme • *n* bodybuilding
culturista • *n* bodybuilder
cuneïforme • *n* cuneiform
cunyat • *n* brother-in-law
cúpula • *n* cupola, dome
cura • *n* care
curandero • *n* quacksalver
cúrcuma • *n* turmeric
curi • *n* curium
curiós • *adj* curious
curiosa • *adj* curious
curiosament • *adv* curiously
curós • *adj* careful
curri • *n* curry
curs • *n* class, course
cursa • *n* race
cursar • *v* course
cursiu • *adj* cursive
cursiva • *n* cursive, italic
curt • *adj* short
cutani • *adj* cutaneous
cúter • *n* cutter
cutxu • *n* dog

D

dácord • *interj* agreed
dávantguerra • *adj* antebellum
dhora • *adj* early
dór • *adj* golden
dactilologia • *n* dactylology
dada • *n* datum
dades • *n* data
daga • *n* dagger, knife
daikon • *n* daikon
dàlia • *n* dahlia
dalmàtica • *n* dalmatic
dalt • *adv* above • *prep* up
daltabaix • *n* downturn
dama • *n* draught
damajoana • *n* demijohn
dames • *n* draughts
damnar • *v* doom
damunt • *prep* above
dansa • *n* dance
dansar • *v* dance
dany • *n* damage, harm
danyar • *v* damage
darrere • *adv* behind • *prep* behind

darreries • *n* dessert
dasyatis • *n* stingray
data • *n* date
dàtil • *n* date
datxa • *n* dacha
dau • *n* die
daurada • *adj* golden
daurar • *v* gild
daurat • *n* gold • *adj* gold, golden
davant • *prep* against, before • *adv* before
davantal • *n* apron
davanter • *n* forward
de • *n* coral • *prep* from, of
deambulatori • *n* ambulatory
debatre • *v* discuss
dèbil • *adj* faint, feeble, weak
debilitar • *v* weaken
debilitar-se • *v* decline, weaken
debilitat • *n* weakness
dèbilment • *adv* weakly
debut • *n* debut
debutar • *v* debut
dècada • *n* decade

decadent • *adj* decadent
decàedre • *n* decahedron
decaedre • *n* decahedron
decàgon • *n* decagon
decalatge • *n* offset
decalatges • *n* offset
decapitació • *n* decapitation
decapitar • *v* behead, decapitate
decatló • *n* decathlon
decebedor • *adj* deceptive
decebre • *v* deceive
decebut • *adj* disappointed
decenni • *n* decade
decentment • *adv* decently
deceptiu • *adj* deceptive
decibel • *n* decibel
decididament • *adv* decidedly
decidir • *v* decide
decidu • *adj* deciduous
dècim • *adj* tenth
decisió • *n* decision
decisiu • *adj* decisive
decisivament • *adv* decisively
declamar • *v* say
declaració • *n* declaration
declarar • *v* state
declinació • *n* declension
declinar • *v* decline
declinar-se • *v* decline
declivi • *n* decline
decoratiu • *adj* decorative
decreixença • *n* decrease
decréixer • *v* decrease
decretar • *v* award
dèdal • *n* labyrinth, maze
deessa • *n* goddess
defecte • *n* bug, defect, fault, shortcoming
defectiu • *adj* defective
defectuós • *adj* defective
defensa • *n* defense
defensor • *n* defender
deficiència • *n* deficiency
deficient • *adj* deficient
dèficit • *n* deficit
definició • *n* definition
definit • *adj* definite
definitiu • *adj* definitive
deflació • *n* deflation
deformació • *n* deformation
deformar • *v* warp
defraudar • *v* defraud
defunció • *n* decease
degà • *n* dean
degudament • *adv* duly
dehiscència • *n* dehiscence
deïficació • *n* deification

deïficar • *v* deify
deïtat • *n* deity, divinity
deixar • *v* abandon, allow, depart, let, quit, stop
dejunar • *v* fast
delegada • *n* delegate
delegat • *n* delegate
deleteri • *adj* deleterious
deliberadament • *adv* deliberately
deliberat • *adj* deliberate
delicat • *adj* delicate
deliciós • *adj* delicious
deliciosament • *adv* deliciously
delicte • *n* crime
delinqüent • *n* felon
deliqüescent • *adj* deliquescent
deliri • *n* delirium
delit • *n* delight
delme • *n* tithe
delta • *n* delta
demà • *n* tomorrow • *adv* tomorrow
demanar • *v* ask, order, request
democràcia • *n* democracy
demòcrata • *n* democrat
democràtic • *adj* democratic
democràticament • *adv* democratically
democratització • *n* democratization
demògraf • *n* demographer
demografia • *n* demography
demogràfic • *adj* demographic
demostrar • *v* demonstrate, show
dempeus • *adv* upright
dena • *n* bead
dendrita • *n* dendrite
denegar • *v* deny
denominador • *n* denominator
denominar • *v* name
dens • *adj* dense
densament • *adv* densely
dent • *n* tooth
dental • *adj* dental
denticulat • *adj* denticulate
dentista • *n* dentist
denunciar • *v* denounce
departir • *v* depart
deplorable • *adj* sad
deplorablement • *adv* deplorably
deport • *n* sport
deportar • *v* transport
deportat • *n* transport
depressió • *n* depression, slump
depressiu • *adj* depressive
depriment • *adj* depressing
deprimir • *v* depress
deprimit • *adj* depressed, down
derivació • *n* bypass
derivar • *v* derive

derma • *n* dermis
dermatòleg • *n* dermatologist
dermatologia • *n* dermatology
dermatològic • *adj* cutaneous
dermis • *n* dermis
derogar • *v* derogate
derogatori • *adj* derogatory
derrota • *n* defeat
derrumbar-se • *v* crumble
desacuradament • *adv* inaccurately
desafiament • *n* challenge
desafiar • *v* challenge
desafiu • *n* challenge
desafortunat • *adj* unfortunate, unlucky
desagradable • *adj* unpleasant
desagraït • *adj* thankless
desaigua • *n* sink
desallotjament • *n* eviction
desallotjar • *v* displace
desaparèixer • *v* go
desaparició • *n* disappearance
desapercebudament • *adv* inconspicuously
desapercebut • *adj* unnoticed
desaprovat • *adj* deprecated
desar • *v* keep, save
desarmat • *adj* unarmed
desastre • *n* disaster
desastrós • *adj* disastrous
desastrosament • *adv* disastrously
desbaratar • *v* thwart
descalç • *adv* barefoot
descans • *n* rest
descansar • *v* rest
descapotable • *n* convertible
descarregar • *v* unload
descendent • *n* descendant
descendir • *v* descend
descentralitzar • *v* decentralize
descobriment • *n* discovery
descobrir • *v* discover
descolonització • *n* decolonization
descompondre • *v* decompose
descomposició • *n* decomposition
desconcertant • *adj* disconcerting
desconcertantment • *adv* disconcertingly
desconcertar • *v* maze
desconcertat • *adj* confused
desconegut • *n* stranger • *adj* unknown
descontaminació • *n* decontamination
descordar • *v* loose
descortès • *adj* uncourteous
descreure • *v* disbelieve
descripció • *n* description
descriptivament • *adv* descriptively
descriure • *v* describe
descuidar-se • *v* forget

desdenyar • *v* contemn
desdenyosament • *adv* disdainfully
desdonar • *v* evict
desè • *adj* tenth
desembocadura • *n* mouth
desembossador • *n* plunger
desemmarcar • *v* unmask
desemmarcar-se • *v* unmask
desencadenar • *v* unchain
desencaminadament • *adv* astray
desendreçat • *adj* frowsy, untidy
desenfrenadament • *adv* unrestrainedly
desengramponador • *n* screwdriver
desentenimentat • *adj* witless
desenterrament • *n* disinterment
desenterrar • *v* disinter
desenvolupament • *n* development
desenvolupar • *v* develop, evolve
desert • *n* desert
desertar • *v* desert
desertor • *n* deserter
desesperació • *n* despair
desesperadament • *adv* desperately
desesperat • *adj* desperate, hopeless
desfer • *v* undo
desfilar-se • *v* fray
desforestació • *n* deforestation
desgastar • *v* chafe
desgraciat • *adj* infelicitous, miserable
desguàs • *n* outlet
deshidratació • *n* dehydration
deshonest • *adj* dishonest
deshonestament • *adv* dishonestly
desig • *n* desire, wish
desigual • *adj* unequal, uneven
desigualment • *adv* unevenly
desigualtat • *n* inequality
desinfecció • *n* disinfection
desinteressadament • *adv* disinterestedly
desinteressat • *adj* disinterested, unselfish
desitjable • *adj* desirable
desitjar • *v* desire, will, wish
deslleial • *adj* disloyal
deslleialment • *adv* disloyally
deslleialtat • *n* disloyalty
deslligar • *v* loose, untie
deslluït • *adj* lackluster
desmai • *n* faint, fainting
desmanyotat • *adj* ungainly
desmentiment • *n* denial
desmoralitzar • *v* demoralize
desmoronar-se • *v* crumble
desmuntable • *adj* removable
desnerit • *adj* puny
desnivell • *n* inclination
desnonament • *n* eviction

desnonar • *v* displace
desobedient • *adj* disobedient
desobeir • *v* disobey
desocupat • *adj* free, idle
desodorant • *n* deodorant
desodorar • *v* deodorize
desodoritzar • *v* deodorize
desordenat • *adj* disorderly, untidy
desordre • *n* disorder, disruption
desorganització • *n* disorganization
desorganitzat • *adj* disorganized
desossar • *v* bone
desoxiribosa • *n* deoxyribose
despectiu • *adj* derogatory
despectivament • *adv* pejoratively
despedida • *n* valediction
despedir • *v* dismiss, sack
despert • *adj* awake
despertador • *n* alarm
despertar • *v* awake
despesa • *n* expenditure
despietadament • *adv* mercilessly
despietat • *adj* merciless
despit • *n* spite
desplaçament • *n* displacement
desplaçar • *v* displace
desplantador • *n* trowel
despotisme • *n* despotism
despreocupat • *adj* carefree
després • *adv* after, afterwards, then
desproporcionadament • *adv* disproportionately
desproporcionat • *adj* disproportionate
despullat • *adj* naked
dessuadora • *n* sweatshirt
destacat • *adj* outstanding
desterrament • *n* exile
desterrar • *v* exile
destí • *n* destiny, fate, fortune
destilar • *v* brew
destilleria • *n* distillery
destituir • *v* cashier, dismiss, sack
destorbar • *v* hinder
destre • *adj* dexterous
destresa • *n* dexterity
destructible • *adj* destructible
destructiu • *adj* destructive
destructivament • *adv* destructively
destructor • *n* destroyer
destruir • *v* go
desvergonyit • *adj* shameless
desvestit • *adj* unclothed
desvetllat • *adj* restless
desviació • *n* bypass
desviar • *v* deflect, divert
desviar-se • *v* deflect, digress
detall • *n* detail

detecció • *n* detection
detectar • *v* detect
detectiu • *n* detective
detenir • *v* detain
deterioració • *n* deterioration
determinadament • *adv* determinedly
determinar • *v* determine, set
determinat • *adj* determined
detestar • *v* loathe
detindre • *v* detain
déu • *n* god
deu • *n* ten
deure • *n* duty • *v* must
deures • *n* homework
deute • *n* debt
deutor • *n* debtor
deutora • *n* debtor
devastar • *v* devastate
devorar • *v* devour, gorge
dia • *n* day, daylight, daytime
diabètic • *n* diabetic • *adj* diabetic
diabetis • *n* diabetes
diable • *n* demon, devil, fiend
diabòlic • *adj* diabolical
diabòlicament • *adv* diabolically
diaca • *n* deacon
diacrític • *adj* diacritical
diacrònic • *adj* diachronic
diagnòstic • *adj* diagnostic
diagonal • *n* diagonal • *adj* diagonal
diagonalment • *adv* diagonally
dialecte • *n* dialect
dialècticament • *adv* dialectically
dialogar • *v* dialogue
diamant • *n* diamond
diametralment • *adv* diametrically
diàmetre • *n* diameter
diana • *n* reveille
diari • *n* daily, diary, journal, news, newspaper • *adj* daily
diàriament • *adv* daily
diarrea • *n* shit
diatomea • *n* diatom
diatòmic • *adj* diatomic
dibuix • *n* drawing, tread
dibuixar • *v* draw
dicció • *n* diction
diccionari • *n* dictionary
dicotomia • *n* dichotomy
dicroic • *adj* dichroic
dicroisme • *n* dichroism
dictadura • *n* dictatorship
didàctic • *adj* didactic, educational
didàcticament • *adv* didactically
didal • *n* thimble
didalera • *n* foxglove
diencèfal • *n* diencephalon

dieta • *n* diet
dietètic • *adj* dietary
difamació • *n* defamation
difamador • *adj* defamatory
difamant • *adj* defamatory
difamatori • *adj* defamatory
diferència • *n* difference
diferent • *adj* different
diferentment • *adv* differently
difícil • *adj* difficult, hard, rough, uneasy
dificultar • *v* hinder
dificultat • *n* difficulty
dificultats • *n* hardship
diftèria • *n* diphtheria
diftong • *n* diphthong
difunt • *n* deceased • *adj* deceased
digerible • *adj* digestible
digestiu • *n* digestive • *adj* digestive
digitació • *n* fingering
digital • *adj* digital
digitalització • *n* digitization
digitalment • *adv* digitally
dignament • *adv* worthily
digne • *adj* dignified, worthy
dignitat • *n* dignity
digressió • *n* digression, discursion
digui • *interj* hello
dihuitè • *n* eighteenth • *adj* eighteenth
diletantisme • *n* dilettantism
diligentment • *adv* diligently
diluvi • *n* deluge
dimensió • *n* dimension
dímer • *n* dimer
diminut • *adj* minute
dimoni • *n* demon, devil, fiend, monster
dina • *n* dyne
dinàmic • *adj* dynamic
dinàmica • *n* dynamic
dinàmicament • *adv* dynamically
dinamita • *n* dynamite
dinamitar • *v* dynamite
dinar • *n* dinner, lunch • *v* lunch
dinastia • *n* dynasty
dinàstic • *adj* dynastic
diner • *n* denier, money
dinosaure • *n* dinosaur
dinovè • *adj* nineteenth
dins • *prep* in, inside, within • *adv* in, inside • *adj* inside
díode • *n* diode
diorita • *n* diorite
diòxid • *n* dioxide
diplodoc • *n* diplodocus
diploma • *n* degree
diplomàcia • *n* diplomacy
diplomàtic • *n* diplomat • *adj* diplomatic
diplomàtica • *n* diplomat

diplomàticament • *adv* diplomatically
dipòsit • *n* deposit, depot, tank
dipositar • *v* deposit
díptic • *n* diptych
dir • *v* go, say, tell, utter
dir-se • *v* call, hight
direcció • *n* direction, management
directament • *adv* directly, outright
directe • *adj* direct
directiu • *adj* managerial
director • *n* conductor, director, head
directora • *n* director, head
dirigent • *n* leader
dirigir • *v* cast, direct, head, lead, steer
disc • *n* circle, disk, puck
discontinuïtat • *n* discontinuity
discret • *adj* tactful
discretament • *adv* discreetly
discriminatori • *adj* discriminatory
disculpa • *n* apology
disculpes • *interj* sorry
discurs • *n* speech, utterance
discussió • *n* discussion
discutible • *adj* arguable, moot
discutir • *v* discuss, quarrel
disenteria • *n* dysentery
disfòria • *n* dysphoria
disfrutar • *v* bask
disgustat • *adj* upset
dislèxia • *n* dyslexia
disminució • *n* decrease
disminuir • *v* decrease, lower
disparar • *v* fire, gun, shoot
dispers • *adj* sparse
dispersar • *v* disperse
disponible • *adj* available, out
disposat • *adj* prepared, ready, willing
dispositiu • *n* device
disprosi • *n* dysprosium
disputa • *n* argument
dissecar • *v* dissect
dissecció • *n* dissection
disseny • *n* design
dissenyador • *n* designer
dissenyar • *v* design
dissetè • *n* seventeenth
dissident • *n* dissident
dissimular • *v* palliate
dissipar • *v* dispel
dissociar • *v* dissociate
dissuasiu • *adj* dissuasive
distància • *n* distance
distant • *adj* distant
distinció • *n* distinction
distingible • *adj* distinguishable
distingir • *v* distinguish
distingit • *adj* distinguished

distint • *adj* distinct
distintament • *adv* distinctly
distintiu • *adj* distinctive
distracció • *n* distraction
distreure • *v* amuse, distract, entertain
districte • *n* district
dit • *n* digit, finger, toe
dita • *n* proverb, saying
diürn • *adj* diurnal
divergència • *n* divergence
divers • *adj* diverse
diversificació • *n* diversification
diversificar • *v* diversify
diverticle • *n* diverticulum
divertir • *v* amuse, entertain
divertit • *adj* amusing, droll, entertaining, fun, funny • *n* wit
diví • *adj* divine
dividir • *v* split
divinitat • *n* deity, divinity
divisa • *n* motto
divisar • *v* devise
divisió • *n* chapter
divorci • *n* divorce
divorciar • *v* divorce
divorciat • *adj* divorced
divuitè • *n* eighteenth • *adj* eighteenth
divulgar • *v* disclose, divulge
do • *n* do
doblar • *v* double
doble • *adj* double
doblec • *n* lap
dobleg • *n* plait
doblegar • *v* bow, fold
doblement • *adv* doubly
dobles • *n* doubles
dobra • *n* dobra
docilitat • *n* docility
doctrina • *n* doctrine
doctrinal • *adj* doctrinal
doctrinalment • *adv* doctrinally
document • *n* document
documentació • *n* documentation
documental • *n* documentary • *adj* documentary
documentar • *v* document
dodecaedre • *n* dodecahedron
dodecàedre • *n* dodecahedron
dodecàgon • *n* dodecagon
dofí • *n* dolphin
dogma • *n* dogma
dogmàtic • *adj* dogmatic
dogmatisme • *n* dogmatism
dol • *n* bereavement
dòlar • *n* dollar
dolç • *adj* soft, sweet • *n* sweet
dolçamara • *n* bittersweet

dolçament • *adv* sweet, sweetly
dolçor • *n* sweetness
doldre • *v* hurt
dolent • *adj* bad, evil
doler • *v* hurt
dolor • *n* dolor, pain
dolorós • *adj* painful
dolorosament • *adv* painfully
domador • *n* tamer
domar • *v* tame
domàs • *n* damask
domèstic • *adj* domestic
domesticat • *adj* domesticated
domesticitat • *n* domesticity
domicili • *n* domicile
dominar • *v* dominate
domini • *n* realm
dominical • *adj* dominical
dona • *n* wife, woman
donació • *n* donation
donar • *v* give
dònat • *n* doughnut
donatiu • *n* donation
doncs • *interj* so
donzell • *n* absinthe, wormwood
dormilega • *n* sleeper
dormint • *n* sleeping
dormir • *v* sleep
dormitori • *n* bedroom
dos • *n* two
dosi • *n* dose
dot • *n* dowry
dotor • *adj* nosy • *n* snoop
dotoreig • *n* snoop
dotorejar • *v* pry
dotzè • *n* duodecimo, twelfth • *adj* twelfth
dotzena • *adj* twelfth
drac • *n* dragon
dracma • *n* drachma
draconià • *adj* draconian
draga • *n* dredge
dragamines • *n* minesweeper
dragar • *v* dredge
dragó • *n* dragoon, gecko
dramàticament • *adv* dramatically
dramaturg • *n* playwright
dramaturga • *n* playwright
drap • *n* cloth, tatter
drassana • *n* shipyard
dràstic • *adj* drastic
drecera • *n* shortcut
dret • *n* law, right • *adj* right, upright
dretà • *n* right-handed
driblar • *v* dribble
driblatge • *n* dribble
dring • *n* clink

dringar • *v* clink, ring
drissa • *n* halyard
droga • *n* drug
drogat • *adj* high
dromedari • *n* dromedary
druida • *n* druid
dubtar • *v* doubt, hesitate
dubte • *n* doubt, dubitation
dubtós • *adj* doubtful
dubtosament • *adv* doubtfully
duc • *n* duke
ducado • *n* duchy
ducat • *n* ducat, duchy
duel • *v* duel • *n* duel
duet • *n* duet
dulces • *n* sweets
dulcimer • *n* dulcimer
duo • *n* duet

duodè • *n* duodenum
duplicació • *n* duplication
duplicar • *v* duplicate, mirror
duplicat • *n* duplicate
duquessa • *n* duchess
dur • *adj* hard • *v* steer
dura • *adj* hard
durabilitat • *n* durability
durable • *adj* durable
duració • *n* duration
durada • *n* duration
durador • *adj* durable
durant • *prep* during
durian • *n* durian
dutxa • *n* shower
dutxar-se • *v* shower

E

e • *n* e
eben • *n* ebony
eclèctic • *adj* eclectic
eclesiàstic • *adj* ecclesiastical
eclipsar • *v* eclipse
eclipsi • *n* eclipse
eclíptica • *n* ecliptic
eco • *n* echo
ecòleg • *n* ecologist
ecologia • *n* ecology
ecològic • *adj* ecological
ecològicament • *adv* ecologically
ecologista • *n* environmentalist
economia • *n* economics
econòmic • *adj* economic
econòmicament • *adv* economically
economista • *n* economist
ecosistema • *n* ecosystem
ecs • *interj* yuck
ectòpic • *adj* adventitious
eculi • *n* thorn
ecumènic • *adj* ecumenical
edat • *n* age
edició • *n* edit, editing, edition
edificar • *v* build
edifici • *n* building
editar • *v* edit
editorial • *adj* editorial
educació • *n* education
educat • *adj* educated
educatiu • *adj* educational
efecte • *n* effect, spin
efectiu • *n* cash • *adj* effective
efervescent • *adj* effervescent

eficaç • *adj* effective
eficàcia • *n* effectiveness, efficacy
eficiència • *n* efficiency
eficient • *adj* efficient
eficientment • *adv* efficiently
efímer • *adj* ephemeral
egocèntric • *adj* egocentric
egoista • *adj* selfish
egua • *n* mare
eguí • *n* neigh
eguinar • *v* neigh
eh • *interj* hey
ei • *interj* hey
eina • *n* tool
einsteini • *n* einsteinium
eix • *n* axis, axle
eixam • *n* swarm
eixàrcia • *n* rigging
eixir • *v* quit
eixugar • *v* wipe
eixut • *adj* dry
eixutesa • *n* dryness
eixutor • *n* dryness
ejaculació • *n* ejaculation
ejacular • *v* cum, ejaculate
ejecció • *n* ejection
el • *art* the
ela • *n* el
elàstic • *adj* elastic, resilient
elasticitat • *n* elasticity
elecció • *n* election
elector • *n* elector
electoral • *adj* electoral
electre • *n* electrum

elèctric • *adj* electric, electrical
elèctricament • *adv* electrically
electricitat • *n* electricity
electró • *n* electron
elèctrode • *n* electrode
electrodinamòmetre • *n* electrody-namometer
electròlit • *n* electrolyte
electromagnètic • *adj* electromagnetic
electromagnetisme • *n* electromagnetism
electrònic • *adj* electronic
electrònica • *n* electronics
electrònicament • *adv* electronically
electroscopi • *n* electroscope
elefant • *n* elephant
elegant • *adj* elegant
elegantment • *adv* elegantly
elegible • *adj* eligible
elegir • *v* choose
elemental • *adj* elemental
elevació • *n* elevation
elevat • *adj* high
eliminació • *n* out
eliminar • *v* eliminate
elit • *n* elite
elitista • *n* elitist • *adj* elitist
elixir • *n* elixir
ell • *pron* he
ella • *pron* she
elles • *pron* they
ells • *pron* they
elm • *n* helmet
eloqüència • *n* eloquence, utterance
eloqüent • *adj* eloquent
els • *art* the • *pron* them
eludir • *v* escape
em • *pron* me, myself
emancipació • *n* emancipation
emancipar • *v* emancipate
emascular • *v* emasculate
embà • *n* wall
embadalit • *adj* rapt, spellbound
embaràs • *n* pregnancy
embarassada • *adj* pregnant
embeinar • *v* sheath
embetumar • *v* beguile
emblemàtic • *adj* emblematic
embocadura • *n* mouth
embolcall • *n* sheath
embolicar • *v* wrap
embotellar • *v* bottle
embragatge • *n* clutch
embriac • *n* drunk • *adj* drunk
embriaguesa • *n* drunkenness
embrió • *n* embryo
embrionari • *adj* embryonic
embrolla • *n* claptrap

embruixament • *n* spell
embruixar • *v* bewitch
embrutar • *v* defile, dirty
embull • *n* claptrap
embut • *n* funnel
emergència • *n* emergence, emergency
emergir • *v* emerge
emèrit • *adj* emeritus
emetre • *v* broadcast, emit, utter
èmfasi • *n* emphasis, stress
emfasitzar • *v* highlight
emfàtic • *adj* emphatic
emfàticament • *adv* emphatically
emfatitzar • *v* emphasize
emigrar • *v* emigrate
eminència • *n* eminence
emirat • *n* emirate
emissió • *n* broadcast, emission
emmagatzemar • *v* store
emmarcar • *v* frame
emmascarar • *v* mask
emmetzinar • *v* poison
emmidonar • *v* starch
emmudit • *adj* speechless
emmurallar • *v* wall
emoció • *n* emotion
emocional • *adj* emotional
emocionalment • *adv* emotionally
emocionar • *v* move
emocionat • *adj* excited
empaperar • *v* paper
empaquetar • *v* box, case, package
empaquetat • *adj* packed
empaquetatge • *n* package
empastifar • *v* smear
empat • *n* tie
empatar • *v* draw
empatia • *n* empathy, sympathy
empedrar • *v* pave
empenta • *n* shove
empentar • *v* shove
empentejar • *v* shove
empènyer • *v* push, shove
empenyorar • *v* pawn, pledge
emperador • *n* emperor
emperadriu • *n* empress
empipador • *adj* tiresome
empitjorament • *n* worsening
empitjorar • *v* suffer
empleat • *n* employee
emprendre • *v* undertake
empresa • *n* enterprise
empresonament • *n* imprisonment
empresonar • *v* imprison
empunyadura • *n* hilt
empunyar • *v* grip
emú • *n* emu

en • *prep* in, within • *adv* thereof
ena • *n* en
enamorar • *v* enamor
enboirat • *adj* foggy
ençà • *adv* far
encalentir • *v* mull
encallar • *v* hang
encallar-se • *v* hang
encallat • *adv* aground • *adj* stuck
encant • *n* charm
encantador • *adj* delightful, lovely
encantament • *n* spell
encantat • *adj* delighted
encanteri • *n* enchantment
encapçalar • *v* head, lead
encapsar • *v* box
encara • *adv* even, still, yet
encarar • *v* look
encarcarat • *adj* stiff
encarcerament • *n* incarceration
encarnació • *n* incarnation
encàrrec • *n* charge, errand
encastar • *v* embed
encendre • *v* light
encenedor • *n* lighter
encens • *n* incense
encenser • *n* censer
encerar • *v* wax
encertar • *v* ascertain, hit
enciam • *n* lettuce
enciclopèdia • *n* encyclopedia
enciclopèdic • *adj* encyclopedic
encinta • *adj* pregnant
encís • *n* spell
encistellada • *n* basket
enclusa • *n* anvil, incus
encobrir • *v* palliate
encomanadís • *adj* contagious
encomiable • *adj* praiseworthy
encoratjador • *adj* encouraging
encreuament • *n* crossroads
encuny • *n* die
encunyar • *v* mint
endauat • *adj* checkered
endemés • *adv* furthermore
endèmic • *adj* endemic
enderrocar • *v* topple
endeutament • *n* indebtedness
endeutat • *adj* indebted
endevinar • *v* guess
endocardi • *n* endocardium
endocrí • *adj* endocrine
endocrinologia • *n* endocrinology
endolcir • *v* sweeten
endoll • *n* outlet, plug, point
endometri • *n* endometrium
endorfina • *n* endorphin

endoteli • *n* endothelium
endreçat • *adj* tidy
endurir • *v* harden
endurir-se • *v* harden
ènema • *n* enema
enemic • *n* enemy • *adj* enemy
energètic • *adj* energetic
energia • *n* energy
enèrgic • *adj* energetic
enèrgicament • *adv* energetically
enèsim • *adj* nth
enfadar • *v* anger
enfadat • *adj* angry
enfarinar • *v* flour
enfat • *n* anger
enfiladissa • *n* climber
enfilar • *v* thread
enfocar • *v* focus
enfonsar • *v* sink
enfony • *n* hovel
engabiar • *v* cage
engalba • *n* slip
enganar • *v* fool
enganxar • *v* hook, paste, stick
enganyar • *v* cheat, delude, trick
enganyós • *adj* deceptive
engendrar • *v* beget, breed
enginy • *n* ingenuity
enginyer • *n* engineer
enginyeria • *n* engineering
enginyós • *adj* ingenious, inventive, neat
engoliment • *n* swallow
engolir • *v* swallow
engonal • *n* groin
engrapadora • *n* stapler
engreixador • *adj* fattening
engrillonar • *v* fetter
engronsar • *v* swing
engruna • *n* crumb
enguixat • *n* cast
enigma • *n* enigma
enigmàtic • *adj* enigmatic
enjovar • *v* yoke
enllà • *adv* far
enllaç • *n* anchor, link
enllaçar • *v* link
enllaunar • *v* can
enlloc • *adv* nowhere
enneàgon • *n* nonagon
ennegrir • *v* blacken
ennuar • *v* tie
ennuvolat • *adj* cloudy
enorme • *adj* enormous, great, huge
enormement • *adv* enormously
enquitranar • *v* tar
enrabiada • *n* tantrum
enrajolar • *v* tile

enredada • *n* scam
enredar • *v* entangle
enrere • *adv* backward
enrevessat • *adj* convoluted
ens • *pron* ourselves
ensabonar • *v* lather
ensenyament • *n* teaching
ensenyant • *n* teacher
ensenyar • *v* show, teach
ensordidor • *adj* deafening
ensordir • *v* deafen
ensota • *adv* below
ensucrat • *adj* sweet
ensulsiada • *n* landslide
ensumar • *v* smell
ensutzar • *v* begrime
entallament • *n* carving
entebenar • *v* stun
entendre • *v* get, understand
enteniment • *n* wit
enter • *adj* entire • *n* integer
enterament • *adv* entirely
enteresa • *n* integrity
enterrament • *n* burial, funeral, interment
enterramorts • *n* gravedigger
enterrar • *v* bury, inter
enterrat • *adj* buried
entollar • *v* puddle
entomòleg • *n* entomologist
entomologia • *n* entomology
entomològic • *adj* entomological
entonació • *n* intonation
entorn • *n* environment
entrada • *n* entrance, inning, tackle
entrar • *v* enter
entre • *prep* between
entrebancar-se • *v* trip
entremaliat • *adj* mischievous
entrenador • *n* coach, trainer
entrenament • *n* training
entrenar • *v* train
entrepà • *n* sandwich
entresòl • *n* entresol
entretenir • *v* amuse, entertain
entretingut • *adj* amusing
entrevista • *n* interview
entrevistador • *n* interviewer
entrevistar • *v* interview
entusiasmadís • *adj* excitable
entusiasta • *adj* keen
entusiàstic • *adj* enthusiastic
entusiàsticament • *adv* enthusiastically
enuig • *n* anger
enunciat • *n* utterance
enutjar • *v* anger
enutjat • *adj* angry

envair • *v* encroach, invade
envant • *adv* forth
enveja • *n* envy
envejar • *v* envy
envellir • *v* age
enverinament • *n* poisoning
enverinar • *v* poison
enviar • *v* send, swallow
envinagrat • *n* pickle
envoltar • *v* surround
enyorar • *v* long, miss
enyorat • *adj* homesick
enzim • *n* enzyme
eòlic • *adj* aeolian
ep • *interj* hey
epicicle • *n* epicycle
epidemiòleg • *n* epidemiologist
epidemiologia • *n* epidemiology
epidemiològic • *adj* epidemiologic
epidèrmic • *adj* cutaneous
epidermis • *n* epidermis
epidídim • *n* epididymis
epífisi • *n* epiphysis
epiglotis • *n* epiglottis
epígraf • *n* epigraph
epigrafia • *n* epigraphy
epíleg • *n* epilogue
epilèpsia • *n* epilepsy
epinefrina • *n* adrenaline
episodi • *n* episode
epístola • *n* epistle
Epístola • *n* epistle
epitafi • *n* epitaph
epiteli • *n* epithelium
epitelial • *adj* epithelial
epitèlic • *adj* epithelial
època • *n* epoch, era
epònim • *adj* eponymous
èpsilon • *n* epsilon
equació • *n* equation
equador • *n* equator
eqüestre • *adj* equestrian
equidna • *n* echidna
equilibrar • *v* balance
equilibri • *n* balance, equilibrium
equilibrista • *n* acrobat
equinocci • *n* equinox
equinoderm • *n* echinoderm
equip • *n* crew, equipment, team
equipament • *n* equipment
equipar • *v* tool
equipat • *adj* furnished
equipatge • *n* equipment, luggage
equipol·lència • *n* equipollence
equitatiu • *adj* fair
equivalència • *n* equipollence
equivalent • *adj* tantamount

era • *n* era
erbi • *n* erbium
erecció • *n* erection
erecte • *adj* erect
erèctil • *adj* erectile
erg • *n* erg
ergonòmic • *adj* ergonomic
eriçó • *n* hedgehog
erm • *n* moor
ermini • *n* ermine
ermità • *n* hermit
erosió • *n* erosion
eròtic • *adj* erotic
eròticament • *adv* erotically
errada • *n* fault
erroni • *adj* erroneous
erròniament • *adv* wrongly
error • *n* bug, fault
eruga • *n* caterpillar
erupció • *n* eruption
es • *pron* herself, himself, itself, oneself,
themselves • *art* the
és • *v* is
esbandir • *v* rinse
esbarzer • *n* blackberry, bramble
esborrany • *n* draft, sketch, stub
esborronador • *adj* creepy
esbós • *n* draft, sketch
esbossos • *n* sketch
esbronc • *n* rebuke
esbroncada • *n* boo, rebuke
esbroncar • *v* boo, rebuke
escacat • *adj* checkered
escacs • *n* chess
escadalós • *adj* shameful
escafoide • *adj* scaphoid
escaig • *adj* odd
escala • *n* ladder, staircase, stairs, straight
escalable • *adj* scalable
escalar • *v* climb
escamarlà • *n* lobster
escampar • *v* smear
escandalós • *adj* boisterous, outrageous
escandi • *n* scandium
escandir • *v* scan
escàndol • *n* scandal
escanejar • *v* scan
escapar • *v* escape
escapar-se • *v* abscond
escàpol • *adj* single
escapolir-se • *v* abscond
escarabat • *n* beetle, cockroach
escarabeu • *n* scarab
escaramussa • *n* skirmish
escaramussar • *v* skirmish
escarapelůla • *n* cockade
escarransit • *adj* puny

escàs • *adj* scarce, sparse
escassedat • *n* scarcity
escassesa • *n* scarcity
escassetat • *n* scarcity
escatologia • *n* eschatology
escaure • *v* become
escena • *n* scene, stage, venue
escenari • *n* backdrop, scenario, stage
escènic • *adj* scenic
escèptic • *n* skeptic • *adj* skeptical
escepticisme • *n* skepticism
escindir • *v* split
esclafidors • *n* castanet
esclatar • *v* explode
esclau • *n* slave, thrall
esclava • *n* slave
esclavatge • *n* slavery
esclavitud • *n* slavery
escleròmetre • *n* sclerometer
esclop • *n* clog
escola • *n* school
escolar-se • *v* run
escollir • *v* choose, name, take
escoltar • *v* listen
escombra • *n* broom
escombrar • *v* sweep
escondir • *v* abscond
escopeta • *n* gun, shotgun
escopir • *v* spit
escorça • *n* bark, crust, rind
escorcollar • *v* scan
escorpí • *n* scorpion
escorreguda • *n* cum, spunk
escórrer-se • *v* come, cum, ejaculate
escorta • *n* escort, guard
escorxador • *n* shrike, skinner
escorxar • *v* skin
escot • *n* cleavage, share
escota • *n* sheet
escriny • *n* casket
escriptor • *n* writer
escriptori • *n* desktop
escriptura • *n* deed
escrit • *adj* written
escriure • *v* write
escrot • *n* scrotum
escrotal • *adj* scrotal
escrutar • *v* scrutinize
escuder • *n* armiger, squire
escull • *n* reef
escullera • *n* breakwater
escultor • *n* sculptor
escultora • *n* sculptor
escultura • *n* sculpture
escultural • *adj* sculptural
escuma • *n* foam
escurçó • *n* adder, varmint, viper

escusat • *n* toilet
escut • *n* buckler, shield
escúter • *n* scooter
esdevenir • *v* become, get
esència • *n* scent
esfera • *n* sphere
esfèric • *adj* spherical
esferòmetre • *n* spherometer
esfigmomanòmetre • *n* sphygmo-manometer
esfínter • *n* sphincter
esfinx • *n* sphinx
esforç • *n* effort, endeavor
esforçar-se • *v* try
esgarrapar • *v* scratch
esgarrar • *v* tear
esgarrifós • *adj* chilling, horrible
esglaó • *n* step
església • *n* church
esgrima • *n* fencing
esguerrat • *adj* crippled
eslògan • *n* slogan
esma • *n* judgment
esmaixada • *n* dunk, jam, slam, smash
esmaixar • *v* dunk, slam
esmalt • *n* enamel
esmaltar • *v* enamel
esmaragda • *n* emerald
esmena • *n* amendment
esmicolar-se • *v* crumble
esmoladora • *n* hone
esmolat • *adj* sharp
esmorzar • *v* breakfast • *n* breakfast
esnap • *n* snap
esòfag • *n* gullet
esotèric • *adj* esoteric
espadatxí • *n* swordsman
espagueti • *n* spaghetti
espai • *n* room
espai-temps • *n* spacetime
espaiós • *adj* roomy, spacious
espantall • *n* scarecrow
espantaocells • *n* scarecrow
espantar • *v* frighten, scare
espantós • *adj* eerie
esparreguera • *n* asparagus
espars • *adj* sparse
espasa • *n* epee, sword
espasmòdic • *adj* spasmodic
espatla • *n* shoulder
espatlla • *n* shoulder
espàtula • *n* spatula
espaventar • *v* frighten, scare
espècia • *n* spice
especial • *adj* special
especialista • *n* specialist
especialitat • *n* specialty

especialment • *adv* especially, specially
espècie • *n* specie, species
específic • *adj* specific
específicament • *adv* specifically
especificar • *v* name, specify
espectacle • *n* display, show
espectacular • *adj* spectacular
espectre • *n* spectrum
espectroscòpia • *n* spectroscopy
especulació • *n* speculation
especulatiu • *adj* speculative
espelma • *n* candle
espelta • *n* spelt
esperança • *n* hope
esperar • *v* await, hope, wait
esperar-se • *v* wait
esperit • *n* spirit
esperma • *n* semen, sperm
esperó • *n* spur
esperonar • *v* spur
espia • *n* spy
espiadimonis • *n* dragonfly
espiar • *v* spy
espiciar • *v* mull
espiera • *n* peephole
espiga • *n* ear, spike
espígol • *n* lavender
espill • *n* mirror
espín • *n* spin
espina • *n* fishbone, spine, thorn
espinac • *n* spinach
espinada • *n* backbone, spine
espinel • *n* spinel
espineta • *n* spinet
espinós • *adj* prickly
espionatge • *n* espionage
espiral • *n* spiral
espiritual • *adj* spiritual
espiritualitat • *n* spirituality
espiròmetre • *n* spirometer
espitjar • *v* shove
espitllera • *n* loophole
esplandit • *n* splay
esplèndid • *adj* splendid
esplèndit • *adj* gorgeous
espoliar • *v* spoil
esponja • *n* sponge
esponjar • *v* sponge
esponjós • *adj* spongy
espontaneïtat • *n* spontaneity
espontàniament • *adv* spontaneously
espora • *n* spore
esporàdic • *adj* sporadic
esporàdicament • *adv* sporadically
esport • *n* sport
espòs • *n* spouse
esposa • *n* spouse

esprémer • *v* squeeze
esprintar • *v* dash
espuri • *adj* spurious
espurna • *n* spark
espurnejar • *v* sizzle
esquaix • *n* squash
esquelet • *n* skeleton
esquelètic • *adj* skeletal
esquena • *n* back
esquer • *n* bait
esquerda • *n* crack
esquerra • *n* left
esquerrà • *adj* left • *n* left-handed
esquerre • *adj* left
esquetx • *n* sketch
esquí • *n* ski, skiing
esquiador • *n* skier
esquinçar • *v* tear
esquirol • *n* squirrel
esquist • *n* schist, shale
esquizofrènia • *n* schizophrenia
essencial • *adj* essential
essencialitat • *n* essentiality
ésser • *v* be • *n* being
est • *n* east
està • *v* is
estabilitat • *n* stability
estable • *n* stable • *adj* stable
establert • *adj* set
establiment • *n* establishment
establir • *v* establish, set
estabornit • *adj* dazed
estaca • *n* stake
estacament • *n* stagnation
estació • *n* season, station
estacional • *adj* seasonal
estacionari • *adj* stationary
estada • *n* sojourn
estadi • *n* stadium, stage
estafa • *n* scam
estafar • *v* defraud, scam
estalactita • *n* stalactite
estalagmita • *n* stalagmite
estalonar • *v* heel
estalviador • *adj* thrifty
estalviar • *v* save
estalzí • *n* soot
estam • *n* stamen
estampar • *v* stamp
estanc • *n* newsagent
estancada • *adj* stagnant
estancament • *n* stagnation
estancat • *adj* stagnant
estàndard • *n* standard • *adj* standard
estanquer • *n* newsagent
estant • *n* shelf
estany • *n* tin

estar • *v* be
estat • *n* state
estàtic • *adj* static
estàtua • *n* statue
estatura • *n* stature
esteganografia • *n* steganography
estegosaure • *n* stegosaur
estel • *n* kite, star
estela • *n* stele
estelat • *adj* starry
estella • *n* splinter
estendard • *n* banner, standard
estenedor • *n* clotheshorse, clothesline
estepa • *n* steppe
èster • *n* ester
estereotip • *n* stereotype
estèril • *adj* sterile
esterilització • *n* sterilization
esterilitzar • *v* sterilize
esterlí • *adj* sterling
esternal • *adj* sternal
esternudar • *v* sneeze
esternut • *n* sneeze
estès • *adj* far-flung
estètic • *adj* aesthetic
estètica • *n* aesthetics
estic • *n* stick
estigmatitzar • *v* stigmatize
estimada • *adj* beloved • *n* darling
estimat • *adj* beloved, dear • *n* darling
estimulació • *n* stimulation
estimulador • *n* stimulant
estimulant • *n* stimulant
estipendi • *n* wage
estirabot • *n* nonsense
estirada • *n* dive
estirar • *v* stretch
estiu • *n* summer
estiuejar • *v* summer
estival • *adj* estival
estoc • *n* rapier
estocàstic • *adj* stochastic
estoic • *adj* stoical
estola • *n* stole
estómac • *n* maw, stomach
estona • *n* while
estora • *n* mat
estorament • *n* astonishment
estorat • *v* wonder
estornell • *n* starling
estrafolari • *adj* bizarre
estranger • *adj* foreign • *n* foreigner, stranger
estrangera • *adj* foreign • *n* foreigner
estrangulació • *n* strangulation
estrangular • *v* strangle
estrany • *n* alien, chrysanthemum •

adj alien, bizarre, foreign, odd, queer, strange, weird
estranya • n alien • adj alien, foreign
estranyament • adv strangely
estrat • n stratum, stratus
estrateg • n tactician
estratega • n tactician
estratègia • n strategy
estratègic • adj strategic
estratègicament • adv strategically
estratosfera • n stratosphere
estratus • n stratus
estrella • n star
estrena • n release
estrenar • v release
estrènyer • v squeeze
estrep • n stapes, stirrup
estrès • n stress
estressar • v stress
estressat • adj stressed
estret • adj narrow
estreta • adj narrow
estribor • n starboard
estrident • adj loud
estripar • v tear
estronci • n strontium
estruç • n ostrich
estructura • n frame, skeleton, structure
estructural • adj structural
estuc • n stucco
estudi • n study
estudiant • n student
estudiar • v learn, read, study
estufa • n stove
estúpid • n nincompoop • adj stupid
estúpidament • adv stupidly
estupidesa • n stupidity
esvalot • n commotion, stir
esvàstica • n swastika
et • n ampersand • pron yourself
eta • n eta
età • n ethane
etanamida • n acetamide
etapa • n stage
etern • adj eternal, undying
eternal • adj eternal
eternitat • n eternity, lifetime
ètic • adj ethical
ètica • n ethics
etil • n ethyl
etimòleg • n etymologist
etimòloga • n etymologist
etimologia • n etymology
etimològic • adj etymological
etimologista • n etymologist
etiologia • n aetiology
etiqueta • n label, tag

etiquetar • v label, tag
ètnia • n ethnicity
ètnic • adj ethnic
etnocèntric • adj ethnocentric
etnocentrisme • n ethnocentrism
etnografia • n ethnography
ets • art the
eucaliptus • n eucalyptus
eucariota • n eukaryote
eufemisme • n euphemism
eufoni • n euphonium
eufòria • n euphoria
eufòric • adj euphoric
euga • n horse, mare
eugenèsia • n eugenics
eureka • interj eureka
europi • n europium
eutanàsia • n euthanasia
evangeli • n gospel
eventual • n temporary
evidència • n witness
evident • adj evident
evitar • v circumvent
evolució • n evolution
exactament • adv accurately, exactly, quite
exacte • adj accurate, exact
exagerar • v exaggerate
examen • n examination
exasperar • v exasperate
excavació • n dig, excavation
excavador • n digger, excavator
excavadora • n digger
excavar • v dig
excedir • v exceed
excel·lència • n excellence
excel·lent • adj capital, excellent, swell
excel·lentment • adv excellently
excel·lir • v excel
excèntric • adj eccentric
excepció • n exception
excepcional • adj exceptional, outstanding
excepcionalment • adv exceptionally
excepte • conj but
excés • n excess
excessiu • adj excessive
excitable • adj excitable
excitant • adj exciting
excitat • adj excited
exclamar • v exclaim
excloure • v exclude
exclusiu • adj exclusive
excomunicar • v excommunicate
excrement • n shit
excretar • v excrete
excretori • adj excretory

execució • *n* performance
executar • *v* execute
exegesi • *n* exegesis
exemple • *n* example
exempt • *adj* exempt
exercici • *n* exercise
exercir • *v* exercise
exèrcit • *n* army, military
exercitar • *v* exercise
exhalació • *n* exhalation
exhauriment • *n* depletion
exhaust • *adj* exhausted
exhaustiu • *adj* exhaustive
exhibicionisme • *n* exhibitionism
exhibicionista • *n* exhibitionist • *adj* exhibitionist
exhibir • *v* display, exhibit
exhumació • *n* exhumation
exhumar • *v* exhume
exigència • *n* requirement
exigent • *adj* exigent
exigir • *v* demand
exili • *n* exile
exiliar • *v* exile
exiliat • *n* exile
existència • *n* existence
existent • *adj* existent, existing, extant
existir • *v* exist
èxit • *n* hit, success
exitós • *adj* successful
exogen • *adj* adventitious
exorcisme • *n* exorcism
exorcista • *n* exorcist
exorcitzar • *v* exorcise
exosfera • *n* exosphere
exosquelet • *n* exoskeleton
exòtic • *adj* exotic
expelùlir • *v* expel
experimental • *adj* experimental
explicació • *n* explanation
explicar • *v* explain, narrate, tell
explícit • *adj* explicit

explícitament • *adv* explicitly
exploració • *n* exploration
explorador • *n* explorer
explorar • *v* explore
explosió • *n* explosion
explosiu • *n* explosive • *adj* explosive
explotar • *v* explode, exploit
exposar • *v* exhibit
expressar • *v* express
expressió • *n* expression, utterance
expressionista • *n* expressionist • *adj* expressionist
expressiu • *adj* expressive
expressivament • *adv* expressively
exquisit • *adj* exquisite
extasiat • *adj* rapt
extendre • *v* extend
extens • *adj* extensive
extensament • *adv* extensively
extensió • *n* extension, tract
exterior • *n* outfielder
extern • *adj* external, inessential
externa • *adj* external
extinció • *n* extinction
extingir • *v* extinguish
extint • *adj* extinct
extracelùlular • *adj* extracellular
extraïble • *adj* removable
extraordinari • *adj* extraordinary
extraterrestre • *n* alien • *adj* extraterrestrial
extravagant • *adj* extravagant
extrem • *n* extreme, winger • *adj* extreme, far
extremisme • *n* extremism
extremista • *n* extremist • *adj* extremist
extremitat • *n* extremity
extreure • *v* extract
extrovertit • *adj* outgoing
exultant • *adj* exultant
exultar • *v* exult

F

fabricant • *n* maker
fabulós • *adj* great
fabulosament • *adv* fabulously
faç • *n* face
faceta • *n* face
fàcil • *adj* easy, effortless
fàcilment • *adv* easily
facoquer • *n* warthog
factible • *adj* feasible
factici • *adj* factitious

factura • *n* bill
fada • *n* fairy
fagot • *n* bassoon
faig • *n* beech
faisà • *n* pheasant
falùlàcia • *n* fallacy
falùlibilitat • *n* fallibility
falùlible • *adj* fallible
fàlùlic • *adj* phallic
falùlus • *n* phallus

falaguera • *n* fern
falange • *n* phalanx
falç • *n* sickle
falca • *n* wedge
falciot • *n* swift
falcó • *n* falcon, hawk, kestrel
faldilla • *n* skirt
falguera • *n* fern
falla • *n* fault
fallar • *v* award
fals • *adj* artificial, false, spurious
falsament • *adv* falsely
falsejar • *v* fake, falsify
falsificar • *v* falsify
falta • *n* fault, foul, lack
faltar • *v* lack
fam • *n* hunger
fama • *n* fame
família • *n* family, people
familiar • *adj* familiar • *n* family
familiaritzar • *v* familiarize
familiarment • *adv* familiarly
familiars • *n* household
famós • *adj* famous
fanàtic • *adj* fanatical
fanàticament • *adv* fanatically
fanfara • *n* fanfare
fanfarró • *n* braggart
fang • *n* clay, mud
fangós • *adj* muddy
fantasia • *n* fancy, fantasy
fantasma • *n* phantom
fantàstic • *adj* fantastic
far • *n* headlight, lighthouse
faraó • *n* faro, pharaoh
faraònic • *adj* pharaonic
farcell • *n* bundle
farga • *n* forge
farigola • *n* thyme
farina • *n* flour
farinetes • *n* porridge
farmacèutic • *n* pharmacist
farmàcia • *n* pharmacy
farmacologia • *n* pharmacology
farmacològic • *adj* pharmacological
farola • *n* lamppost, streetlight
farragós • *adj* unwieldy
farratge • *n* fodder
fascinador • *adj* fascinating
fascinant • *adj* fascinating
fase • *n* stage
fàstic • *n* disgust
fastigós • *adj* disgusting
fastiguejar • *v* harass
fastiguejat • *adj* screwed
fat • *adj* dull
fatal • *adj* fatal

fatalisme • *n* fatalism
fatigar • *v* tire
fatigar-se • *v* tire
fauna • *n* fauna
faune • *n* faun
fava • *n* nincompoop • *adj* silly
favorable • *adj* auspicious
favorit • *adj* favorite
fax • *n* fax
fe • *n* faith
feble • *adj* faint, feeble, puny, weak
feblesa • *n* weakness
febre • *n* bug, fever, temperature
febril • *adj* feverish, hectic
febrilment • *adv* feverishly
fecundació • *n* fertilization
federal • *adj* federal
feijoa • *n* feijoa
feina • *n* job
feix • *n* bundle, sheaf
feixisme • *n* fascism
feixista • *n* fascist
fel • *n* bile
felůlació • *n* fellatio
feldspat • *n* feldspar
felí • *n* cat • *adj* feline
feliç • *adj* happy
felicitat • *n* happiness
felicitats • *interj* congratulations
feliçment • *adv* fortunately, happily
felina • *n* cat
feltre • *n* baize, felt
fem • *n* dung
femella • *n* female • *adj* female
femení • *adj* female • *n* feminine
femenina • *adj* female
feminisme • *n* feminism
feminitat • *n* femininity
femoral • *adj* femoral
femta • *n* excrement, shit
fèmur • *n* femur
fenc • *n* hay
fènix • *n* phoenix
fenomen • *n* phenomenon
fenomenal • *adj* phenomenal
fenomènic • *adj* phenomenal
fer • *v* be, do, go, make
fer-ho • *v* do
fera • *n* beast
fèretre • *n* coffin
ferida • *n* injury
ferir • *v* hurt, injure, wound
feristela • *n* varmint
ferm • *adj* fast, firm
fermament • *adv* fast
fermar • *v* tie
ferment • *n* ferment

fermentació • *n* fermentation
fermesa • *n* firmness
fermi • *n* fermium
fermió • *n* fermion
feroç • *adj* fierce
feroçment • *adv* fiercely
ferotge • *adj* ferocious, fierce
ferradura • *n* horseshoe
ferrar • *v* shoe
ferrer • *n* blacksmith, smith
ferrera • *n* smith
fèrric • *adj* ferric
ferro • *n* iron • *adj* iron
ferromagnètic • *adj* ferromagnetic
ferromagnetisme • *n* ferromagnetism
fèrtil • *adj* fertile
fertilització • *n* fertilization
fertilitzar • *v* fertilize
fesol • *n* bean
festa • *n* feast, holiday, party
festuc • *n* pistachio
fet • *n* deed, fact
fetal • *adj* fetal
fetge • *n* liver
fetgera • *n* liverwort
fètid • *adj* fetid
fetiller • *n* mage, magician, sorcerer, wizard
feu • *n* feud, fief
fi • *n* end, finish, phi
fiabilitat • *n* reliability
fiable • *adj* dependable
fiasco • *n* fiasco
fiblada • *n* zap
fibló • *n* thorn
fibrós • *adj* fibrous
fíbula • *n* fibula
ficar • *v* put
ficció • *n* fiction
ficcional • *adj* fictional
fictici • *adj* fictitious
fidedigne • *adj* trustworthy
fidel • *adj* faithful
fidelment • *adv* faithfully
fideu • *n* noodle
fiduciari • *n* fiduciary
figa • *n* fig
figle • *n* ophicleide
figuera • *n* fig
figura • *n* figure
figurar-se • *v* figure
figurativament • *adv* figuratively
fil • *n* thread, yarn
filacteri • *n* phylactery
filantrop • *n* philanthropist
filantropia • *n* philanthropy
filantròpic • *adj* philanthropic

filatèlic • *adj* philatelic
filferro • *n* wire
filharmònic • *n* philharmonic
filigrana • *n* filigree, watermark
filigranar • *v* filigree
filisteu • *adj* philistine
fill • *n* son
filla • *n* daughter
fillastra • *n* stepdaughter
fillastre • *n* stepson
fillol • *n* godson
fillola • *n* goddaughter
film • *n* movie
filogènia • *n* phylogeny
filòleg • *n* philologist
filologia • *n* philology
filològic • *adj* philological
filòsof • *n* philosopher
filòsofa • *n* philosopher
filosofia • *n* philosophy
filosòfic • *adj* philosophical
filosòficament • *adv* philosophically
filtració • *n* spoiler
filtrar • *v* filter, sieve
filtre • *n* filter
fílum • *n* phylum
final • *n* end, final • *adj* final
finalista • *n* finalist
finalitzar • *v* finish
finalment • *adv* eventually, finally, ultimately
financer • *adj* financial
financerament • *adv* financially
finances • *n* finance
finestra • *n* window
finestró • *n* shutter
fingiment • *n* simulation
fingir • *v* feign, pretend
finir • *v* finish
finit • *adj* finite
fins • *prep* until
fiola • *n* vial
fiord • *n* fjord
firma • *n* firm
fiscal • *adj* fiscal • *n* prosecutor
fiscorn • *n* flugelhorn
físic • *adj* physical
físicament • *adv* physically
fisiòleg • *n* physiologist
fisiologia • *n* physiology
fisiològic • *adj* physiological
fisiològicament • *adv* physiologically
fissura • *n* fissure
fita • *n* exploit, finish, milestone
fitó • *n* bullseye
fitòfag • *adj* phytophagous
fitxa • *n* counter

fitxer • *n* file
fix • *adj* fixed
fixar • *v* set
flàccid • *adj* limp
flàccida • *adj* limp
flagell • *n* flail
flageolet • *n* flageolet
flairar • *v* smell
flaire • *n* smell
flama • *n* flame, light
flamant • *adj* flamboyant
flamenc • *n* flamenco, flamingo
flatulent • *adj* flatulent
flauta • *n* flute
fleca • *n* bakery
flegma • *n* phlegm
flegmàtic • *adj* phlegmatic
fletxa • *n* arrow
flexibilitat • *n* flexibility
flexible • *adj* flexible
flexió • *n* inflection
floc • *n* flock, jib, lock
floema • *n* phloem
flor • *n* blossom, flower
floració • *n* blossom
floral • *adj* floral
florera • *n* vase
floret • *n* foil
floridura • *n* mold
florir • *v* blossom, flower
florista • *n* florist
flotació • *n* flotation
flotar • *v* float
fluctuar • *v* fluctuate
fluid • *n* fluid
fluidament • *adv* fluently
fluir • *v* flow, run
fluor • *n* fluorine
flux • *n* flow
foc • *n* fire
foca • *n* cow, seal
focal • *adj* focal
focus • *n* focus
foganya • *n* fireplace
folůlicle • *n* follicle
folklore • *n* folklore
follador • *n* fucker
follar • *v* fuck, screw
follet • *n* gnome, goblin, sprite
folre • *n* lining
fonament • *n* base
fonamental • *n* fundamental, primary • *adj* fundamental
fonamentalisme • *n* fundamentalism
fonaments • *n* foundation
fondo • *adj* deep
fondre • *v* cast, melt

fonedor • *n* founder
fonema • *n* phoneme
fonètic • *adj* phonetic
fonètica • *n* phonetics
fonèticament • *adv* phonetically
fong • *n* fungus, mushroom
fònic • *adj* phonic
fonòleg • *n* phonologist
fonoll • *n* fennel
fonologia • *n* phonology
fonològic • *adj* phonological
fons • *n* background, bottom, ground
font • *n* fountain, spring
fontanelůla • *n* fontanelle
fora • *adv* outside
foradar • *v* bore, drill, hole, pierce
foraster • *n* alien, foreigner, stranger • *adj* foreign
forastera • *n* alien, foreigner • *adj* foreign
forat • *n* hole
força • *adv* fairly, pretty, rather • *n* force, strength
forca • *n* fork, gibbet
forçadament • *adv* forcibly
forçar • *v* take
forçat • *adj* contrived, forced
forense • *adj* forensic
forest • *n* forest
forja • *n* forge
forjar • *v* forge
forma • *n* form
formal • *adj* formal
formalment • *adv* formally
formar • *v* form, shape
formatge • *n* cheese
formiga • *n* ant
formigó • *n* concrete
formiguer • *n* anthill
formós • *adj* beautiful
formósa • *adj* beautiful
fórmula • *n* formula
formulari • *n* form
forn • *n* bakery, oven
fornejar • *v* bake
forner • *n* baker
fornir • *v* furnish, supply
forquilla • *n* fork
fort • *n* fort, strength • *adj* loud, strong • *adv* strong, strongly
fortalesa • *n* fortress, stronghold
fortuna • *n* fortune
fòrum • *n* forum
fosa • *n* font
fosc • *adj* black, dark
fosca • *n* night
foscor • *n* dark, darkness
fosfat • *n* phosphate

fòsfor • *n* phosphorus
fosforós • *adj* phosphorous
fossat • *n* moat
fòssil • *n* fossil
fossilització • *n* fossilization
fotesa • *n* trifle
fotja • *n* coot
foto • *n* photo, photograph, picture
fotó • *n* photon
fotocòpia • *n* photocopy
fotocopiadora • *n* photocopier
fotocopiar • *v* photocopy, xerox
fotògraf • *n* photographer
fotografia • *n* photograph, photography, picture
fotografiar • *v* photograph
fotogràfic • *adj* photographic
fotogràficament • *adv* photographically
fotòmetre • *n* photometer
fotoquímic • *adj* photochemical
fotosfera • *n* photosphere
fotosíntesi • *n* photosynthesis
fotosintètic • *adj* photosynthetic
fotovoltaic • *adj* photovoltaic
fotre • *v* fuck, screw
fotre-li • *v* do
fotut • *adj* screwed
fracàs • *n* dud, failure
fracassar • *v* fail
fracció • *n* fraction
fractal • *n* fractal • *adj* fractal
fragant • *adj* fragrant
fragata • *n* frigate
fràgil • *adj* brittle, fragile
fragilitat • *n* fragility
fragment • *n* fragment, snippet
fragmentar • *v* fragment
fragmentari • *adj* fragmentary
franc • *n* franc • *adj* frank
francament • *adv* fairly, outright
franci • *n* francium
franctirador • *n* sniper
franelŭla • *n* flannel
frare • *n* friar, harvestman
frase • *n* phrase, sentence
fraseologia • *n* phraseology
fratern • *adj* fraternal
fraternitat • *n* brotherhood
fraternitzar • *v* fraternize
frau • *n* fraud
fraudulència • *n* fraudulence
fraudulent • *adj* fraudulent
fraudulentament • *adv* fraudulently
fre • *n* brake
fred • *n* cold • *adj* cold, cool
freda • *adj* cool
fredeluga • *n* lapwing

fredor • *n* coldness
fregar • *v* rub
fregir • *v* fry
frenesí • *n* frenzy
frenètic • *adj* frenetic, hectic
frenèticament • *adv* frantically
frenologia • *n* phrenology
freqüència • *n* frequency
freqüentar • *v* frequent
freqüentment • *adv* frequently
fresa • *n* spawn
fresc • *adj* cool, fresh, recent • *n* fresco
fresca • *adj* fresh
frescor • *n* freshness
freula • *n* strawberry
fricció • *n* friction
frigorífic • *n* refrigerator
fris • *n* frieze
frívol • *adj* frivolous
frívolament • *adv* frivolously
frivolitat • *n* frivolity
front • *n* forehead, front
frontal • *adj* frontal
frontera • *n* border, boundary, frontier
fronterer • *adj* frontier
frontispici • *n* frontispiece
frontó • *n* pediment
fructosa • *n* fructose
frugal • *adj* frugal
fruit • *n* fruit
fruita • *n* fruit
frustrar • *v* thwart
frustrat • *adj* frustrated
fúcsia • *n* fuchsia
fuet • *n* slapstick, whip
fuetejar • *v* whip
fugir • *v* abscond, flee
fuita • *n* escape
fulano • *n* random
full • *n* foil, leaf, sheet
fulla • *n* leaf
fullet • *n* brochure, tract
fum • *n* smoke
fumador • *n* smoker
fumar • *v* smoke
fumejar • *v* smoke
funció • *n* function
funcionar • *v* function, go, run
funcionari • *n* official
fundació • *n* foundation
funeral • *n* funeral
funerals • *n* funeral
funerari • *adj* funerary
fungible • *adj* fungible
fura • *n* ferret
furgoneta • *n* van
furiós • *adj* furious

furó • *n* ferret
furtivitat • *n* stealth
fus • *n* spindle
fusell • *n* rifle
fuster • *n* carpenter, joiner
fustera • *n* carpenter
futbol • *n* football, soccer

fútil • *adj* futile
futilesa • *n* futility
futilitat • *n* futility
futur • *n* future • *adj* future
futurisme • *n* futurism
futurista • *adj* futuristic

G

gàbia • *n* cage
gabinet • *n* cabinet
gablet • *n* gable
gadolini • *n* gadolinium
gafarró • *n* serin
gai • *n* gay • *adj* gay
gaia • *adj* gay
gaieta • *n* jet
gaig • *n* jay
gairebé • *adv* almost, nearly
gaita • *n* bagpipes
galůli • *n* gallium
galàctic • *adj* galactic
galàctica • *adj* galactic
galactosa • *n* galactose
galàxia • *n* galaxy
galena • *n* galena
galera • *n* galley
galeta • *n* cookie
galimaties • *n* claptrap
galindó • *n* bunion
galió • *n* galleon
gall • *n* chicken, rooster
galleda • *n* bucket
gallet • *n* popcorn, trigger
gallina • *n* chicken, hen
galopar • *n* run
galta • *n* cheek
galvanitzar • *v* galvanize
galvanòmetre • *n* galvanometer
gamarús • *n* owl
gamba • *n* shrimp
gàmeta • *n* gamete
gamma • *n* gamma, gamut
gana • *n* appetite, hunger
gangli • *n* ganglion
ganivet • *n* knife
ganivetada • *n* stab
ganxo • *n* hook
ganxut • *adj* hooked
ganyota • *n* mop
garantia • *n* guarantee, pledge
garantir • *v* guarantee
garatge • *n* garage
garba • *n* sheaf

garbell • *n* sieve
garbuix • *n* mess
garfi • *n* hook
gargamella • *n* gorge
gàrgola • *n* gargoyle
garita • *n* box
garjola • *n* pokey
garra • *n* claw
garrafa • *n* carafe
garrepa • *adj* stingy
garrí • *n* piglet
garrot • *n* stick
garrova • *n* carob
garrover • *n* carob
garroví • *n* carob
garsa • *n* magpie
gaseta • *n* gazette, journal
gasolina • *n* gasoline
gasós • *adj* gaseous
gasosa • *n* lemonade
gastar • *v* spend
gàstric • *adj* gastric
gastritis • *n* gastritis
gastrointestinal • *adj* gastrointestinal
gastronomia • *n* gastronomy
gastronòmic • *adj* gastronomic
gat • *n* cat, jack, tom
gata • *n* cat, queen
gatara • *n* uproar
gatejar • *v* crawl
gatet • *n* kitten
gateta • *n* kitten
gatosa • *n* gorse
gatzara • *n* brouhaha, fuss, hubbub, stir
gaudir • *v* bask, enjoy
gautxo • *n* gaucho
gavany • *n* paletot
gavià • *n* gull
gavina • *n* gull
ge • *n* gee
gebre • *n* frost
gegant • *n* giant • *adj* giant
gegantesc • *adj* gigantic
gegantí • *adj* gigantic
gegantisme • *n* gigantism

gel • *n* ice
gelada • *n* freeze, frost
gelar • *v* freeze
gelat • *adj* frozen
gelatina • *n* jelly
gelatinós • *adj* gelatinous
gelós • *adj* jealous
gelosament • *adv* jealously
gema • *n* bud
gemar • *v* bud
gemec • *n* moan
gemegar • *v* groan, moan
gemma • *n* gem
gendre • *n* son-in-law
genealogia • *n* genealogy
genealògicament • *adv* genealogically
genealogista • *n* genealogist
general • *n* general • *adj* general
generalment • *adv* generally
gènere • *n* gender, genre, genus, kind, sort
genèric • *adj* generic
generós • *adj* generous
genet • *n* jockey
geneta • *n* genet
genètic • *adj* genetic
genètica • *n* genetics
genèticament • *adv* genetically
genetista • *n* geneticist
geni • *n* genius
genial • *adj* great, groovy
genitiu • *n* genitive • *adj* genitive
geniva • *n* gum
genocidi • *n* genocide
genoll • *n* knee
genoma • *n* genome
gent • *n* people
gentilesa • *n* kindness
genuí • *adj* genuine
geògraf • *n* geographer
geografia • *n* geography
geogràficament • *adv* geographically
geòleg • *n* geologist
geologia • *n* geology
geològicament • *adv* geologically
geòmetra • *n* geometer
geometria • *n* geometry
geomètric • *adj* geometric
gep • *n* hump
geperuda • *n* humpback
geperut • *n* humpback
gerd • *n* raspberry
gerdera • *n* raspberry
gerència • *n* management
geriatria • *n* geriatrics
germà • *n* brother, germane, sibling
germana • *n* sibling, sister

germanastre • *n* stepbrother
germani • *n* germanium
germania • *n* jacquerie
germen • *n* germ
germinal • *adj* germinal
germinar • *v* germinate, sprout
gerra • *n* jug, pitcher
gerro • *n* vase
gerundi • *n* gerund
gespa • *n* turf
gest • *n* face
gesta • *n* exploit
gesticular • *v* gesticulate
gestió • *n* management
getó • *n* counter
gigantisme • *n* gigantism
gimnàs • *n* gymnasium
gimnasta • *n* gymnast
gimnàstic • *adj* gymnastic
gimnàstica • *n* gymnastics
gin • *n* gin
ginebra • *n* gin
ginebre • *n* juniper
ginecologia • *n* gynecology
ginecològic • *adj* gynecological
ginesta • *n* broom
gingebre • *n* ginger
gingivitis • *n* gingivitis
gínjol • *n* jujube
ginjoler • *n* jujube
gipó • *n* doublet
gir • *n* gyre
gira-sol • *n* sunflower
girafa • *n* giraffe
girar • *v* turn
gitano • *n* gypsy
gla • *n* acorn
glaçada • *n* freeze, frost
glaçador • *adj* chilling
glaçar • *v* freeze
glacera • *n* glacier
glacial • *adj* glacial
gladiador • *n* gladiator
gladiol • *n* gladiolus
gland • *n* glans
glàndula • *n* gland
glandular • *adj* glandular
gleva • *n* divot
glicina • *n* glycine
glicòlisi • *n* glycolysis
glicoproteïna • *n* glycoprotein
global • *adj* global
globalment • *adv* globally
globular • *adj* global
globus • *n* balloon, lob
glop • *n* drink, sip, tot
gloriós • *adj* glorious

glotis • *n* glottis
glucosa • *n* glucose
gluó • *n* gluon
glutamina • *n* glutamine
gnom • *n* gnome
go • *n* go
gol • *n* goal
gola • *n* gluttony, gorge, gorget, throat
golafre • *n* pig
golejador • *n* scorer
golf • *n* golf, gulf
golfes • *n* attic
golfista • *n* golfer
golut • *n* wolverine
goma • *n* eraser, rubber
gomfaró • *n* banner
góndola • *n* gondola
gong • *n* gong
goniòmetre • *n* goniometer
gonocòccia • *n* gonorrhea
gorilûla • *n* gorilla
gorra • *n* cap
gos • *n* dog
gossa • *n* bitch, dog
got • *n* glass
gota • *n* drop, goutte
goteta • *n* droplet
gòtic • *n* goth
govern • *n* government
governador • *n* governor
governamental • *adj* governmental
governant • *n* ruler
governar • *v* govern, rule
Goy • *n* goy
gràcies • *interj* thanks
graciosament • *adv* gracefully
gradual • *adj* gradual
gradualment • *adv* gradually
gràfic • *n* graph, graphic • *adj* graphic
gràfica • *n* plot
gràfics • *n* graphic
gralla • *n* jackdaw
gram • *n* gram
gramàtica • *n* grammar
gramatical • *adj* grammatical
gran • *adj* big, great, old
grana • *n* carmine
granada • *n* grenade
granat • *n* garnet
grandesa • *n* grandeur
grandiloqüent • *adj* grandiloquent
grandiós • *adj* grandiose
graner • *n* granary
granger • *n* farmer
granític • *adj* granitic
granja • *n* farm
granota • *n* frog

grans • *n* elder
grapa • *n* staple
grapat • *n* handful
grappa • *n* grappa
gras • *adj* fat
grassonet • *adj* chubby
gratacel • *n* skyscraper
gratar • *v* scratch
gratificant • *adj* rewarding
gratitud • *n* gratitude
grau • *n* degree
graula • *n* rook
grava • *n* gravel
gravar • *v* engrave, etch
gravat • *n* engraving, gravure
gravetat • *n* gravity
gravitació • *n* gravitation
gravitacional • *adj* gravitational
gravitatori • *adj* gravitational
gravós • *adj* burdensome
gregari • *adj* gregarious
greixar • *v* oil
greixós • *adj* greasy
greu • *adj* deep, grave, heavy
greument • *adv* gravely
grèvol • *n* holly
grif • *n* griffin
grill • *n* cricket
grilló • *n* fetter
grinyol • *n* screech
grip • *n* influenza
gripau • *n* toad
gris • *n* gray • *adj* gray
griu • *n* griffin
groc • *n* yellow • *adj* yellow
grog • *n* grog
grogor • *n* yellowness
groller • *adj* coarse, crude, filthy
grollera • *adj* coarse
gronxador • *n* swing
grop • *n* knot
grosella • *n* currant
grossa • *n* gross
grosset • *adj* chubby
grup • *n* group, set
gruta • *n* grotto
guai • *adj* cool
guant • *n* glove
guanyador • *n* winner
guanyadora • *n* winner
guanyar • *v* earn
guarda • *n* guard, watch
guardabosc • *n* ranger
guardaespatlles • *n* bodyguard
guardar • *v* keep
guardià • *n* watch
guardó • *n* award

guardonar • *v* award
guarnició • *n* garnish, garrison
guarniment • *n* garnish
guarnir • *v* garnish, tire
guatlla • *n* quail
guèiser • *n* geyser
guepard • *n* cheetah
guerra • *n* war
guerrejar • *v* war
guerrer • *n* warrior
guerrilla • *n* guerrilla
guerxo • *adj* cross-eyed
guiar • *v* steer
guilla • *n* fox, vixen
guillotina • *n* guillotine
guillotinar • *v* guillotine
guímel • *n* gimel

guineu • *n* fox
guió • *n* dash, script
guionet • *n* hyphen
guitarra • *n* guitar
guitarrista • *n* guitarist
guix • *n* chalk, gypsum
gulag • *n* gulag
guru • *n* guru
guspira • *n* spark
gust • *n* taste
gustar • *v* taste
gustatiu • *adj* gustatory
gustatori • *adj* gustatory
gustós • *adj* delicious
gustosament • *adv* gladly, willingly

H

hàbil • *adj* skillful
habilitar • *v* enable
habilitat • *n* proficiency, skill
hàbit • *n* habit, robe
habitable • *adj* habitable
habitació • *n* room
habitant • *n* inhabitant
habitar • *v* inhabit
hàbitat • *n* habitat
habitatge • *n* dwelling
habitualment • *adv* habitually
haca • *n* nag
hadal • *adj* hadal
hadró • *n* hadron
hafni • *n* hafnium
haixix • *n* hashish
halogen • *n* halogen
halterofília • *n* weightlifting
halterofilista • *n* weightlifter
ham • *n* fishhook
hamaca • *n* hammock
hamburguesa • *n* hamburger
hàmster • *n* hamster
handbol • *n* handball
handicapar • *v* handicap
haploide • *adj* haploid
harem • *n* harem
harmònica • *n* harmonica
harmoniosament • *adv* harmoniously
harmonitzar • *v* harmonize
harmònium • *n* harmonium
harpia • *n* harpy
hebdomadari • *n* hebdomadary
hectàrea • *n* hectare
hedonisme • *n* hedonism

hedonista • *n* hedonist
hedra • *n* ivy
hegemònic • *adj* hegemonic
heli • *n* helium
hèlice • *n* propeller, screw
helicó • *n* helicon
helicòpter • *n* helicopter
heliòmetre • *n* heliometer
heliosfera • *n* heliosphere
hèlix • *n* helix
hematològic • *adj* hematologic
hemiplegia • *n* hemiplegia
hemisferi • *n* hemisphere
hemofílic • *adj* haemophilic
hemorroide • *n* hemorrhoid
hendíadis • *n* hendiadys
hepàtic • *adj* hepatic
hepatitis • *n* hepatitis
heptàgon • *n* heptagon
herald • *n* harbinger
heràldica • *n* heraldry
herba • *n* grass, herb
herbaci • *adj* grassy, herbaceous
herbacol • *n* cardoon
herbari • *n* herbarium
herbívor • *n* herbivore • *adj* herbivorous
herboritzar • *v* herborize
hereditari • *adj* hereditary
heretar • *v* inherit
heretge • *n* heretic
heretgia • *n* heresy
herètic • *adj* heretical
hereu • *n* heir
hermafrodita • *n* hermaphrodite
hermètic • *adj* airtight

heroi • *n* hero
heroic • *adj* heroic
heroïna • *n* hero, heroin, heroine
heroisme • *n* heroism
herpes • *n* herpes
herpetologia • *n* herpetology
hesitació • *n* hesitation
hesitar • *v* hesitate
heterogeni • *adj* heterogeneous
heterosexisme • *n* heterosexism
heterosexual • *adj* heterosexual
heterosexualitat • *n* heterosexuality
heura • *n* ivy
heurístic • *adj* heuristic
heurística • *n* heuristic
hexàedre • *n* hexahedron
hexaedre • *n* hexahedron
hexàgon • *n* hexagon
hiat • *n* hiatus
hibernació • *n* hibernation
hibernar • *v* hibernate
híbrid • *n* hybrid • *adj* hybrid
hidràulic • *adj* hydraulic
hidràulica • *n* hydraulics
hidroavió • *n* seaplane
hidrocarbur • *n* hydrocarbon
hidrodinàmic • *adj* hydrodynamic
hidrodinàmica • *n* hydrodynamics
hidrogen • *n* hydrogen
hidrosfera • *n* hydrosphere
hidrostàtic • *adj* hydrostatic
hidrur • *n* hydride
hiena • *n* hyena
higiene • *n* hygiene
higiènic • *adj* hygienic
higròmetre • *n* hygrometer
hil • *n* hilum
hilarant • *adj* hilarious
hilaritat • *n* hilarity
himen • *n* hymen
himnari • *n* hymnal
himne • *n* anthem, hymn
hipàl·lage • *n* hypallage
hiperactiu • *adj* hyperactive
hipèrbaton • *n* hyperbaton
hipèrbola • *n* hyperbola
hipèrbole • *n* hyperbola, hyperbole
hiperbòlic • *adj* hyperbolic
hiperglicèmia • *n* hyperglycemia
hiperglucèmia • *n* hyperglycemia
hiperònim • *n* hypernym
hipersensibilitat • *n* hypersensitivity
hipertext • *n* hypertext
hipertròfia • *n* hypertrophy
hipnosi • *n* hypnosis
hipnòtic • *n* hypnotic, soporific • *adj* hypnotic, soporific

hipnotisme • *n* hypnotism
hipnotitzador • *n* hypnotist
hipocamp • *n* hippocampus
hipocaust • *n* hypocaust
hipocondria • *n* hypochondria
hipocresia • *n* hypocrisy
hipòcrita • *n* hypocrite • *adj* hypocritical
hipodèrmic • *adj* hypodermic
hipòdrom • *n* hippodrome
hipònim • *n* hyponym
hipopòtam • *n* hippopotamus
hipotalàmic • *adj* hypothalamic
hipotàlem • *n* hypothalamus
hipoteca • *n* mortgage
hipotecar • *v* mortgage
hipotenusa • *n* hypotenuse
hipòtesi • *n* hypothesis
hipotètic • *adj* hypothetical
hipotèticament • *adv* hypothetically
hipòxia • *n* hypoxia
hissar • *v* hoist
histerectomia • *n* hysterectomy
histèria • *n* hysteria
histèric • *adj* hysterical
histèricament • *adv* hysterically
història • *n* history
historiador • *n* historian
historial • *n* history
històric • *adj* historic, historical
històricament • *adv* historically
histriònic • *adj* histrionic
hivern • *n* winter
hivernar • *v* winter
hola • *interj* hello, hi
holístic • *adj* holistic
holmi • *n* holmium
hom • *pron* you
home • *n* boy, man
homenatge • *n* homage, keep
homeòpata • *n* homeopath
homeopatia • *n* homeopathy
homicidi • *n* homicide
homofòbia • *n* homophobia
homòfon • *n* homophone
homofonia • *n* homophony
homogeni • *adj* homogeneous
homògraf • *n* homograph
homologar • *v* homologate
homònim • *n* homonym • *adj* homonymous
homonímia • *n* homonymy
homosexual • *n* homosexual • *adj* homosexual
homosexualitat • *n* homosexuality
honestament • *adv* honestly
honestedat • *n* honesty
honor • *n* honor

honorable • *adj* honorable
honorari • *adj* honorary • *n* wage
honradesa • *n* honesty
hoquei • *n* hockey
hora • *n* hour, time
horari • *n* schedule
horitzó • *n* horizon
horitzontal • *adj* horizontal
horitzontalment • *adv* horizontally
hormona • *n* hormone
hormonal • *adj* hormonal
horòscop • *n* horoscope
horrible • *adj* horrible, lousy
horriblement • *adv* horribly
hòrrid • *adj* horrible
horroritzat • *adj* aghast
horrorós • *adj* awful
hortalissa • *n* vegetable
horticultura • *n* horticulture
hosanna • *interj* hosanna
hospital • *n* hospital
hospitalització • *n* hospitalization
host • *n* army

hoste • *n* guest
hostessa • *n* steward, stewardess
hostil • *adj* hostile, unfriendly
hotel • *n* hotel
hui • *n* today
huit • *n* eight
humà • *n* human • *adj* human, humane
humanisme • *n* humanism
humanístic • *adj* humanistic
humanitari • *adj* humanitarian
humanitària • *adj* humanitarian
humanitat • *n* humanity
húmer • *n* humerus
humida • *adj* moist
humil • *adj* humble
humiliar • *v* humble
humilment • *adv* humbly
humit • *adj* damp, humid, moist
humitat • *n* damp, moisture
humor • *n* mood, temper
huracà • *n* hurricane
hússar • *n* hussar

I

i • *conj* and • *n* i
iac • *n* yak
iaia • *n* crone, grandmother
iambe • *n* iamb
iàmbic • *adj* iambic
iarda • *n* yard
ibis • *n* ibis
ibuprofèn • *n* ibuprofen
iceberg • *n* iceberg
icona • *n* icon
icosaedre • *n* icosahedron
icosàedre • *n* icosahedron
ics • *n* ex
ictiòleg • *n* ichthyologist
ictiologia • *n* ichthyology
idea • *n* idea
ideal • *n* ideal • *adj* ideal
idealització • *n* idealization
idealment • *adv* ideally
idèntic • *adj* identical
idènticament • *adv* identically
identificable • *adj* identifiable
identificació • *n* identification
identificar • *v* identify
identificar-se • *v* identify
identitat • *n* identity
ideograma • *n* ideogram, ideograph
ideologia • *n* ideology
idíl·lic • *adj* idyllic

idili • *n* idyll
idiòcia • *n* idiocy
idiolecte • *n* idiolect
idioma • *n* language
idiosincràtic • *adj* idiosyncratic
idiota • *n* fool, idiot, nincompoop
idiotisme • *n* idiom
ídol • *n* idol
idòlatra • *n* idolater • *adj* idolatrous
idolatria • *n* idolatry
iglú • *n* igloo
ignorància • *n* ignorance
ignorant • *adj* ignorant, oblivious
igual • *adj* equal, even
igualitarisme • *n* egalitarianism
igualment • *adv* equally
iguals • *n* deuce
igualtat • *n* equality
il·legal • *adj* illegal
il·legalment • *adv* illegally
il·legible • *adj* illegible
il·legítim • *adj* illegitimate
il·lícit • *adj* illicit
il·limitat • *adj* limitless, unlimited
il·lògic • *adj* illogical
il·lògicament • *adv* illogically
il·luminar • *v* light
il·lusió • *n* illusion
il·lustre • *adj* illustrious

ili • *n* ileum, ilium
ilíac • *adj* iliac
illa • *n* block, island
illegible • *adj* illegible
illenc • *n* islander
illenca • *n* islander
illetrat • *adj* illiterate
illusió • *n* illusion
imaginació • *n* imagination
imaginar • *v* imagine
imaginari • *adj* imaginary
imaginatiu • *adj* imaginative
imam • *n* imam
imant • *n* magnet
imatge • *n* image
imatgeria • *n* imagery
imbatible • *adj* unbeatable
imbècil • *n* imbecile, nincompoop
imbecilůlitat • *n* imbecility
imbricar • *v* imbricate
imbuir • *v* imbue
imitació • *n* imitation
imitar • *v* imitate
immadur • *adj* immature
immaduresa • *n* immaturity
immaterial • *adj* immaterial
immaterialitat • *n* immateriality
immediat • *adj* immediate
immediatament • *adv* immediately, outright
immediatesa • *n* immediacy
immenjable • *adj* inedible
immens • *adj* immense
immensitat • *n* immensity
immersió • *n* plunge
immigrant • *n* immigrant
imminència • *n* imminence
imminent • *adj* imminent
immòbil • *adj* immobile, stationary
immoble • *adj* immobile
immolar • *v* immolate
immoral • *adj* base, immoral, outrageous
immoralment • *adv* immorally
immortal • *adj* immortal
immortalitat • *n* immortality
immundícia • *n* filth
immune • *adj* immune
immunitat • *n* immunity
immunòleg • *n* immunologist
immunologia • *n* immunology
immunològic • *adj* immunological
impacient • *adj* impatient
impacientment • *adv* impatiently
impactar • *v* impact
impala • *n* impala
imparable • *adj* unstoppable
imparcial • *adj* impartial

imparcialment • *adv* impartially
imparell • *adj* odd
impecable • *adj* impeccable
impecablement • *adv* impeccably
impedir • *v* fetter
impenetrabilitat • *n* impenetrability
impensable • *adj* unthinkable
imperceptible • *adj* imperceptible
imperceptiblement • *adv* imperceptibly
imperfecció • *n* imperfection
imperfectament • *adv* imperfectly
imperfecte • *adj* imperfect
imperfet • *n* imperfect
imperi • *n* empire
imperial • *adj* imperial
imperialista • *n* imperialist • *adj* imperialist, imperialistic
imperiós • *adj* imperious
impermeabilització • *n* waterproofing
impermeable • *adj* impermeable, waterproof
impersonalment • *adv* impersonally
impertinent • *adj* impertinent
impetuós • *adj* impetuous
implacable • *adj* relentless
implicar • *v* imply
implícit • *adj* implicit
implícitament • *adv* implicitly
implosió • *n* implosion
impopularitat • *n* unpopularity
important • *adj* important
importantment • *adv* importantly
importú • *adj* importunate
impossible • *n* impossible • *adj* impossible
impossiblement • *adv* impossibly
impost • *n* tax
imposta • *n* ledge
impotent • *adj* impotent
impracticabilitat • *n* impracticability
impracticable • *adj* impracticable
imprecís • *adj* inaccurate
impregnar • *v* imbue, permeate
imprès • *adj* impressed
impressió • *n* impression
impressionable • *adj* impressionable
impressionant • *adj* impressive
impressionantment • *adv* impressively
impressionat • *adj* impressed
impressionisme • *n* impressionism
impressionista • *n* impressionist
impressora • *n* press
imprevisible • *adj* unpredictable
imprevist • *adj* unforeseen
imprimible • *adj* printable
improbabilitat • *n* improbability
improbable • *adj* improbable, unlikely

improductiu • *adj* unproductive
impropi • *adj* improper, infelicitous
improvisació • *n* improvisation
improvisar • *v* improvise
imprudència • *n* imprudence
imprudent • *adj* careless, imprudent, unwise
imprudentment • *adv* imprudently
impudència • *n* impudence
impudent • *adj* impudent
impuls • *n* impulse, momentum
impulsió • *n* impulse
impulsiu • *adj* impulsive
impur • *adj* filthy, impure, unclean
impuresa • *n* impurity
inacabable • *adj* endless
inacabat • *adj* unfinished
inacceptabilitat • *n* unacceptability
inacceptable • *adj* unacceptable
inacceptablement • *adv* unacceptably
inaccessibilitat • *n* inaccessibility
inaccessible • *adj* inaccessible
inacció • *n* inaction
inactiu • *adj* idle, inactive
inactivitat • *n* inactivity
inadequadament • *adv* inadequately
inadequat • *adj* inadequate, infelicitous, unsuitable
inadmissible • *adj* inadmissible
inalienable • *adj* inalienable
inanimat • *adj* inanimate
inaplicable • *adj* inapplicable
inapropiat • *adj* inappropriate
inauguració • *n* inauguration
inaugural • *adj* inaugural
incandescent • *adj* incandescent
incapaç • *adj* incapable, unable
incautament • *adv* incautiously
incendi • *n* fire
incendiari • *adj* incendiary
incentiu • *n* incentive
incert • *adj* uncertain
incertament • *adv* uncertainly
incessant • *adj* incessant, unremitting
incestuós • *adj* incestuous
incinerar • *v* incinerate
incisió • *n* incision
incisiu • *adj* incisive • *n* incisor
incitar • *v* prompt
inclinació • *n* bow, inclination
inclinar • *v* incline, lean, tilt
inclusió • *n* inclusion
inclusiu • *adj* inclusive
incoherent • *adj* incoherent
incoherentment • *adv* incoherently
incòlume • *adj* unscathed
incombustible • *adj* incombustible

incomestible • *adj* inedible
incòmodament • *adv* uncomfortably
incòmode • *adj* uncomfortable
incomparable • *adj* incomparable
incompatible • *adj* incompatible
incompetent • *adj* incompetent
incomplet • *adj* incomplete
incompletament • *adv* incompletely
incomprensible • *adj* incomprehensible
inconcebible • *adj* inconceivable
inconclús • *adj* unfinished
incondicional • *adj* unconditional, utter
incongruent • *adj* incongruous
inconscient • *adj* oblivious, unconscious
• *n* unconscious
inconsideradament • *adv* inconsiderately
inconsiderat • *adj* inconsiderate
inconstància • *n* inconstancy
inconstant • *adj* fickle, inconstant
inconstitucional • *adj* unconstitutional
inconveniència • *n* inconvenience
inconvenient • *adj* inconvenient
inconvenientment • *adv* inconveniently
incorporar • *v* incorporate
incorporar-se • *v* coalesce
incorrectament • *adv* incorrectly
incorrecte • *adj* false, incorrect
incrèdul • *adj* incredulous
increïble • *adj* incredible, unconvincing
increïblement • *adv* incredibly, unbelievably
incremental • *adj* incremental
íncub • *n* incubus
incubació • *n* incubation
incubadora • *n* incubator
íncube • *n* incubus
incurable • *adj* incurable
indagació • *n* inquiry
indecent • *adj* indecent
indecís • *adj* indecisive
indefens • *adj* defenseless, helpless
indefensable • *adj* indefensible
indefinidament • *adv* indefinitely
indefinit • *adj* indefinite, undefined
indegudament • *adv* unduly
indeleble • *adj* indelible
independència • *n* independence
independent • *adj* independent
independentment • *adv* independently
indescriptible • *adj* indescribable
indesitjable • *adj* undesirable
indestructible • *adj* indestructible
índex • *n* forefinger, index
indi • *n* indium
indicatiu • *adj* indicative
indici • *n* tip
indiferent • *adj* indifferent

indígena • *adj* indigenous
indigència • *n* destitution
indigent • *n* indigent • *adj* indigent
indignació • *n* indignation, outrage
indignar • *v* outrage
indignat • *adj* indignant
indigne • *adj* base, unworthy
indignitat • *n* indignity
indiot • *n* turkey
indirectament • *adv* indirectly
indirecte • *adj* indirect
indiscret • *adj* indiscreet, tactless
indiscriminat • *adj* indiscriminate
indiscutible • *adj* indisputable
indispensable • *adj* indispensable
indisponible • *adj* unavailable
indistingible • *adj* indistinguishable
indistint • *adj* indistinct
individu • *n* individual
individual • *adj* individual
individualista • *adj* maverick
individualment • *adv* individually
individuals • *n* singles
indivisible • *adj* indivisible
indolent • *adj* indolent
indolor • *adj* painless
indomable • *adj* indomitable
indret • *n* place
indubtable • *adj* indubitable
indubtablement • *adv* undoubtedly, un-questionably
induir • *v* induce
indulgent • *adj* indulgent
indult • *n* pardon
indultar • *v* pardon
industrial • *adj* industrial
industrialisme • *n* industrialism
industrialitzat • *adj* industrialized
inèdit • *adj* unpublished
ineficaç • *adj* ineffective
inelàstic • *adj* inelastic
inepte • *adj* inept
ineptitud • *n* ineptitude
inequívoc • *adj* unambiguous, unequivo-cal
inequívocament • *adv* unambiguously
inèrcia • *n* inertia
inert • *adj* inert
inescrutable • *adj* inscrutable
inesperadament • *adv* unexpectedly
inesperat • *adj* unexpected
inessencial • *adj* inessential
inestabilitat • *n* instability
inestable • *adj* unstable
inevitable • *adj* inevitable, unavoidable
inevitablement • *adv* inevitably
inexacte • *adj* inexact

inexcusablement • *adv* inexcusably
inexistència • *n* nonexistence
inexistent • *adj* nonexistent
inexorable • *adj* inexorable
inexpert • *adj* inexperienced
inexplicable • *adj* inexplicable
infalúlibilitat • *n* infallibility
infalúlible • *adj* bulletproof, infallible
infame • *adj* infamous
infàmia • *n* infamy
infant • *n* tot
infantil • *adj* infantile
infatuació • *n* infatuation
infecció • *n* infection
infecciós • *adj* infectious
infeliç • *adj* infelicitous, unhappy
inferioritat • *n* inferiority
infermer • *n* nurse
infermera • *n* sister
infidel • *n* infidel • *adj* unfaithful
infidelitat • *n* infidelity
infidelment • *adv* unfaithfully
infiltrar • *v* infiltrate
infinit • *adj* infinite
infinitat • *n* infinity
infinitiu • *n* infinitive
inflamable • *adj* inflammable
inflamació • *n* inflammation
inflar • *v* inflate
inflar-se • *v* swell
inflexibilitat • *n* inflexibility
inflexible • *adj* inflexible
inflexiblement • *adv* inflexibly
inflexió • *n* inflection
inflorescència • *n* inflorescence
influència • *n* influence
informació • *n* data, information
informal • *adj* casual, informal
informalitat • *n* informality
informalment • *adv* informally
informar • *v* report
informatiu • *adj* informative • *n* news
informe • *n* report
infortunat • *adj* unlucky
infraestructura • *n* framework, infras-tructure
inframón • *n* afterlife
infranquejable • *adj* impassable
infraroig • *n* infrared • *adj* infrared
infreqüent • *adj* infrequent
infructuós • *adj* fruitless
infundat • *adj* unfounded
infusió • *n* infusion
ingrat • *adj* thankless
ingredient • *n* ingredient
inhabitable • *adj* uninhabitable
inhalació • *n* inhalation

inhalar • _v_ inhale
inherent • _adj_ inherent
inhibició • _n_ inhibition
inhibir • _v_ inhibit
inhumà • _adj_ inhuman
inhumació • _n_ inhumation
inici • _n_ beginning, inception, outset
inicial • _n_ initial • _adj_ initial
inicials • _n_ initial
iniciar • _v_ begin
iniciativa • _n_ initiative
inimaginable • _adj_ unimaginable
inintelůligent • _adj_ unintelligent
inintelůligentment • _adv_ unintelligently
inintelůligibilitat • _n_ unintelligibility
inintelůligible • _adj_ unintelligible
inintelůligiblement • _adv_ unintelligibly
ininterrompudament • _adv_ uninterruptedly
ininterromput • _adj_ uninterrupted
injecció • _n_ injection
injectar • _v_ inject
injúria • _n_ slander
injuriar • _v_ slander
injust • _adj_ unfair, unjust
injustament • _adv_ unjustly
injustificable • _adj_ unjustifiable
innat • _adj_ inborn, innate
innecessari • _adj_ needless, unnecessary
innecessàriament • _adv_ unnecessarily
innegable • _adj_ undeniable
innoble • _adj_ base
innocència • _n_ innocence
innocent • _adj_ innocent
innocentment • _adv_ innocently
innocu • _adj_ innocuous
innovador • _adj_ innovative
inoblidable • _adj_ unforgettable
inofensiu • _adj_ harmless, inoffensive
inorgànic • _adj_ inorganic
inqüestionable • _adj_ unquestionable
inquiet • _adj_ restless
inquilí • _n_ tenant
insaciable • _adj_ insatiable
insalubre • _adj_ unhealthy
insanitat • _n_ craziness, insanity
insatisfactori • _adj_ unsatisfactory
insatisfet • _adj_ dissatisfied
inscripció • _n_ inscription
inscriure • _v_ inscribe
insecte • _n_ insect
insegur • _adj_ insecure, unsafe
inseminació • _n_ insemination
insensible • _adj_ insensible, insensitive
inseparable • _adj_ inseparable
inseparablement • _adv_ inseparably
inserció • _n_ insertion

insignificant • _adj_ insignificant, trifling
insinuar • _v_ imply
insípid • _adj_ insipid
insípidament • _adv_ insipidly
insistència • _n_ insistence
insolent • _adj_ insolent
insoluble • _adj_ insoluble
insolvent • _adj_ insolvent
insomne • _adj_ insomniac
insomni • _n_ insomnia
insondable • _adj_ inscrutable
insostenible • _adj_ unsustainable
inspecció • _n_ check, inspection
inspeccionar • _v_ inspect, search
inspirador • _adj_ inspiring
inspirar • _v_ inhale
instalůlació • _n_ installation
instalůlar • _v_ install
instant • _n_ moment, second
instantani • _adj_ instantaneous
instigació • _n_ instigation
instintiu • _adj_ instinctive
instrucció • _n_ instruction
instructiu • _adj_ instructive
instrumentista • _n_ instrumentalist
insubstituïble • _adj_ irreplaceable
insuficient • _adj_ insufficient
insuficientment • _adv_ insufficiently
insular • _adj_ insular
insulina • _n_ insulin
insuls • _adj_ dull
insult • _n_ insult
insultant • _adj_ insulting
insultar • _v_ insult
insuportable • _adj_ impossible, unbearable
insurgent • _n_ insurgent • _adj_ insurgent
intacte • _adj_ intact
intangible • _adj_ intangible
integrar • _v_ integrate
integritat • _n_ integrity
intelůlectual • _adj_ highbrow, intellectual
• _n_ intellectual
intelůligència • _n_ intelligence
intelůligent • _adj_ intelligent
intelůligentment • _adv_ intelligently
intelůligibilitat • _n_ intelligibility
intelůligible • _adj_ intelligible
intelůligiblement • _adv_ intelligibly
intempestivitat • _n_ intempestivity
intenció • _n_ intention
intencionadament • _adv_ intentionally
intencionat • _adj_ intentional
intens • _adj_ deep, intense
intensament • _adv_ intensely
intensificar • _v_ intensify
intensitat • _n_ intensity

intensiu • *adj* intensive
intensivament • *adv* intensively
intent • *n* down, go
intentar • *v* try
interacció • *n* interaction
intercalar • *adj* intercalary
intercanvi • *n* exchange
intercanviable • *adj* interchangeable
intercanviar • *v* exchange
intercepció • *n* interception
intercontinental • *adj* intercontinental
interdisciplinari • *adj* interdisciplinary
interès • *n* interest
interessant • *adj* interesting
interessat • *adj* interested
interferència • *n* interference
interferir • *v* interfere
intergalàctic • *adj* intergalactic
interí • *adj* interim
interior • *adj* domestic, inner, interior • *n* infielder, inside, interior
interiorment • *adv* internally
interjecció • *n* interjection
interludi • *n* interlude
intermedi • *adj* intermediate
interminable • *adj* endless, interminable, neverending
intermitent • *adj* intermittent
intermitentment • *adv* intermittently
intern • *n* boarder, inmate • *adj* internal
internacional • *adj* international
internacionalment • *adv* internationally
internament • *adv* internally
internat • *n* inmate
interpersonal • *adj* interpersonal
interplanetari • *adj* interplanetary
interpolar • *v* interpolate
intèrpret • *n* interpreter
interpretar • *v* interpret
interrogativament • *adv* interrogatively
interrompre • *v* interrupt
interrupció • *n* disruption
interruptor • *n* switch
intersexual • *n* intersexual • *adj* intersexual
intervenció • *n* intervention
intervenir • *v* intervene
interviu • *n* interview
intestí • *n* intestine
intestinal • *adj* intestinal
intestins • *n* bowels
íntim • *adj* intimate
intimidar • *v* browbeat, intimidate
intimitat • *n* intimacy
intocable • *n* pariah
intolerable • *adj* intolerable
intolerant • *adj* intolerant

intracelŭlular • *adj* intracellular
intranquil • *adj* restless
intransigent • *adj* uncompromising
intransitiu • *adj* intransitive
intransitivament • *adv* intransitively
intravenós • *adj* intravenous
intrèpid • *adj* intrepid
intricat • *adj* intricate
intriga • *n* intrigue
intrigant • *adj* intriguing
intrigar • *v* intrigue
intrínsec • *adj* intrinsic
introducció • *n* introduction
introductori • *adj* introductory
introduir • *v* set
introspectiu • *adj* introspective
intuïció • *n* intuition
intuïtiu • *adj* intuitive
inundació • *n* flood
inundar • *v* inundate
inusual • *adj* unusual
inútil • *adj* useless
invàlid • *adj* disabled, invalid
invalidar • *v* invalidate
invariable • *adj* invariable
invasió • *n* invasion
invasiu • *adj* invasive
invasor • *n* invader
invencible • *n* invincible • *adj* invincible
invenció • *n* invention
inventar • *v* invent
inventari • *n* inventory
inventariar • *v* inventory
inventiu • *adj* inventive
invers • *adj* inverse
inversemblant • *adj* implausible
invertebrat • *n* invertebrate • *adj* invertebrate
invertir • *v* invert, invest
investigació • *n* investigation, research
investigar • *v* investigate
investir • *v* invest
inveterat • *adj* inveterate
invicte • *adj* unbeaten
invisibilitat • *n* invisibility
invisible • *adj* invisible
invisiblement • *adv* invisibly
invitació • *n* invite
invitar • *v* invite
invitat • *n* guest
invocar • *v* invoke
involuntari • *adj* involuntary, unintentional
involuntàriament • *adv* involuntarily, unintentionally
invulnerable • *adj* invulnerable
ió • *n* ion

io-io • *n* yo-yo
iod • *n* yodh
iode • *n* iodine
ioga • *n* yoga
iogurt • *n* yogurt
iònic • *adj* ionic
ionosfera • *n* ionosphere
iot • *n* yacht
iota • *n* iota
ípsilon • *n* upsilon
ira • *n* anger, ire
irat • *adj* irate
iridescència • *n* iridescence
iridi • *n* iridium
iris • *n* iris
ironia • *n* irony
irònic • *adj* ironic
irònicament • *adv* ironically
irracional • *adj* irrational
irracionalment • *adv* irrationally
irreconeixible • *adj* unrecognizable
irreemplaçable • *adj* irreplaceable
irrefutable • *adj* irrefutable
irregular • *adj* irregular
irregularitat • *n* irregularity
irregularment • *adv* irregularly
irrellevant • *adj* moot
irremeiable • *adj* irremediable
irreparable • *adj* irreparable
irreparablement • *adv* irreparably

irreprimible • *adj* irrepressible
irresistible • *adj* irresistible
irresponsable • *adj* irresponsible
irreverent • *adj* irreverent
irrigar • *v* irrigate
irritabilitat • *n* irritability
irritable • *adj* irritable
irritació • *n* irritation
irritant • *adj* irritating
irrupció • *n* irruption
isard • *n* chamois
isolació • *n* isolation
isolament • *n* isolation
isolar • *v* insulate, isolate
isolat • *adj* insular
isomètric • *adj* isometric
isotònic • *adj* isotonic
isòtop • *n* isotope
isqui • *n* ischium
ísquium • *n* ischium
istme • *n* isthmus
iteratiu • *adj* iterative
iterbi • *n* ytterbium
itinerant • *adj* itinerant
itinerari • *n* course
itri • *n* yttrium
ivori • *n* ivory
ixent • *adj* rising

J

ja • *adv* already • *interj* now
jaciment • *n* deposit
jade • *n* jade
jaqueta • *n* jacket
jardí • *n* garden
jardiner • *n* gardener
jardinera • *n* gardener
jaspi • *n* jasper
javelina • *n* javelin
jazz • *n* jazz
jejú • *n* jejunum
jerbu • *n* jerboa
jeroglífic • *n* hieroglyph • *adj* hieroglyphic
jeure • *v* lie
jihad • *n* jihad
jo • *n* ego
joc • *n* game, play, set
joguet • *n* toy
joguina • *n* toy
joia • *n* glee, joy
joier • *n* jeweler

joiós • *adj* joyful
joquei • *n* jockey
jòquer • *n* joker
jorn • *n* day
jornada • *n* day
jou • *n* collar, yoke
joule • *n* joule
jove • *adj* young • *n* youth
joventut • *n* youth
jovial • *adj* jovial
jubilar • *v* retire
judici • *n* judgment
judicial • *adj* judicial
judiciari • *adj* judicial
judo • *n* judo
jugador • *n* gambler, player
jugar • *v* play
julivert • *n* parsley
jull • *n* darnel
jungla • *n* jungle
junt • *adv* together
juntura • *n* joint

júnyer • *v* yoke
junyir • *v* yoke
jurament • *n* oath, pledge
jurar • *v* swear, vow
jurat • *n* juror, jury
jurisdicció • *n* venue
just • *adj* fair, just • *adv* just
justament • *adv* fairly, justly
justar • *v* joust
justesa • *n* justice

justícia • *n* justice
justificable • *adj* justifiable
justificació • *n* justification
justificar • *v* justify
justificat • *adj* justified
jute • *n* jute
jutge • *n* judge
jutjar • *v* adjudicate, judge, try

K

kamikaze • *n* kamikaze
kaó • *n* kaon
kappa • *n* kappa
khi • *n* chi
kiwi • *n* kiwi

koiné • *n* koine
kolkhoz • *n* kolkhoz
ksi • *n* xi
kumis • *n* koumiss

L

léndemà • *n* morrow
la • *n* la • *art* the
laberint • *n* labyrinth, maze, spaghetti
laberíntic • *adj* labyrinthine
labial • *adj* labial
labirintitis • *n* labyrinthitis
labor • *adj* menial
laboratori • *n* laboratory
laboriós • *adj* laborious
laboriosament • *adv* laboriously
laca • *n* lacquer, lake
laceració • *n* laceration
lacrimal • *adj* lacrimal
lacrosse • *n* lacrosse
lactosa • *n* lactose
laic • *adj* lay, secular
lama • *n* lama
lambda • *n* lambda
lament • *n* lament
lamentable • *adj* pitiful, regrettable, sad
lamentar • *v* lament
làmia • *n* lamia
làmpada • *n* lamp
lànguid • *adj* languid
lantani • *n* lanthanum
làpida • *n* gravestone
lapsus • *n* lapse
laringe • *n* larynx
laringofaringe • *n* laryngopharynx
làrix • *n* larch
lasanya • *n* lasagna
lasciu • *adj* lewd

làser • *n* laser
latent • *adj* dormant
lateral • *n* wing
làtex • *n* latex
latitud • *n* latitude
latrina • *n* latrine
laurenci • *n* lawrencium
lava • *n* lava
lavabo • *n* sink, toilet, washbasin
lecitina • *n* lecithin
lector • *n* reader
legal • *adj* legal
legalitat • *n* legality
legalització • *n* legalization
legalment • *adv* legally
legió • *n* legion
legislació • *n* legislation
legislador • *n* legislator
legislar • *v* legislate
legislatiu • *adj* legislative
legítim • *adj* legitimate
legítimament • *adv* legitimately
lema • *n* motto
lèmming • *n* lemming
lèmur • *n* lemur
lent • *n* lens • *adj* slow
lentament • *adv* slowly
lentitud • *n* slowness
lepra • *n* leprosy
leptó • *n* lepton
les • *art* the • *pron* them
lesbià • *adj* lesbian

lesbiana • *n* lesbian • *adj* lesbian
lesió • *n* lesion
lesionar • *v* lesion
letal • *adj* deadly
letargia • *n* lethargy
letàrgic • *adj* lethargic
levitació • *n* levitation
lexema • *n* lexeme
lèxic • *adj* lexical
lexicògraf • *n* lexicographer
lexicògrafa • *n* lexicographer
lexicografia • *n* lexicography
lexicogràfic • *adj* lexicographic
lexicologia • *n* lexicology
libació • *n* libation
libèlůlula • *n* dragonfly
libidinal • *adj* libidinal
libidinoso • *adj* libidinous
licantropia • *n* lycanthropy
líder • *n* head, leader, ruler
liderar • *v* head
ligni • *adj* wooden
lignit • *n* lignite
lila • *n* lilac • *adj* lilac
limfa • *n* lymph
limfàtic • *adj* lymphatic
límit • *n* bound, limit
limitar • *v* limit
limusina • *n* limousine
lingot • *n* ingot
lingüista • *n* linguist
lingüístic • *adj* linguistic
lingüística • *n* linguistics
link • *n* link
linx • *n* lynx
liofilitzar • *v* lyophilize
lípid • *n* lipid
liquen • *n* lichen
líquid • *n* liquid • *adj* liquid
liquidar • *v* liquidate
lira • *n* lyre
liró • *n* dormouse
lisina • *n* lysine
literalment • *adv* literally
literari • *adj* literary
literatura • *n* literature
liti • *n* lithium
lític • *adj* lithic
litigar • *v* litigate
litigi • *n* lawsuit
litosfera • *n* lithosphere
lítote • *n* litotes
litúrgia • *n* liturgy
litúrgic • *adj* liturgical
llaç • *n* noose
llac • *n* lake
lladrar • *v* bark

lladre • *n* burglar, robber, thief
lladruc • *n* bark
llagosta • *n* grasshopper, lobster, locust
llàgrima • *n* tear
llama • *n* llama
llamàntol • *n* lobster
llamborda • *n* cobblestone
llambric • *n* earthworm
llamentar-se • *v* moan
llaminadura • *n* candy, sweet
llaminadures • *n* sweets
llamp • *n* lightning
llampec • *n* bolt, lightning
llampresa • *n* lamprey
llana • *n* wool
llança • *n* lance, spear
llançador • *n* pitcher
llançaflames • *n* flamethrower
llançament • *n* cast, launch, pitch, shot
llançar • *v* launch, pitch, release, throw
llancer • *n* lancer
llanceta • *n* lancet
llangardaix • *n* lizard
llanguir • *v* languish
llanós • *adj* woolly
llanterna • *n* flashlight, torch
llanxa • *n* launch
llapis • *n* pencil
llar • *n* hearth, home
llard • *n* lard
llarg • *adj* large
llàstima • *n* pity, shame
llastimós • *adj* sorry
llauna • *n* can
llaurar • *v* plough
llaüt • *n* lute
llautó • *n* brass
llavar • *v* wash
llavi • *n* lip
llavor • *n* seed
llavors • *adv* then
llebre • *n* hare, jackrabbit
llebrer • *n* greyhound
lledoner • *n* hackberry
llegar • *v* will
llegenda • *n* legend
llegendari • *adj* legendary
llegible • *adj* legible
llegir • *v* read
llegir-se • *v* read
llegum • *n* legume, vegetable
llei • *n* fineness, law
lleial • *adj* faithful, loyal
lleialment • *adv* loyally
lleialtat • *n* loyalty
lleig • *adj* ugly
lleixiu • *n* lye

llémena • *n* nit
llenç • *n* canvas
llençar • *v* cast
llençolet • *n* diaper
llengua • *n* language, tongue
llenguatge • *n* language
llengüeta • *n* bootstrap
llentilla • *n* lentil
llenya • *n* firewood
lleó • *n* lion
lleona • *n* lioness
llepada • *n* lick
llepar • *v* blow, lick
llesca • *n* bun, slice
llest • *adj* clever, ready, set
llestesa • *n* intelligence
llet • *n* cum
lleter • *n* milkman
lletera • *n* churn
lletgesa • *n* ugliness
lletjor • *n* ugliness
lletós • *adj* milky
lletra • *n* letter
lletrat • *adj* literate
lletrejar • *v* spell
lletuga • *n* lettuce
lleuger • *adj* light, soft
lleugerament • *adv* lightly, slightly
lleure • *n* leisure
lleva • *n* levy
llevadora • *n* midwife
llevant • *adj* eastern
llevar-se • *v* awake
llevat • *adj* awake • *n* leaven, yeast
llevataps • *n* corkscrew
lli • *n* flax, linen
llibertat • *n* freedom, liberty
llibre • *n* book
llibrer • *n* bookseller
llibreria • *n* bookshop
llibres • *n* book
llibret • *n* libretto
llibreter • *n* bookseller
llibretera • *n* bookseller
lliga • *n* alloy, league
lligabosc • *n* honeysuckle
lligacama • *n* garter
lligadura • *n* tie
lligam • *n* tie
lligament • *n* ligament
lligar • *v* cable, link, tie
llim • *n* silt
llima • *n* file
llimac • *n* slug
llimona • *n* lemon
llimonada • *n* lemonade
llimoner • *n* lemon

llimonera • *n* lemon
llinatge • *n* ancestry, lineage
llinda • *n* lintel
llindar • *n* sill, threshold
lliri • *n* lily
llis • *adj* smooth
lliscant • *adj* slippery
llíssera • *n* mullet
llista • *n* list
llistar • *v* list
llistat • *adj* striped
llit • *n* bed
lliura • *n* pound, sterling
lliurar • *v* issue
lliure • *adj* free
lliurement • *adv* freely
lloable • *adj* praiseworthy
lloar • *v* praise
lloc • *n* place, room
llogar • *v* hire, rent
llogater • *n* tenant
lloguer • *n* rent
llom • *n* spine
llombrígol • *n* navel
llong • *adj* long
llop • *n* wolf
llorer • *n* laurel
lloro • *n* parrot
llosa • *n* flagstone, slab
llot • *n* mud
llotja • *n* box
lluç • *n* hake, pike
llúdria • *n* otter
llúdriga • *n* otter
lluentor • *n* shine
lluerna • *n* glowworm, skylight
lluir • *v* shine
lluïssor • *n* shine
lluita • *n* fight, struggle
lluitador • *n* wrestler
lluitadora • *n* wrestler
lluitar • *v* fight
llum • *n* highlight, light
lluna • *n* moon
llunàtic • *adj* lunatic
lluny • *adv* far
llunyà • *adj* far, long
llúpol • *n* hop
lo • *art* the
lòbul • *n* lobe
local • *adj* local • *n* venue
localitzar • *v* localize
localment • *adv* locally
locomotora • *n* locomotive
logaritme • *n* logarithm
lògic • *adj* logical
lògicament • *adv* logically

logístic • *adj* logistic
logorrea • *n* logorrhea
lona • *n* canvas
longitud • *n* length, longitude
losange • *n* lozenge
lubricació • *n* lubrication
lubricar • *v* lubricate
lubricitat • *n* lechery
lubrificació • *n* lubrication
lúcid • *adj* lucid

lucidesa • *n* lucidity
lumbago • *n* lumbago
lúnula • *n* lunula
luteci • *n* lutetium
luvar • *n* louvar
luxós • *adj* luxurious
luxúria • *n* lust
luxuriós • *adj* luxurious

M

mà • *n* hand, quire
mac • *adj* hand-held
maça • *n* mace, pestle
macadàmia • *n* macadamia
maco • *adj* cute, kind
maçoneria • *n* masonry
màcula • *n* macula
madrastra • *n* stepmother
maduixa • *n* strawberry
maduixer • *n* strawberry
maduixera • *n* strawberry
madur • *adj* mature, ripe
madura • *adj* mature
madurar • *v* mature
maduresa • *n* maturity
mag • *n* mage, magician, magus, sorcerer, wizard
màgia • *n* magic
màgic • *n* mage, magician, sorcerer, wizard • *adj* magic, magical
màgicament • *adv* magically
magnànim • *adj* magnanimous
magnànimament • *adv* magnanimously
magnat • *n* mogul
magnesi • *n* magnesium
magnèsia • *n* chalk
magnètic • *adj* magnetic
magnetisme • *n* magnetism
magnetitzar • *v* magnetize
magnetòmetre • *n* magnetometer
magnetosfera • *n* magnetosphere
magnífic • *adj* gorgeous, magnificent
magníficament • *adv* magnificently
magnòlia • *n* magnolia
magrana • *n* pomegranate
magraner • *n* pomegranate
magre • *adj* lean, skinny
mai • *adv* never
maionesa • *n* mayonnaise
maixella • *n* jaw
majestat • *n* majesty
majestuós • *adj* imperial, majestic

majestuosament • *adv* majestically
major • *n* major • *adj* major
majordom • *n* butler
majoria • *n* majority
majúscula • *adj* capital
mal • *adj* bad • *adv* badly • *n* evil
malabarisme • *n* juggling
malabarista • *n* juggler
malacologia • *n* malacology
malaïdament • *adv* damn
malalt • *adj* ill
malaltia • *n* disease, illness
malaltís • *adj* sickly
malaltós • *adj* sickly
malaltús • *adj* sickly
malament • *adv* badly
malauradament • *adv* unfortunately
malaurat • *adj* unlucky
maldestre • *adj* awkward, infelicitous, maladroit
maledicció • *n* curse
malèfic • *adj* evil
maleir • *v* damn
maleït • *adj* damn
malentendre • *v* misunderstand
maleta • *n* case
maleter • *n* trunk
malèvol • *adj* malevolent
malfactor • *n* wrongdoer
malgirbat • *adj* scruffy
malgrat • *prep* despite • *conj* while
malhumorós • *adj* prickly
malícia • *n* malice
maliciós • *adj* evil, malicious, spiteful
maliciosament • *adv* maliciously
maligne • *adj* malignant
malla • *n* mesh, net
malson • *n* nightmare
malt • *n* malt
maluc • *n* hip
malva • *n* mallow
malvat • *adj* evil

malversar • *v* embezzle
malvolença • *n* venom
mama • *n* mamma, mum
mamella • *n* mamma, udder
mamífer • *n* mammal
mamografia • *n* mammography
mamut • *n* mammoth
manaire • *adj* bossy
manament • *n* commandment
manar • *v* command, rule
manat • *n* command
manatí • *n* manatee
manc • *adj* one-armed
manca • *n* lack
mancança • *n* shortcoming
mancar • *v* lack
mandat • *n* mandate
mandíbula • *n* jaw, mandible
mandolina • *n* mandolin
mandonguilla • *n* dumpling, meatball
mandra • *n* sloth
mandràgora • *n* mandrake
mandrós • *adj* lazy
mandrosament • *adv* lazily
mànec • *n* handle
mànega • *n* hose, sleeve
maneig • *n* management
manejar • *v* steer
manera • *n* way
maneta • *n* crank, hand, handle
manganès • *n* manganese
mangle • *n* mangrove
mango • *n* mango
maniñ • *interj* hello
mania • *n* bug, mania
maníac • *adj* maniacal
manifest • *n* manifest, manifesto • *adj* manifest
manifestació • *n* march
manifestar • *v* manifest
màniga • *n* sleeve
manilles • *n* handcuffs
manipulació • *n* handling
manipulador • *adj* manipulative
manipular • *v* manipulate
manllevador • *n* borrower
manllevar • *v* borrow
mannitol • *n* mannitol
manòmetre • *n* manometer
mans • *adj* tame
mansuetud • *n* mansuetude
manta • *n* bedspread, blanket
mantega • *n* butter
mantegós • *adj* buttery
manteguera • *n* churn
manteniment • *n* maintenance
mantenir • *v* maintain

mantissa • *n* mantissa
manumetre • *v* manumit
manuscrit • *n* manuscript • *adj* manuscript
manxa • *n* bellows
manyà • *n* locksmith
maó • *n* brick
maqueta • *n* model
maquillatge • *n* makeup
màquina • *n* machine
maquinari • *n* hardware
maquíssim • *adj* gorgeous
mar • *n* sea
maragda • *n* emerald
marató • *n* marathon
marbre • *n* marble
marc • *n* frame, mark
marca • *n* march, mark
marcadament • *adv* markedly
marcar • *v* highlight, plot, score
marcgravi • *n* margrave
marcir • *v* wither
marcolfa • *n* tart
marduix • *n* marjoram
mare • *n* mother
marea • *n* tide
mareal • *adj* tidal
marejador • *adj* giddy
marejat • *adj* dizzy, giddy
marfanta • *n* tart
marfil • *n* ivory
marga • *n* loam
marge • *n* margin
marginal • *adj* fringe
marí • *adj* marine • *n* sailor
marica • *n* fag • *adj* queer
maricó • *n* fag, fruit
marieta • *n* fag, fruit, queen • *adj* family, queer
marihuana • *n* marijuana
marina • *n* navy, seascape
mariner • *n* seaman
marineria • *n* crew
marit • *n* husband
marital • *adj* marital
marjal • *n* plot, wetland
marmota • *n* marmot
marquès • *n* margrave, marquess
marquesa • *n* marchioness
marqueteria • *n* marquetry
marrà • *n* hog, ram
marrada • *n* detour
marraix • *n* porbeagle
marraixa • *n* carafe
marró • *n* brown, chestnut, coffee, cow • *adj* brown, chestnut, coffee
marsopa • *n* porpoise

marsupial • *n* marsupial • *adj* marsupial
marta • *n* marten
martell • *n* hammer, malleus
martellejar • *v* hammer
martinet • *n* egret
màrtir • *n* martyr
marxa • *n* march
marxar • *v* march
màscara • *n* mask
mascarada • *n* mask, masquerade
mascarell • *n* gannet
mascla • *adj* male
mascle • *n* male, tom • *adj* male
masclisme • *n* machismo
mascota • *n* pet
masculí • *adj* male, masculine, virile
masculina • *adj* male
masmorra • *n* dungeon
masoquisme • *n* masochism
masoquista • *n* masochist • *adj* masochistic
massa • *n* crust, dough, mass • *adv* too
massacrar • *v* massacre
massacre • *n* massacre
massapà • *n* marzipan
massatge • *n* massage
massatgista • *n* masseur
massiu • *adj* bulk, massive
mastectomia • *n* mastectomy
mastegar • *v* chew
masticar • *v* chew
mastodòntic • *adj* mammoth
mastografia • *n* mammography
masturbació • *n* masturbation
matacà • *n* machicolation
matafaluga • *n* anise
matalàs • *n* mattress
mateix • *pron* herself, himself, itself, myself, ourselves, same, themselves, yourself • *adj* one, own, same
matemàtic • *adj* mathematical
matemàtica • *n* mathematics
matemàtiques • *n* mathematics
matèria • *n* subject
material • *adj* material
materialisme • *n* materialism
materialista • *n* materialist • *adj* materialistic
materialització • *n* materialization
matí • *n* morning
matinada • *n* morning
matís • *n* nuance
matràs • *n* flask
matriarcal • *adj* matriarchal
matrícula • *n* plate
matrimoni • *n* marriage
matriu • *n* matrix, womb

matx • *n* match
mausoleu • *n* mausoleum
màxim • *adj* maximum
me • *pron* me
mecànic • *adj* mechanical
mecànica • *n* mechanics
mecanisme • *n* device, mechanism
medalla • *n* award, badge
medalló • *n* locket, medallion
medi • *n* environment, medium
mediambiental • *adj* environmental
mediastí • *n* mediastinum
mèdic • *adj* medical
medicinal • *adj* medicinal
medieval • *adj* medieval
mediocre • *adj* indifferent, mediocre
mediocritat • *n* mediocrity
meditació • *n* meditation
mèdium • *n* medium
medulŭla • *n* marrow
medusa • *n* jellyfish
megàlit • *n* megalith
megalòman • *adj* megalomaniacal
megalòpoli • *n* megalopolis
megalòpolis • *n* megalopolis
meiosi • *n* meiosis
meiòtic • *adj* meiotic
meitat • *n* half
mel • *n* honey
melancòlic • *adj* melancholic
melca • *n* sorghum
melé • *n* scrum
melic • *n* navel
melisse • *n* melissa
melmelada • *n* jelly, marmalade
meló • *n* melon
melodia • *n* riff, tune
melòdic • *adj* melodic
melodiós • *adj* melodious
melodramàtic • *adj* melodramatic
melós • *adj* mellow
melsa • *n* spleen
mem • *n* meme
membrana • *n* membrane, web
membranós • *adj* membranous
membre • *n* limb, member
memorable • *adj* memorable
memorablement • *adv* memorably
memòria • *n* memory, remembrance
memorització • *n* memorization
memoritzar • *v* memorize
mena • *n* ore, sort
mendelevi • *n* mendelevium
mendicant • *n* beggar
mendicar • *v* beg
menester • *n* requirement
menhir • *n* menhir

meninge • *n* meninx
menisc • *n* meniscus
menjador • *n* eater
menjar • *v* eat • *n* food
mensualment • *adv* monthly
ment • *n* head, mind, wit
menta • *n* mint • *adj* mint
mental • *adj* mental
mentalment • *adv* mentally
mentida • *n* lie
mentir • *v* cheat, lie
mentó • *n* chin
mentre • *conj* while
mentrestant • *adv* meanwhile, then
menú • *n* menu
menut • *adj* minute
menys • *conj* but, minus • *adj* less • *adv* less • *prep* less
menyspreable • *adj* despicable, disgusting, nasty
menysprear • *v* despise
menyspreuar • *v* contemn
mer • *adj* mere
merament • *adv* merely
meravella • *n* wonder
meravellós • *adj* marvelous, wonderful
meravellosament • *adv* wonderfully
mercader • *n* merchant
mercantil • *adj* mercantile
mercat • *n* market
mercenari • *n* mercenary
mercès • *interj* thanks
merci • *interj* thanks
mercuri • *n* mercury
merda • *n* shit • *interj* shit
merda! • *interj* fuck
mereixedor • *adj* deserving
merèixer • *v* deserve
meritar • *v* deserve
merla • *n* blackbird
merlà • *n* whiting
mes • *n* month
més • *adj* else, plus • *adv* more • *conj* plus
mesa • *n* board
mescla • *n* blend
mesclar • *v* mix, shuffle
mesenteri • *n* mesentery
mesó • *n* meson
mesosfera • *n* mesosphere
mesquita • *n* mosque
messies • *n* messiah
mestre • *n* master
mestressa • *n* mistress, schoolmistress
mesura • *n* measure
mesurar • *v* clock, measure
metà • *n* methane
meta • *n* finish, goal

metabòlic • *adj* metabolic
metabolisme • *n* metabolism
metacarp • *n* metacarpus
metacarpià • *n* metacarpal • *adj* metacarpal
metafísica • *n* metaphysics
metàfora • *n* metaphor
metafòric • *adj* metaphorical
metafòricament • *adv* metaphorically
metàlůlic • *adj* metallic
metalůlografia • *n* metallography
metalůloide • *n* metalloid
metalůlúrgia • *n* metallurgy
metalůlúrgic • *adj* metallurgical
metall • *n* brass, metal
metatars • *n* metatarsus
metatarsià • *n* metatarsal • *adj* metatarsal
meteor • *n* meteor
meteòric • *adj* meteoric
meteorit • *n* meteorite
meteorologia • *n* meteorology
metge • *n* doctor, physician
metgessa • *n* doctor, physician
meticulós • *adj* meticulous
meticulosament • *adv* meticulously
metil • *n* methyl
metionina • *n* methionine
mètode • *n* method
metre • *v* put
metro • *n* metro, subway
metrologia • *n* metrology
metròpoli • *n* archbishopric, metropolis
metròpolis • *n* archbishopric, metropolis
metropolità • *adj* metropolitan
metxa • *n* light
metzina • *n* poison
mèu • *interj* meow
mi • *pron* me • *n* mi, mu
mica • *n* bit, crumb • *adj* quiet
mico • *n* monkey
micòleg • *n* mycologist
micologia • *n* mycology
microbi • *n* microbe
microbiologia • *n* microbiology
micròcit • *n* microcyte
microcosmos • *n* microcosm
microfilm • *n* microfilm
microfilmar • *v* microfilm
micròfon • *n* microphone
microgram • *n* microgram
micròmetre • *n* micrometer
microona • *n* microwave
microorganisme • *n* microorganism
microprocessador • *n* microprocessor
microscopi • *n* microscope
microscòpia • *n* microscopy
microscòpic • *adj* microscopic

midó • n starch
mig • adj half, mean
migdia • n noon, south
migdiada • n siesta
migjorn • n south
migratori • adj migratory
milůlenni • n millennium
milůlèsim • adj thousandth
milůligram • n milligram
milà • n kite
milè • adj thousandth
milfulles • n yarrow
militar • adj military
militarment • adv militarily
mill • n millet
millor • adj best, better
millora • n improvement
millorar • v better, improve
milpeu • n millipede
mina • n mine
minar • v mine
mineral • n mineral • adj mineral
mineralogia • n mineralogy
mineralogista • n mineralogist
mini • n minium
miniaplicació • n applet
mínim • adj minimal
minimalista • adj minimal
ministeri • n ministry
ministre • n minister
minoria • n minority
minoritat • n minority
minotaure • n minotaur
minuciós • adj meticulous, thorough
minúscul • adj minuscule, minute, tiny
minusvàlid • adj disabled
minut • n minute
minyó • n boy
minyona • n menial
miocardi • n myocardium
miocardiopatia • n cardiomyopathy
miolar • v meow
miop • n myope • adj myopic
miopia • n myopia
miosi • n meiosis
mira • n scope
mira-sol • n sunflower
miracle • n miracle
miraculós • adj miraculous
miraculosament • adv miraculously
mirada • n look
mirall • n mirror
mirar • v behold, look, watch
miratge • n mirage
miríada • n myriad
mirlitó • n kazoo
mirra • n myrrh

mirtil • n blueberry
misantrop • n misanthrope
misantropia • n misanthropy
misantròpic • adj misanthropic
miscelůlani • adj miscellaneous
miserable • adj miserable, pitiful
misèria • n misery
misericòrdia • n mercy
misogàmia • n misogamy
misogin • n misogynist
misogínia • n misogyny
misologia • n misology
misopèdia • n misopedia
missa • n mass
missatge • n message
missatger • n messenger
missatgera • n messenger
míssil • n missile
missió • n mission
missioner • n missionary
missiva • n missive
misteri • n mystery
misteriós • adj eerie, mysterious
misteriosament • adv mysteriously
místic • adj mystic, mystical
misto • n match
mite • n myth
mites • n myth
mític • adj mythical
mitigar • v alleviate, mitigate, palliate
mitjà • n medium, way • adj medium, middle
mitjan • adj mid
mitjana • n average, mean, median
mitjançant • prep through
mitjanit • n midnight
mitjó • n sock
mitocondri • n mitochondrion
mitologia • n mythology
mitosi • n mitosis
mix • n cat
mixa • n cat
mnemònic • adj mnemonic
mòbil • adj mobile
mobiliari • adj movable
mobilitat • n mobility
mobilització • n mobilization
moblat • adj furnished
moc • n mucus, snood
mocador • n handkerchief
moda • n mode
model • n model, pattern
mòdem • n modem
moderadament • adv moderately
moderar • v moderate
moderat • adj moderate
modern • adj modern

modernització • *n* modernization
modernitzar • *v* modernize
modest • *adj* modest
modestament • *adv* modestly
modificació • *n* edit
modificar • *v* change, modify
modular • *v* modulate
mofar • *v* circumvent
mofeta • *n* skunk
moix • *n* cat • *adj* down
moixa • *n* cat
moixet • *n* kitten
moixeta • *n* kitten
mol • *n* maul, mole
mola • *n* millstone, sunfish
molar • *adj* molar
moldre • *v* grind, mill
molècula • *n* molecule
molecular • *adj* molecular
molest • *adj* upset
molestar • *v* annoy, bother, disturb, harass
molí • *n* mill
molibdèn • *n* molybdenum
moliner • *n* miller
moll • *n* marrow • *adj* wet
molla • *n* crumb, spring
molsa • *n* moss
molt • *adv* much, very
moment • *n* moment, second
momeria • *n* mummery
mòmia • *n* mummy
món • *n* world
monacal • *adj* monastic
monaquisme • *n* monasticism
monarca • *n* monarch
monarquia • *n* monarchy
monàrquic • *n* monarchist
monàstic • *adj* monastic
moneda • *n* coin, currency
moneder • *n* purse
monestir • *n* monastery
monetari • *adj* monetary, pecuniary
mongeta • *n* bean
monitor • *n* display, monitor
monja • *n* nun
monjo • *n* monk
monocrom • *adj* monochrome
monocromàtic • *adj* monochromatic
monoeci • *adj* monoecious
monògam • *adj* monogamous
monogàmia • *n* monogamy
monòleg • *n* monologue
monolingüe • *adj* monolingual
monòlit • *n* monolith
monòmer • *n* monomer
monopatí • *n* skateboard

monopoli • *n* monopoly
monopolitzar • *v* monopolize
monosacàrid • *n* monosaccharide
monosíl·lab • *n* monosyllabic • *adj* monosyllabic
monosil·làbic • *adj* monosyllabic
monoteisme • *n* monotheism
monoteista • *n* monotheist • *adj* monotheistic
monòton • *adj* monotone, monotonous
monotonia • *n* monotony
monotrema • *n* monotreme
monòxid • *n* monoxide
monstre • *n* monster
monstruós • *adj* monster, monstrous
monstruosament • *adv* monstrously
monument • *n* bomb, monument
monumental • *adj* monumental
monya • *n* bun
mooli • *n* daikon
moqueta • *n* carpet
móra • *n* blackberry, mulberry
moralment • *adv* morally
morat • *n* murrey
mòrbid • *adj* morbid
mòrbida • *adj* morbid
mordaç • *adj* acrimonious, cutting
mordent • *n* mordant
mordentar • *v* mordant
morella • *n* nightshade
morera • *n* mulberry
morfema • *n* morpheme
morfina • *n* morphine
morfologia • *n* morphology
morfològicament • *adv* morphologically
morir • *v* die
morrió • *n* morion, muzzle
morro • *n* snout
morrut • *n* weevil
morsa • *n* walrus
mort • *adj* dead, deceased • *n* death, deceased, kill
mortal • *adj* deadly, mortal • *n* mortal
mortalitat • *n* mortality
morter • *n* mortar
mortífer • *adj* deadly
mos • *n* bit, mouthful
mosaic • *n* mosaic
mosca • *n* fly
moscovita • *n* muscovite
mosquet • *n* musket
mosqueter • *n* musketeer
mosquit • *n* gnat, mosquito
mossa • *n* wench
mossegada • *n* bite, mouthful
mossegar • *v* bite
mostassa • *n* mustard

mostatxo • *n* moustache
mostra • *n* pattern, sample
mostrar • *v* show
mostratge • *n* sampling
mot • *n* word
mota • *n* mound
motel • *n* motel
motiu • *n* motif, motive
motivació • *n* motivation
motle • *n* mold
motlle • *n* cast, mold
motmot • *n* motmot
moto • *n* bike, motorcycle
motocicleta • *n* motorcycle
motor • *n* engine, motor • *adj* motor
motorista • *n* motorist
motxilla • *n* backpack
moure • *v* move
moviment • *n* movement
muda • *n* mute
mudament • *n* move
mudança • *n* move
mudar • *v* move
mufló • *n* mouflon
mugir • *v* moo
mugit • *n* moo
mugró • *n* nipple
mújol • *n* mullet
mul • *n* mule
mullar • *v* wet
mullar-se • *v* wet
muller • *n* wife
multilingüe • *adj* multilingual
multimèdia • *n* multimedia • *adj* multimedia
multinacional • *n* multinational • *adj* multinational

múltiple • *n* multiple • *adj* multiple
multitud • *n* crowd
mundà • *adj* worldly
mundial • *adj* global, worldwide
mundialment • *adv* worldwide
municipal • *adj* municipal
municipi • *n* municipality
muntanya • *n* mountain
muntanyós • *adj* hilly, mountainous
muntar • *v* ride
muó • *n* muon
mur • *n* wall
muralla • *n* wall
murar • *v* wall
muricec • *n* bat
murri • *adj* cunning
murta • *n* myrtle
musaranya • *n* shrew
muscle • *n* shoulder
múscul • *n* muscle
muscular • *adj* muscular
musculós • *adj* muscular
musell • *n* snout
museu • *n* museum
músic • *n* musician
música • *n* music
musical • *adj* musical
musicalitat • *n* musicality
mussol • *n* owl
musteir • *v* wither
mustiar • *v* wilt, wither
mut • *n* mute • *adj* mute
mutació • *n* mutation
mutant • *n* mutant • *adj* mutant
mutilació • *n* mayhem, mutilation
mutu • *adj* mutual, reciprocal

N

nabinera • *n* bilberry, blueberry
nabiu • *n* bilberry, blueberry, cranberry
nació • *n* nation
nacional • *adj* national
nacionalisme • *n* nationalism
nacionalista • *adj* nationalist
nacionalment • *adv* nationally
nadó • *n* baby
naftalina • *n* naphthalene
nàiada • *n* naiad
naïf • *adj* naive
naixença • *n* birth
naixent • *adj* rising
nan • *n* dwarf, gnome
nana • *n* dwarf

nanisme • *n* dwarfism
nano • *n* dwarf
nanosegon • *n* nanosecond
nansa • *n* handle
nàpia • *n* snout
narcís • *n* narcissist, narcissus
narcisista • *n* narcissist
narcolèpsia • *n* narcolepsy
narcòtic • *n* soporific • *adj* soporific
nariu • *n* nostril
narració • *n* narrative
narrar • *v* narrate
narratiu • *adj* narrative
narrativa • *n* narrative
nàrtex • *n* narthex

narval • *n* narwhal
nas • *n* nose, snout
nasal • *adj* nasal
nasalització • *n* nasalization
nat • *adj* born
nata • *n* cream
natació • *n* swimming
natalici • *n* birthday
natja • *n* butt, buttock, tail
natura • *n* nature
natural • *adj* plain
naturalment • *adv* naturally
nau • *n* aisle, nave, ship
nàufrag • *adj* shipwrecked
naufragar • *v* shipwreck
naufragi • *n* shipwreck
nàusea • *n* nausea
nauseabund • *adj* nauseating
nàutic • *adj* nautical
naval • *adj* naval
navalla • *n* razor
navegar • *v* sail
neandertal • *n* neanderthal
neboda • *n* niece
nebot • *n* nephew
nebulós • *adj* cloudy, nebulous
nebulosa • *n* nebula
necessari • *adj* necessary
necessàriament • *adv* necessarily
necessitar • *v* need
necessitat • *n* necessity, need
necròpolis • *n* necropolis
necrosi • *n* necrosis
nèctar • *n* nectar
nectarina • *n* nectarine
nedador • *n* swimmer
nedadora • *n* swimmer
nedar • *v* swim
negar • *v* deny
negatiu • *adj* negative
negativa • *n* no
negligència • *n* neglect, negligence
negligent • *adj* careless, neglectful, negligent
negligentment • *adv* negligently
negligible • *adj* negligible
negligir • *v* neglect
negoci • *n* business
negociable • *adj* negotiable
negociació • *n* negotiation
negociar • *v* negotiate
negra • *n* black
negre • *n* black • *adj* black
negrenc • *adj* blackish
negreta • *adj* bold
negror • *n* blackness, darkness
negrós • *adj* blackish

néixer • *v* dawn
nen • *n* child
nena • *n* girl
neó • *n* neon
neoclassicisme • *n* neoclassicism
neodimi • *n* neodymium
neologisme • *n* neologism
nepotisme • *n* nepotism
neptuni • *n* neptunium
nereida • *n* nereid
nervi • *n* nerve
nerviós • *adj* nervous
nerviosament • *adv* nervously
nét • *n* grandson
net • *adj* clean, neat, net, plain
néta • *n* granddaughter
netament • *adv* cleanly
netbol • *n* netball
netedat • *n* cleanliness
neteja • *n* cleanup
netejar • *v* clean
neu • *n* snow
neula • *n* wafer
neumàtic • *n* tyre
neural • *adj* neural
neuràlgic • *adj* neuralgic
neurastènia • *n* neurasthenia
neurobiologia • *n* neurobiology
neuroblast • *n* neuroblast
neurocirurgia • *n* neurosurgery
neurocirurgià • *n* neurosurgeon
neurofisiologia • *n* neurophysiology
neuròleg • *n* neurologist
neurologia • *n* neurology
neurològic • *adj* neurological
neuromotor • *adj* neuromotor
neuromuscular • *adj* neuromuscular
neuropsiquiatria • *n* neuropsychiatry
neurosi • *n* neurosis
neuròtic • *n* neurotic • *adj* neurotic
neurotransmissor • *n* neurotransmitter
neurotropisme • *n* neurotropism
neutral • *adj* neutral
neutralitat • *n* neutrality
neutre • *adj* neutral
neutrí • *n* neutrino
neutró • *n* neutron
nevar • *v* snow
nexe • *n* nexus
ni • *n* nu
nigromància • *n* necromancy
nihilisme • *n* nihilism
nimbe • *n* nimbus
nina • *n* doll
ningú • *n* nobody
nínxol • *n* niche
niobi • *n* niobium

níquel • *n* nickel
nit • *n* night
nitrogen • *n* nitrogen
niu • *n* nest
no • *n* no • *adv* not
nobeli • *n* nobelium
noble • *adj* noble
noblesa • *n* nobility
noció • *n* notion
nociu • *adj* harmful
nocturn • *adj* nocturnal
nòdul • *n* nodule
nogensmenys • *adv* however, nevertheless
noguera • *n* walnut
noi • *n* boy
noia • *n* bird, girl
nom • *n* name
nòmada • *n* nomad • *adj* nomadic
nomadisme • *n* nomadism
nombre • *n* number
nombrós • *adj* numerous
nomenament • *n* appointment
només • *adv* alone, just, only
nominar • *v* nominate
nominatiu • *adj* nominative
nonat • *adj* unborn
nònius • *n* nonius
nora • *n* daughter-in-law
noradrenalina • *n* noradrenaline
nord • *n* north
nord-est • *n* northeast
nord-oest • *n* northwest
norma • *n* rule
normal • *n* normal • *adj* normal
normalment • *adv* normally, usually
normatiu • *adj* normative
nosaltres • *pron* we
nostàlgia • *n* nostalgia
notable • *adj* notable
notablement • *adv* importantly, notably
notar • *v* notice
notícia • *n* message

notícies • *n* news
notificació • *n* notification
notificar • *v* report
notori • *adj* notorious
notòriament • *adv* notoriously
notorietat • *n* notoriety
nou • *adj* new • *n* nine, nut
nouvinguda • *n* newcomer
nouvingut • *n* newcomer
novament • *adv* anew, newly
novè • *n* ninth • *adj* ninth
novel·la • *n* novel
novel·lista • *n* novelist
novell • *n* newcomer
novena • *n* ninth
nòvia • *n* girlfriend
nu • *adj* naked, nude
núbil • *adj* nubile
nuca • *n* nape
nuclear • *adj* nuclear
nucleó • *n* nucleon
nucli • *n* nucleus
nuesa • *n* nudity
numerador • *n* numerator
numerar • *v* number
numèric • *adj* numerical
número • *n* number, numeral
numismàtica • *n* numismatics
nuós • *adj* knotty
nupcial • *adj* bridal
nus • *n* knot
nutrici • *adj* nutritious
nutricional • *adj* nutritional
nutrient • *adj* nutritious
nutritiu • *adj* nutritional, nutritious
nuvi • *n* bridegroom
núvia • *n* bride
núvol • *n* cloud
nuvolós • *adj* cloudy
nyam • *n* yam • *adj* yum
nyoqui • *n* dumpling
nyu • *n* gnu

O

o • *n* o • *conj* or
oasi • *n* oasis
obediència • *n* obedience
obedient • *adj* obedient
obelisc • *n* obelisk
obertament • *adv* openly
obertura • *n* initial, opening
obès • *adj* obese
obesitat • *n* obesity

objecte • *n* object
objectiu • *n* goal • *adj* objective
oblic • *adj* oblique
oblidable • *adj* forgettable
oblidadís • *adj* forgetful, oblivious
oblidar • *v* forget
oblidar-se • *v* forget
oblidós • *adj* forgetful, oblivious
obligació • *n* duty

obligar • v oblige
obligatori • adj compulsory, obligatory
obliqüitat • n obliquity
oblit • n oversight
obliteració • n obliteration
oblong • adj oblong
oboè • n oboe
oboista • n oboist
obra • n play
obrer • n worker
obscè • adj filthy, obscene, rude
obscenament • adv obscenely
obscenitat • n obscenity
obscur • adj dark
obscurantisme • n obscurantism
obscuritat • n dark, night
obsequiós • adj obsequious
observació • n observation
observar • v observe
observatori • n observatory
obsessió • n obsession
obsidiana • n obsidian
obsolescència • n obsolescence
obsolet • adj obsolete
obstacle • n fetter, hurdle, obstacle
obstètric • adj obstetric
obstinadament • adv obstinately
obstinat • adj obstinate
obstructiu • adj obstructive
obtenir • v achieve, guess
obtindre • v get
obtús • adj obtuse
obús • n gun, howitzer
obvi • adj obvious
òbviament • adv obviously
obvietat • n obviousness, truism
oca • n goose
ocapi • n okapi
ocarina • n ocarina
ocasional • adj casual, occasional
ocasionalment • adv occasionally
occidental • adj western
occípit • n occiput
occipital • n occipital • adj occipital
oceà • n ocean
oceànic • adj oceanic
oceanògraf • n oceanographer
oceanografia • n oceanography
oceanologia • n oceanography
ocell • n bird
ocelot • n ocelot
oci • n leisure
oclusiva • n plosive
ocórrer • v happen
octàedre • n octahedron
octaedre • n octahedron
octàgon • n octagon

octau • n octavo
octava • n octave
octet • n octet
octogenari • n octogenarian • adj octogenarian
ocular • adj ocular
ocult • n occult • adj occult
ocultar • v abscond, occult
ocultisme • n occult
ocupació • n occupation
ocupar • v encroach
ocupat • adj busy
oda • n poem
odalisca • n odalisque
odi • n hatred
odiar • v hate
odiós • adj hateful, odious
odorar • v smell
oest • n west
ofagar • v suffocate
ofegar • v drown, suffocate
ofegar-se • v suffocate
ofensiu • adj offensive
ofensiva • adj offensive
oferiment • n offering
oferir • v offer, sacrifice
oferta • n offer
ofici • n profession
oficial • adj official
oficialment • adv officially
oficina • n office
oftàlmic • adj ophthalmic
oftalmòleg • n ophthalmologist
oftalmòloga • n ophthalmologist
oftalmologia • n ophthalmology
ogre • n ogre
oïble • adj audible
oïda • n hearing
oir • v hear
okapi • n okapi
olfacte • n olfaction, scent, smell
olfactiu • adj olfactory
olfactori • adj olfactory
oli • n oil
òliba • n owl
oligarca • n oligarch
oligarquia • n oligarchy
oligàrquic • adj oligarchic
olisbe • n dildo
oliva • n olive
olla • n casserole, pot
olm • n elm
olor • n smell
olorar • v smell
om • n elm
ombra • n shade, shadow
ombrelůla • n parasol, umbrella

omega • *n* omega
ometre • *v* omit
òmicron • *n* omicron
ominós • *adj* ominous
omissió • *n* omission
omnidireccional • *adj* omnidirectional
omnipotència • *n* omnipotence
omnipotent • *adj* almighty, omnipotent
omnipresència • *n* omnipresence
omnipresent • *adj* omnipresent
omnisciència • *n* omniscience
omniscient • *adj* omniscient
omnívor • *n* omnivore • *adj* omnivorous
on • *adv* where • *conj* where
ona • *n* ripple
onagre • *n* onager
oncle • *n* uncle
oncòleg • *n* oncologist
oncologia • *n* oncology
ondina • *n* undine
ondulat • *adj* corrugated
oneirologia • *n* oneirology
onejar • *v* flutter, ripple
onerós • *adj* onerous
ònix • *n* onyx
onomatopeia • *n* onomatopoeia
onomatopeic • *adj* onomatopoeic
onsevol • *conj* wherever
onsevulga • *adv* anywhere • *conj* wherever
onsevulla • *adv* wherever • *conj* wherever
ontologia • *n* ontology
ontològic • *adj* ontological
onzè • *n* eleventh • *adj* eleventh
onzena • *n* eleventh
oòcit • *n* oocyte
oosfera • *n* oosphere
opac • *adj* opaque
òpal • *n* opal
opció • *n* option, switch
opcional • *adj* optional
operació • *n* operation, surgery
operatiu • *adj* operational
opercle • *n* operculum
opi • *n* opium
opinió • *n* opinion
oponent • *n* opponent
oportú • *adj* opportune, timely
oportunitat • *n* chance, opportunity
oposar • *v* oppose
oposat • *adj* opposite
oposició • *n* opposition
opressió • *n* oppression
òptic • *adj* optic
optimisme • *n* optimism
optimista • *n* optimist • *adj* optimistic
opulència • *n* opulence

opulent • *adj* opulent
opuscle • *n* brochure
or • *n* gold
oració • *n* prayer
oral • *adj* oral
oralment • *adv* orally
orangutan • *n* orangutan
oratori • *n* oratory
oratòria • *n* oratory
orb • *adj* blind
òrbita • *n* circle, orbit
orbital • *adj* orbital
orbitar • *v* orbit
orc • *n* orc
orde • *n* order
ordenada • *n* ordinate
ordenar • *v* clean, command, order, sort
ordi • *n* barley
ordinador • *n* computer
ordinari • *adj* ordinary
ordre • *n* command, order
orella • *n* ear
oreneta • *n* swallow
orenga • *n* oregano
orfe • *n* orphan
òrfena • *n* orphan
òrgan • *n* organ
orgànic • *adj* organic
organisme • *n* organism
organització • *n* organization
organitzar • *v* arrange, organize
organitzat • *adj* organized
orgànul • *n* organelle
orgasme • *n* climax, orgasm
orgue • *n* organ
orgull • *n* pride
orgullós • *adj* haughty, proud
orgullosament • *adv* proudly
oriental • *adj* eastern
orientalista • *n* orientalist
original • *n* manuscript
originalitat • *n* originality
originàriament • *adv* originally
orina • *n* urine
orinar • *v* pee
òrix • *n* oryx
orla • *n* border, fringe
ornamental • *n* ornamental • *adj* ornamental
ornitòleg • *n* ornithologist
ornitologia • *n* ornithology
ornitològic • *adj* ornithological
ornitorinc • *n* platypus
orologia • *n* horology
orquestra • *n* orchestra
orquestral • *adj* orchestral
orsa • *n* luff

ortiga • *n* nettle
ortodòncia • *n* orthodontics
ortodontologia • *n* orthodontics
ortodox • *adj* orthodox
ortodòxia • *n* orthodoxy
ortogonal • *adj* orthogonal
ortogràfic • *adj* orthographic
ortopèdic • *adj* orthopedic • *n* orthopedist
ortopedista • *n* orthopedist
os • *n* bone
ós • *n* bear
osca • *n* notch
oscar • *v* notch
oscil·lació • *n* oscillation
oscil·lar • *v* oscillate
oscil·loscopi • *n* oscilloscope
osmi • *n* osmium
osmosi • *n* osmosis
osmòtic • *adj* osmotic
ossanna • *interj* hosanna
ossi • *adj* bony, osseous

ossicle • *n* ossicle
ossificar • *v* ossify
ostatge • *n* hostage
ostentós • *adj* ostentatious, pretentious
ostracisme • *n* ostracism
ostres • *interj* gosh
otàlgia • *n* otalgia
òtic • *adj* otic
otitis • *n* otitis
ou • *n* egg, eggshell, nut
ous • *n* balls, plum
oval • *n* oval • *adj* oval
ovari • *n* ovary
ovella • *n* ewe
ovoide • *adj* egg-shaped, ovoid
òvul • *n* ovum
ovular • *adj* oval
òxid • *n* oxide, rust
oxidar • *v* rust
oxigen • *n* oxygen
oxímoron • *n* oxymoron

P

pa • *n* bread
paciència • *n* patience
pacient • *n* patient • *adj* patient
pacientment • *adv* patiently
pacífic • *adj* peaceful
pacíficament • *adv* peacefully
pacifista • *adj* peaceable
pacte • *n* agreement, pact
padellàs • *n* potsherd
padrastre • *n* stepfather
padrí • *n* godfather
paella • *n* paella
pagà • *adj* ethnic, pagan • *n* pagan
paga • *n* wage
pagament • *n* payment
paganisme • *n* paganism
pagar • *v* pay
pagell • *n* pandora
pàgina • *n* page
pagoda • *n* pagoda
paio • *n* dude, guy
país • *n* country
paisatge • *n* landscape
pal • *n* mast, pale, stake
pal·ladi • *n* palladium
pal·liar • *v* alleviate, palliate
pal·liatiu • *adj* palliative
pàl·lid • *adj* pale, pallid
pala • *n* paddle, shovel
paladí • *n* paladin

palau • *n* palace
paleoantropologia • *n* paleoanthropology
paleobotànica • *n* paleobotany
paleontòleg • *n* paleontologist
paleontologia • *n* paleontology
paleontològic • *adj* paleontological
paleozoologia • *n* paleozoology
palestra • *n* palaestra
palet • *n* pallet
paleta • *n* bricklayer, trowel
palíndrom • *n* palindrome
palissada • *n* palisade
palla • *n* masturbation, straw
pallasso • *n* clown
paller • *n* haystack
pallús • *n* chaff
palmell • *n* palm
palmito • *n* fan
paloma • *n* butterfly
palometa • *n* butterfly
palpable • *adj* palpable
palput • *n* hoopoe
paltó • *n* paletot
pam • *n* span
panacea • *n* panacea
pancarta • *n* banner
pancreàtic • *adj* pancreatic
pàncrees • *n* pancreas
pandereta • *n* tambourine

panellet • *n* bun
panerola • *n* cockroach
pànic • *n* panic
panoli • *n* nincompoop
panoràmic • *adj* panoramic
panotxa • *n* corncob
pansa • *n* raisin
pansir • *v* wilt, wither
pantà • *n* swamp
pantalla • *n* screen
pantaló • *n* pantaloons, pants
pantalons • *n* pants
pantanós • *adj* boggy
panteó • *n* pantheon
panxa • *n* abdomen, belly, paunch
panxell • *n* calf
paó • *n* peacock
Papa • *n* pope
papa • *n* pop
papaió • *n* butterfly
papal • *adj* papal
papalló • *n* butterfly
papallona • *n* butterfly
papaorelles • *n* earwig
paparra • *n* tick
papat • *n* papacy
paper • *n* paper
paperada • *n* paperwork
paperassa • *n* paperwork
papereria • *n* stationery
papers • *n* papers
papi • *n* pop
paquet • *n* package
para-sol • *n* parasol, sunshade, umbrella
para-xocs • *n* bumper
paràbola • *n* parable, parabola
parabòlic • *adj* parabolic
paracaigudes • *n* parachute
paracaigudista • *n* parachutist, para-trooper
parada • *n* stop
paradigma • *n* paradigm
paradís • *n* paradise
paradoxa • *n* paradox
paradoxal • *adj* paradoxical
paradoxalment • *adv* paradoxically
parafang • *n* mudguard
parafràstic • *adj* paraphrastic
parafràstica • *adj* paraphrastic
paraigua • *n* umbrella
paralŭlel • *adj* parallel
paralŭlelogram • *n* parallelogram
paralelepípede • *n* parallelepiped
paràlisi • *n* paralysis
paralític • *n* paralytic • *adj* paralytic
paralitzar • *v* paralyze
parameci • *n* paramecium

paramilitar • *n* paramilitary • *adj* paramil-itary
paranoic • *n* paranoid • *adj* paranoid
paranormal • *adj* paranormal
paraplegia • *n* paraplegia
paraplègic • *n* paraplegic • *adj* paraplegic
parar • *v* set, stop
paràsit • *n* parasite
paraula • *n* word
parc • *n* garden, park
parcament • *adv* sparingly
parcial • *adj* partial
parcialment • *adv* partially
pardal • *n* sparrow
pare • *n* father
parèixer • *v* seem
parell • *adj* even
parella • *n* couple, pair
parèmia • *n* proverb
parent • *n* relative
parentela • *n* kith
parèntesi • *n* parenthesis
parer • *n* view
paret • *n* wall
pària • *n* pariah
parla • *n* speech, utterance
parlament • *n* parliament
parlamentari • *adj* parliamentary
parlant • *n* speaker
parlar • *v* speak, talk
paròdia • *n* parody
parodiar • *v* parody
parpella • *n* eyelid
parpelleig • *n* blip
parrell • *n* gypsum
parròquia • *n* parish
part • *n* birth, part, party
participar • *v* play
participi • *n* participle
partícula • *n* particle
partida • *n* game
partir • *v* split
partit • *n* match
partitura • *n* score
pas • *n* march, stage, step
passable • *adj* passable
passadís • *n* aisle
passant • *prep* around
passaport • *n* passport
passar • *v* happen, pass, spend
passarelŭla • *n* gateway
passatemps • *n* pastime
passatge • *n* passage
passatger • *n* passenger • *adj* passing
passeig • *n* stroll, walk
passejada • *n* stroll, walk
passejar • *v* stroll

passejar-se • *v* stroll
passiu • *adj* passive
passius • *n* liabilities
passivament • *adv* passively
passivitat • *n* passivity
pasta • *n* brass, bun, dough, pasta
pastanaga • *n* carrot
pasteuritzar • *v* pasteurize
pastilla • *n* lozenge, pastille
pastís • *n* cake, pie
pastissos • *n* pastry
pastitx • *n* pastiche
pastor • *n* shepherd
pasturar • *v* pasture
patacada • *n* crash
patata • *n* potato
patent • *n* patent • *adj* patent
patentar • *v* patent
patern • *adj* paternal
patètic • *adj* pathetic, sad
patge • *n* page
patí • *n* skate
pati • *n* court
patiment • *n* suffering
pàtina • *n* patina
patinar • *v* skate
patinatge • *n* skating
patinet • *n* scooter
patir • *v* suffer
patogen • *n* pathogen
patologia • *n* pathology
patològic • *adj* pathological
pàtria • *n* fatherland
patriarca • *n* patriarch
patriarcal • *adj* patriarchal
patriarcat • *n* patriarchy
patriarquia • *n* patriarchy
patrici • *n* patrician
patrimoni • *n* patrimony
patriota • *n* patriot
patriòtic • *adj* patriotic
patriòticament • *adv* patriotically
patriotisme • *n* patriotism
patró • *n* boss, pattern
patronímic • *n* patronymic
patrulla • *n* patrol
pau • *n* peace
paüra • *n* fear
pavimentar • *v* pave
peana • *n* pedestal
pebre • *n* pepper
pebrot • *n* pepper
pebrotera • *n* pepper
pebrots • *n* guts
peça • *n* piece, room
pecador • *n* sinner
pecar • *v* sin

pecat • *n* misdeed, sin
pectina • *n* pectin
peculiar • *adj* peculiar
pedagog • *n* pedagogue
pedagògic • *adj* pedagogical
pedal • *n* pedal
pedalejar • *v* pedal
pedant • *adj* pedantic
pederasta • *n* pederast
pederàstia • *n* pederasty
pedestal • *n* pedestal
pedòmetre • *n* pedometer
pedra • *n* cow, rock, stone
pedrenc • *adj* stone
pedrenyal • *n* flint
pedrenyera • *n* flint
pedrer • *n* gizzard
peduncle • *n* peduncle
pegar • *v* hit, marry
pegàs • *n* pegasus
peix • *n* fish
peixater • *n* fishmonger
pejoratiu • *adj* derogatory
pejorativament • *adv* pejoratively
pèl • *n* hair
pèl-roig • *adj* ginger, red, redheaded
pèlůlet • *n* pellet
pelůlícula • *n* film, movie
pelar • *v* chafe, pod
pelat • *adj* broke
pelegrí • *n* pilgrim
pelegrina • *n* pilgrim
pelegrinatge • *n* pilgrimage
pelfa • *n* fleece
pelicà • *n* pelican
pell • *n* skin
pelussa • *n* fringe
pelvià • *adj* pelvic
pelvis • *n* pelvis
pena • *n* pain, time
pendent • *adj* outstanding, pending
penedir-se • *v* repent
penedit • *adj* penitent
penetrar • *v* soak
penicilůlina • *n* penicillin
península • *n* peninsula
penis • *n* penis
penitència • *n* penance
penitent • *n* penitent • *adj* penitent
penjar • *v* hang
penjar-se • *v* hang
penjat • *n* hangman
penjoll • *n* pendant
pensament • *n* thought
pensar • *v* think
pensarós • *adj* thoughtful
pensatiu • *adj* pensive

pensionista • *n* boarder
pentàedre • *n* pentahedron
pentaedre • *n* pentahedron
pentàgon • *n* pentagon
pentagrama • *n* staff
pentatleta • *n* pentathlete
pentatló • *n* pentathlon
pentatònic • *adj* pentatonic
pentinar • *v* comb, tease
penúltim • *adj* penultimate
penya-segat • *n* cliff
penyora • *n* pledge
penyorar • *v* pledge
peó • *n* pawn
pèptid • *n* peptide
per • *conj* for • *prep* for, per, toward
pera • *n* pear
percebe • *n* barnacle
percebre • *v* perceive
percentatge • *n* percentage
percepció • *n* perception
percussió • *n* percussion
perdigó • *n* pellet
perdiu • *n* partridge
perdó • *n* pardon • *interj* pardon, sorry
perdonar • *v* forgive, pardon
perdre • *v* lose
pèrdua • *n* loss
perdut • *adj* lost
perenne • *adj* perennial
perennifoli • *n* perennial
perepunyetes • *adj* fussy
perera • *n* pear
peresa • *n* sloth
peresós • *adj* lazy • *n* sloth
peresosament • *adv* lazily
perfecció • *n* perfection
perfeccionar • *v* perfect
perfeccionisme • *n* perfectionism
perfeccionista • *n* perfectionist
perfectament • *adv* flawlessly, perfectly
perfecte • *adj* flawless
perfídia • *n* perfidy
perforar • *v* bore, drill
perfum • *n* fragrance, perfume
pergelisòl • *n* permafrost
perifèria • *n* fringe, periphery
perífrasi • *n* periphrasis
perill • *n* danger, jeopardy, peril
perillós • *adj* dangerous, perilous
perillositat • *n* dangerousness
perineu • *n* perineum
període • *n* era, period, span
periòdic • *n* newspaper
periòdicament • *adv* periodically
periodisme • *n* journalism
periodista • *n* journalist

periodístic • *adj* journalistic
periquito • *n* budgerigar, parakeet
perir • *v* perish
peristil • *n* peristyle
perit • *adj* professional, proficient
peritoneu • *n* peritoneum
perjudicial • *adj* damaging
perla • *n* pearl
permanència • *n* permanence
permanent • *adj* permanent
permanentment • *adv* permanently
permeable • *adj* permeable
permetre • *v* let
permís • *n* leave, permission
pernil • *n* ham
però • *conj* albeit, but
perpendicular • *adj* perpendicular
perpendicularment • *adv* perpendicularly
perpetrar • *v* perpetrate
perpetu • *adj* perpetual
perpetual • *adj* perpetual
perpetualment • *adv* perpetually
perpètuament • *adv* perpetually
perpetuar • *v* perpetuate
perplex • *adj* puzzled
perquè • *conj* because, so • *n* why
perquisició • *n* inquiry
persecució • *n* chase
perseguiment • *n* pursuit
perseguir • *v* prosecute
perseverança • *n* perseverance
perseverància • *n* pluck
perseverar • *v* persevere
persiana • *n* blind, louver
persimó • *n* persimmon
persona • *n* person
personal • *adj* personal, private
personalitzat • *adj* custom-built, custom-made
personalment • *adv* personally
personatge • *n* character
personificar • *v* personify
perspicaç • *adj* perspicacious
perspicàcia • *n* perspicacity
persuadir • *v* persuade
persuasiu • *adj* persuasive
persuasivament • *adv* persuasively
pertànyer • *v* pertain
pertinença • *n* property
pertinent • *adj* relevant
pertorbar • *v* derange
perviure • *v* linger
perxa • *n* hanger
pesar • *v* weigh
pesat • *adj* heavy
pesca • *n* fishing

pescador • *n* fisher, fisherman
pescar • *v* fish
pèsol • *n* pea
pesolera • *n* pea
pessebre • *n* manger
pesseta • *n* peseta
pessic • *n* pinch
pessigar • *v* pinch
pèssim • *adj* lousy
pessimisme • *n* pessimism
pessimista • *n* pessimist • *adj* pessimistic
pesta • *n* pest
pestanya • *n* eyelash
pesticida • *n* pesticide
pet • *n* fart
pètal • *n* petal
petar • *v* fart
petge • *n* leg
petició • *n* request
petit • *adj* little, small
petjada • *n* footprint, step
petjapapers • *n* paperweight
petó • *n* kiss
petonejar • *v* kiss
petri • *adj* stone
petrificar • *v* petrify
petroli • *n* oil
petroquímic • *adj* petrochemical
petulant • *adj* smug
peu • *n* foot
peülla • *n* hoof
pi • *n* pine
pianista • *n* pianist
piano • *n* piano
pic • *n* peak, pick
pica • *n* basin, pike, sink, washbasin
pica-soques • *n* nuthatch
picador • *n* picador
picant • *adj* spicy
picar • *v* mull
picot • *n* woodpecker
picota • *n* pillory
pidolar • *v* beg
pietat • *n* piety
piezòmetre • *n* piezometer
pífia • *n* dud
pifre • *n* fife
piga • *n* freckle, mole
pigment • *n* pigment
pigmentar • *v* pigment
pigota • *n* smallpox
pijama • *n* pajamas
pila • *n* cell, pile
pilar • *n* pillar, prop
pilastra • *n* pilaster
pilot • *n* pilot • *adj* pilot
pilota • *n* ball, football

pilotar • *v* pilot
piloteig • *n* rally
pilotes • *n* ball, plum
píndola • *n* pill
pinguejar • *v* ping
pingüí • *n* penguin
pinsà • *n* chaffinch, finch
pinso • *n* feed, fodder
pintallavis • *n* lipstick
pintar • *v* paint
pintor • *n* painter
pintura • *n* paint, painting
pinya • *n* cone, pineapple
pinyol • *n* pit
pió • *n* pion
pipa • *n* pipa
pipeta • *n* pipette
pipí • *n* piss
piramidal • *adj* pyramidal
piràmide • *n* pyramid
pirata • *n* pirate
piratejar • *v* pirate
pírcing • *n* piercing
piròman • *n* pyromaniac
piromania • *n* pyromania
piròmetre • *n* pyrometer
pirotècnia • *n* pyrotechnics
pirotècnic • *adj* pyrotechnic
pis • *n* apartment
pisa • *n* earthenware
pissarra • *n* blackboard
pista • *n* ring, runway, trail
pistatxer • *n* pistachio
pistatxo • *n* pistachio
pistola • *n* gun, pistol
pit • *n* boob, breast, chest
pit-roig • *n* robin
pitjor • *adj* worse
pitrera • *n* jug, rack
pituïtari • *adj* pituitary
pitxer • *n* ewer
piulada • *n* tweet
piular • *v* tweet
pivot • *n* center, post
pivotar • *v* pivot
pixada • *n* piss
pixar • *v* piss
pixat • *n* piss
pixo • *n* piss
pizza • *n* pizza
pizzeria • *n* pizzeria
pla • *adj* even, flat, shallow • *n* plain
plaça • *n* plaza, square
placa • *n* slab
placar • *v* tackle
placatge • *n* tackle
placebo • *n* placebo

placenta • *n* placenta
plaent • *adj* pleasant
plaer • *n* delight
plaga • *n* pest
plagi • *n* plagiarism
plaguicida • *n* pesticide
planador • *n* glider
plançó • *n* sapling
plàncton • *n* plankton
planejar • *v* flatten, plan, plot
planeta • *n* destiny, fate, planet
planetari • *n* planetarium • *adj* planetary
planetoide • *n* asteroid
planificació • *n* planning
planificar • *v* arrange
planta • *n* plant
plantar • *v* plant
plantejar • *v* moot
plantilla • *n* staff, template
plantofa • *n* slipper
planxa • *n* iron
planxar • *v* iron
plany • *n* dirge
plànyer-se • *v* moan
planyívol • *adj* mournful
plaqueta • *n* platelet
plàstic • *n* plastic • *adj* plastic
plasticitat • *n* plasticity
plat • *n* course, dish, plate
plata • *n* argent, silver
plataforma • *n* platform
plàtan • *n* banana
platejat • *adj* silver
platerets • *n* cymbal
platí • *n* platinum
platirí • *adj* platyrrhine
platja • *n* beach, sand, strand
plató • *n* set
platònic • *adj* platonic
plaure • *v* please
plausible • *adj* plausible
ple • *adj* full • *n* strike
plebea • *n* commoner
plebeu • *n* commoner
plec • *n* fold
plegament • *n* fold
plegar • *v* fold
plenament • *adv* fully
plenari • *adj* plenary
plet • *n* lawsuit
plètora • *n* plethora
pletòric • *adj* plethoric
plom • *n* lead
ploma • *n* feather, sugar
plomall • *n* panache
plorar • *v* cry, weep
ploure • *v* rain

pluja • *n* rain
plujós • *adj* rainy
plumí • *n* nib
plural • *n* plural • *adj* plural
pluralitat • *n* plurality
plurilingüe • *adj* multilingual
plutoni • *n* plutonium
pluviòmetre • *n* pluviometer
pneumàtic • *n* tyre
pneumatòmetre • *n* pneumatometer
pneumònia • *n* pneumonia
població • *n* population
poblar • *v* people
poblar-se • *v* people
poble • *n* people, town, village
poblet • *n* hamlet
pobre • *adj* poor
pobres • *n* poor
pobresa • *n* poverty
poc • *adv* little • *adj* quiet
podar • *v* prune
poder • *v* can • *n* power
poderós • *adj* mighty, powerful
poderosament • *adv* powerfully
podòmetre • *n* pedometer
podrir • *v* rot
podrit • *adj* rotten
poema • *n* poem
poesia • *n* poem, poetry
poeta • *n* poet
poetastre • *n* poetaster
poetessa • *n* poetess
poètic • *adj* poetic
poètica • *adj* poetic
poèticament • *adv* poetically
poeticitat • *n* poetry
pogrom • *n* pogrom
polůlen • *n* pollen
polůlinització • *n* pollination
polůlució • *n* pollution
polůluent • *n* pollution
polůluir • *v* defile
polaina • *n* spat
polca • *n* polka
polèmic • *adj* polemic, polemical
policia • *n* police
policrom • *adj* polychromatic
policromàtic • *adj* polychromatic
poliedre • *n* polyhedron
políedre • *n* polyhedron
polietilè • *n* polyethylene
polifosfat • *n* polyphosphate
polígam • *n* polygamist
poligàmia • *n* polygamy
polígon • *n* polygon
poliinsaturat • *adj* polyunsaturated
polímer • *n* polymer

polinomi • *n* polynomial
polinomial • *adj* polynomial
polit • *n* curlew
politeisme • *n* polytheism
politeista • *n* polytheist • *adj* polytheistic
polític • *adj* political • *n* politician
política • *n* policy, politician, politics
políticament • *adv* politically
poll • *n* louse
polla • *n* dick
pollancre • *n* poplar
pollastre • *n* chicken, cockerel
polleguera • *n* hinge
pollet • *n* chick, cockerel
pollí • *n* foal
pollós • *adj* lousy
polo • *n* polo
polonesa • *n* polonaise
poloni • *n* polonium
polpós • *adj* fleshy
pols • *n* dust
poltra • *n* filly
poltre • *n* colt, foal, rack
pólvora • *n* gunpowder
polzada • *n* inch
polze • *n* thumb
poma • *n* apple
pomada • *n* ointment, salve
pompós • *adj* pompous
pomposament • *adv* pompously
pòmul • *n* cheekbone
poncella • *n* button
poncem • *n* citron
pondreś • *v* set
ponent • *n* west
poni • *n* pony
pont • *n* bridge
pontífex • *n* pontiff
pontificat • *n* papacy
ponxo • *n* poncho
pop • *n* octopus
popa • *n* jug, stern
popular • *adj* popular
pòquer • *n* poker
poquet • *n* bit
por • *adj* afraid • *n* fear
porc • *n* pig
porca • *n* sow
porcatera • *n* pigsty
porcell • *n* piglet
porcellana • *n* china, porcelain
porcellera • *n* pigsty
porcí • *adj* porcine
porció • *n* portion
pornista • *n* pornographer
pornògraf • *n* pornographer
pornografia • *n* pornography

pornogràfic • *adj* pornographic
porós • *adj* porous
porositat • *n* porosity
porpra • *adj* purple
porqueria • *n* filth
porquet • *n* piglet
porquí • *adj* porcine
porra • *n* baton
porret • *n* joint
porro • *n* leek
port • *n* port
porta • *n* door, gate
portabilitat • *n* portability
portable • *adj* portable
portador • *n* carrier
portadora • *n* carrier
portaequipatge • *n* trunk
portar • *v* act, bear, bring, carry, lead, take, wear
portàtil • *n* laptop • *adj* portable
portaveu • *n* spokesperson
porter • *n* goalkeeper
porteria • *n* goal
porticó • *n* shutter
posar • *v* put, set
posició • *n* position
pòsit • *n* dregs, lees
positiu • *adj* plus, positive • *n* positive
positivament • *adv* positively
positró • *n* positron
positura • *n* attitude
posposar • *v* adjourn, postpone
posseïr • *v* possess
possessió • *n* ownership, possession, property
possessiu • *adj* possessive
possibilitat • *n* possibility
possible • *adj* possible
possiblement • *adv* possibly
postal • *n* postcard
Postdata • *n* postscript
pòster • *n* poster
posterior • *adj* hind
posteriorment • *adv* later
postilló • *n* postilion
postís • *adj* false
postmodernitat • *n* postmodernism
postpart • *adj* postnatal
postres • *n* dessert
pòstum • *adj* posthumous
posturer • *adj* prim
pota • *n* foot, paw
potable • *adj* drinkable, potable
potassi • *n* potassium
potència • *n* power
potencial • *n* potential • *adj* potential
potent • *adj* powerful

potentment • *adv* powerfully
poterna • *n* postern
potser • *adv* maybe, perhaps
pou • *n* well
pràctic • *adj* handy, practical
pràctica • *n* practice
practicable • *adj* negotiable
pràcticament • *adv* practically
practicar • *v* practice
pragmàtic • *adj* pragmatic
pragmàtica • *adj* pragmatic
praseodimi • *n* praseodymium
prat • *n* meadow, pasture
precari • *adj* precarious
precàriament • *adv* precariously
precarietat • *n* precariousness
precedent • *n* precedent
preciós • *adj* lovely, precious
precipici • *n* precipice
precipitadament • *adv* abruptly
precipitat • *adj* hasty
precís • *adj* accurate, exact, precise
precisament • *adv* accurately, precisely
precisar • *v* name
precoç • *adj* precocious
preconcebut • *adj* preconceived
predestinació • *n* predestination
predilecció • *n* predilection
predisposat • *adj* prone
predominant • *adj* predominant
predominantment • *adv* predominantly
prefaci • *n* preface
preferències • *n* like
preferible • *adj* preferable
preferiblement • *adv* preferably, rather
preferit • *adj* favorite
pregar • *v* beg, pray
pregària • *n* prayer
pregon • *adj* deep
pregunta • *n* question
preguntar • *v* ask
preguntar-se • *v* wonder
prehistòria • *n* prehistory
prehistòric • *adj* prehistoric
preliminar • *adj* preliminary
preludi • *n* prelude
prematur • *adj* previous
prémer • *v* press
premi • *n* award, prize
premiar • *v* award
premsa • *n* press
prenatal • *adj* prenatal
prendre • *v* take
prènsil • *adj* prehensile
prenyada • *adj* pregnant
prenyat • *n* pregnancy • *adj* pregnant
preocupació • *n* concern, worry

preocupada • *adj* worried
preocupant • *adj* worrying
preocupar • *v* concern, worry
preocupar-se • *v* worry
preocupat • *adj* worried
preparat • *adj* prepared, set
preposició • *n* preposition
prepuci • *n* prepuce
pres • *n* prisoner
presa • *n* hurry, prey, quarry, take
presbícia • *n* presbyopia
present • *n* present • *adj* present
presentable • *adj* presentable
presentació • *n* introduction
presentar • *v* present, submit
presentar-se • *v* report
preservar • *v* preserve
preservatiu • *n* condom
presidència • *n* presidency
presidencial • *adj* presidential
president • *n* president
presidenta • *n* president
presó • *n* prison
presoner • *n* prisoner
pressa • *n* haste
préssec • *n* peach
presseguer • *n* peach
pressentiment • *n* hunch, presentiment
pressupost • *n* budget
prestador • *n* lender
prestar • *v* loan
prestatge • *n* shelf
préstec • *n* loan
presumiblement • *adv* presumably
presumptament • *adv* allegedly
presumpte • *adj* alleged
presumptuós • *adj* conceited
pretenciós • *adj* pretentious
pretendre • *v* mean
pretensió • *n* claim
preu • *n* charge, cost, price
preventiu • *adj* preventive
preveure • *v* devise
previ • *adj* former, previous
prèviament • *adv* previously
previsible • *adj* foreseeable
prim • *adj* slim
primari • *n* primary • *adj* primary
primària • *n* primary • *adj* primary
primàriament • *adv* primarily
primat • *n* primate
primavera • *n* primrose, spring
primer • *n* first • *adj* first, prime, pristine • *adv* first
primigeni • *adj* primeval
primitiu • *adj* primitive, pristine
primitivament • *adv* primitively

primogènit • *n* firstborn • *adj* firstborn
primogènita • *n* firstborn
prímula • *n* primrose
príncep • *n* prince
princesa • *n* princess
principal • *adj* chief, main
principalment • *adv* chiefly, mainly
principi • *n* base, beginning
principiant • *n* beginner
pristí • *adj* pristine
privacitat • *n* privacy
privadament • *adv* privately
privadesa • *n* privacy
privat • *adj* private
privilegi • *n* privilege
privilegiat • *adj* privileged
pro • *n* pro • *prep* pro
proa • *n* bow, prow
probabilitat • *n* chance, probability
probable • *adj* probable
probablement • *adv* probably
problema • *n* problem
probòscide • *n* proboscis
procediment • *n* procedure
procés • *n* process
processar • *v* process
processió • *n* procession
proclamació • *n* proclamation
procliu • *adj* prone
prodigi • *n* prodigy
prodigiós • *adj* prodigious
producte • *n* product
productiu • *adj* productive
productor • *n* producer
productora • *n* producer
produir • *v* produce
proesa • *n* exploit
profà • *adj* lay, profane
profanar • *v* profane
profecia • *n* prophecy
professió • *n* profession
professional • *n* professional • *adj* professional
professionalment • *adv* professionally
professor • *n* professor
professora • *n* professor
profeta • *n* prophet
profètic • *adj* prophetic
profetitzar • *v* prophesy
profilàctic • *adj* preventive, prophylactic
profitós • *adj* profitable
profund • *adj* deep
profundament • *adv* deeply
profunditat • *n* depth
profunditzar • *v* deepen
profunditzar-se • *v* deepen
progènie • *n* progeny

prògnat • *adj* prognathous
programa • *n* platform, program, schedule
programador • *n* programmer
programari • *n* software
progrés • *n* progress
progressar • *v* evolve
progressió • *n* progression
progressisme • *n* progressivism
progressista • *adj* progressive
progressiu • *adj* progressive
prohibir • *v* prohibit
prohibit • *adj* forbidden
projecte • *n* project
projectil • *n* missile, projectile
pròleg • *n* prologue
prolífic • *adj* prolific
prolix • *adj* prolix
promesa • *n* pledge, promise
prometedor • *adj* promising
prometi • *n* promethium
prometre • *v* pledge, promise
prominent • *adj* prominent
promiscu • *adj* promiscuous
promíscuament • *adv* promiscuously
promiscuïtat • *n* promiscuity
promoció • *n* class
pronom • *n* pronoun
pronosticar • *v* foresee
pronúncia • *n* pronunciation
pronunciació • *n* pronunciation, utterance
pronunciar • *v* pronounce, utter
propà • *n* propane
propens • *adj* prone
proper • *adj* next
propi • *adj* own
propici • *adj* auspicious
propícia • *adj* auspicious
propietari • *n* owner
propietat • *n* estate, ownership, possession, property, propriety
propina • *n* tip
proporció • *n* proportion
proporcional • *adj* proportional, proportionate
proposar • *v* propose
proposta • *n* proposal
prosa • *n* prose
prosceni • *n* proscenium
prosimi • *n* prosimian
prosòdia • *n* prosody
prospeccions • *n* prospect
prospecte • *n* brochure
pròsper • *adj* prosperous
prosperar • *v* prosper
pròstata • *n* prostate

prostatectomia • *n* prostatectomy
prostatitis • *n* prostatitis
pròstil • *n* prostyle
prostitució • *n* prostitution
prostituta • *n* hooker, prostitute
protactini • *n* protactinium
protagonista • *n* protagonist
protecció • *n* protection
protectorat • *n* protectorate
protegir • *v* protect
proteïna • *n* protein
protesta • *n* protest
protestar • *v* protest
protó • *n* proton
protozou • *n* protozoan
protrombina • *n* prothrombin
protur • *n* proturan
prou • *adv* enough • *pron* enough
prou! • *interj* enough
prova • *n* evidence, proof, witness
provar • *v* pilot, test, try, witness
proveir • *v* supply
proverbi • *n* proverb, saying
província • *n* province
provisional • *adj* makeshift, provisional
provisionalment • *adv* provisionally
provocador • *adj* provocative
provocatiu • *adj* provocative
pròxim • *adj* close, immediate
prudentment • *adv* deliberately, prudently
pruna • *n* plum
pruner • *n* plum
prunera • *n* plum
psalm • *n* psalm
psalmejar • *v* psalm
pseudociència • *n* pseudoscience
pseudòpode • *n* pseudopod
psi • *n* psi
psicoanàlisi • *n* psychoanalysis
psicodèlic • *adj* psychedelic
psicòleg • *n* psychologist
psicologia • *n* psychology
psicològic • *adj* psychological
psicològicament • *adv* psychologically
psicoteràpia • *n* psychotherapy
psicròmetre • *n* psychrometer
psiquiatre • *n* psychiatrist
psiquiatria • *n* psychiatry
psiquiàtric • *adj* psychiatric
psoriasi • *n* psoriasis
pterodàctil • *n* pterodactyl
pterosaure • *n* pterosaur
pua • *n* quill

púber • *n* pubescent
pubertat • *n* puberty
pubescent • *n* pubescent
pubis • *n* pubis
públic • *n* audience • *adj* public
publicació • *n* publication
públicament • *adv* publicly
publicar • *v* publish, release
publicitat • *n* publicity
puça • *n* flea
pudor • *n* pudor
pugilista • *n* pugilist
pugnaç • *adj* pugnacious
puig • *n* hill
puix • *conj* because
pujar • *v* rise
pulcre • *adj* neat
pulmó • *n* lung
pulmonar • *adj* pulmonary
pulmonia • *n* pneumonia
púlpit • *n* pulpit
púlsar • *n* pulsar
pumicita • *n* pumice
punició • *n* punishment
puniment • *n* punishment
punir • *v* punish
punitiu • *adj* punitive
punt • *n* dot, point, stitch, stop
punta • *n* butt, head, tip
puntuació • *n* punctuation
puntual • *adj* punctual
puntualitat • *n* punctuality
punxa • *n* tip
punxada • *n* flat
punxegut • *adj* pointed
puny • *n* cuff, fist
punyal • *n* dagger, knife
punyalada • *n* stab
pupil • *n* pupil
pupiŀla • *n* pupil
puput • *n* hoopoe
pur • *adj* clean, neat, pure
puresa • *n* purity
purgatiu • *adj* purgative
purgatori • *n* purgatory
purificar • *v* purify
purpuri • *adj* purple
pus • *n* pus
puta • *n* tart, whore
putatiu • *adj* putative
putejat • *adj* screwed
pútrid • *adj* putrid
putxero • *n* casserole

Q

quadern • *n* signature
quaderna • *n* rib
quadragèsim • *adj* fortieth
quadrant • *n* quadrant
quadrar • *v* square
quadrat • *n* square • *adj* square
quadre • *n* painting
quadrícula • *n* grid
quadrilàter • *n* quadrilateral • *adj* quadrilateral
quadriplègic • *n* quadriplegic
quàdruple • *adj* quadruple
quadruplicar • *v* fourfold
qual • *pron* whose
qualificació • *n* qualification
qualificat • *adj* qualified
qualitat • *n* quality
qualitatiu • *adj* qualitative
quality • *n* quality
qualque • *pron* any
quan • *adv* when
quantitat • *n* quantity, quantum
quàntum • *n* quantum
quarantè • *n* fortieth • *adj* fortieth
quarantena • *n* quarantine
quark • *n* quark
quars • *n* quartz
quart • *n* barrel, quart, quarter, quarto •
adj fourth
quarter • *n* quarter
quasi • *adv* almost • *adj* rough
quaternari • *adj* quaternary
quaternària • *adj* quaternary
quatre • *n* four
que • *adv* how, what • *prep* than • *conj*
that
què • *pron* what
quedar • *v* date
quedar-se • *v* remain, stay
queixa • *n* complaint
queixar-se • *v* complain
quelació • *n* chelation
quelcom • *pron* anything, something
quequeig • *n* stutter

quequejar • *v* stutter
quer • *n* rock
qüestió • *n* question
qüestionari • *n* questionnaire
quetzal • *n* quetzal
qui • *pron* who, whose
quiasme • *n* chiasmus
quibuts • *n* kibbutz
quiet • *adj* quiet, still
quil • *n* chyle
quilla • *n* keel
quilogram • *n* kilogram
quilooctet • *n* kilobyte
quilotona • *n* kiloton
quilovolt • *n* kilovolt
quilowatt • *n* kilowatt
quim • *n* chyme
quimera • *n* chimera
químic • *adj* chemical • *n* chemist
química • *n* chemist, chemistry
químicament • *adv* chemically
quimono • *n* kimono
quinari • *adj* quinary
quinària • *adj* quinary
quinina • *n* quinine
quint • *n* fifth • *adj* fifth
quinta • *n* fifth
quintar • *n* quintal
quintet • *n* quintet
quinzè • *adj* fifteenth
quinzenal • *adj* fortnightly
quinzenalment • *adv* fortnightly
quiquiriquic • *interj* cock-a-doodle-doo
quirat • *n* carat, karat
quiròfan • *n* surgery
quirúrgic • *adj* surgical
quirúrgicament • *adv* surgically
quitina • *n* chitin
quitó • *n* chiton
quitrà • *n* tar
quixotesc • *adj* quixotic
quotidià • *adj* quotidian

R

rabassut • *adj* stocky
rabí • *n* rabbi
ràbia • *n* anger, chafe, outrage, rabies,
rage
rabínic • *adj* rabbinical

rabiós • *adj* rabid
rabosa • *n* fox
raça • *n* breed, race
racial • *adj* racial
raciocinació • *n* ratiocination

racional • *adj* rational
racionalment • *adv* rationally
racisme • *n* racism
racista • *n* racist • *adj* racist
racó • *n* angle
radar • *n* radar
radi • *n* radium, radius
radiació • *n* radiation
radiant • *n* radiant • *adj* radiant, sunny
radical • *n* fringe, radical • *adj* radical
radicalment • *adv* radically
ràdio • *n* radio, wireless
radioactiu • *adj* radioactive
radioactivitat • *n* radioactivity
radiocarboni • *n* radiocarbon
radiodifusió • *n* broadcasting
radiodirigit • *adj* radio-controlled
radiolari • *n* radiolarian
radiòleg • *n* radiologist
radiòmetre • *n* radiometer
radó • *n* radon
ràfec • *n* eaves
rai • *n* ferry, raft
raig • *n* ray, spout, spurt
raïm • *n* bunch, grape, raceme
rajada • *n* ray
rajola • *n* tile
ramat • *n* flock, herd, multitude
ramificació • *n* ramification
rampí • *n* rake
ranci • *adj* rancid, rank
rancuniós • *adj* spiteful
rànquing • *n* ranking
raó • *n* reason
raonable • *adj* reasonable
raonablement • *adv* reasonably
raonada • *adj* mature
raonament • *n* reasoning
raonar • *v* reason
raonat • *adj* mature
rap • *n* angler, monkfish
rapar • *v* shave
ràpid • *adj* fast, prompt, speedy, swift • *adv* fast
ràpidament • *adv* fast, quickly
rapidesa • *n* speed
raptar • *v* kidnap
rapte • *n* kidnap, rapture
raqueta • *n* racket
raquis • *n* spine
raquític • *adj* rachitic
raquitisme • *n* rickets
rar • *adj* rare, weird
rarament • *adv* rarely, seldom
rascar • *v* scratch
rasclet • *n* rake
raspall • *n* brush

raspallar • *n* brush
rastre • *n* trail
ratapinyada • *n* bat
ratera • *n* mousetrap
ratlla • *n* dash
ratllador • *n* grater
ratllat • *adj* striped
ratolí • *n* mouse
ratpenat • *n* bat
ratxe • *n* gust
rauc • *n* croak
raucar • *v* croak
rave • *n* radish
ravenera • *n* radish
reacció • *n* reaction
reaccionari • *n* reactionary • *adj* reactionary
reaci • *adj* unwilling
reactiu • *n* reagent
real • *adj* actual
realisme • *n* realism
realista • *adj* realistic
realitat • *n* reality
realment • *adv* really
rebaixat • *adj* deprecated
rebel • *n* rebel • *adj* rebellious
rebel·lar-se • *n* rising
rebel·lió • *n* rebellion
rebequeria • *n* tantrum
rebombori • *n* brouhaha, fuss, hubbub, stir, uproar
rebost • *n* larder, pantry
rebot • *n* rebound
rebotir • *v* swell
rebotre • *v* rebound
rebre • *v* get, receive
rebuda • *n* receipt
rebuig • *n* clearance, clearing, refuse, rejection
rebut • *n* receipt
rebutjar • *v* clear, dismiss, refuse, reject, repel
recapitulació • *n* recapitulation
recapitular • *v* summarize
recar • *v* grudge
recent • *adj* recent
recentment • *adv* recently
recepta • *n* recipe
receptiu • *adj* receptive
receptor • *n* catcher
recerca • *n* research
recessiu • *adj* recessive
recíproc • *adj* reciprocal
recitar • *v* say
reclutament • *n* recruitment
recollidor • *n* dustpan
recollir • *v* collect, gather

recolsar-se • *v* lean
recolzar • *v* support
recomanar • *v* recommend
recompensar • *v* reward
reconeixement • *n* acknowledgement
reconquerir • *v* regain
reconstruir • *v* rebuild, reconstruct
reconstruit • *adj* reconstructed
record • *n* memory, recollection, souvenir
recordar • *v* recall, recollect, remember, remind
recordatori • *n* remembrance
recorregut • *n* course, run
recórrer • *v* course
recta • *n* line
rectangle • *n* rectangle
rectangular • *adj* rectangular
recte • *adj* upright
rectoria • *n* rectory
recuperació • *n* recovery
recuperar • *v* retrieve
redacció • *n* composition
redactar • *v* word
redempció • *n* atonement
rèdit • *n* revenue
redreçar • *v* straighten
reducte • *n* redoubt
reduir • *v* lower, reduce
redundància • *n* redundancy
redundant • *adj* redundant
reemborsament • *n* reimbursement
reemborsar • *v* reimburse
reemplaçable • *adj* replaceable
reemplaçar • *v* replace, supersede
refectori • *n* refectory
referèndum • *n* referendum
refinar • *v* refine
refinat • *adj* refined
reflexió • *n* reflection
reforç • *n* reinforcement
refracció • *n* refraction
refractòmetre • *n* refractometer
refrany • *n* proverb
refredat • *n* cold
refrescant • *adj* chilling
refrigerar • *v* refrigerate
refugi • *n* refuge
refugiar-se • *v* refuge
refugiat • *n* refugee
refús • *n* rejection
refusar • *v* decline, refuse, reject, repel
refutar • *v* refute
regal • *n* gift
regalèssia • *n* licorice
reganyar • *v* rebuke
règim • *n* regime
regiment • *n* regiment

regió • *n* belt, region
regional • *adj* regional
registre • *n* observation
regla • *n* rule, ruler
regna • *n* rein
regnar • *v* reign, rule
regnat • *n* reign
regne • *n* kingdom
regularitat • *n* regularity
regularment • *adv* regularly
rei • *n* king
reial • *adj* regal, royal
reietó • *n* goldcrest
reïna • *n* resin
reina • *n* queen
reincidir • *v* recidivate
reinstal·lar • *v* reinstall
reiterar • *v* reiterate
reixat • *n* gate
rejoveniment • *n* rejuvenation
relació • *n* relationship
relatiu • *adj* relative
relativament • *adv* relatively
relaxació • *n* relaxation
relaxar • *v* relax
relaxat • *adj* easygoing, relaxed
relé • *n* relay
religió • *n* religion
religiós • *adj* religious
religiosament • *adv* religiously
reliquiari • *n* reliquary
rellamp • *n* lightning
relleu • *n* relief
relleus • *n* relay
rellevància • *n* relevance
rellevant • *adj* relevant
rellevar • *v* relay
relliscada • *n* slip
rellogar • *v* sublease
rellotge • *n* clock, watch
rellotger • *n* watchmaker
rellotgera • *n* watchmaker
reluctància • *n* reluctance
rem • *n* oar, rowing
remant • *n* rowing
remar • *v* row
remarcable • *adj* remarkable
remarcar • *v* highlight
remei • *n* remedy
remeiar • *v* palliate, remedy
rememorar • *v* recollect, remember
remolcador • *n* tugboat
remolcar • *v* tow
remolí • *n* swirl, vortex, whirlpool
remordiment • *n* remorse
remot • *adj* far-flung, remote
remoure • *v* stir

remugant • *n* ruminant • *adj* ruminant
remuneració • *n* remuneration, wage
ren • *n* reindeer
rendible • *adj* profitable
rendiment • *n* efficiency
reni • *n* rhenium
renill • *n* neigh
renillar • *v* neigh
renovable • *adj* renewable
rentable • *adj* washable
rentamans • *n* washstand
rentaplats • *n* dishwasher
rentar • *v* wash
renyir • *n* scold
reomplir • *v* refill
reorganitzar • *v* reorganize
reparació • *n* reparation
reparar • *v* sort
repartiment • *n* cast
repartir • *v* deal, split
repelůlent • *adj* repellent
repelůlir • *v* repel
repeló • *n* hangnail
repenjar-se • *v* lean
repetible • *adj* repeatable
repetició • *n* repetition
repetidament • *adv* repeatedly
repetidor • *n* repeater
repetir • *v* repeat
replegar • *v* collect
replet • *adj* packed, replete
repleta • *adj* replete
repòs • *n* rest
reposar • *v* rest
reprendre • *v* rebuke, resume
reprensió • *n* rebuke
representació • *n* depiction, performance, representation
representant • *n* steward
representar • *v* represent
reproductiu • *adj* reproductive
reproductor • *adj* reproductive
reproduir • *v* rehearse
reprovable • *adj* guilty
rèptil • *n* reptile
república • *n* republic
republicà • *adj* conservative, republican
repugnant • *adj* disgusting, revolting
reputació • *n* name, reputation
requerir • *v* need
requisat • *adj* impressed
requisit • *n* requirement
rereguarda • *n* rearguard
rerelínia • *n* linebacker
rerequart • *n* quarterback
rés • *n* prayer
res • *pron* anything, nothing • *n* love, zero

resar • *v* pray
rescat • *n* ransom, rescue
rescatar • *v* rescue
resclosa • *n* lock
reservar • *v* book
reservat • *adj* reserved
residència • *n* residence
residencial • *adj* residential
resident • *n* inmate
residir • *v* reside
resina • *n* resin
resinós • *adj* resinous
resistència • *n* resistance, resistor
resistent • *adj* resilient, resistant • *n* resistant, resistor
resistible • *adj* resistible
resoldre • *v* resolve, solve
resolució • *n* resolve
resolut • *adj* resolute
respectable • *adj* respectable
respecte • *n* fear
respectiu • *adj* respective
respectivament • *adv* respectively
respectuós • *adj* respectful
respir • *n* respite
respiració • *n* breath
respirar • *v* breathe
respiratori • *adj* respiratory
respondre • *v* answer, respond
responsabilitat • *n* accountability, liability, responsibility
responsable • *adj* liable, responsible
responsablement • *adv* responsibly
resposta • *n* answer, feedback
ressaca • *n* hangover
ressaltar • *v* highlight
ressec • *adj* parched
ressonant • *adj* resounding
ressort • *n* spring
resta • *n* rest
restant • *adj* remaining
restar • *v* remain, return, stay
restaurant • *n* restaurant
restrenyiment • *n* constipation
restrictiu • *adj* restrictive
restringir • *v* restrict
resultat • *n* result, score
resum • *n* abstract, summary
resumir • *v* summarize
resumit • *adj* abridged
resurrecció • *n* resurrection
ret • *n* hairnet
retallar • *v* cut
reticent • *adj* reticent
retirat • *adj* secluded
retoc • *n* retouch
retopar • *v* ricochet

retòric • *adj* rhetorical
retorta • *n* retort
retractable • *adj* retractable
retrat • *n* portrait
retribució • *n* wage
retrovirus • *n* retrovirus
reumàtic • *n* rheumatic • *adj* rheumatic
reunió • *n* meeting
reunir • *v* collect
revelador • *adj* telltale
revelar • *v* reveal
revenja • *n* revenge
revenjar-se • *v* revenge
reverberar • *v* reverberate
reverència • *n* bow, reverence
reverenciar • *v* revere
reverent • *adj* reverent
reverir • *v* revere
revetlla • *n* merrymaking, revel
revista • *n* magazine
revocació • *n* revocation
revolt • *n* curve
revolta • *n* revolt
revoltar • *v* revolt
revolució • *n* revolution
revolucionari • *n* revolutionary • *adj* revolutionary
revòlver • *n* revolver
rialla • *n* laughter
riba • *n* shore
ribosa • *n* ribose
ribot • *n* plane
ric • *adj* rich
ricor • *n* richness
rictus • *n* face
ridícul • *adj* ludicrous, ridiculous
riera • *n* creek, torrent
rierol • *n* creek, stream
riff • *n* riff
rifle • *n* rifle
rígid • *adj* rigid, stiff
rígidament • *adv* rigidly
rigidesa • *n* rigidity
rigiditat • *n* rigidity
rigorosament • *adv* rigorously
rima • *n* rhyme
rimar • *v* rhyme
ring • *n* ring
rinoceront • *n* rhinoceros
riquesa • *n* richness
risc • *n* jeopardy, risk
rissaga • *n* bore
ritme • *n* rhythm
rítmicament • *adv* rhythmically
ritual • *adj* ritual
ritus • *n* rite
riu • *n* current, river

riure • *v* laugh • *n* laugh, laughter
rival • *n* rival
rivalitat • *n* rivalry
rivalitzar • *v* vie
rizoma • *n* rhizome
ro • *n* rho
roba • *n* clothes, clothing
robar • *v* steal
robatori • *n* steal, theft
robí • *n* ruby
robòtica • *n* robotics
robust • *adj* rude, sturdy
roc • *n* rock
roca • *n* rock, stone
rock • *n* rock
rococó • *n* rococo
roda • *n* wheel
rodamón • *n* globetrotter, hobo, tramp, wanderer
rodanxa • *n* ring
rodar • *v* wheel
rodejar • *v* circumvent, surround
rodi • *n* rhodium
rodó • *adj* round
rogenc • *adj* reddish
rogent • *adj* ablaze
roí • *adj* evil
roig • *n* red • *adj* red
roja • *n* red
rojor • *n* redness
rom • *adj* blunt • *n* rum
romandre • *v* linger
romanent • *adj* remaining
romaní • *n* rosemary
romàntic • *adj* romantic
romànticament • *adv* romantically
rombe • *n* lozenge, rhombus
romboedre • *n* rhombohedron
rombòedre • *n* rhombohedron
romboèdric • *adj* rhombohedral
romer • *n* rosemary
ronc • *adj* husky
roncar • *v* purr, snore
ronda • *n* bypass
rondinaire • *adj* grumpy
ronronejar • *v* purr
ronyó • *n* kidney
ros • *n* blond
rosa • *n* pink, popcorn, rose • *adj* pink
rosada • *n* dew
rosari • *n* rosary
rosat • *adj* rose
rosegador • *n* rodent
rosegar • *v* gnaw
rosella • *n* poppy
roser • *n* rose
roseta • *n* popcorn

rossí • *n* nag
rossinyol • *n* chanterelle, nightingale
rostit • *adj* roast
rot • *n* burp
rotar • *v* belch
rotonda • *n* roundabout
roure • *n* oak
rovell • *n* rust, yolk
rovellar • *v* rust
rovellat • *adj* rusty
rubicund • *adj* ruddy
rubicunda • *adj* ruddy
rubidi • *n* rubidium
ruc • *n* donkey
ruca • *n* donkey, rocket
ruda • *n* rue
rude • *adj* rough, rude
rudimentari • *adj* obsolete
rugir • *v* roar

rugós • *adj* uneven
ruïna • *n* ruin, wreck
ruïnós • *adj* ruinous
ruixador • *n* sprinkler
ruixar • *v* sprinkle
ruleta • *n* roulette
rumb • *n* course
rumiar • *v* linger, mull
rumor • *n* rumor
ruptura • *n* rupture
rural • *adj* rural
rusc • *n* beehive
rústic • *adj* rustic
ruta • *n* course, route, run
ruteni • *n* ruthenium
rutherfordi • *n* rutherfordium
rutinari • *adj* routine

S

sa • *adj* clean, sound • *art* the
saba • *n* sap
sabata • *n* shoe
sabater • *n* shoemaker
sabatilla • *n* slipper
saber • *v* know
sabó • *n* soap
sabonera • *n* lather
sabor • *n* taste
saborós • *adj* delicious
sabotatge • *n* sabotage
sabotejar • *v* sabotage
sacabutx • *n* sackbut
sacarina • *n* saccharin
sacarosa • *n* sucrose
sacerdot • *n* priest
sacerdotessa • *n* priestess
saciar • *v* satiate
sacietat • *n* satiety
sacre • *adj* sacral • *n* sacrum
sacrificar • *v* immolate, sacrifice
sacrificar-se • *v* sacrifice
sacrifici • *n* sacrifice
sacrificial • *adj* sacrificial
sacríleg • *adj* sacrilegious
sacrílegament • *adv* sacrilegiously
sacrilegi • *n* sacrilege
sacrosant • *adj* sacrosanct
sacsejador • *n* rattle, shaker
sàdic • *adj* sadistic
sadollar • *v* quench
sadomasoquista • *adj* sadomasochistic
safir • *n* sapphire

safrà • *n* saffron • *adj* saffron
safranera • *n* saffron
saga • *n* saga
sagaç • *adj* sagacious
sagacitat • *n* sagacity
sageta • *n* arrow
sagnant • *adj* bloody
sagnar • *v* bleed
sagrada • *adj* holy
sagrat • *adj* hallowed, holy, sacred
sagristà • *n* sexton
sal • *n* salt
sala • *n* room
salar • *v* salt
salari • *n* salary, wage
salat • *adj* salty
salconduit • *n* safe-conduct
salí • *adj* saline
saliva • *n* saliva
salm • *n* psalm
salmejar • *v* psalm
salmó • *n* salmon
salsitxa • *n* sausage
salt • *n* jump, leap
saltamartí • *n* grasshopper
saltar • *v* jump, leap, spring
saltiri • *n* psalter, psaltery
salts • *n* diving
salubre • *adj* healthy
saludablement • *adv* healthily
saludar • *v* greet, wave
salut • *interj* cheers • *n* health
salv • *adj* safe

salvació • *n* salvation
salvar • *v* save
salvatge • *n* savage • *adj* savage, wild
salvatgement • *adv* savagely
sàlvia • *n* sage
salze • *n* willow
samari • *n* samarium
samarreta • *n* singlet, vest
sandàlia • *n* sandal
sandvitx • *n* sandwich
sanefa • *n* border
sang • *n* blood
sangonera • *n* leech
sanguinyol • *n* dogwood
sanitat • *n* health
sant • *adj* holy • *n* saint
santa • *adj* holy • *n* saint
santedat • *n* sainthood
santificar • *v* canonize
sapador • *n* sapper
sarau • *n* party
sarbatana • *n* blowgun
sarcasme • *n* sarcasm
sarcàstic • *adj* sarcastic
sarcàsticament • *adv* sarcastically
sarcòfag • *n* sarcophagus
sargantana • *n* lizard
sartori • *n* sartorius
sastre • *n* tailor
sastressa • *n* tailor
satànic • *adj* satanic
satèŀlit • *n* satellite
sàtir • *n* satyr
satíric • *adj* satirical
satíricament • *adv* satirically
satisfacció • *n* satisfaction
satisfactori • *adj* satisfactory
satisfactòriament • *adv* satisfactorily
satisfer • *v* satisfy
satisfet • *adj* happy, satisfied
saturat • *adj* saturated
saturní • *adj* plumbic
saüc • *n* elder
sauna • *n* sauna
savi • *adj* sage, wise
sàviament • *adv* wisely
saviesa • *n* lore, wisdom
saxofonista • *n* saxophonist
sebaci • *adj* sebaceous
séc • *n* fold
sec • *adj* dry
seca • *n* drought, mint
secada • *n* drought
secció • *n* section
secor • *n* dryness
secreció • *n* secretion
secret • *adj* arcane, secret • *n* secret

secretament • *adv* secretly
secretar • *v* secrete
secretina • *n* secretin
secretisme • *n* secrecy
secta • *n* sect
secular • *adj* secular
secundari • *adj* secondary
secundària • *adj* secondary
seda • *n* silk
sedant • *n* sedative • *adj* sedative
sedàs • *n* sieve
sedentari • *adj* sedentary
sedició • *n* sedition
sedós • *adj* silky
seductor • *adj* seductive • *n* tempter
segar • *v* mow, reap
segell • *n* bull, seal, stamp
segellar • *v* seal, stamp
segle • *n* century
sègoll • *n* rye
segon • *adj* latter, second • *n* second
segona • *n* accompaniment, second
segons • *prep* per
segregació • *n* segregation
segregar • *v* segregate
segrest • *n* kidnap, kidnapping
segrestar • *v* kidnap
següent • *adj* following, next
seguici • *n* household, retinue
seguir • *v* follow, keep, observe
segur • *adj* safe, sure
segurament • *adv* surely
seguretat • *n* safety, security
selecció • *n* selection
seleccionar • *v* select
seleni • *n* selenium
sella • *n* saddle
selva • *n* forest
semàfor • *n* semaphore
semàntic • *adj* semantic
semàntica • *n* semantics
semblança • *n* resemblance, similarity
semblant • *adj* akin, like, similar
semblantment • *adv* similarly
semblar • *v* appear, look, resemble, seem
sembrar • *v* sow
semen • *n* cum
sement • *n* cum
semicercle • *n* semicircle
semiconductor • *n* semiconductor
semideessa • *n* demigod
semidéu • *n* demigod
seminari • *n* workshop
sempre • *adv* always
senador • *n* senator
senadora • *n* senator
senar • *adj* odd

senari • *adj* senary
senària • *adj* senary
senat • *n* senate
sencer • *adj* full, unbroken
senda • *n* footpath
sender • *n* footpath, path
sendera • *n* footpath
senil • *adj* senile
senilitat • *n* senility
sensació • *n* sense
sensacional • *adj* sensational
sensacionalisme • *n* sensationalism
sensacionalista • *adj* sensationalist
sensat • *adj* sensible
sense • *prep* without
sensori • *adj* sensory
sensorial • *adj* sensory
sensual • *adj* sensual
sentència • *n* sentence
sentenciar • *v* award
sentimental • *adj* sentimental
sentimentalment • *adv* sentimentally
sentir • *v* hear, read, sense
sentit • *n* sense
seny • *n* head, intelligence, judgment
senyal • *n* sign, signal
senyor • *n* liege, lord, mister
senyora • *n* lady
senyorejar • *v* lord
senzill • *adj* plain, simple
senzillament • *adv* simply
separadament • *adv* separately
separar • *v* separate, shed, split
separat • *adj* divorced, separate
sépia • *n* cuttlefish
sèpia • *n* cuttlefish, sepia • *adj* sepia
septe • *n* septum
septentrió • *n* north
septentrional • *adj* northern
sèptic • *adj* septic
sèptim • *n* seventh • *adj* seventh
sèptima • *n* seventh
sepulcre • *n* grave
sequedat • *n* dryness
seqüència • *n* sequence
sequera • *n* drought
sequoia • *n* redwood
ser • *v* be, get
serac • *n* serac
serè • *adj* serene
sèrie • *n* series
serietat • *n* seriousness
seriós • *adj* earnest, grave, serious
seriosament • *adv* seriously
serjant • *n* clamp
serotonina • *n* serotonin
serp • *n* serpent, snake

serpent • *n* serpent, snake
serpentó • *n* serpent
serra • *n* saw
serradora • *n* sawmill
serradures • *n* sawdust
serrar • *v* saw, squeeze
serrell • *n* fringe
sèrum • *n* serum
servei • *n* bathroom, duty, serve, service, throw-in
servici • *n* bathroom
servir • *v* serve, service
servitud • *n* easement
ses • *art* the
sèsam • *n* sesame
sèssil • *adj* sessile
sessió • *n* session
sesta • *n* siesta
set • *n* set, seven, thirst
setciències • *n* know-it-all
setè • *n* seventh • *adj* seventh
setge • *n* siege
setmana • *n* week
setmanal • *adj* weekly • *adv* weekly
setmanalment • *adv* weekly
setrill • *n* cruet
setrilleres • *n* cruet
setzè • *n* sextodecimo, sixteenth
seu • *n* base, headquarters, seat, see, venue
sèu • *n* sebum, tallow
seure • *v* sit
sever • *adj* harsh, stern
severa • *adj* harsh
severament • *adv* severely
sexar • *v* sex
sexe • *n* gender, sex
sexisme • *n* sexism
sexista • *n* sexist • *adj* sexist
sext • *n* sixth • *adj* sixth
sexta • *n* sext, sixth
sexual • *adj* sexual
sexualment • *adv* sexually
sí • *adv* yeah
si • *n* heart, si, sinus • *interj* hello • *conj* if
sigma • *n* sigma
signar • *v* ink
signatura • *n* signature
significar • *v* mean
significat • *n* sense, significance
significatiu • *adj* significant
significativament • *adv* significantly
sílŭlaba • *n* syllable
silŭlàbic • *adj* syllabic
silŭlogisme • *n* syllogism
silenci • *n* silence
silenciador • *n* muffler

silenciós • *adj* quiet
silenciosament • *adv* quietly, silently
sílex • *n* chert, flint
silicat • *n* silicate
silici • *n* silicon
silicona • *n* silicone
silueta • *n* silhouette
silur • *n* catfish
simbiosi • *n* symbiosis
simbiòtic • *adj* symbiotic
símbol • *n* symbol
simbòlic • *adj* symbolic
simbòlicament • *adv* symbolically
simbolisme • *n* symbolism
simbolitzar • *v* symbolize
simetria • *n* symmetry
simètric • *adj* symmetrical
simètricament • *adv* symmetrically
similar • *adj* similar
similitud • *n* similarity
simpatia • *n* sympathy
simpàtic • *adj* sympathetic
simple • *adj* plain, simple, single
simplement • *adv* just, merely, simply
símplex • *adj* simplex
simplificació • *n* simplification
símptoma • *n* symptom
simptomàtic • *adj* symptomatic
simulació • *n* simulation
simulacre • *n* simulacrum
simultani • *adj* simultaneous
simultàniament • *adv* simultaneously
sinagoga • *n* synagogue
sinapsi • *n* synapse
sincer • *adj* sincere
sincerament • *adv* sincerely
sinceritat • *n* sincerity
sinclinal • *n* synclinal
sincronitzar • *v* synchronize
síndria • *n* watermelon
sindriera • *n* watermelon
síndrome • *n* syndrome
sinècdoque • *n* synecdoche
single • *n* single
singlot • *n* hiccup
singular • *n* singular • *adj* singular
singularment • *adv* uniquely
sínia • *n* noria
sínode • *n* synod
sinònim • *n* synonym • *adj* synonymous
sinopsi • *n* synopsis
sintàctic • *adj* syntactic
sintàcticament • *adv* syntactically
sintagma • *n* phrase
sintaxi • *n* syntax
síntesi • *n* synthesis
sintetitzador • *n* synthesizer

sinus • *n* sine
sipai • *n* sepoy
sípia • *n* cuttlefish
sirena • *n* mermaid, siren
sis • *n* six
sisè • *n* sixth • *adj* sixth
sísmic • *adj* seismic
sismògraf • *n* seismograph
sismòleg • *n* seismologist
sismologia • *n* seismology
sismològic • *adj* seismological
sismòmetre • *n* seismometer
sistema • *n* system
sistemàtic • *adj* systematic
sistemàticament • *adv* systematically
sitja • *n* silo
situació • *n* lie
situat • *adj* situated
sivella • *n* buckle
sloop • *n* sloop
so • *n* sound • *art* the
soberg • *adj* superb
sobirà • *n* sovereign • *adj* sovereign
sobirania • *n* sovereignty
sobre • *prep* about, on, toward • *n* envelope
sobreacceleració • *n* jerk
sobreestimar • *v* overestimate
sobremenjar • *v* overeat
sobrenatural • *adj* supernatural
sobrenom • *n* nickname
sobrer • *adj* remaining
sobresalt • *n* jump
sobresaltar • *v* jump
sobresortint • *adj* outstanding
sobretaula • *n* desktop
sobretot • *adv* especially • *n* paletot
sobreviure • *v* survive
sobri • *adj* sober
sobtadament • *adv* suddenly
sobtat • *adj* sudden
sociable • *adj* sociable
social • *adj* social
socialisme • *n* socialism
socialista • *n* socialist • *adj* socialist
socialment • *adv* socially
societat • *n* society
sociòleg • *n* sociologist
sociologia • *n* sociology
sociològic • *adj* sociological
sòcol • *n* plinth
socorrista • *n* lifeguard
socors • *n* succor
sodi • *n* sodium
sodomia • *n* sodomy
sodomita • *n* sodomite
sofà • *n* sofa

soforífic • *n* soporific
sofre • *n* sulfur
sofrir • *v* suffer
softbol • *n* softball
sogra • *n* mother-in-law
sogre • *n* father-in-law
soia • *n* soy
soja • *n* soy
sol • *adj* alone, neat, sole • *adv* alone • *n* sol, sun
sòl • *n* floor, ground, soil
solůlicitud • *n* request
sola • *n* sole
solament • *adv* only
solar • *n* plot
solatge • *n* dregs
solc • *n* furrow
soldador • *n* welder
soldar • *v* weld
soldat • *n* soldier
soldats • *n* troop
solemne • *adj* formal, solemn
solemnement • *adv* solemnly
solemnitat • *n* solemnity
sòlid • *n* solid, solidus • *adj* solid, sound
sòlidament • *adv* solidly
solidificar • *v* solidify
soliloqui • *n* soliloquy
solitari • *adj* lonely, solitaire, solitary • *n* patience, solitary
Solitari • *n* solitaire
solitud • *n* solitude
soll • *n* pigsty
sols • *adv* just, only
solstici • *n* solstice
solter • *n* bachelor • *adj* sole, unmarried
soluble • *adj* soluble
solucionar • *v* resolve, solve
solut • *n* solute
somera • *n* donkey
somiar • *v* dream
sommelier • *n* butler
somnambulisme • *n* sleepwalking, somnambulism
somni • *n* dream
somnífer • *n* soporific • *adj* soporific
somnolent • *adj* sleepy
somrient • *adj* smiling
somrís • *n* smile
somriure • *v* smile • *n* smile
son • *n* sleep
sonar • *n* sonar • *v* sound
sondejar • *v* fathom
sonet • *n* sonnet
sònic • *adj* sonic
sonor • *n* voice
sopar • *n* dinner, supper • *v* supper

sopesar • *v* mull
soporífer • *adj* soporific
soporífic • *adj* soporific
soprano • *n* soprano
sor • *n* sister
sord • *adj* deaf
sordesa • *n* deafness
sòrdid • *adj* sordid
sorgir • *v* emerge
soroll • *n* noise
sorollós • *adj* boisterous, noisy
sorollosament • *adv* loudly, noisily
sorprendre • *v* surprise
sorprendreś • *v* wonder
sorprenent • *adj* astonishing, surprising
sorprenentment • *adv* surprisingly
sorpresa • *n* astonishment, surprise
sorra • *n* sand
sorrenc • *adj* sandy
sorrera • *n* sandbox
sort • *n* luck
sortida • *n* exit, outlet
sortint • *adj* outgoing
sortir • *v* appear, date, exit, quit
sortir-seń • *v* manage
sos • *art* the
sospir • *n* sigh
sospirar • *v* sigh
sospita • *n* suspicion
sospitar • *v* suspect
sospitós • *adj* suspect, suspicious
sospitosament • *adv* suspiciously
sostenible • *adj* sustainable
sostenidor • *n* bra
sostenir • *v* hold, support, sustain
sostracció • *n* subtraction
sostre • *n* ceiling, roof
sota • *adv* below, beneath, under, underneath • *prep* below, beneath, under, underneath
soterrani • *n* basement
sotmetre • *v* submit
sotmetreś • *v* submit
sotsarrendament • *n* sublease
sotsarrendar • *v* sublease
sotsobrar • *v* capsize
sou • *n* salary, wage
sovint • *adv* often
staff • *n* staff
suar • *v* sweat
suau • *adj* mild, soft
suaument • *adv* gently, softly
subatòmic • *adj* subatomic
subconsciència • *n* subconscious
subconscient • *n* subconscious • *adj* subconscious
subcontinent • *n* subcontinent

subcutani • *adj* subcutaneous
súbdit • *n* subject
subestimar • *v* underestimate
subhasta • *n* auction
subhastar • *v* auction
subjacent • *adj* underlying
subjecte • *adj* liable, subject • *n* subject
subjectiu • *adj* subjective
subjectivament • *adv* subjectively
subjectivitat • *n* subjectivity
subjugar • *v* subjugate
sublim • *adj* sublime
submarí • *n* submarine • *adj* submarine
submergible • *adj* waterproof
submergir • *v* drown, submerge
submergir-se • *v* sink
subministrar • *v* supply
subordre • *n* suborder
subratllar • *v* highlight
subscriure̱ • *v* subscribe
subsegüent • *adj* subsequent
subseqüentment • *adv* subsequently
subsidi • *n* subsidy
subsòl • *n* subsoil
substància • *n* substance
substantiu • *n* noun
substituir • *v* substitute, supersede
substitut • *n* substitute, surrogate
substrat • *n* substrate, substratum
subterrani • *adj* subterranean, underground
subtil • *adj* subtle
subtilesa • *n* subtlety
subtilment • *adv* subtly
subtítol • *n* subtitle
subtítols • *n* subtitle
subtracció • *n* subtraction
suburbà • *n* suburban
suburbi • *n* suburb
subvenció • *n* subsidy
subvencionar • *v* subsidize
suc • *n* juice
succeir • *v* happen
successiu • *adj* successive
successivament • *adv* successively
succint • *adj* succinct
succintament • *adv* succinctly
sucós • *adj* juicy
sucre • *n* sugar
súcub • *n* succubus
súcube • *n* succubus
suculent • *adj* succulent
sud • *n* south
sud-est • *n* southeast
suficient • *adj* sufficient

suficientment • *adv* enough, sufficiently
sufocar • *v* suffocate
suggeriment • *n* suggestion
suggestió • *n* suggestion
suïcidi • *n* suicide
suid • *n* hog
suma • *n* total
sumac • *n* sumac
sumar • *v* add, number
sumari • *n* summary • *adj* summary
sumàriament • *adv* summarily
sumptuós • *adj* sumptuous
suor • *n* sweat
superar • *v* overwhelm
superàvit • *n* surplus
superb • *adj* haughty
superego • *n* superego
superficial • *adj* shallow, superficial
superficialment • *adv* superficially
superfície • *n* surface
superflu • *adj* superfluous
supèrfluament • *adv* superfluously
superior • *adj* superior, upper
superioritat • *n* superiority
superjò • *n* superego
superlatiu • *adj* superlative
supermercat • *n* supermarket
superstició • *n* superstition
supersticiós • *adj* superstitious
supersticiosament • *adv* superstitiously
supervisió • *n* oversight
supervivent • *n* survivor
suplantar • *v* displace
suplementar • *v* supplement
suplementari • *adj* supplementary
suplent • *n* surrogate
suplicar • *v* beg
suportable • *adj* bearable
suportar • *v* bear, stand
suposar • *v* guess, suppose
supositori • *n* suppository
suprem • *adj* supreme
supremacia • *n* supremacy
suprimir • *v* abolish
surfista • *n* surfer
surrealisme • *n* surrealism
susceptibilitat • *n* susceptibility
susceptible • *adj* susceptible
sushi • *n* sushi
suspendre • *v* adjourn
suspicaç • *adj* suspicious
sutge • *n* grime, soot
sutja • *n* grime, soot

T

tabac • *n* tobacco
tabalet • *n* tabor
tabú • *n* taboo • *adj* taboo
tabular • *adj* tabular
tac • *n* cue
taca • *n* spot, stain
tacany • *n* hog
tàcit • *adj* tacit
tàcitament • *adv* tacitly
taciturn • *adj* taciturn
tacòmetre • *n* tachometer
tàctica • *n* tactic
tàctil • *adj* tactile
taigà • *n* taiga
talůli • *n* thallium
talaia • *n* watchtower
talc • *n* talc
tàlem • *n* thalamus
talent • *n* talent
talentós • *adj* talented
talismà • *n* phylactery
talla • *n* stature
tallador • *n* trencher
tallahams • *n* tailor
tallanassos • *n* dragonfly
tallar • *v* cut, shred
tallat • *adj* light
taller • *n* workshop
taló • *n* cheque, heel
talonador • *n* hooker
talp • *n* mole
talpó • *n* vole
talús • *n* talus
també • *adv* also, too
tambor • *n* drum
tamboret • *n* stool
tamborinejar • *v* drum
tampoc • *adv* either
tamponar • *v* tampon
tan • *adv* as, so
tanatofòbia • *n* thanatophobia
tanc • *n* tank
tanca • *n* boards, fence
tancada • *n* sit-in
tancar • *v* close
tancat • *adj* acute, closed
tangent • *n* tangent
tangible • *adj* tangible
tango • *n* tango
tanmateix • *conj* albeit, yet • *adv* however, nevertheless
tàntal • *n* tantalum
tantalitzar • *v* tantalize
tany • *n* sucker

tap • *n* spigot
tapa • *n* cover, lid
taquilla • *n* gate
taquímetre • *n* tachymeter
tard • *adj* late • *adv* late
tarda • *n* afternoon, evening
tardor • *n* autumn
targeta • *n* card
tarima • *n* platform
taronger • *n* orange
taronja • *n* orange
tars • *n* tarsus
tarsal • *adj* tarsal
tarser • *n* tarsier
tarsià • *adj* tarsal
tartamudejar • *v* stutter
tartana • *n* bomb
tascó • *n* wedge
tassa • *n* cup, mug
tast • *n* sample, taste
tastar • *v* taste, try
tatuar • *v* ink, tattoo
tatuatge • *n* tattoo
tau • *n* tau
taula • *n* table
tauler • *n* backboard
tauló • *n* slab
tauó • *n* tauon
tauró • *n* shark
taüt • *n* coffin
taverna • *n* pub
taxa • *n* duty, tax
taxi • *n* taxi
taxidèrmia • *n* taxidermy
taxímetre • *n* taximeter
taxonomia • *n* taxonomy
te • *n* tea
teatral • *adj* theatrical
teatre • *n* simulation, theater
tebi • *adj* lukewarm, tepid
tèbia • *adj* lukewarm
tecla • *n* key
teclat • *n* keyboard
teclejar • *v* keyboard, type
tecneci • *n* technetium
tècnic • *adj* technical
tècnicament • *adv* technically
tecnocràcia • *n* technocracy
tecnologia • *n* technology
tecnològic • *adj* technological
tecnològicament • *adv* technologically
tectònic • *adj* tectonic
tediós • *adj* humdrum, tedious
teix • *n* yew

teixeda • *n* yew
teixidor • *n* dragonfly
teixir • *v* weave
teixit • *n* tissue
teixó • *n* badger
tela • *n* canvas
telecinesi • *n* telekinesis
telèfon • *n* phone, telephone
telefonada • *n* call
telefonar • *v* call, telephone
telegrafia • *n* telegraphy
telenotícies • *n* news
teleologia • *n* teleology
telepatia • *n* telepathy
telepàtic • *adj* telepathic
telescopi • *n* telescope
telescòpic • *adj* telescopic
televisió • *n* television
televisor • *n* television
tell • *n* linden
telluri • *n* tellurium
teló • *n* curtain
telofase • *n* telophase
tema • *n* thread
témer • *v* dread
temerari • *adj* daredevil
temeràriament • *adv* recklessly
temor • *n* fear
temperança • *n* temperance
temperat • *adj* temperate
temperatura • *n* temperature
tempesta • *n* rainstorm, storm, tempest, thunderstorm
tempestat • *n* storm
tempestejar • *v* tempest
tempestuós • *adj* stormy
temple • *n* temple
temporal • *n* storm, temporal • *adj* temporal, temporary
temporalment • *adv* temporarily
temps • *n* tense, time, weather
temptació • *n* temptation
temptador • *n* tempter • *adj* tempting
temptadora • *n* tempter • *adj* tempting
temptar • *v* tempt
temptativa • *n* attempt, go
tenaç • *adj* tenacious
tenda • *n* shop, tent
tendència • *n* tendency
tendenciós • *adj* tendentious
tendenciosament • *adv* tendentiously
tendó • *n* tendon
tendrament • *adv* tenderly
tendre • *adj* tender
tendresa • *n* endearment
tenebres • *n* darkness
tenir • *v* have • *adj* old

tennis • *n* tennis
tens • *adj* taut, tense
tensió • *n* stress
tentacle • *n* tentacle
téntol • *n* time-out
tènue • *adj* faint, tenuous
tenyir • *v* dye
teocràcia • *n* theocracy
teocràtic • *adj* theocratic
teòleg • *n* theologian
teologia • *n* theology
teològic • *adj* theological
teorema • *n* theorem
teoria • *n* theory
teòric • *adj* theoretical
teòricament • *adv* theoretically
teoritzar • *v* theorize
tequila • *n* tequila
terapeuta • *n* therapist
terapèutic • *adj* therapeutic
teràpia • *n* therapy
terbi • *n* terbium
terbolí • *n* whirlwind
tercer • *n* mediator, third, tierce • *adj* third • *adv* thirdly
tercera • *n* third
tercerament • *adv* thirdly
terme • *n* term
terminal • *n* shell, terminal • *adj* terminal
terminar • *v* finish
terminologia • *n* terminology
tèrmit • *n* termite
termiter • *n* anthill
termodinàmic • *adj* thermodynamic
termoelèctric • *adj* thermoelectric
termoelectricitat • *n* thermoelectricity
termòmetre • *n* thermometer
termosfera • *n* thermosphere
terna • *n* triple
ternari • *adj* triple
terra • *n* deck, dirt, earth, floor, ground, land, world
terrassa • *n* terrace
terratinent • *n* landowner
terratrèmol • *n* earthquake
terreny • *n* field, land, plot
terrestre • *adj* terrestrial
terrible • *adj* terrible
terriblement • *adv* terribly
terrissa • *n* pottery
terrissaire • *n* potter
territ • *n* sandpiper
territori • *n* territory
territorial • *adj* territorial
terror • *n* terror
terrorisme • *n* terrorism
terrorista • *n* terrorist • *adj* terrorist

tesar • *v* tense
tesaurus • *n* thesaurus
tesi • *n* thesis
tesla • *n* tesla
tesor • *n* treasure
tesselůlació • *n* tessellation
testament • *n* will
testicular • *adj* testicular
testificar • *v* witness
testimoni • *n* baton, witness
testimoniatge • *n* witness
tetera • *n* teakettle
tetraedre • *n* tetrahedron
tetràedre • *n* tetrahedron
tetràgon • *n* tetragon
tetralogia • *n* tetralogy
tetrámetro • *n* tetrameter
tetraplegia • *n* quadriplegia
tetraplègic • *n* quadriplegic
teula • *n* tile
teulada • *n* roof
teular • *v* tile
textual • *adj* textual
textura • *n* texture
theta • *n* theta
tia • *n* aunt
tibant • *adj* taut
tic • *n* tic
tifa • *n* shit
tifó • *n* typhoon
tifus • *n* typhus
tigra • *n* tigress
tigre • *n* tiger
tigressa • *n* tigress
timbre • *n* doorbell
tímid • *adj* timid
tímidament • *adv* shyly
timó • *n* helm, rudder
timpà • *n* eardrum, tympanum
tina • *n* cask
tinamú • *n* tinamou
tinent • *adj* lieutenant
tint • *n* dye
tinta • *n* ink
tintar • *v* ink
tinter • *n* inkwell
tinya • *n* ringworm
tio • *n* dude, uncle
tiorba • *n* theorbo
tip • *adj* full
típic • *adj* typical
típicament • *adv* typically
tipogràfic • *adj* typographical
tipus • *n* kind, sort, type
tirà • *n* tyrant
tirador • *n* handle
tirania • *n* tyranny

tirànic • *adj* tyrannical
tiranitzar • *v* tyrannize
tirar • *v* loose, pull, throw
tirar-se • *v* fuck
tiro • *n* draught
tirosina • *n* tyrosine
tiroteig • *n* shooting
tisi • *n* phthisis
tísic • *adj* phthisic
tisora • *n* scissor
tisores • *n* scissors, shears
tisoreta • *n* earwig
tità • *n* titan
titani • *n* titanium
titànic • *adj* titanic
titlla • *n* tilde
títol • *n* degree, title
titola • *n* dick
titubar • *n* stagger • *v* stammer, titubate
titubejar • *v* hesitate, stammer, teeter,
titubate • *n* stagger
titular • *n* incumbent • *adj* incumbent
to • *n* tone
tobogan • *n* slide
toc • *n* bunt
tocar • *v* call, play, touch
tocata • *n* toccata
tòfona • *n* truffle
toga • *n* robe
toix • *adj* stupid
tolerable • *adj* tolerable
tolerant • *adj* tolerant
tolerar • *v* tolerate
toll • *n* puddle
tom • *n* tome
tomaquera • *n* tomato
tomàquet • *n* tomato
tomba • *n* tomb
tombar • *v* topple
tonada • *n* tune
tondre • *v* shear
tòner • *n* toner
tònic • *adj* stressed
tonsilito • *n* tonsillitis
tontina • *n* tontine
tonto • *adj* frivolous • *n* nincompoop
tonyina • *n* tuna
topazi • *n* topaz
tòpic • *n* truism
tora • *n* aconite
tòrax • *n* chest, thorax
torba • *n* peat
torcaboques • *n* napkin
torçada • *n* sprain
torçar • *v* warp
tord • *n* thrush
tori • *n* thorium

torn • *n* go, turn
tornado • *n* tornado
tornar • *v* return
tornar-se • *v* wax
tornavís • *n* screwdriver
torneig • *n* tournament
torniquet • *n* tourniquet, turnstile
toro • *n* bull
torpede • *n* torpedo
torpedinar • *v* torpedo
torrada • *n* toast
torrar • *v* toast
torre • *n* rook, tower
torrencial • *adj* torrential
torrent • *n* torrent
tòrrid • *adj* sultry
tors • *n* torso
tort • *adj* bent, crooked, one-eyed
tortita • *n* pancake
tortuga • *n* tortoise, turtle
tortuós • *adj* crooked
tortura • *n* torture
torturador • *n* torturer
torturar • *v* torture
torxa • *n* link, torch
tos • *n* cough
tosc • *adj* rough
tossar • *v* butt
tossir • *v* cough
tossudament • *adv* stubbornly
tossut • *adj* stubborn
tot • *n* all, whole • *pron* anything, everything • *adj* whole
total • *adj* full, utter • *n* total
totalitari • *adj* totalitarian
totalitat • *n* whole
totalment • *adv* altogether, completely, entirely, quite, totally
tothom • *pron* everybody, everyone
tou • *adj* soft
tova • *n* adobe
tovalló • *n* napkin
tovallola • *n* towel
tòxic • *adj* poisonous, toxic
toxicitat • *n* toxicity
trabuc • *n* blunderbuss
trabuquet • *n* trebuchet
traçada • *n* plot
traçar • *v* plot
tracoma • *n* trachoma
tractable • *adj* agreeable, tractable
tractament • *n* treatment
tractar • *v* deal
tractat • *n* tract
tracte • *n* deal, tract
tractor • *n* tractor
tradició • *n* tradition

tradicional • *adj* traditional
tradicionalment • *adv* traditionally
traducció • *n* translation
traductor • *n* translator
traduir • *v* translate
tràfic • *n* traffic
tragèdia • *n* tragedy
tràgic • *adj* tragic
tragicòmic • *adj* tragicomic
traïció • *n* treason
traïdor • *n* traitor • *adj* traitor, traitorous
trair • *v* betray, traitor
trajectòria • *n* course, trajectory
trama • *n* plot
trametre • *v* send
trampejar • *v* cheat
trampós • *n* cheat
tramvia • *n* tram
tranqui • *adj* cool
tranquil • *adj* easygoing, quiet
tranquilůlitzar • *v* reassure
transalpí • *adj* transalpine
transatlàntic • *adj* transatlantic
transcendentalment • *adv* transcendentally
transcripció • *n* transcription
transexual • *adj* transsexual
transformació • *n* conversion, transformation
transformar • *v* transform
transició • *n* transition
transistor • *n* transistor
transitable • *adj* passable
transitar • *v* travel
transitiu • *adj* transitive
transitivament • *adv* transitively
transitori • *adj* transitional, transitory
transliteració • *n* transliteration
translúcid • *adj* translucent
transmetre • *v* broadcast
transmissor • *n* transmitter
transparent • *adj* transparent
transparentment • *adv* transparently
transport • *n* transport
transportar • *v* transport • *n* transpose
transsepte • *n* transept
transversal • *adj* transverse
trapa • *n* trapdoor
trapella • *adj* naughty
trapezi • *n* trapeze, trapezium, trapezoid
trapezoide • *n* trapezoid
tràquea • *n* trachea
traqueal • *adj* tracheal
traqueïtis • *n* tracheitis
trasbalsat • *adj* upset
traslladar • *v* move
trasplantar • *v* transplant

trastorn • *n* disorder
traumàtic • *adj* traumatic
travessa • *n* sleeper
travesser • *n* crossbar
treball • *n* job, toil, work
treballador • *adj* hardworking • *n* worker
treballadora • *n* worker
treballat • *adj* wrought
trèmol • *n* aspen
tremolar • *v* quiver, tremble
tremolor • *v* quake • *n* tremble
tremolós • *adj* tremulous
tremp • *n* temper
tren • *n* train
trena • *n* plait
trenca • *n* shrike
trencable • *adj* breakable
trencadís • *adj* brittle
trencaglaç • *n* icebreaker
trencat • *adj* broken • *n* cedilla
trepitjada • *n* tread
trepitjar • *v* tread
tres • *n* three
tresor • *n* treasure
tret • *n* feature
treure • *v* remove
trèvol • *n* clover, club
tria • *n* choice
triangle • *n* triangle
triangulació • *n* triangulation
triar • *v* choose
tribal • *adj* tribal
tribú • *n* tribune
tribu • *n* tribe
tribuna • *n* tribune
tribunal • *n* court
tricicle • *n* tricycle
tricotilomanía • *n* trichotillomania
trident • *n* trident
tridimensional • *adj* three-dimensional
triglicèrid • *n* triglyceride
trígon • *n* trigon
trigonometria • *n* trigonometry
trigonomètric • *adj* trigonometric
trillar • *v* thresh
trilogia • *n* trilogy
trimarà • *n* trimaran
trímer • *n* trimer
trimestral • *adj* quarterly
trimestralment • *adv* quarterly
trimestre • *n* trimester
trinat • *n* trill
trinc • *n* clink
trineu • *n* sledge
trinquet • *n* foremast
trinxar • *v* shred
trinxera • *n* trench

triomfador • *adj* triumphant
triomfant • *adj* triumphant
tripartit • *adj* tripartite
triple • *adj* triple
triplicar • *v* triple
tríptic • *n* triptych
triptòfan • *n* tryptophan
tripulació • *n* crew
tripulant • *n* crew
trisecar • *v* trisect
trist • *adj* miserable, sad
trista • *adj* sad
tristament • *adv* sadly
tristesa • *n* sadness
tritó • *n* merman, newt
triturar • *v* grind, shred
triumvirat • *n* triumvirate
trivial • *adj* frivolous, trivial
tro • *n* thunder
troana • *n* privet
trobada • *n* meeting
trobador • *n* troubadour
trobadora • *n* troubadour
trobar • *v* ascertain, find
trobar-se • *v* lie
trocejar • *v* shred
trofeu • *n* award, trophy
troica • *n* troika
trombó • *n* trombone
trompa • *n* squinch, trunk
trompeta • *n* trumpet, trumpeter
trompeter • *n* trumpeter
trompetista • *n* trumpeter
tron • *n* throne
tronar • *v* thunder
tronc • *n* frustum
tronera • *n* embrasure, pocket
tropa • *n* troop
tropopausa • *n* tropopause
troposfera • *n* troposphere
trossa • *n* bun
truc • *n* cheat
trucada • *n* call
trucar • *v* call, ring, telephone
truisme • *n* truism
truita • *n* trout
truja • *n* sow
trumfar • *v* trump
tsar • *n* tsar
tsuga • *n* hemlock
tu • *pron* thou, you
tub • *n* tube
tuba • *n* tuba
tubercle • *n* tuber
tuberculosi • *n* tuberculosis
tuli • *n* thulium
tulipa • *n* tulip

tumor • *n* tumor
túmul • *n* barrow, mound
tumult • *n* mayhem
túnel • *n* nutmeg
tungstè • *n* tungsten
túnica • *n* tunic
turbant • *n* turban
turbojet • *n* turbojet
turca • *n* drunkenness
turisme • *n* tourism

turmell • *n* ankle
turment • *n* torment
turmentador • *n* tormentor
turmentar • *v* torment
turó • *n* hill, polecat
turquesa • *n* turquoise • *adj* turquoise
tutoria • *n* tutorial
tutorial • *n* tutorial

U

u • *n* one, u • *adj* one • *pron* you
ua • *interj* boo
ualabi • *n* wallaby
ubic • *adj* ubiquitous
ubicació • *n* location
ucàs • *n* ukase
udol • *n* howl
udolar • *v* howl
udòmetre • *n* pluviometer
ufà • *adj* smug
uixer • *n* usher
ull • *n* eye
ullada • *n* look
ullal • *n* fang, tusk
ullblau • *adj* blue-eyed
ulleres • *n* circle, spectacles
ulna • *n* ulna
ultratge • *n* outrage
ultratomba • *n* afterlife
ultraviolat • *n* ultraviolet • *adj* ultraviolet
umbilical • *adj* umbilical
un • *art* an • *adj* one
una • *art* an • *adv* o'clock
unànime • *adj* unanimous
unànimement • *adv* unanimously
unça • *n* ounce
unflar • *v* inflate
unflar-se • *v* swell
ungla • *n* fingernail, nail
ungüent • *n* salve
únic • *adj* alone, one, only, singular, unique
únicament • *adv* only, uniquely
unicel·lular • *adj* unicellular
unicorn • *n* unicorn
uniforme • *adj* level
unilateral • *adj* unilateral
unilateralment • *adv* unilaterally
unilingüe • *adj* monolingual
unió • *n* join
unir • *v* unite

unir-se • *v* coalesce, join
unisex • *adj* unisex
unitari • *adj* unitarian, unitary
unitat • *n* unit, unity
univers • *n* universe
universitat • *n* university
untar • *v* smear
ur • *n* aurochs
uracil • *n* uracil
urani • *n* uranium
urbà • *adj* urban
urea • *n* urea
uretra • *n* urethra
urgència • *n* emergency
urgent • *adj* urgent
urgentment • *adv* urgently
úric • *adj* uric
urinari • *adj* urinary
urna • *n* casket
uròleg • *n* urologist
urologia • *n* urology
urpa • *n* claw, spike, talon
ús • *n* use
usar • *v* use
usual • *adj* usual
usuari • *n* user
usurpar • *v* encroach, usurp
utensili • *n* utensil
úter • *n* womb
uterí • *adj* uterine
útil • *adj* helpful, useful
utilitari • *n* utilitarian • *adj* utilitarian
utilitària • *n* utilitarian
utilitat • *n* usefulness
utilitzar • *v* use
útilment • *adv* usefully
utopia • *n* utopia
utòpic • *adj* utopian
úvula • *n* uvula

V

va • *adj* vain
vaca • *n* cow
vacances • *n* holiday
vacant • *adj* vacant
vaccí • *n* vaccine
vacilŭlació • *n* hesitation, vacillation
vacilŭlar • *v* vacillate
vacu • *adj* vacant
vacuna • *n* vaccine
vaga • *n* strike
vagament • *adv* vaguely
vagar • *n* drift • *v* wander
vagarejar • *n* drift
vagina • *n* vagina
vagó • *n* car, carriage
vague • *adj* vague
vaguetat • *n* vagueness
vaguista • *n* striker
vaina • *n* pod
vaixell • *n* boat, ship
vaixella • *n* crockery, dish
valdre • *v* count
valent • *adj* brave, courageous, valiant
valentament • *adv* bravely
vàlid • *adj* valid
vall • *n* valley
valor • *n* courage, value, worth
valoració • *n* appraisal
valquíria • *n* valkyrie
valuós • *adj* valuable
vàlvula • *n* valve
vampir • *n* vampire
vanadi • *n* vanadium
vanadinita • *n* vanadinite
vanagloriós • *adj* boastful
vanament • *adv* vainly
vàndal • *n* vandal • *adj* vandal
vandalisme • *n* vandalism
vanitat • *n* vanity
vanitós • *adj* vain
vano • *n* fan
vànova • *n* bedspread
vapor • *n* vapor
vaquer • *n* cowherd
varec • *n* kelp
variable • *n* variable • *adj* variable
variablement • *adv* variably
variació • *n* variation
variant • *n* bypass
varietat • *n* breed, sort, variety
varis • *adj* various
vas • *n* glass
vascular • *adj* vascular
vasectomia • *n* vasectomy

vassall • *n* liege
vàter • *n* bathroom, loo, toilet
veça • *n* vetch
vector • *n* vector
vedat • *n* park
vedell • *n* calf
vedella • *n* beef
vegà • *n* vegan • *adj* vegan
vegada • *n* time
vegetació • *n* vegetation
vegetal • *n* vegetable • *adj* vegetable
vegetarià • *n* vegetarian • *adj* vegetarian
vegetariana • *n* vegetarian
vegetarianisme • *n* vegetarianism
vehicle • *n* vehicle
velŭleïtat • *n* velleity
vela • *n* sail
velar • *n* velar
veler • *n* barque
vell • *n* fleece • *adj* old
vella • *n* crone
velló • *n* fleece
vellut • *n* velvet
vellutat • *adj* velvety
veloç • *adj* fast, speedy
velocímetre • *n* speedometer
velocitat • *n* speed, velocity
veloçment • *adv* fast
vena • *n* vein
vèncer • *v* defeat
vencer • *v* mature
vencible • *adj* vincible
venciment • *n* defeat
venda • *n* sale
vendre • *v* deal, sell
venedor • *n* salesman, vendor
veneració • *n* worship
venerar • *v* worship
venir • *v* come
venjar • *v* avenge
vent • *n* wind
ventall • *n* fan
ventar • *v* fan
ventilador • *n* fan
ventre • *n* abdomen, belly
verat • *n* mackerel
verb • *n* verb
verbal • *adj* oral, verbal
verbós • *adj* verbose
verd • *adj* blue, green • *n* green
verdaderament • *adv* fairly, quite
verdós • *adj* greenish
verdura • *n* vegetable
veredicte • *n* award, judgment

verema • *n* vintage
verga • *n* rod
verge • *n* virgin • *adj* virgin
vergonya • *n* shame
vergonyós • *adj* shameful, shy
verí • *n* poison, venom
verificació • *n* verification
verificar • *v* check
verinós • *adj* poisonous, toxic, venomous
veritable • *adj* true
veritablement • *adv* truly
veritat • *n* truth
vermell • *n* red • *adj* red
vermellor • *n* redness
vermellós • *adj* reddish, sandy
vermut • *n* vermouth
vern • *n* alder
vernís • *n* varnish
verola • *n* smallpox
verra • *n* sow
verro • *n* boar
versat • *adj* proficient
versàtil • *adj* versatile
versatilitat • *n* versatility
versemblança • *n* likelihood
versió • *n* release
vèrtebra • *n* vertebra
vertebrat • *n* vertebrate • *adj* vertebrate
vèrtex • *n* vertex
vertical • *adj* vertical
verticalment • *adv* vertically
vertiginós • *adj* dizzy
vesc • *n* mistletoe
vescomte • *n* viscount
vesícula • *n* vesicle
vespa • *n* wasp
vespre • *n* evening, night
vessar • *v* shed, spill
vestigi • *n* vestige
vestigial • *adj* vestigial
vestir • *v* dress
vestir-se • *v* dress
vestit • *n* dress, suit
vetlla • *n* vigil
vetllada • *n* night
vetust • *adj* ancient
veu • *n* voice
veure • *v* see, view, witness
vexar • *v* harass
vexatori • *adj* vexatious
vi • *n* wine
via • *prep* per • *n* way
viable • *adj* viable
vianant • *n* pedestrian
viarany • *n* footpath
viatge • *n* voyage
viatjar • *v* travel • *n* travel

vibra • *n* wyvern
vibràfon • *n* vibraphone
vibrato • *n* vibrato
víbria • *n* dragon, wyvern
vibrissa • *n* whisker
vici • *n* vice
víctima • *n* victim
victòria • *n* victory, win
victoriós • *adj* victorious
victoriosament • *adv* victoriously
vicunya • *n* vicuna
vida • *n* life
vidre • *n* glass
vidu • *n* widow, widower
vigèsim • *adj* twentieth
vigilància • *n* vigilance
vigilant • *adj* alert, vigilant
vigilantment • *adv* vigilantly
vigilar • *v* behold
vigília • *n* vigil
vigorosament • *adv* vigorously
vil • *adj* base, vile
vímet • *n* wicker
vinagre • *n* vinegar
vinagrera • *n* cruet
vinclar • *v* bow, link, topple
vincle • *n* link
vint-i-dosè • *n* twenty-second • *adj* twenty-second
vint-i-unè • *n* twenty-first • *adj* twenty-first
vintè • *n* twentieth • *adj* twentieth
vinya • *n* vine, vineyard
viola • *n* leapfrog, viola
violació • *n* rape
violar • *v* take
violència • *n* violence
violent • *adj* violent
violentament • *adv* violently
violeta • *n* violet • *adj* violet
violí • *n* violin
violinista • *n* violinist
violoncel • *n* cello
viral • *adj* viral
virginal • *n* virginal
virginitat • *n* virginity
víric • *adj* viral
viril • *adj* manly, masculine, virile
virilitat • *n* virility
virologia • *n* virology
virrei • *n* viceroy
virtual • *adj* virtual
virtualment • *adv* virtually
virtuós • *n* virtuoso • *adj* virtuous
virtuosa • *n* virtuoso
virtuosament • *adv* virtuously
virtuosisme • *n* virtuosity

virtut • *n* virtue
virulent • *adj* virulent
virulentament • *adv* virulently
virus • *n* virus
visat • *n* visa
víscera • *n* offal, viscera
viscós • *adj* viscous
viscosímetre • *n* viscometer
viscositat • *n* viscosity
visibilitat • *n* visibility
visible • *adj* visible
visiblement • *adv* visibly
visió • *n* vision
visir • *n* vizier
visita • *n* call
visitar • *v* call
visó • *n* mink
vista • *n* eyesight, view, vision
visual • *adj* visual
vital • *adj* vital
vitalisme • *n* vitalism
vitalitat • *n* vitality
vitamina • *n* vitamin
vitrina • *n* case
viu • *adj* alive, live, living
viure • *v* live
vivaç • *adj* lively, vivacious
vivacitat • *n* vivacity
vivaçment • *adv* vivaciously
vivenda • *n* dwelling
vivent • *adj* alive
vívid • *adj* vivid
vivípar • *adj* viviparous
vocal • *adj* vocal • *n* vowel
vocalment • *adv* vocally
vociferació • *n* vociferation
vociferar • *v* vociferate
vodka • *n* vodka
vodú • *n* voodoo
vol • *n* flight
volador • *v* flying
voladora • *v* flying
volant • *n* shuttlecock, winger
volateria • *n* poultry

volcà • *n* volcano
volcànic • *adj* volcanic
volea • *n* volley
vòlei • *n* volleyball
voleibol • *n* volleyball
voler • *v* want
volta • *n* go, round, vault
voltar • *v* surround, wheel
voltor • *n* vulture
volum • *n* volume
voluminós • *adj* bulky
voluntari • *adj* voluntary
voluntàriament • *adv* voluntarily
voluntat • *n* will
voluptuós • *adj* voluptuous
vòmit • *n* vomit
vomitar • *v* boot, vomit
vora • *n* border, brim, edge, hem, shore
voràgine • *n* maelstrom
voral • *n* shoulder
vorejar • *v* border
vorera • *n* pavement, shore, sidewalk
vori • *n* ivory
vòrtex • *n* vortex
vós • *pron* you
vosaltres • *pron* you
vostè • *pron* you
vostès • *pron* you
vot • *n* voice, vote, vow
votant • *n* voter
votar • *v* cast, vote
vou-verivou • *n* lullaby
voyeurisme • *n* voyeurism
vudú • *n* voodoo
vuit • *n* eight
vuitada • *n* octave
vuitè • *adj* eighth
vulcanització • *n* vulcanization
vulcanologia • *n* volcanology
vulgar • *adj* base, vulgar
vulnerabilitat • *n* vulnerability
vulva • *n* vulva

W

watt • *n* watt
whisky • *n* whiskey

X

xabec • *n* xebec
xacal • *n* jackal
xafardejar • *v* blab, blabber, gossip
xafarder • *n* blabber, gossip
xafarderia • *n* gossip
xafogós • *adj* sultry
xafogosa • *adj* sultry
xai • *n* lamb
xaloc • *n* sirocco
xaman • *n* shaman
xamanisme • *n* shamanism
xamba • *n* fluke
xampany • *n* champagne
xampú • *n* shampoo
xanca • *n* stilt
xantatge • *n* blackmail
xantatgista • *n* blackmailer
xàquima • *n* hackamore
xarampió • *n* measles
xarlatà • *n* charlatan
xarop • *n* syrup
xarrasclet • *n* garganey
xarrupar • *v* sip
xarxa • *n* net, network, screen, web
xarxet • *adj* teal
xat • *n* chat
xato • *adj* flat, pug-nosed
xec • *n* cheque
xef • *n* chef, cook
xeic • *n* sheik
xemeneia • *n* chimney, fireplace
xenó • *n* xenon
xenòfob • *adj* xenophobic
xenòfoba • *adj* xenophobic
xenofòbia • *n* xenophobia
xerès • *n* sherry
xeringa • *n* syringe
xerinola • *n* revelry
xerografia • *n* xerography
xerrac • *n* handsaw
xerrar • *v* chat
xic • *n* boy
xicana • *n* chicane

xicot • *n* boy, boyfriend
xicota • *n* girlfriend
xifra • *n* abstract, cipher, digit, figure, number, numeral
xilema • *n* xylem
xillar • *v* call
xilòfon • *n* xylophone
ximpanzé • *n* chimpanzee
ximple • *adj* foolish, silly • *n* nincompoop
ximpleries • *n* drivel
ximplet • *adj* silly
xinxa • *n* bedbug, bug
xinxilla • *n* chinchilla
xiprer • *n* cypress
xiquet • *n* boy
xiqueta • *n* girl
xisclar • *v* call
xiscle • *n* call
xiulada • *n* whistle
xiular • *v* whistle
xiulet • *n* whistle
xiulo • *n* whistle
xiuxiueig • *n* whisper
xiuxiuejar • *v* whisper
xo • *interj* whoa
xoc • *n* crash, shock
xocant • *adj* outrageous
xocar • *v* hit, shock
xocolata • *n* chocolate • *adj* chocolate
xocolatina • *n* chocolate
xop • *adj* drenched
xoriguer • *n* kestrel
xovinista • *n* chauvinist • *adj* chauvinist, chauvinistic
xuclar • *v* suck
xucrut • *n* sauerkraut
xufa • *n* chufa
xufla • *n* chufa
xurma • *n* mob
xusma • *n* mob
xutador • *n* kicker

Z

zebra • *n* zebra
zel • *n* zeal
zero • *n* love, nought, zero
zeta • *n* zee, zeta
zeugma • *n* zeugma
zig-zag • *n* zigzag
ziga-zaga • *n* zigzag
zigoma • *n* cheekbone
zigot • *n* zygote

zigzaguejar • *v* zigzag
zinc • *n* zinc
zirconi • *n* zirconium
zitzània • *n* darnel
zoantropia • *n* zoanthropy
zodíac • *n* zodiac
zombi • *n* zombie
zona • *n* zone
zoòleg • *n* zoologist

zoologia • *n* zoology
zoològic • *n* zoo • *adj* zoological
zoòspora • *n* zoospore

zopilot • *n* buzzard